Joseph Chi
May 22.
Toronto.

EVERYONE IN THE BIBLE

EVERYONE IN THE BIBLE

WILLIAM P. BARKER

FLEMING H. REVELL COMPANY • OLD TAPPAN • NEW JERSEY

To the Church Family at Bower Hill—

fellow workers, whose names are in the book of life (PHILIPPIANS 4:3)

A SPECIAL NOTE OF THANKS:

to Mrs. Howard E. Betts and Mrs. Fred F. Smoot for their incredible patience in deciphering my handwriting, and for typing, retyping, and proofreading; to John B. Barker, Donald T. Kauffman, and Fred M. Rogers for their many excellent suggestions; to Jean, Jock, and Ellen for their interest and encouragement.

PREFACE

The purpose of this volume is to provide Bible readers with a concise, accurate, and readable biographical account of every person named in the Bible.

Obviously, many of these persons are merely "names" on a list. There is little than can be said about those who are merely "names," apart from identifying their tribe or family (if given in the Bible) and mentioning the event in Biblical history involving those "names." For example, many of those listed who returned after the Exile in Babylon are people who are remembered only as descendants of certain tribal leaders.

There are many persons of the same name in the Bible. There is considerable confusion about the identity of many of these, especially those who happened to live at the same time. In spite of careful detective work, sometimes we can only tentatively identify certain persons. Some of the identifications listed in this book are based on educated guesses. For example, Alexander of Ephesus (Acts 19:33), Alexander "the coppersmith" (II Timothy 4:14), and the Alexander who made a "shipwreck" of the faith of other Christians (I Timothy 1:1—2) appear to this writer to have been three separate individuals, and have been treated as such in this book. Other scholars, however, have built strong cases for believing that two of these three, or even all three, were really the same person.

The situation is further complicated by the fact that many persons were known by two names. For example, King Uzziah, the great monarch of Judah in Isaiah's time, was also known by the name "Azariah." In such cases, the writer has tried to give cross-references, so that one biographical paragraph will suffice for both names.

English spellings of Hebrew and Greek names are another difficulty. The problem is made worse when we remember that even in Hebrew there were variant spellings of the same name. For instance, to take the name "Uzziah" again, that name can be, and was, rendered in the Hebrew to be the equivalent of "Uzzi" and "Uzzia." Every Bible dictionary, encyclopedia, and reference book has a different list of "Uzziahs," "Uzzis," and "Uzzias."

In general, the writer has used the Revised Standard Version of the Bible in compiling his names, except in the cases of names which are most commonly known in English in the forms given in earlier translations. As far as possible, cross-references have been included to give every alternate spelling of every name. The writer, being human, however, undoubtedly has unintentionally omitted certain variations of some names.

Some readers will be rightfully critical because too little material is given on some names and too much on others. The writer can only answer that the real use of this book, as of any book, is to help us all to a deeper understanding of the meaning of the Name "above every name that is named, not only in this age but also in that which is to come." (Ephesians 1:21)

A

AARON Moses' brother and a fluent speaker, Aaron was appointed by God to go with Moses and do the talking for his tongue-tied brother. He shared the responsibilities of leading the children of Israel from captivity in Egypt, even propping up Moses' arm during a battle with Amalek to help inspire the Israelites to victory. Moses took Aaron and other leaders up Mount Sinai, and appointed him and his family to the priesthood. Aaron was not only the first high priest of Israel, but was appointed temporary judge of the people when Moses was on Sinai. It was at this time that Aaron finally gave in to the people's wishes, supervised the fabrication of the golden calf, and permitted a wild celebration around it. When Moses returned and angrily reproached his brother, Aaron shifted the blame to the people. In spite of this lapse into idolatry, Aaron was looked up to as "the priest" during the forty years of wandering after leaving Egypt. He died on Mount Hor shortly before the Israelites crossed over to the Promised Land. EXODUS 4 —40; LEVITICUS 1—24; NUMBERS 1— 33; DEUTERONOMY 9

ABADDON The king of the bottomless pit described in lurid detail by John, the writer of the Revelation, Abaddon appeared after the fifth angel blew his trumpet. Abaddon's Greek name was Apollyon, meaning "Destroyer." John was personifying the word *abaddon*, meaning "ruin" or "destruction," mentioned by Job and the Psalmist. REVELATION 9:11

ABAGTHA One of seven royal servants of Persian King Ahasuerus or Xerxes, Abagtha was one of those ordered to escort Queen Vashti to the king's presence during a lavish, seven-day banquet. ESTHER 1:10

13

ABDA

1 Father of the chief of Solomon's forced labor battalions, Adoniram. 1 KINGS 4:6

2 One of the Levites listed by Nehemiah who returned from exile in Babylonia to Jerusalem. NEHEMIAH 11:17

ABDEEL Father of Shelemiah, the man sent by King Jehoiakim to arrest Jeremiah the prophet and his secretary, Baruch. JEREMIAH 36:26

ABDI

1 Grandfather of Ethan, one of David's principal song leaders. 1 CHRONICLES 6:44; II CHRONICLES 29:12

2 One of the many who married a non-Jewish girl during the Exile, a thing that was forbidden by the Law. EZRA 10:26

ABDIEL One of those listed in the genealogies in 1 Chronicles, Abdiel was the founder of a family of Gadites who lived in Gilead. 1 CHRONICLES 5:15

ABDON

1 Hillel's son, Abdon was the last of the minor judges, ruling eight years. JUDGES 12:13—15

2 Son of Shasak, Abdon was one of the family of Benjamin residing in Jerusalem and was listed by the Chronicler. I CHRONICLES 8:23

3 Another man, also living in Jerusalem, this Abdon was the son of Jeiel, another descendant of Benjamin. I CHRONICLES 8:30

4 King Josiah's messenger, this Abdon was sent to Huldah the prophetess by Josiah to ask what he should do about the book of the Law that had just been found in the Temple during the renovations. II CHRONICLES 34:20

ABEDNEGO Abednego was the nickname given Azariah, one of the four young princes of Judah hauled off to Babylonia in 607 B.C., by one of the Babylonian court. Abednego stubbornly refused to bow down before the golden image of the Babylonian king, and was thrown, with Shadrach and Meshach, into the fiery furnace by the irate king. Because of their faith, however, they emerged unhurt. DANIEL 1—3

ABEL Adam and Eve's son, Abel was the younger twin brother of Cain, and was a shepherd. When God asked an offering, Abel picked out the best of his flock. Because his sacrifice of the best he had was preferred by God to what Cain presented, Cain flew into a jealous rage and killed Abel, thus committing the first murder in the Bible. GENESIS 4

ABI A well-known eighth-century B.C. queen and queen mother, Abi was the daughter of Zechariah, the wife of Ahaz, and the mother of Hezekiah. II KINGS 18:2

ABIA, ABIAH See ABIJAH

ABIALBON A member of "The Thirty," the third contingent of David's elite group of guards, Abialbon "the Arbathite" came from a village named Arabah or Betharabah in northern Judah. II SAMUEL 23:31

ABIASAPH A son of Korah, great-great-great grandson of Jacob, Abiasaph was one of the heads of families of Levites that left Egypt with Moses. EXODUS 6:24

ABIATHAR The high priest during David's reign, Abiathar was the eleventh high priest after Aaron, and was from a famous family of priests. He was the sole survivor of the slaughter of eighty-five priests at Nob by Doeg the Edomite. Escaping to David when David was still a guerilla fighter, Abiathar was David's fast friend until near the end of David's reign. Abiathar stayed with David during the critical days of Absalom's revolt, was sent back to Jerusalem with the Ark, and helped smooth the way for David's return to Jerusalem. Possibly because of his jealousy of other leaders and of his co-high priest, Zadok, Abiathar supported Adonijah's conspiracy. Although other leaders of this conspiracy were executed, Abiathar's sentence was reduced to banishment out of consideration for his past loyalty and service. I SAMUEL 22, 23, 30; II SAMUEL 8, 15, 17, 19, 20; I KINGS 1, 2, 4; I CHRONICLES 15, 18, 24, 27

ABIDA Grandson of Abraham and Keturah, Abida is mentioned in the genealogies as a son of Midian. GENESIS 25:4; I CHRONICLES 1:33

ABIDAN One of the tribe of Benjamin, Abidan was selected as one of twelve "princes" who were to represent the twelve tribes and help with the census when Moses took a head count in the wilderness. NUMBERS 1, 2, 7, 10

ABIEL
1 One of the tribe of Benjamin, this Abiel was remembered primarily as the man who was Saul's grandfather and Kish's father. I SAMUEL 9:1; 14:15

2 This Abiel was a member of David's 3rd elite corps of guards, called "The Thirty," probably the same man as the "Abialbon" listed in II SAMUEL 23:31. I CHRONICLES 11:32

ABIEZER
1 A head of a family of the tribe of Manassah, Abiezer is recorded as receiving an allotment of land after the conquest of the Promised Land by Joshua. He also went by the name of Iezer, as mentioned in NUMBERS 26:39. JOSHUA 17:2; I CHRONICLES 7:18
2 This Abiezer hailed from Anathoth, and was one of David's leading warriors and a member of "The Thirty," the third division of David's elite group of guards. Abiezer was assigned as commander of David's army for the ninth month. II SAMUEL 23:27; I CHRONICLES 11:28, 27:12

ABIGAIL
1 The resourceful and charming wife of Nabel of Carmel, Abigail realized how foolish her husband had been in turning away David's messengers so churlishly. Unknown to her husband, Abigail brought gifts to pacify David, and thus averted a raid on Nabel. After Nabel's death, David married Abigail. She shared David's hardships at Gath, and was even captured once. Later, she lived at Hebron with David and was mother of his son, Chileab or Daniel. I SAMUEL 25, 27, 30; II SAMUEL 2:2
2 This Abigail was a sister of David. She married Ithra, and their son, Amasa, was remembered as the man Absalom appointed in place of Joab as commander. II SAMUEL 17:25; I CHRONICLES 2:16—17

ABIHAIL

1 A Levite, Abihail's son, Zuriel, was appointed chief of the Merari clan in Moses' time. The Meraris were assigned to camp on the north side of the tabernacle, and to carry certain parts of the tabernacle during the wandering in the wilderness. NUMBERS 3:35

2 A woman of the same name who married Abishur, one of those listed as a descendant of Judah. I CHRONICLES 2:29

3 A man who is listed in the genealogies as a head of a family in the tribe of Gad. I CHRONICLES 5:14

4 David's niece, who married Rehoboam, successor to Solomon. II CHRONICLES 11.18

5 Father of the beautiful and famous Esther, the Jewish girl who became queen of Persia. ESTHER 2:15; 9:29

ABIHU One of Aaron's sons, Abihu was a priest who accompanied Moses to Sinai, but who later died with his brother Nadab when they offered unholy fire to the Lord. EXODUS 6, 24, 28; LEVITICUS 10:1; NUMBERS 3, 26; I CHRONICLES 6; 24:1—2

ABIHUD Benjamin's grandson and Bela's son, Abihud is listed in the genealogies. I CHRONICLES 8:3

ABIJAH

1 Great-grandson of David, Abijah was the favorite son of Rehoboam. He ruled Judah for about two years at a time when Jeroboam had been king of the northern kingdom, Israel, for about twenty years. The Book of Kings states that Abijah continued all the sins of his ancestors. Chronicles, however, portrays him as a defender of the faith whose moment of glory came when he defeated Jeroboam's larger army and captured three Israelite cities and great booty. II CHRONICLES 11—14; I KINGS 14, 15

2 This Abijah was the second son of the great Samuel. Along with his brother, Joel, he was a judge at Beersheba, but so corrupt that pressure grew to elect a king in Israel. I CHRONICLES 8:2

3 The young son of King Jeroboam, Abijah took ill and died. During his illness his mother had gone in disguise to the prophet Ahijah to ask whether the boy would recover and was told that he would not. I KINGS 14:1

4 A priest in David's time, this Abijah drew the lot to be eighth when his turn came to be officer of the sanctuary. I CHRONICLES 24:10; 26:20

5 Benjamin's grandson, son of Becher, listed in the genealogies. I CHRONICLES 7:8

6 The mother of Hezekiah, and daughter of Zechariah, Abijah was a famous queen and queen mother in the eighth century B.C. She is listed in II Kings 18:2 as ABI. II CHRONICLES 29:1

7 One of the priests who returned from captivity in Babylonia with Zerubbabel, this Abijah was one of those who put his seal on the covenant drawn up by Nehemiah in Jerusalem to keep the Law. NEHEMIAH 10:7; 12:1—4, 12—17

ABIJAM See ABIJAH 1

ABIMAEL One of Noah's numerous descendants, Abimael is listed as one of the grandsons of Shem through Shem's son, Joktan. GENESIS 10:26—28; I CHRONICLES 1:20—22

ABIMELECH

1 A king of Gerar, this Abimelech was told by Abraham that Sarah, Abraham's wife, was Abraham's sister. After Abimelech took Sarah into his harem, he was warned in a dream that Sarah was actually Abraham's wife, and that his taking Sarah was the cause of temporary sterility among Abimelech's people and flocks. Indignant at Abraham's deceit, Abimelech sent Sarah back to her husband, gave him gifts, and asked him to leave. Later, after a squabble over a well, Abraham and Abimelech made a treaty at Beersheba. A variation of the stories of Abimelech and Abraham portrays Abimelech and Isaac going through exactly the same situations. GENESIS 20, 21, 26

2 This Abimelech was one of Gideon's sons, and was listed as one of the judges of Israel. A brutal ruler, Abimelech rose to power by executing all of his seventy brothers except Jotham, who escaped, and ruthlessly suppressed revolt by killing everyone in Shechem. Abimelech was fatally injured in the seige of Thebez when a woman dropped a millstone on him from the city wall. JUDGES 8, 9; II SAMUEL 11:21

3 Another Abimelech was the Philistine king of Gath when David fled for refuge and pretended to be insane. In I Samuel 21:10, this king is called Achish. PSALM 34:1

ABINADAB

1 The owner of the house in the village of Kirjath-jearim in which the Ark was placed after the disaster at Beth-Shemesh, Abinadab was a member of the tribe of Judah. His son Eleazar looked after the Ark until it was removed by David. Two other sons, Ahio and Uzzah, helped take the Ark to Jerusalem. I SAMUEL 7:1; II SAMUEL 6:3—4; I CHRONICLES 13:7

2 This Abinadab was David's older brother, Jesse's second son, who fought the Philistines alongside his brothers Eliab and Shammah. I SAMUEL 16:8; 17:13; I CHRONICLES 2:13

3 Another Abinadab, this was one of Saul's sons, who, with his brother Jonathan, died in the slaughter on Mount Gilboa when Saul was crushed by the Philistines. I SAMUEL 31:2; I CHRONICLES 8—10

4 An obscure Abinadab is mentioned as the father of one of Solomon's officials who supervised government in Dor in the territory of Issachar. I KINGS 4:11

ABINOAM
The father of Barak, the hero who defeated the Canaanites mentioned in Deborah's Song in the era of the judges of Israel. JUDGES 4, 5

ABIRAM

1 One of those who plotted against Moses in the desert, Abiram joined with his brother Dathan, and with On and Korah, but died after the conspiracy failed. NUMBERS 16, 26; DEUTERONOMY 11:6

2 The oldest son of Hiel of Bethel, this young man named Abiram died because his father disobeyed Joshua's

orders and started to rebuild Jericho. I KINGS 16:34

ABISHAG A pretty girl from Shunem, Abishag was hired to nurse David in his old age. After David's death, David's son Adonijah wanted to marry her, but was forbidden by Solomon because of the possible threat to Solomon's throne. I KINGS 1, 2

ABISHAI David's nephew and a bold and loyal follower of David, Abishai was always in the thick of the battles against the Philistines, the Edomites, the Ammonites, and Absalom's forces. He is given special mention in all the records and is listed as one of "The Thirty," David's elite corps of guardsmen-officers. I SAMUEL 26; II SAMUEL 2, 3, 10, 16, 18—21, 23; I CHRONICLES 2, 11, 18, 19

ABISHALOM King Jeraboam's father-in-law, sometimes known as Absalom, Abishalom was the father of Maachah. I KINGS 15: 2, 10

ABISHUA
1 Aaron's grandson and Phineas' son, Abishua is listed in the genealogies or family tree in Chronicles and Ezra. I CHRONICLES 6:4, 5, 50; EZRA 7:5
2 Another Abishua, this man is also one of those listed in the genealogical tables of Chronicles. He is Benjamin's grandson and Bela's son. I CHRONICLES 8:4

ABISHUR Judah's great-grandson, Abishur's place in the family tree of Judah is carefully listed by Chronicles, along with that of his father, Shammai, and his children. I CHRONICLES 2:28

ABITAL One of David's wives, Abital stayed with David at Hebron and was the mother of his fourth son, Shephatiah. II SAMUEL 3:4; I CHRONICLES 3:3

ABITUB One of the tribe of Benjamin listed in the genealogical charts, Abitub was the son of Shaharaim and was also known as Ahitub. I CHRONICLES 8:11

ABIUD One of Zerubbabel's sons, according to the list in Matthew. However, the name does not occur in the roll of Zerubbabel's sons in I Chronicles 3:19. MATTHEW 1:13

ABNER Saul's cousin and a valiant officer of Saul's army, Abner continued the war against David after Saul's death, but finally negotiated a peace. While received hospitably by David, Abner was resented by David's general, Joab. Joab, vengeful because of Abner's killing of Joab's associate Ashael, murdered Abner at the gate of Hebron. I SAMUEL 14, 17, 20, 26; II SAMUEL 2—4; I KINGS 2: I CHRONICLES 26, 27

ABRAHAM The patriarch who was the father of the people of God, Abraham left the security and comfort of Ur because of the call of God. Promised a land and descendants, Abraham lived most of his life without either, having to live on trust. God entered into a covenant with Abraham, assuring him that He kept His word. Finally, in his old age, a son called Isaac was born to Abraham and his wife, Sarah. Abraham's supreme test of faith came when God apparently went against His own promise and ordered Abraham to sacrifice the boy. Abraham obediently prepared to carry out the orders, but was stayed at the last minute when God intervened. Abraham finally secured a piece of land in the Promised Land when he bought a plot with a cave at Machpelah, where both Sarah and he were buried. Appropriately, his name in Hebrew means "father of a multitude," and he is revered as the spiritual ancestor of all Jews and Christians. GENESIS 11—25

ABRAM See ABRAHAM

ABSALOM The son of David, Absalom was a handsome and talented leader who broke his father's heart by leading a revolt against him. Avenging his sister Tamar, who had been attacked by his half-brother Amnon, Absalom killed Amnon and was forced to flee. Although attempts were made to bring David and Absalom together again, Absalom felt slighted and began to use his charm to win followers. His plot against David nearly succeeded, even causing David to flee from Jerusalem. II SAMUEL 3, 13—19; I KINGS 1, 2; I CHRONICLES 3:2

ACHAICUS With Stephanas and Fortunatus, Achaicus visited the Apostle Paul at Ephesus. He was a Corinthian Christian who cheered Paul and who was well regarded in the Corinthian church. I CORINTHIANS 16:17

ACHAN A greedy, deceitful man, Achan disobeyed Joshua's orders and the nation's pact against looting Jericho, and secretly stole some of the booty. When Israel's next assault was bloodily repulsed, the leaders suspected a breakdown of the community vow. Achan was tried and executed, along with his entire family. JOSHUA 7

ACHAR See ACHAN

ACHBOR

1 The father of the seventh king of Edom, Baal-hanan. GENESIS 36; I CHRONICLES 1:49
2 When a long-lost book was found during the repair of the Temple in King Josiah's reign in 640 B.C., Josiah sent Achbor as mesenger to ask the prophetess Huldah about the contents of the book. He is known as Abdon in II Chronicles 34:20. II KINGS 22: 12, 14
3 Father of Elnathan, the man sent by King Jehoikim to bring back the prophet Urijah from Egypt in 600 B.C. JEREMIAH 36

ACHIM One of Joseph's distant ancestors, Achim is mentioned only by Matthew in his genealogical table. MATTHEW 1:14

ACHISH

1 The first of two kings of Gath of the same name, this Achish allowed David to come to Gath after the massacre of the priests at Nob. When it was learned that David was the killer of Goliath, David pretended to be mad, but Achish generously befriended David. He let David settle in Ziglag and would have let David participate

in the final campaign against Saul if the other Philistine leaders had not vetoed the idea. I SAMUEL 21, 27—29
2 Another king of Gath, this Achish lived about forty-five years later, in Solomon's time. When two of Shimei's slaves ran away to Gath, Shimei broke his parole by going to Achish to bring them back. I KINGS 2: 39—40

ACHSA Caleb's daughter, Achsa was promised as bride to the man who captured Debir in 1440 B.C. Othniel took the town and claimed Achsa as his prize. She shrewdly persuaded her father to throw in some fresh springs for water in addition to her other dowry of lands. JOSHUA 15: 16—17; JUDGES 1: 12—13; I CHRONICLES 2: 49

ACHSAH   See ACHSA

ADAH
1 One of Lamech's two wives, Adah was the mother of Jabal and Jubal. GENESIS 4: 19—23
2 Another Adah, this woman was the daughter of Elon the Hittite, and became the wife of Esau. GENESIS 36: 2—16

ADAIAH
1 A native of Boscath, this Adaiah's daughter was the mother of King Josiah; thus Adaiah was Josiah's grandfather. II KINGS 22: 1
2 A Levite who was listed by the Chronicler as the distant ancestor of Asaph, one of David's temple singers. I CHRONICLES 6:41
3 One of the sons of Shimei, a Benjaminite listed in the rolls of that tribe. I CHRONICLES 8:21
4 Another Adaiah, this one was a

son of Jeroham, a Levite descended from Aaron, and was the head of a family listed as living in Jerusalem. I CHRONICLES 9:12; NEHEMIAH 11:12
5 This Adaiah was remembered as the father of the official named Maaseiah who helped Athaliah put Joash on the throne as king of Judah. II CHRONICLES 23:1
6 Another Adaiah, this man, the son of Bani, was listed as one of the many who married a non-Jewish girl during the Babylonian captivity and exile. EZRA 10:29
7 Yet another Adaiah lived during the Exile and broke the law by marrying a non-Jew. EZRA 10:39
8 One of the tribe of Judah, this Adaiah's descendant, Athaiah, was listed in Nehemiah's roster of those living in Jerusalem. NEHEMIAH 11:9

ADALIA The fifth of the ten sons of the vicious Haman, the Persian official, Adalia was hung with his father and brothers when Queen Esther saved the Jews. ESTHER 9:8

ADAM As the meaning of his name in Hebrew, "of the ground," implies, Adam was created from dust and given life by God's breath into his nostrils. Adam was put on earth to live obediently and responsibly before God and given freedom to enjoy every part of creation except the tree of knowledge of good and evil. Persuaded to sample the fruit of the forbidden tree by Eve his wife, Adam disobeyed God. His disobedience alienated him from God, his wife, and all of nature, and set off the chain-reaction of sin. GENESIS 2—5

ADAR One of Bela's sons, Benjamin's grandson, listed in the genealogies. I CHRONICLES 8:3

ADBEEL The third son of Ishmael, Adbeel's name is one of those included in the roll of Abraham's descendants. GENESIS 25:13; I CHRONICLES 1:29

ADDAR See ADAR

ADDI One of Joseph's remote ancestors, listed by Luke. LUKE 3:28

ADER One of Berah's sons, included in the roll of the tribe of Benjamin by the Chronicler. I CHRONICLES 8:15

ADIEL
1 One of the tribe of Simeon, Adiel joined with other members of his tribe to drive out nomads from the grazing lands of Gedor and take over their territory. I CHRONICLES 4:36
2 The ancestor of one of the priests taken into exile to Babylonia. I CHRONICLES 9:12
3 The father of David's treasurer, Azmaveth. I CHRONICLES 27:25

ADIN One of the heads of families carried off to Babylonia during the Exile. Adin's family returned to Jerusalem, one contingent with Zerubbabel, another with Ezra, and joined with Nehemiah in putting their seal to the covenant to keep the Law. EZRA 2:15; 8:6; NEHEMIAH 7:20; 10:14—16

ADINA A Reubenite fighter, Adina was one of David's "mighty men of the armies." I CHRONICLES 11:42

ADLAI Father of Shaphat, David's chief herdsman in the valleys. I CHRONICLES 27:29

ADMATHA One of seven Persian royal advisors, Admatha was one of those few who were admitted to the king's presence and allowed to look at the king. ESTHER 1:14

ADNA
1 A member of the family of Pahath-moab, Adna married a non-Jewish woman during the Exile, breaking the Law. EZRA 10:30
2 A grandson of Jozadak and son of Jeshua, this Adna was head of the priestly family of Harim in the days of high priest Joiakim, at the time the Jews rebuilt the wall of Jerusalem after the Exile. NEHEMIAH 12:15

ADNAH
1 One of Saul's army officers from the tribe of Manasseh, Adnah left Saul to join David at Ziglag. I CHRONICLES 12:20
2 King Jehoshaphat's commander-in-chief over the troops of Judah, which numbered some three hundred thousand men. II CHRONICLES 17:14

ADONIBEZEK The head of a Canaanite tribe in southern Palestine, Adonibezek was captured after a battle with the tribe of Judah. He had frequently boasted of having chopped off the thumbs and big toes of seventy kings, and so he received similar torture and mutilation from Judah. JUDGES 1:5—7

ADONIJAH
1 David's fourth son, Adonijah was in line to succeed David as king. Bathsheba, however, prevailed upon the aged, dying David to name Solomon as his successor. Adonijah went

ADONIKAM

ahead with schemes to have himself crowned. His conspiracy was blocked by the prophet Nathan, who hurried to have David and Bathsheba approve a speedy coronation of Solomon. Although Adonijah pledged loyalty to Solomon, Solomon quickly became alarmed at Adonijah's bold and somewhat treasonous request to marry Abishag, David's nurse, and had him executed. II SAMUEL 3:4; I KINGS 1—2
2 A Levite, this Adonijah was sent by King Jehoshaphat to teach the Law in the cities of Judah in an effort to reform the nation in 914 B.C. II CHRONICLES 17:8
3 Another Adonijah was one of the chiefs who signed the covenant with Nehemiah after the Exile, promising to keep the Law. NEHEMIAH 10:16

ADONIKAM One of those whose clan returned to Jerusalem after the Exile in Babylonia. EZRA 2:13; 8:13; NEHEMIAH 7:18; 10:16

ADONIRAM The superintendent of the levies of forced laborers during the reigns of David, Solomon, and Rehoboam, Adoniram was an important person in the ambitious building programs of his masters. The freedom-loving populace resented being drafted as laborers, and hated Adoniram. He was finally stoned to death in Israel when the northern provinces revolted during Rehoboam's reign. I KINGS 4—5

ADONIZEDEK A king of the Canaanites who ruled Jerusalem at the time Joshua was invading the Promised Land, Adonizedek persuaded four other Canaanite chiefs to unite and try to repel Joshua. They were brilliantly outmaneuvered and defeated by Joshua, and were subsequently put to death. JOSHUA 10:1—3

ADORAM See **ADONIRAM**

ADRAMMELECH One of the sons of the Assyrian King Sennacherib, Adrammelech joined with his brother Sharezer to murder Sennacherib in the Temple of Nisroch in 721 B.C. II KINGS 19:37; ISAIAH 37:38

ADRIEL The man who married Merab, Saul's oldest daughter, who had been promised as David's bride for killing Goliath, Adriel fathered five sons who were hung by the Gibeonites to even the account for Saul's atrocities. I SAMUEL 18:19; II SAMUEL 21:8

AENEAS A paralytic in Lydda who had been bedridden for eight years, Aeneas was healed in the name of Jesus Christ by Peter. ACTS 9:33—34

AGABUS A Christian prophet from Jerusalem, Agabus went to Paul in Antioch in 44 A.D. and predicted a famine. Some years later, perhaps 59 A.D., Agabus warned Paul that he would be imprisoned if he went to Jerusalem. In spite of Agabus' warning, Paul went—and was seized. ACTS 11:28; 21:10

AGAG A ruler of the Amalekites who was captured by Saul, Agag was at first spared by Saul, against the prophet Samuel's instructions. Later, Samuel personally hacked him to pieces. I SAMUEL 15

AGEE The father of Shammah, one of David's great warriors. Shammah's one-man stand at Lehi won the day against the Philistines. II SAMUEL 23:11

AGRIPPA Great-grandson of Herod the Great, Marcus Julius Agrippa was the son of Agrippa I and was only seventeen when he succeeded his father in 44 A.D. as ruler of Galilee, Abilene, Iturea, and Trachonitis. He dabbled enough in both Greek and Jewish lore to prompt the compliment from St. Paul that he was an expert in Jewish customs. Agrippa heard Paul's case, and would have dismissed it had not Paul already appealed to Caesar. Agrippa lived until 100 A.D., and was the last of the Herods. ACTS 25—26

AGUR A Jewish sage mentioned only as "son of Jakeh" in Proverbs 30, Agur was a collector of many of the sayings in the Book of Proverbs. PROVERBS 30:1

AHAB
1 Queen Jezebel's husband and Omri's son, Ahab was seventh king of Israel from about 919 B.C. to 897 B.C. Under Jezebel's influence, he tried to promote Baal and Astarte worship and to silence the Lord's prophets. This brought the great Elijah into conflict with Ahab and Jezebel. Ahab was warrior enough to defeat and capture Banhadad, the Syrian king, but witless enough to let him go free, to the prophet's disgust. On another occasion, Ahab was guilty of appropriating Naboth's vineyard, thus angering Elijah. He died in battle in an ill-advised war against the Syrians. I KINGS 16—22; II CHRONICLES 18

2 A false prophet and a contemporary of Jeremiah this Ahab was carried off to Babylon around 600 B.C., and burned to death by King Nebuchadnezzar. JEREMIAH 29:21—22

AHARAH The third son of Benjamin, listed in the family genealogy by the Chronicler. I CHRONICLES 8:1

AHARHEL A son of Harum who is listed in the rolls of the tribe of Judah. I CHRONICLES 4:8

AHASAI See AHZAI

AHASBAI The father of Eliphelet, one of the members of David's crack corps of "The Thirty." II SAMUEL 23:34

AHASUERUS
1 The Persian monarch better known as Xerxes, 485-465 B.C. Cruel, capricious, and extravagant, Ahasuerus is best remembered in the Bible for the pogrom which was averted through the efforts of his wife Esther, the Jewish queen. ESTHER 1—3; 6—10; EZRA 4:6
2 A Persian ruler referred to in the Book of Daniel as the father of Darius the Mede, this Ahasuerus cannot be clearly identified by Biblical scholars and historians. DANIEL 9:11

AHAZ
1 Eleventh king of Judah, Ahaz was Jotham's son and Hezekiah's father. His sixteen-year reign (about 735 B.C. to about 720 B.C.) was the backdrop for the prophet Isaiah's great career. Ahaz preferred to play international politics rather than heed Isaiah's sound advice, even scorning a sign from God,

Immanuel, whom Isaiah promised. Inevitably, Ahaz and Judah came out as losers, paying expensive "presents" to the larger powers. A superstitious dabbler in idolatrous cults, Ahaz left his country weakened morally and financially. II KINGS 15—17; I CHRONICLES 9:42; II CHRONICLES 27:9, 28; ISAIAH 1, 7; HOSEA 1:1; MICAH 1:1

2 One of the tribe of Benjamin this Ahaz belonged to Saul's branch of the family tree. I CHRONICLES 8:35—36; I CHRONICLES 9:41—42

AHAZIAH

1 Son of Jezebel and Ahab, Ahaziah became king of Israel when his father was killed in his ill-planned alliance with Jehoshaphat against the Syrians. As superstitious and idolatrous as his parents, Ahaziah reigned only two years before dying as a result of injuries from a fall. I KINGS 22; II KINGS 1; I CHRONICLES 3:11; II CHRONICLES 20

2 Another king, this Ahaziah was fifth ruler of Judah, the southern kingdom, succeeding his father Jehoram. During his one-year reign, however, the real ruler was the queen mother Athaliah, an evil woman who corrupted the nation. II KINGS 8—12; I CHRONICLES 3:11; II CHRONICLES 22

AHBAN One of the clan of Jerahmeel of the tribe of Judah listed in the genealogies by the Chronicler. I CHRONICLES 2:29

AHER One of those on the rolls of the tribe of Benjamin listed by the Chronicler. I CHRONICLES 7:12

AHI

1 One of the tribe of Gad who was head of a family. I CHRONICLES 5:15

2 An Asherite, listed in the genealogies by the Chronicler. I CHRONICLES 7:34

AHIAH   See AHIJAH

AHIAM The son of Sharar, and one of David's thirty greatest fighting men, Ahaim was sometimes known as Sacar. II SAMUEL 23:33; I CHRONICLES 11:35

AHIAN One of the tribe of Manassah listed in the family rolls by the Chronicler. I CHRONICLES 7:19

AHIEZER

1 A son of Ammishaddai, Ahiezer was selected to represent the tribe of Dan when Moses decided to count all those who were with him in the Exodus from Egypt. NUMBERS 1:12; 2:25; 7:66, 71; 10:25

2 A chieftain from the tribe of Benjamin this Ahiezer, although a relative of Saul, decided to throw in his lot with David and brought his troop of expert archers to David at Ziglag. I CHRONICLES 12:3

AHIHUD

1 One of Ehud's clan, this Ahihud was head of a family in the tribe of Benjamin, according to the Chronicler's list. I CHRONICLES 8:7

2 A member of the tribe of Asher, this Ahihud, a son of Shelomi, was selected to represent his tribe when Moses divided the Promised Land. NUMBERS 34:27

AHIJAH

1 Great-grandson of the great priest Eli and grandson of Phineas, this Ahijah was the priest who carried the ephod for Saul and accompanied his army as oracle-consultant. I SAMUEL 14:3, 18

2 The prophet of the Lord who lived in Jeroboam's time, Ahijah ripped his coat into twelve pieces, giving Jeroboam ten, dramatically promising that on Solomon's death the kingdom would divide. Years later, Jeroboam sent his wife in disguise to ask about their sick child. Ahijah was not fooled by the deception, and cooly announced that Jeroboam's line would die out. I KINGS, 11, 12, 14, 15; II CHRONICLES 9:29; 10:15

3 A son of Shisha, Ahijah, with his brother Elihoreph, was one of Solomon's secretaries, carrying on the family occupation which Shisha had begun under David. I KINGS 4:3

4 The father of Baasha, the man who successfully conspired against Jeroboam's son Nadab and made himself king of Israel about 953 B.C. I KINGS 27:33; 21:22; II KINGS 9:9

5 One of Jerahmeel's sons listed in the roster of Judah's family. I CHRONICLES 2:25

6 One of Ehud's sons listed in the roll of the tribe of Benjamin. I CHRONICLES 8:7

7 The Pelonite who was one of David's great fighting men, listed in the roll of "The Thirty," the top heroes in David's army. I CHRONICLES 11:36

8 A Levite, who was put in charge of David's Temple treasury and given oversight of the special offerings for the Temple. I CHRONICLES 26:20

9 One of the heads of a family who returned from the Exile in Babylon, and joined with Nehemiah to sign the covenant promising to keep the Law in Jerusalem in 445 B.C. NEHEMIAH 10:26

AHIKAM An official in King Josiah's court, Ahikam was one of those sent by Josiah to Huldah the prophetess to ask for advice when the book we now call Deuteronomy was discovered during renovations in the Temple. Some years later, he protected Jeremiah from mob violence. He was also remembered as the father of Gedaliah, whom Nebuchadnezzar appointed as governor of Judah. II KINGS 22; II CHRONICLES 34:20; JEREMIAH 26:24; 39:14; 40:5—16

AHILUD Ahilud was the father of two prominent civil servants. One son, Jehoshaphat, was a keeper of records under David and Solomon; another son, Baana, was one of Solomon's commissary officers, responsible for providing food for the palace for one month each year. II SAMUEL 8:16; 20:24; I KINGS 4:3, 12; I CHRONICLES 18:15

AHIMAAZ

1 Father of Ahinoam, who married King Saul. I SAMUEL 14:50

2 A son of Zadok the priest, Ahimaaz was such a fast long-distance runner that he became a famous and trusted messenger for David. He played a key part in saving David during Absalom's revolt, and was the man who brought the sad news of Absalom's death to David. II SAMUEL 15—18

3 Another Ahimaaz, this man was one of Solomon's commissary officers responsible for getting food for the entire palace household for one month every year, and was given the province of Naphtali as his territory. I KINGS 4:15

AHIMAN

1 A son of Anak, Ahiman lived in Hebron at the time of the conquest of the Promised Land and was one of the Canaanites pushed out by the invading tribes of Israel. NUMBERS 13: 22; JOSHUA 15:14; JUDGES 1:10

2 A Levite who was one of those appointed a gatekeeper of the Levites' camp in David and Solomon's time. I CHRONICLES 9:17

AHIMELECH

1 The priest of Nob who looked after David when he was a fugitive from Saul, Ahimelech broke the rules by feeding the hungry David some of the holy bread and by giving David Goliath's sword. When Ahimelech's acts were reported to Saul, Saul ordered Ahimelech and eighty-five other priests executed. I SAMUEL 21—22

2 A Hittite fighter who joined David's guerrilla forces and became a leader. I SAMUEL 26:6

3 One of Abiathar's sons, this Ahimelech was the grandson of 1, above. His father was the only survivor of the massacre of priests at Nob. Ahimelech carried on the family tradition and became a priest in David's time. II SAMUEL 8:17; I CHRONICLES 18:16; 24:6

AHIMOTH One of the tribe of Levi listed under the descendants of Kohath by the Chronicler. I CHRONICLES 6:25

AHINADAB Son of Iddo, Ahinadab

was one of Solomon's twelve commissary officers responsible for getting food for the entire palace household for one month every year, and was assigned the area of Mahanaim. I KINGS 4:14

AHINOAM

1 Daughter of Ahamaaz, Ahinoam married King Saul. I SAMUEL 14:50

2 A woman of Jezreel, this Ahinoam married David and joined him at Gath and Ziglag along with his other wife, Abigail. She and Abigail were captured briefly by the Amalekites and were later rescued. Ahinoam subsequently lived with David at Hebron where she gave birth to David's oldest son, Amnon. I SAMUEL 25:43; 27:3; 30:5; II SAMUEL 2:2; 3:2; I CHRONICLES 3:1

AHIO

1 A son of Abinadab, the man who housed the Ark after it was sent back by the Philistines, Ahio and his brother Uzzah drove the cart carrying the Ark from their home in Kirjathjearim to Jerusalem during David's reign. II SAMUEL 6:3, 4; I CHRONICLES 13:7

2 One of the men listed in the family tree in the genealogy of the house of Benjamin. I CHRONICLES 8:14

3 Another Ahio, this one is remembered as one of Saul's uncles. I CHRONICLES 8:31; 9:37

AHIRA A son of Enan, the man selected to represent the tribe of Naphtali when Moses asked for leaders to help him conduct a census of those accompanying him in the wilderness.

NUMBERS 1:15; 2:29; 7:78; 7:83; 10:27

AHIRAM The name of a man in the tribe of Benjamin who was founder of a large family. NUMBERS 26:38; I CHRONICLES 8:1

AHISAMACH One of the tribe of Dan at the time of Moses, Ahisamach's son helped prepare the tabernacle for worship. EXODUS 31:6; 35:34; 38:23

AHISHAHAR One of the sons of Bilhan and a grandson of Benjamin, listed in the genealogical tables of the tribe of Benjamin. I CHRONICLES 7:10

AHISHAR The man who had the heavy responsibility of being superintendent of Solomon's palace. I KINGS 4:6

AHITHOPHEL One of David's most influential advisors, Ahithophel was an astute, crafty politician who later encouraged Absalom to rebel against David. When Absalom turned down the key part of the plan that Ahithophel had prepared, Ahithophel shrewdly knew the revolt was doomed and hung himself—the only suicide in the Old Testament that was not motivated by war. II SAMUEL 15—17; II CHRONICLES 27

AHITUB
1 The grandson of Eli the priest, this Ahitub was also a priest, and is best remembered as the father of another priest, Ahimelech, who was killed by Saul for aiding the fugitive David. I SAMUEL 14:3; 22:9—20
2 Perhaps the same as 1, Ahitub is mentioned as the father of the high priest Zadok in David's reign. II SAMUEL 8:17; I CHRONICLES 6:7—8; 18:16; EZRA 7:2
3 Another Ahitub, this man lived seven generations later than 2 and was also listed in the family tree of Levi. I CHRONICLES 6:11—12
4 An ancestor of Azariah, who was one of the priests to return to Jerusalem from the Exile in Babylon. I CHRONICLES 9:11; NEHEMIAH 11:11

AHLAI
1 One of Shashan's family listed in the genealogy of Perez's tribe by the Chronicler. I CHRONICLES 2:31
2 The father of Zabad, one of David's fighters in the elite corps of "The Thirty." I CHRONICLES 11:41

AHOAH A son of Bela, one of the tribe of Benjamin listed in the genealogies by the Chronicler. I CHRONICLES 8:4

AHOLIAB A member of the tribe of Dan, Aholiab was a skilled designer and builder appointed by Moses to work with Bezaleel in constructing the tabernacle. EXODUS 31:6; 35:34; 36:1—2; 38:23

AHOLIBAMAH
1 The daughter of Anah, a Canaanite, who was one of Esau's wives. GENESIS 36
2 One of Esau's numerous descendants, this Aholibamah was a head of a family or clan giving allegiance to Esau. GENESIS 36:41; I CHRONICLES 1:52

AHUMAI Judah's great-grandson, listed in the family tree of the tribe of Judah. I CHRONICLES 4:2

AHUZAM One of Ashur's sons, and a descendant of Judah through Caleb, Ahuzam was named in the rolls of the tribe of Judah. I CHRONICLES 4:6

AHUZZAM See **AHUZAM**

AHUZZATH A friend and advisor of the Philistine King Abimelech of Gerar, Ahuzzath was present and active in the treaty negotiations between Isaac and King Abimelech at Beersheba. GENESIS 26:26

AHZAI A priest, Ahzai was the ancestor of Amashai, one of the priests who returned to Jerusalem after the Exile. NEHEMIAH 11:13; I CHRONICLES 9:12

AIAH
1 One of the sons of Zibeon, Aiah was a descendant of Seir, a Horite chief listed among Esau's descendants. GENESIS 36:24; I CHRONICLES 1:40
2 The father of Rizpah, one of Saul's mistresses. II SAMUEL 3:7; 21:8—11

AKAN A son of Ezer, Akan was a descendant of Seir, a Horite chief who was one of the descendants of Esau. GENESIS 36:27; I CHRONICLES 1:42

AKKUB
1 One of David's many descendants, Akkub is listed by the Chronicler as one of Elioeni's sons. I CHRONICLES 3:24
2 A Levite, this Akkub was appointed one of the gatekeepers on the east side of the city of the Lord in David's time. His descendants returned to Jerusalem after the Exile. I CHRONICLES 9:17; EZRA 2:42, 45; NEHEMIAH 7:45; 11:19; 12:25
3 Another Akkub, this man was one of the Levites selected by Ezra to teach and explain the Law to those who had returned from Exile in Babylon. NEHEMIAH 8:7

ALAMETH See **ALEMETH**

ALEMETH
1 A grandson of Benjamin and son of Becher, Alemeth is listed in the genealogy of the tribe of Benjamin. I CHRONICLES 7:8
2 One of Saul's descendants through Jonathan, listed in the rolls of the tribe of Benjamin. I CHRONICLES 8:36; 9:42

ALEXANDER
1 Alexander was the son of Simon of Cyrene, the man who was compelled to bear Jesus' cross. Alexander and his brother Rufus were apparently well known to Mark's readers, and were probably Jewish Christians, active in the church. MARK 15:21
2 A leading public figure in Jerusalem, this Alexander was one of the high priest's clique who conducted the hearing when Peter and John were arrested after the resurrection and accused of healing and preaching. ACTS 4:6
2 A well-known Jew in Ephesus who became one of Paul's converts to Jesus Christ, this Alexander was present at the riot in Ephesus, and tried unsuccessfully to calm the mob and defend Paul the Apostle's companions. ACTS 19:33
4 This Alexander, along with Hymenaeus, was one of the converts who

later renounced their belief in Christ and were described by Paul as people who made a "shipwreck of their faith." I TIMOTHY 1:1—2

5 A coppersmith, possibly of Ephesus, this Alexander seriously hampered Paul's ministry. Paul warned Timothy to beware of this Alexander as a malicious character. Possibly Alexander **4** and **5** are the same. II TIMOTHY 4:14

ALIAH One of Esau's descendants who was an Edomite chieftain. GENESIS 36:40; I CHRONICLES 1:51

ALIAN One of the sons of Shobal, listed among Seir's descendants in the family tree of Esau. GENESIS 36:23; I CHRONICLES 1:40

ALLON The head of one of thhe families listed in the rolls of the tribe of Simeon. I CHRONICLES 4:37

ALMODAD One of Joktan's sons, a descendant of Noah through Noah's son, Shem. GENESIS 10:26; I CHRONICLES 1:20

ALPHAEUS
1 The father of Matthew, Jesus' disciple. MARK 2:14
2 The father of the second James in the list of Jesus' disciples. Scholars are not certain whether Alphaeus **1** and **2** are the same man. If so, it would mean that Matthew and James "the Less" were brothers. MATTHEW 10:3; MARK 3:18; LUKE 6:15; ACTS 1:13

ALVAH See ALIAH

ALVAN See ALIAN

AMAL Asher's grandson, Beriak's son, listed in the genealogy of Asher. I CHRONICLES 7:35

AMALEK The grandson of Esau and son of Eliphaz, Amalek was the founder of a large clan of fierce desert warriors known as the Amalekites who bitterly fought the Israelites' entrance into Canaan. GENESIS 36:12, 16; I CHRONICLES 1:36

AMARIAH
1 The grandfather of Zadok, and son of Meraiioth, high priest in David's reign. I CHRONICLES 6:7, 52; EZRA 7:3
2 Another Amariah, also a high priest, was a son of Azariah, and was high priest in the time of Solomon. I CHRONICLES 6:11; EZRA 7:3
3 This Amariah, a son of Hebron, was a Levite of the family of Kohath and lived in David's time. I CHRONICLES 23:19; 24:23
4 Still another Amariah, a high priest in the time of Jehoshaphat, was appointed by the king to preside over a supreme court to pass on "all matters of the Lord." II CHRONICLES 19:11
5 A Levite who lived in King Hezekiah's time, this Amariah was responsible for distributing the offerings fairly among all the other Levites. II CHRONICLES 31:15
6 One of Bani's family in the tribe of Judah, this Amariah married a non-Jewish girl during the Exile, breaking the Law. EZRA 10:42
7 A priest who headed a large and influential family, this Amariah joined with Nehemiah in signing the covenant to keep the Law after the return

from Exile in Babylon. NEHEMIAH 10:3; 12:2; 13

8 One of Perez's descendants in the tribe of Judah, this Amariah's descendant, Athaiah, was one of those who volunteered to stay on in Jerusalem during the Exile. NEHEMIAH 11:4

9 One of the prophet Zephaniah's distant ancestors, who lived at the time of King Josiah. ZEPHANIAH 1:1

AMASA

1 David's nephew, Amasa joined Absalom's revolt and was made an army officer. Amasa's forces were routed by Joab, David's able general, and the revolt was quashed. David not only forgave Amasa but even appointed him to take Joab's place. He was later assassinated by Joab when Joab came to take over the royal army. II SAMUEL 17—20

2 An outspoken member of the tribe of Ephraim, Amasa was one of those who criticized King Pekah of Israel for bringing fellow Jews who had been captured in the skirmishes with King Ahab of Judah into Samaria. II CHRONICLES 28:12

AMASAI

1 One of Kohath's descendants listed in the genealogies of the tribe of Levi. I CHRONICLES 6:25, 35

2 A chieftain of the tribe of Benjamin who deserted King Saul and brought his squad of thirty fighters to join David at Ziglag. I CHRONICLES 12:18

3 A priest who blew a trumpet and participated in the celebration when David brought the Ark to Jerusalem. I CHRONICLES 15:24

AMASHAI See AMASHSAI

AMASHSAI
A priest, the son of Immer, who was one of those volunteering to settle in Jerusalem during the Exile. NEHEMIAH 11:13

AMASIAH
One of the staff in Jehoshaphat's army, Amasiah patriotically volunteered and later rose to be in charge of two hundred thousand men. II CHRONICLES 17:16

AMAZIAH

1 A king of Judah, this Amaziah came to the throne when his father, Joash, was assassinated (800 B.C.). Amaziah beat a group of desert raiders from Edom and rashly decided he would challenge the larger, stronger King Jehoash of Israel. Jehoash tried to talk Amaziah out of attacking, using the famous parable of the cedar and the thistle. Amaziah ignored the advice, went to war, and suffered complete and humiliating defeat. II KINGS 12—15

2 One of the tribe of Simeon, this Amaziah was chieftain of a clan that slaughtered the shepherds in the valley near Gedor and settled in that area during King Hezekiah's time. I CHRONICLES 4:34

3 A member of the tribe of Levi through Merari, this Amaziah was founder of a family which served in the house of the Lord in David's time. I CHRONICLES 6:45

4 A turncoat priest who had sold out to the nationalistic, idolatrous cult at Bethel backed by Jeroboam II, this Amaziah tried to intimidate and silence the prophet Amos when Amos appeared at Bethel to denounce the cult. AMOS 7:10—14

AMI Ami was one of Solomon's staff of servants. His descendants returned with Zerubbabel to Jerusalem after Exile in Babylon. EZRA 2:57

AMINADAB See AMMINADAB

AMITTAI One of the tribe of Zebulon, Amittai was the father of the missionary-prophet, Jonah. II KINGS 14:25; JONAH 1:1

AMMIEL
1 A member of the tribe of Dan who was sent out by Moses to spy in the Promised Land of Canaan, Ammiel was one of the majority of spies who advised against invading the land. NUMBERS 13:12
2 One of the tribe of Manassah who lived at Lodebar, this Ammiel was the father of Machir, the man who took in Jonathan's orphaned, crippled son. II SAMUEL 9:4—5; 17:27
3 The father of Bathshela, one of David's wives, this Ammiel (or Eliam as he was sometimes called) was the maternal grandfather of Solomon. I CHRONICLES 3:5; II SAMUEL 11:3 (where the name is "Eliam").
4 A Levite, this fourth Amiel was one of Korah's descendants, and served as south gatekeeper in the tabernacle in David's time. I CHRONICLES 26:5

AMMIHUD
1 One of the tribe of Ephraim, Ammihud was the father of a strong chief called Elisham who was selected to represent his tribe in the census Moses was ordered to take. NUMBERS 1:10; 2:18; 7:48; 7:53; 10:22 I CHRONICLES 7:26
2 One of the tribe of Simeon, this Ammihud was the father of Shemuel

the man picked by Moses from the tribe of Simeon to help divide the land equitably among all tribes. NUMBERS 34:20
3 One of the tribe of Naphtali, this third man by the same name was the father of Pedahel, the man picked by Moses from the tribe of Naphtali to help divide the land equitably among all tribes. NUMBERS 34:28
4 This man was the father of Talmai, the king of Geshur, to whom David's fugitive son Absalom fled after murdering his brother Amnon. II SAMUEL 13:37
5 One of the tribe of Judah, a descendant of Perez, this Ammihud was an ancestor of Uthai, one of the first to return to Jerusalem after the Exile. I CHRONICLES 9:4

AMMIHUR See AMMIHUD 4

AMMINADAB
1 A member of the tribe of Levi, Amminadab was the father of Elisheba, Aaron's wife. EXODUS 6:23
2 Perhaps the same as 1, Amminadab was an ancestor of David, according to Ruth's genealogy, and the father of Nahshon, a chief of Judah in Moses' time. NUMBERS 1:7; 2:3; 7:12; 7:17; RUTH 4:19—20; I CHRONICLES 2:10
3 A son of Kohath and the father of Korah, an Amminadab is listed in the rolls of the tribe of Levi who is possibly the same man as 1 and 2. I CHRONICLES 6:22
4 A different Amminadab, this one was a Levite who was part of the crew of priests and Levites which David gathered to bring the Ark to Jerusalem. I CHRONICLES 15:10—11

AMMISHADDAI One of the tribe of Dan, Ammishaddai was the father of the leader, Ahiezer, one of those picked by Moses to help in the census of the tribes leaving Egypt. NUMBERS 1:12; 2:25; 7:66; 7:71; 10:25

AMMIZABAD Son of one of David's renowned commanders and most famous warriors, Benaiah, Ammizabad was in charge of a division of David's troops, but apparently was never as famous as his father. I CHRONICLES 27:6

AMMON The son of Lot by the incestuous relationship of Lot and his youngest daughter, Ammon was the ancestor of a depraved, cruel tribe called Ammonites, who were the mortal enemies of the Israelites. Ammon was also known as Benammi. GENESIS 19:38

AMNON
1 David's oldest son, Amnon seduced his half-sister, Tamar, and was murdered by her indignant brother, Absalom. II SAMUEL 3:2; 13:1—39; I CHRONICLES 3:1
2 A son of Shimon of the family of Caleb, listed in the genealogy of the tribe of Judah by the Chronicler, this Amnon was an ancient clan chief in the tribe. I CHRONICLES 4:20

AMOK The head of a respected family of priests. Amok returned from Babylon with Zerubbabel and worked to rebuild Jerusalem. NEHEMIAH 12:7, 20

AMON
1 Mayor of the city of Samaria in the reign of Jezebel and Ahab (900 B.C.), Amon was given custody of the prophet Micaiah when Ahab joined with Jehoshaphat in the fatal skirmish against the Syrians. I KINGS 22:26; I CHRONICLES 18:25
2 The king of Judah who succeeded Manassah, Amon reigned two years in a dreary repeat of his father Manassah's immorality, luxury, and corruption. He was assassinated in a palace intrigue (639 B.C.), and died unmourned. II KINGS 21; I CHRONICLES 3:14; II CHRONICLES 33
3 A servant of Solomon whose descendants were named among those who returned from Exile in Babylon with Zerubbabel, Amon is also listed as Ami. EZRA 2:57; NEHEMIAH 7:59

AMOS
1 One of the great prophets of the eighth century B.C., whose Book in the Bible is one of the most eloquent denunciations of injustice and cruelty in history, Amos was not from the prophets' caste, but was a rough shepherd and dresser of sycamore trees from Tekoa, a village south of Bethlehem in Judah. He burst in on the idolatrous worship at the national shrine of the northern kingdom of Israel at Bethel, and spoke bluntly for God against the social sins of the nation. The high priest at Bethel, Amaziah, accused him of treason and ordered him out. Undeterred, Amos warned of the coming judgment, using the memorable imagery of a basket of summer fruit, lovely without, but rotten within, and of a plumb line. Nothing is known of Amos' later

career, apart from his return to Tekoa and the writing down of his speeches at Bethel. AMOS

2 One of Jesus' remote ancestors on Joseph's side, this otherwise unknown Amos is included in the genealogy in Luke. LUKE 3:25

AMOZ One of the tribe of Judah, Amoz was the father of the famous prophet Isaiah in the eighth century B.C. II KINGS 19:2; ISAIAH 1:1

AMPLIAS See AMPLIATUS

AMPLIATUS One of those mentioned by name at the conclusion of Paul's letter to the Romans, and to whom he sends special greetings, Ampliatus was a beloved and rather prominent member of the church at Rome. "Ampliatus" was a common name for slaves, leading some to think that this person was also a slave. There is a cell in the catacombs of St. Domatilla dating back to the first century A.D. with the name Ampliatus inscribed over the doorway. ROMANS 16:8

AMRAM

1 Levi's grandson through Kothath, Amram was the father of Moses, Aaron, and Miriam, and the husband of Jochebed. He died in Egypt at the age of 137, the head of a large clan. EXODUS 6:18—20; NUMBERS 3:19; 26:58—59; I CHRONICLES 6:2—3, 18; 23:12—13; 24: 20

2 One of Bani's many descendants who married non-Jewish brides during the Exile, thereby breaking the Law. Amram abided by Ezra's strict rule and returned to Jerusalem without his wife to keep the faith pure. EZRA 10:34

3 For the "Amram" in I CHRONICLES 1:41, see HAMRAM

AMRAPHEL The king of "Shinar," a Mesopotamian state whose location is not definitely known, Amraphel joined with three of his chieftain cronies to fight five other chiefs, including the king of Sodom, Lot's protector. In the rout, Lot, Abraham's nephew, was captured. GENESIS 14

AMZI

1 One of Levi's many descendants through Merari, Amzi was an ancestor of Ethan, David's choir leader. I CHRONICLES 6:45

2 The great-grandfather of Adaiah, this Amzi was a priest in the rebuilt temple at the time of Nehemiah. NEHEMIAH 11:12

ANAH

1 One of the sons of Seir, the Horite, a clan head in the land of Canaan, this Anah is listed with Esau's relatives. GENESIS 36:20, 39; I CHRONICLES 1:38

2 A nephew of 1 and the son of Zibeon, Seir's son, this Anah discovered hot springs in the wilderness while looking after his father's flocks. He was Esau's father-in-law through Esau's marriage to Anah's daughter, Oholibama. GENESIS 36:2, 14, 18, 24, 25; I CHRONICLES 1:40—41

ANAIAH

1 One of the priests who stood at Ezra's right hand while he read the Law to the people in 445 B.C., this Anaiah was a prominent man in Jerusalem after the return from Babylon. NEHEMIAH 8:4

2 This Anaiah was the head of a clan or family who joined Nehemiah in signing a solemn covenant promising to keep the Law. NEHEMIAH 10:22

ANAK The son of Arba, Anak was a giant of a man whose children and descendants were renowned for their enormous size. "The sons of Anak" lived in the hill country near Hebron, and were formidable opponents when the children of Israel invaded Canaan. The tribe was later absorbed by the Philistines. NUMBERS 13:22—33; DEUTERONOMY 9:2; JOSHUA 15:13—15; 21:11; JUDGES 1:20

ANAN One of those who returned from Exile in Babylonia, Anan joined with Nehemiah in signing the covenant to keep the Law. NEHEMIAH 10:26

ANANI One of the sons of Elioeni, Anani was a descendant of David listed in the roll of the Chronicler. I CHRONICLES 3:24

ANANIAH A priest, Ananiah was the grandfather of Azariah, one of those who helped rebuild the walls of Jerusalem after the Exile. NEHEMIAH 11:32

ANANIAS
1 A Christian who lived in Damascus, Ananias heard in a vision that Saul of Tarsus, the fiery persecutor of Christians, had been converted. Although frightened and hesitant, Ananias welcomed and baptized Saul, healing him of his temporary blindness. Paul later spoke of Ananias with gratitude and affection. ACTS 9; 22:12

2 Ananias was a hypocrite who, with his wife Sapphira, pretended to turn over all his goods to the church. Ananias and Sapphira secretely broke their promise to the others of the church and kept back a large part of their goods. Peter, on learning the truth, sternly denounced them. Their sudden death shortly afterward was popularly looked upon as proper punishment for lying. ACTS 5

3 The unscrupulous high priest in Jerusalem from 47 to 59 A.D., this Ananias conducted a hearing for the Apostle Paul in which he degraded the office of high priest by ordering Paul struck in the mouth. When the case was remanded to Festus in Caesarea, Ananias joined others in accusing Paul, distorting the facts, and introducing false charges. Ananias' subsequent career was notable mainly for greed and violence. He died at the hands of his resentful fellow-countrymen when Titus invaded Jerusalem in 70 A.D. ACTS 23—24

ANATH The father of Shamgar, Anath was one of the judges who succeeded Joshua. JUDGES 3:31; 5:6

ANATHOTH
1 A grandson of Benjamin and eighth of the nine sons of Becher listed in the family roll of the tribe of Benjamin. Anathoth was an early family head in the tribe. I CHRONICLES 7:8

2 One of the heads of families who signed the covenant with Nehemiah promising to keep the Law, this Anathoth was part of the community of onetime exiles who resettled in Jerusalem. NEHEMIAH 10:19

ANDREW The brother of Simon Peter and the son of Jonas, or John of Bethsaida, in Galilee, Andrew was the first of Jesus' twelve disciples. After his call by Jesus, Andrew promptly enlisted his brother, Simon Peter, as a follower. Although less flamboyant than Peter, Andrew emerged as a leader among the Twelve. It was Andrew who brought the boy with the loaves and fishes to Jesus, providing the materials to feed the five thousand, and who brought to Jesus the Greeks who had asked Philip for an interview. Andrew, as one bringing others to Jesus, was in a sense the first missionary. Tradition is strong that he was martyred at Patrae. His name always appears among the first four in the New Testament lists of the Twelve. MATTHEW 4:18; 10:2; MARK 1:16; 1:29; 3:18; LUKE 6:14; 1:40—44; 6:8; 12:22; ACTS 1:13

ANDRONICUS One of those who was remembered by name in the greetings at the close of Paul's letter to the Romans, Andronicus was a kinsman of the apostle—that is, a relative or fellow-countryman. Andronicus had been a Christian for a long time, far longer than Paul himself, and had been imprisoned at least once with Paul. Paul adds that Andronicus was a man "of note among the apostles." ROMANS 16:7

ANER One of three Amorite chieftains who signed a mutual assistance pact with Abraham at Mamre or Hebron, Aner and his two brothers accompanied Abraham on a raid to rescue Lot and his goods from the kings of the east. GENESIS 14

ANIAM A son of Shemidah listed in the genealogies among the tribe of Manassah by the Chronicler, Aniam was a clan chieftain in his tribe. I CHRONICLES 7:19

ANNA An aged widow who was a prophetess, Anna spent nearly all her time at worship at the Temple, longing to see the promised Messiah. When Mary and Joseph presented the infant Jesus at the Temple, Anna announced publicly that Jesus was the fulfillment of all of God's promises, and thanked God that she had been allowed to live long enough to see that day. LUKE 2:36—38

ANNAS Appointed high priest A.D. 6 and deposed A.D. 15, Annas was a rich Sadducee who continued to exert power through his son-in-law Caiaphas, who replaced him as high priest. After the arrest of Jesus, an informal hearing was held before Annas in which the high priest's party tried to manufacture charges against Jesus which would call for the death penalty. An unscrupulous schemer, Annas violated many canons of Jewish justice to push Jesus to trial and death. He is mentioned also in Acts as one of the high priest's faction at the trial of Peter and John. LUKE 3:2; JOHN 18:13—24; ACTS 4:6

ANTHOTHIJAH A son of Shashak included in the lists of names of the tribe of Benjamin, Anthothijah and his clan settled near Jerusalem after the invasion of Canaan. I CHRONICLES 8: 24

ANTIPAS One of those who died for their faith in Jesus Christ in the city of Pergamum in Asia Minor, Antipas was a brave and famous martyr during the persecutions in the first century A.D. Tradition holds that he was the bishop of Pergamum, and was killed by being thrown into a hollow brass bull which was heated to lethal temperature. REVELATION 2:13

ANTOTHIJAH
See ANTHOTHIJAH

ANUB One of the tribe of Judah, Anub was a son of Koz, who was listed in the genealogies by the Chronicler as an ancestral head of a family. I CHRONICLES 4:8

APELLES One of those to whom Paul sends a special greeting at the close of his letter to the church at Rome, Apelles was described as "approved in Christ." Apelles was also the name of the family and household of a famous tragic actor in Rome. ROMANS 16:10

APHIA Great-great-great-grandfather of King Saul, Aphia was listed among Saul's ancestors in the tribe of Benjamin. I SAMUEL 9:1

APHSES A Levite, Aphses drew the eighteenth lot (of twenty-four) for service in the House of the Lord in David's time. I CHRONICLES 24:15

APOLLOS An Alexandrian Jew who was converted to Christianity, Apollos came to Ephesus during Paul's absence and began to teach in the synagogue. Although eloquent, he was at first ignorant of certain parts of the Christian faith, such as the meaning of Christian baptism. After being tutored by Aquila and Priscilla, he was invited to serve in Corinth. Although there was later an Apollos-faction at Corinth, Paul and Apollos were warm friends and co-workers. St. Jerome indicates that Apollos later returned to Corinth and became the first bishop there. Many scholars believe that Apollos was the author of the Epistle to the Hebrews. ACTS 18:24; 19:1; I CORINTHIANS 1:12; 3:4—22; 4:6; 16:12; TITUS 3:13

APOLLYON See ABADDON

APPAIM A son of Nadab, listed in the genealogies of the tribe of Judah, Appaim was an early family head in the Jerahmeel side of the tribe. I CHRONICLES 2:30—31

APPHIA A Christian woman who was the wife of Philemon and mother of Archippis, Apphia was the recipient, with her family, of a tender letter from the Apostle Paul, in which he pleads for them to receive with lenience a runaway slave, Onesimus. Tradition holds that Apphia and the rest of her household in Colossae were stoned to death during Nero's persecution. PHILEMON

AQUILA One of the Apostle Paul's closest friends and co-workers at tentmaking and evangelizing, Aquila, together with his wife Priscilla, was a

Pontus Jew, converted to Christianity, who was expelled from Rome by the Emperor Claudius' decree. Settling in Corinth, Aquila and Priscilla welcomed Paul and were the nucleus of the church in Corinth. Paul made his home with them for a year and a half. Aquila and Priscilla went with Paul to Ephesus, where their house was a meeting place for a congregation. They later returned to Rome for eight years, then came back again to Ephesus. A mature and tactful man, Aquila, with Priscilla, was able to help the youthful and promising Apollos to a deeper understanding of the faith. ACTS 18:2—26; ROMANS 16:3; I CORINTHIANS 16:19; I TIMOTHY 4:19

ARA A son of Jether, carried in the list of those in tribe of Asher by the Chronicler, Ara was a warrior-chieftain of a clan in the tribe. I CHRONICLES 7:38

ARAD
1 A Canaanite chief who attacked the Israelites when some of the tribe of Judah began to settle near him, Arad was defeated at Hormah. NUMBERS 21:1; 33:40
2 A son of Beriah, who was a head of a family in the town of Aijalon, this Arad joined many of his fellow tribesmen of Benjamin on a raid on the Philistine city of Gath and drove out all the people of Gath. I CHRONICLES 8:15

ARAH
1 One of the sons of Ulla, of the tribe of Asher, this Arah was the ancestor of a family which returned to Jerusalem with Zerubbabel after Exile in Babylon. I CHRONICLES 7:39; EZRA 2:5; NEHEMIAH 7:10
2 This Arah was the grandfather of the woman who married Tobiah the Ammonite, the man who was such a nuisance in trying to stop Nehemiah from rebuilding the Temple after the Exile. NEHEMIAH 6:18

ARAM
1 The son of Shem and grandson of Noah, Aram was the founder of the Semitic tribe of nomads and traders that eventually occupied the area from Syria south to the Arabian border, and spoke the langauge known as Aramean. GENESIS 10:22—23; I CHRONICLES 1:17
2 A grandson of Nahor and son of Abraham's nephew Kemuel this Aram was mentioned in the Genesis genealogies of Abraham's relatives. GENESIS 22:21
3 Still another Aram is listed as a son of Shamer in the rolls of the tribe of Asher. The Gospel writers refer to Aram by the names "Arni" and "Ram" in the lists of Jesus' ancestors. I CHRONICLES 7:34; MATTHEW 1:3—4; LUKE 3:33

ARAN One of Esau's descendants through Seir the Horite, Aran was a son of Dishon, and was listed in the genealogies of Esau's house. GENESIS 36:28; I CHRONICLES 1:42

ARAUNAH A Jebusite, Araunah owned the threshing floor which stood on Mount Moriah and became the site for the Temple in Jerusalem. When a plague that threatened to decimate the population suddenly ended, King David was instructed by the prophet Gad to erect an altar on Araunah's threshing floor. This altar eventually became the center of worship for the nation. Even today, the site (called the Dome of the Rock) is a holy place for Christians, Jews, and Moslems. Araunah is also called "Ornah." II SAMUEL 24; I CHRONICLES 21; II CHRONICLES 3:1

ARBA Founder of the city of Araba, which later came to be called Hebron, and father of a family of giants who frightened Moses' spies by their size, Arba was the biggest and doughtiest warrior of his tribe. Arba's huge son Anak and Anak's sons were ultimately driven out of the area by Caleb. GENESIS. 35:27; JOSHUA 14:15; 15:13; 21:11

ARCHELAUS Probably the worst of King Herod the Great's tyrannical sons, Archelaus succeeded his father as the Roman's puppet king of Idumea, Judea, and Samaria. He offended his Jewish subjects by a sordid affair and marriage with his brother Alexander's widow, and so alienated his subjects by his senseless cruelty and luxury that after nine years the Emperor Augustus banished him. From then until 41 A.D. Palestine was governed by Roman procurators. MATTHEW 2:22

ARCHIPPUS One of those to whom the letter to Philemon was addressed, and a beloved co-worker of Paul, Archippus was probably the son of Philemon and Apphia or their close rela-

tive. Besides being asked to shelter the escaped slave, Onesimus, Archippus was encouraged by Paul in the letter to the Colossians to be faithful in his duties, hinting that he was an officer or leader in the church at Colossae. COLOSSIANS 4:17; PHILEMON 2

ARD
1 On of the sons of Benjamin listed in the family tree of Jacob in Genesis, Ard emigrated to Egypt with the rest of Jacob's family when famine struck Canaan. GENESIS 46:21
2 Another Ard is mentioned as a son of Bela, Benjamin's son, in the genealogy of Jacob's house in Numbers. In I Chronicles 8:3, he is called Addar. NUMBERS 26:40; I CHRONICLES 8:3

ARDON A son of Caleb and grandson of Hezron, Ardon was listed in the rolls of the family of Judah by the Chronicler as a clan head. I CHRONICLES 2:18

ARELI One of the sons of Gad, Jacob's son, who went to live in Egypt at Joseph's invitation during the famine in Palestine, Areli was the founder-ancestor of a clan of Gadites known as Arelites. GENESIS 46:16; NUMBERS 26:17

AREOPOGITE See DIONYSIUS

ARETAS The Arab king of Nabatea, who was in charge of Damascus at the time that Saul of Tarsus was converted to Jesus Christ, Aretas tried to seize the newly-converted Saul. Aretas' plans were foiled by disciples who lowered Paul over the walls in a basket. Under Aretas, the Nabatean kingdom briefly flourished, extending from the Euphrates to the Red Sea. In 28 A.D. he vengefully attacked and defeated Herod Antipas who had divorced Aretas' daughter. The emperor Gaius, unfriendly toward Herod Antipas, allowed Aretas to take over Damascus a few years later and hold it until Aretas died about 40 A.D. II CORINTHIANS 11:32

ARGOB One of King Pekahiah of Israel's officers, Argob and his fellow officer Arieh were assassinated with the wicked Pekahiah in a Samarian palace revolution led by Pekah about 761 B.C. The reference passage is so obscure, however, that we cannot be certain that Argob was not one of the conspirators, or even the name of a place. II KINGS 15:25

ARIDAL One of cruel Haman's sons, Aridal was also his accomplice, and was hung with Haman after Queen Esther interceded for the Jews and saved them at the last minute from Haman's massacre. ESTHER 9:9

ARIDATHA Another of Haman's ten sons, all of whom were executed, Aridatha participated in the planned destruction of the Jews in Persia which was stopped by Queen Esther's eleventh-hour plea to the king. ESTHER 9:8

ARIEH One of King Pekahiah's officers, Arieh and his fellow officer Argob were assassinated with the wicked Pekahiah in a Samarian palace revolution led by Pekah about 761 B.C. The

reference is so obscure, however, that we cannot be certain that Arieh was not one of the conspirators, or even the name of a place. II KINGS 15:25

ARIEL
1 One of the men chosen by Ezra, after the return from Exile in Babylon, for his leadership and insight, Ariel was one of those commissioned to go to Iddo to ask for men to serve in the house of God at a time when there was a severe shortage of ministers. Fortunately, they succeeded in convincing enough to come and serve. EZRA 8:16
2 An obscure passage in II Samuel 23:20 can be interpreted as referring to a man named Ariel, a man of Moab, whose two sons were killed by Benaiah, one of David's mighty heroes. Since the word *ariel* means "lion" in Hebrew, many translations indicate that Benaiah killed a lion's cubs. II SAMUEL 23:20

ARIOCH
1 Ruler of a kingdom called Ellasar, Arioch governed a territory which was a satellite of the king of the Elamites. Arioch, with his superior, the king of the Elamites, and two other rulers, mounted a raid against the five rulers of cities near the Dead Sea, and captured Abraham's nephew Lot. Abraham gathered sufficient forces, and rescued Lot and his property. Cuneiform inscriptions state that Arioch was later conquered by Khammurabi, and his territory annexed by Babylon. GENESIS 14:1
2 A captain in Nebuchadnezzar's guard sent to execute the prophet

Daniel, this Arioch was convinced not to carry out his orders by Daniel, who claimed that he could interpret Nebuchadnezzar's dreams. Later Arioch brought Daniel to the king. DANIEL 2:14—25

ARISAI One of the ten sons of Haman, Arisai was hung for his part in Haman's projected butchery of the Jews in Persia, which was stopped in the nick of time by Queen Esther's intervention. ESTHER 9:9

ARISTARCHUS A loyal co-worker of the Apostle Paul, Aristarchus hailed from Thessalonica, but was in Ephesus and arrested with Gaius during the riot following Paul's first appearance in that city. Aristarchus was Paul's constant companion at the close of the apostle's life, journeying with him from Troas to Jerusalem, and from Jerusalem to Rome, and sharing Paul's imprisonment in Rome. According to tradition Aristarchus, too, died a martyr's death in Rome during Nero's persecution. ACTS 19:29; 20:4; 27:2; COLOSSIANS 4:10; PHILEMON 24

ARISTOBULUS A resident of Rome, whose household contained many Christians who were extended greetings in Paul's letter to the Romans, Aristobulus was probably the grandson of Herod and brother of Agrippa I. Aristobulus was a close friend of the Emperor Claudius, and spent most of his life in Rome as a completely Romanized Jew. ROMANS 16:10

ARMONI One of Saul's sons by Rizpah, Armoni was one of the seven survivors of Saul whom David handed over to the Gibeonites for execution to avenge Saul's atrocities. II SAMUEL 21:8

AROD One of the sons of Gad listed in the genealogy of the tribes, Arod was the ancestor of a family which became the tribe of Arodites. He accompanied his family to Egypt from Canaan when the famine struck. GENESIS 46:14; NUMBERS 26:17

ARODI See AROD

ARPACHSHAD Shem's third son, Arpachshad was the father of Shelah and grandfather of Eber. The Hebrews claimed to have descended from him. Arpachshad is also believed to have given his name to a tribe and region in northern Assyria. GENESIS 10:22—24; 11:10—13; I CHRONICLES 1:17, 18, 24; LUKE 3:36

ARPHAXAD See ARPACHSHAD

ARTAXERXES A Persian king, Artaxerxes succeeded his father Xerxes and reigned from 464-425 B.C. Artaxerxes, in spite of his initial cruelty in pushing aside two older brothers to grab the throne, was enlightened enough to permit groups of the Jewish exiles to return to Jerusalem from Babylon. He even assisted Ezra and other priests to rehabilitate the ruined city by giving them substantial gifts. Thirteen years later, he allowed his own cupbearer, Nehemiah, to resign and go to Jerusalem to rebuild the city walls. His reign was punctuated with the usual revolts and turbulence, and included wars with Egypt and Athens. EZRA 4; 6:14; 7:1—8:1; NEHEMIAH 2:1; 5:14; 13:6

ARTEMAS A close friend and valued co-worker of the Apostle Paul, Artemas was one of Paul's companions, letter-carriers, and messengers in Paul's later years. Some unsubstantiated traditions claim that Artemas was one of the seventy disciples and was later bishop of Lystra. TITUS 3:12

ARZA Superintendent of the royal Israel palace at Tirzah, Arza had the misfortune to oversee a party which turned into a wild brawl during which his royal boss, King Elah, was assassinated by Zimri, about 930 B.C. I KINGS 16:9

ASA
1 The king of Judah from about 918 —877 B.C., Asa was one of the few rulers who tried to bring about some social and religious reforms. He was also an energetic builder, astute statesman, and competent military leader. During most of his long reign, Judah enjoyed a breathing spell of prosperity, peace, and morality. In his old age, however, Asa showed a lack of trust in the Lord by buying protection from the Syrian king, Ben-hadad, when Baasha, king of Israel, mobilized against Judah. Bitterly denounced by the prophet Hanani, Asa irritably tossed Hanani into jail and began to oppress many of Judah's citizens. Not long after, he contracted a painful foot disease, regarded as punishment for his failure to trust. I KINGS 15—16; 22:41—46; I CHRONICLES 3:10; II CHRONICLES 14—17; 20:32; 21:12; JEREMIAH 41:9; MATTHEW 1:7—8
2 Another Asa, a Levite, headed a family in the villages of the Netoph-athites near Jerusalem, and is listed in the genealogies by the Chronicler. I CHRONICLES 9:16

ASAHEL
1 David's nephew, his sister Zeruiah's son, this Asahal was one of Joab's brothers, and was famous for his speed as a runner and his prowess as a fighter. He was listed as a member of "The Thirty," David's elite corps of warriors, and as a commander of an army division. He was killed while chasing Abner, then one of Saul's officers, after a bloody skirmish near Gibeon. His death caused bad feeling between Joab, his brother, and Abner, his killer, which simmered after Abner joined forces with David and resulted finally in Joab's treacherous murder of Abner. II SAMUEL 2:18—3:30; 23:24; I CHRONICLES 2:16; 11:26; 27:7
2 Another Asahel was one of the eleven Levites that King Jehoshaphat sent to teach the Law to the people in the cities of Judah in an intensive religious education program. II CHRONICLES 17:8
3 A Levite by the same name, who lived about two hundred years later than **2**, this Asahel was appointed by Hezekiah to oversee the collections of offerings and tithes. II CHRONICLES 31:13
4 A minor character, this Asahel was the father of the man named Jonathan who opposed Ezra's edict compelling Jews who had married non-Jewish wives during the time of the Exile to divorce these wives. EZRA 10:15

ASAHIAH   See ASAIAH 3

41

ASAIAH

1 One of the chieftains from the tribe of Simeon at the time of the conquest of Canaan, this Asaiah joined with others in driving out the native Canaanite shepherds from the rich grazing land of Gedor, and taking it over for themselves. I CHRONICLES 4:36

2 One of Merari's grandsons, this Asaiah participated in the festivities when David brought the Ark to Jerusalem. I CHRONICLES 6:30; 15:6—11

3 One of King Josiah's messengers, this man was sent by Josiah to the prophetess Huldah to inquire about the book of the Law found during renovations to the Temple about 640 B.C. II KINGS 22:12—14; II CHRONICLES 34:20

4 One of the Shilonites who returned from the Exile, this Asaiah was listed as a head of a family of returned Jews that settled in Jerusalem. I CHRONICLES 9:5

ASAPH

1 A Levite descended from Kohath, Asaph was appointed by David as a director of choral music in the house of the Lord, and was retained in the same capacity by Solomon in the Temple. At first Asaph and his clan, the Asaphites, composed the Temple choir and were set apart specifically for that purpose. Later two other guilds of musicians, Heman's and Ethan's, were added to assist the Asaphites in conducting the musical parts of worship. Asaph's numerous descendants are mentioned frequently in subsequent history. I CHRONICLES 6:39; 15: 17—19; 16:5—7, 39; 25:1—9; II CHRONICLES 5:12; 20:14; 29:13, 30; 35:15; EZRA 2:41; 3:10; NEHEMIAH 7:44; 11:17, 22; 12:35, 46; TITLES OF PSALMS 50, 73—83; I CHRONICLES 9:15; 26:1

2 This Asaph was the father of Joah, the man who kept the records for King Hezekiah. II KINGS 18:18, 37; II CHRONICLES 29:13; ISAIAH 36:3, 22

3 The man who served as King Artaxerxes' head forester in the province of Judah, this Asaph received a letter from Artaxerxes instructing him to supply Nehemiah with lumber to rebuild Jerusalem after the Exile. NEHEMIAH 2:8

ASAREEL   See ASAREL

ASAREL

One of Jehallelel's sons and Caleb's descendants, listed in the genealogies of the tribe of Judah by the Chronicler, Asarel was an early clan head in the tribe. I CHRONICLES 4:16

ASARELAH

One of the singer Asaph's sons, Asarelah was appointed by David to serve in the house of the Lord as a member of the choir. I CHRONICLES 25:2

ASENATH

The daughter of the Egyptian priest of On, Asenath became Joseph's wife when the Pharaoh awarded her to Joseph for his impressive interpretation of the Pharaoh's dreams. Although nothing is known of her, Asenath was made the subject of many romantic stories. GENESIS 41: 45; 41:50, 46:20

ASHARELAH   See JESHARELAH

ASHBEL

The second son of Benjamin and progenitor of a clan carrying the name Ashbel, Ashbel is recorded in the lists of the tribe of Benjamin. GENESIS 46:21; NUMBERS 26:38; I CHRONICLES 8:1

ASHCHENAZ See ASHKENAZ

ASHER Jacob's eighth son, Asher accompanied Jacob's family to Egypt during the famine. Asher's clan grew to be one of the largest of the twelve tribes. Prominent when the tribes left Egypt under Moses, Asher's tribe was expected to have a great role in the conquest of Palestine and was given some of the richest territory. The subsequent history of Asher's tribe, however, was one of inactivity and failure. Probably absorbing the culture and outlook of their Phoenician neighbors, the Asherites made little effort to take over the Canaanite cities allotted to them or to co-operate with the other tribes in the wars threatening them all. The tribe quickly declined, and by David's time did not even appear on the list of David's leaders. GENESIS 30: 13; 35:26; 46:17; 49:20; EXODUS 1:4; NUMBERS 26:46; JOSHUA 17:10—11; I CHRONICLES 2:2; 7:30, 40

ASHHUR One of Caleb's sons, Ashhur was the father of Tekoa, and is listed in the genealogies of the tribe of Judah by the Chronicler. I CHRONICLES 2:24; 4:5

ASHKENAZ One of the sons of Gomer, who was a descendant of Noah's son Japheth, Ashkenaz was the founder of the tribe which settled in Armenia. GENESIS 10:3; I CHRONICLES 1:6

ASHPENAZ An important man in Nebuchadnezzar's court, Ashpenaz was ordered to pick out a group of the brightest young Jewish men carried off to Babylon, including Daniel, Shadrach, Meshach, and Abednego, and subject them to a three year brain-washing designed to change them from Jews to Babylonians. DANIEL 1:3

ASHRIEL See ASRIEL

ASHUR See ASHHUR

ASHVATH A son of Japhlet, Ashvath was one of the tough, ancient clan chieftains listed in the rolls of the tribe of Asher by the Chronicler. I CHRONICLES 7:33

ASIEL The grandfather of Jehu, Asiel was included as a family head in the Chronicler's genealogical table of the family of Simeon. I CHRONICLES 4:35

ASNAH One of the heads of a family of Nethinim, Asnah was a Temple servant whose descendants returned from the Exile in Babylon to Jerusalem with Zerubbabel in 536 B.C. EZRA 2:50

ASNAPPER See OSNAPPAR

ASPATHA The third of Haman's ten sons, Aspatha was hung with his brothers and their father for their savage plot against the Persian Jews, which was prevented at the last minute by the intervention of Queen Esther. ESTHER 9:7

ASRIEL
1 A son of Manasseh and his Ara-

mite concubine, Asriel was an ancient family head of the tribe of Manasseh. His descendants were known as Asrielites. I CHRONICLES 7:14

2 A son of Gilead and a grandson of Manasseh, this Asriel was head of a clan recorded in the lists of the tribe of Manasseh. NUMBERS 26:31; JOSHUA 17:2

ASSHUR

1 A descendant of Ham, Asshur was the founder of the savage warrior tribe that built the city of Ninevah and grew to become the hated and feared state of Assyria. The name "Asshur" was sometimes used interchangeably with "Assyria." GENESIS 10:11

2 One of Shem's sons, this Asshur was listed in the genealogies of the ancestors of the Israelites. GENESIS 10:22; I CHRONICLES 1:17

ASSHURIM

One of Abraham's great grandsons and one of Dedan's sons, Asshurim was the ancestor of an Arab tribe. GENESIS 25:3

ASSIR

1 A son of Korah and a grandson of Kohath of the tribe of Levi, Assir was one of those who left Egypt with Moses to go into the desert and, eventually, to reach the Promised Land. EXODUS 6:24; I CHRONICLES 6:22

2 A grandson of **1**, this Assir was a son of Ebiasaph and was mentioned as a member of the tribe of Levi in the records of the Chronicler. I CHRONICLES 6:23, 37

3 The King James translation mentions another Assir as a son of Jeconiah in I Chronicles 3:17. Most Hebrew scholars, however, believe that this word should be translated as "captive." I CHRONICLES 3:17

ASYNCRITUS

One of five men in one group together with "the brethren who are with them" who was remembered with a personal greeting by Paul in his letter to the Romans, Asyncritus may have been a member of a small congregation, or one of a group of Christians living in a community near Rome. ROMANS 16:14

ATAR   See ATER

ATARAH

A woman who married into the tribe of Judah as one of Jerahmeel's wives, Atarah became the mother of Onam. I CHRONICLES 2:26

ATER

1 A Levite, Ater was an ancestor of a distinguished family of Levites who ministered in the Temple after returning with Zerubbabel from Exile in Babylon in 536 B.C. EZRA 2:16, 42; NEHEMIAH 7:21, 45

2 Another Ater was one of the heads of families who joined with Nehemiah in signing a covenant promising to observe the Law after the rebuilding of the walls of Jerusalem. NEHEMIAH 10:17

ATHALIAH

1 The daughter of Jezebel, Athaliah inherited her mother's cruelty and ruthlessness. She married Jehoram, king of Judah, and influenced him and their son, Ahaziah, to reintroduce Baal worship. Under her prodding, even parts of the Temple were dismantled to build a shrine to Baal. After the deaths of her husband and son, Athaliah took control, turning Judah into a police state and ordering the massacre of all her grandchildren. Joash alone was saved from this bloodbath, and was raised in secret. The High Priest Jehoiada engineered a carefully planned coup which crowned Joash and killed Athaliah. II KINGS 8:26; 11:1—20; II CHRONICLES 22:2—24:7

2 One of the tribe of Benjamin who was a son of Jehoram, this Athaliah lived in Jerusalem and was listed in the genealogies of the Chronicler. I CHRONICLES 8:26

3 Another Athaliah was the father of Jeshiah, one of those who returned from the Exile with Ezra to Jerusalem. EZRA 8:7

ATHAIH One of the tribe of Judah who joined with other volunteers to live in Jerusalem after exiles returned from Babylon to the devastated capital, Athiah traced his lineage back to Judah through Perez. NEHEMIAH 11:4

ATHLAI One of the many who married non-Jewish wives during the time following the Exile in Babylon, thus breaking the Law. Athlai agreed to abide by Ezra's strict regulations against interfaith marriages when returning to Jerusalem. EZRA 10:28

ATTAI

1 A son of Sheshan's daughter, who was married to her father's Egyptian slave Jarha, Attai was considered as a member of the clan of Jerahmeel of the tribe of Judah. I CHRONICLES 2:35 —36

2 An expert and experienced fighter, this Attai was one of those from the tribe of Gad who left Saul and joined David at Ziglag. Attai and the others of his troop from Gad were noted for their speed in the mountains, and were commissioned as officers in David's army. I CHRONICLES 12:8—15

3 One of the sons of King Rehoboam and his favorite wife, Maacah, daughter of Absalom, this Attai received passing mention in the family tree of Rehoboam. II CHRONICLES 11:20

AUGUSTUS

1 The great Roman who succeeded his famed uncle, Julius Caesar, Caius Octavius was awarded the title "Augustus" by the Roman Senate after he became supreme ruler. Augustus was born in 63 B.C., given a good education as a boy, and pushed into prominence when Julius Caesar was assassinated in 44 B.C. At first he was one of a triumvirate, but he eliminated his last rival, Mark Anthony, in 31 B.C. From then until his death in 14 A.D., the empire enjoyed an unparalleled period of peace and prosperity. His personal qualities, except in his old age, were outstanding. Historians rate Augustus as one of the most enlightened and just of all the ancient rulers. Jesus was born during his reign, probably near the time of the second or third of Augustus' four censuses (26 B.C., 6 B.C., 4 A.D., and 14 A.D.) LUKE 2:1

2 After the death of **1**, many of his successors were granted the title "Augustus." The King James version states that the Apostle Paul appealed to "Augustus" when he was seized in Jerusalem. This "Augustus" was the

Emperor Nero. Other translations substitute "Caesar" or "the Emperor" for "Augustus" to avoid confusion. ACTS 25:21—25; 27:1

AZALIAH The father of Shephan, Azaliah was King Josiah's secretary and confidential personal messenger. II KINGS 22:3; II CHRONICLES 34:8

AZANIAH A Levite, Azaniah was the father of one of the heads of a family who joined with Nehemiah in signing the covenant to keep the Law after rebuilding Jerusalem. NEHEMIAH 10:9

AZARAEL See **AZAREL**

AZAREEL See **AZAREL**

AZAREL
1 One of the clan of Korah who deserted Saul and joined David at Ziglag, Azarel, like the others of his group, was an expert marksman with the bow and arrow and the deadly sling, and could handle these weapons either left- or right-handed. I CHRONICLES 12:6
2 One of the sons of the great singer Heman, this Azarel was also a Levite who was appointed to minister in the music program of the sanctuary at the time of David. Azarel drew the eleventh lot, or turn, to serve. I CHRONICLES 25:18
3 A son of Jeroham, this Azarel was a chieftain in the tribe of Dan at the time David conducted his census. I CHRONICLES 27:22
4 One of the many offspring of Bani who had married non-Jewish women during the Exile in Babylon, this Azarel was listed as one who kept the faith pure and returned to Jerusalem without his foreign wife. EZRA 10:41

5 This Azarel was the father of Amashsai, one of the priests who volunteered to settle in Jerusalem after the return from Exile in Babylon. NEHEMIAH 11:13
6 Still another Azarel, sometimes spelled Azarael or Azareel, was a Levite who was one of the group of musicians marching on the right at the time Nehemiah dedicated the rebuilt walls of Jerusalem after the return from Babylon. NEHEMIAH 12:36

AZARIAH As common a name in Hebrew as Smith is in English, *Azariah* in Hebrew means "Whom God aids." There are about two dozen people in the Bible called Azariah.
1 The son of King Amaziah of Judah, Azariah, also known as Uzziah, was crowned when he was only sixteen. He reigned for fifty-two years, part of the time as a contemporary of Jeroboam. He was an energetic organizer, recapturing Elath on the Red Sea to aid commerce in Judah, subduing the Philistines and Arab desert tribes, digging cisterns, and improving the water supplies for herdsmen and farmers. His large, well-equipped army was one of the first to understand and use artillery. Judah grew rich during his long, strong reign. Attacked by a painful form of leprosy in his old age, Azariah retired and put his son Jotham in charge of the kingdom. His death in the middle of the eighth century B.C. was deeply felt by the nation, as the impressionable young Isaiah testified. II KINGS 14:21;

46

15:1—27; I CHRONICLES 3:2; 26:1—23: 27:2; ISAIAH 1:1; 6:1; 7:1; HOSEA 1:1; AMOS 1:1; ZECHARIAH 14:5

2 A Levite who was grandfather of **3**, this Azariah was a member of a long line of distinguished, respected priests. A close study of the genealogies shows generation after generation of this family serving as high priests. One of the most famous among the many famous descendants of this Azariah was the priest Ezra. I CHRONICLES 6:9

3 High priest at the time of Solomon, this Azariah was a grandson of **2**. A member of the tribe of Levites, he was a man of great prestige. His son, Amariah, carried on the family tradition, becoming High Priest under Jehoshaphat. I KINGS 4:2; I CHRONICLES 6:10—11; EZRA 7:3

4 Of the same illustrious family as **2** and **3**, this Azariah was son of Hilkiah, high priest under King Josiah. Azariah's son, Seraiah, was killed by Nebuchadnezzar, and his grandson, Jehozadak, also a high priest, was carried into Exile to Babylon by Nebuchadnezzar. I CHRONICLES 6:13—14; EZRA 7:1

5 The high priest at the time of Hezekiah, this Azariah constructed store rooms in the Temple to hold the offerings. He was mentioned as one of the house of Zadok, which means that he was part of the same family as **2** and **3**. II CHRONICLES 31:10—13

6 This Azariah, no relation to the others, was a son of a man named Nathan, and held the responsible post of supervising Solomon's twelve com-missary officers. In other words, this Azariah had to make sure that provisions were on hand for all of Solomon's large family, staff, and household. I KINGS 4:5

7 One of the sons of Ethan, the man noted for his wisdom, this Azariah is listed on the roster of the tribe of Judah. I CHRONICLES 2:8

8 One of the tribe of Judah who was part Egyptian, this Azariah is numbered with Jerahmeel's clan by the Chronicler. I CHRONICLES 2:38—39

9 A Levite of the tribe of Kohath, this Azariah was an ancestor of the prophet Samuel. He is also listed in the genealogies of the ancestors of those whom David appointed to look after the music in the house of the Lord. I CHRONICLES 6:36

10 A son of Oded, this Azariah was the prophet who met King Asa on his return from his victory over the Ethiopians and called upon Asa to begin a reform movement to clean up the vice and idolatry in Judah. II CHRONICLES 15:1

11 One of Jehoshaphat's sons, this Azariah was given a lavish inheritance by his father. His older brother Jehoram, however, was given the kingdom. Upon Jehoshaphat's death, all of his other sons, including Azariah, were slaughtered by Jehoram. II CHRONICLES 21:2

12 In II Chronicles 22:6, the King James version erroneously translates *Ahaziah* as "Azariah." See AHAZIAH **2**. II CHRONICLES 22:6

13 One of two Azariahs who were key men in the plot to overthrow the evil Queen Athaliah, this Azariah was a son of Jeroham. The high priest Jehoiada, mastermind of the conspiracy, signed a pact with Azariah, who was one of the top men in the royal army, and sent him on a highly secret tour to recruit trusted followers in the revolt. II CHRONICLES 23:1

14 The second Azariah to be brought in to aid in overthrowing the wicked Athaliah, this man was a son of Obed. He also was an army commander, and helped enroll and assign the conspirators. These careful efforts paid off, and Joash was crowned king of Judah. II CHRONICLES 23:1

15 High priest during the reign of Uzziah or Azariah **1**, this man boldly stood up to the king and denounced him for presumptuously trying to play priest. Uzziah, furious at being crossed, persisted, and was suddenly smitten with leprosy. Azariah, the high priest, and his attendants immediately threw the king out of the Temple. II CHRONICLES 26:17—20

16 A chieftain from the tribe of Ephraim, this Azariah lived in the northern kingdom of Israel during the reign of Pekah and was one of the few who backed up the prophet Oded when he opposed the enslavement of Judeans captured after a battle. Azariah returned the prisoners to their homes in Jericho. II CHRONICLES 28:12

17 A Levite of the tribe of Merari, this Azariah was a son of Jehallalel, and was an active participant in cleaning up the Temple during Hezekiah's reform, about 740 B.C. II CHRONICLES 29:12

18 Another Levite, this Azariah was of the tribe of Kohath, and was the father of a man named Joel who joined with Azariah **16** in renovating the Temple during Hezekiah's reform. II CHRONICLES 29:12

19 One of the family of Ananiah who helped Nehemiah rebuild the wall of Jerusalem after the Exile in Babylon, this Azariah was probably a priest. NEHEMIAH 3:23—24

20 This Azariah was listed as one of the twelve leaders of Israel who, with Zerubbabel, brought the first contingent of Exiles home to Jerusalem from Babylon. NEHEMIAH 7:7

21 One of the priests selected by Ezra as an interpreter of the Law, this Azariah joined other Levites in Ezra's program of instructing the people in the meaning of the Law. NEHEMIAH 8:7

22 One of the leading priests who joined with Nehemiah in signing the covenant to keep the Law, this Azariah may be the same as **21**. I CHRONICLES 9:11; NEHEMIAH 10:2

23 In the description of the dedication procession following the rebuilding of the walls of Jerusalem after the return from Exile in Babylon, mention is made of a man named Azariah who was a leading man from the tribe of Judah. Perhaps he is the same as **21** and/or **22**. NEHEMIAH 12:33

24 The son of Hoshaiah, this Azariah insolently called the prophet Jeremiah a liar. Azariah and others had gone through the formality of consulting Jeremiah for advice, although they had already made up their minds to run and hide in Egypt. When Jeremiah urged them not to run, but to stay in Judea, Azariah accused Jeremiah of being a false prophet and dragged him with them to Egypt. JEREMIAH 42—43

25 One of the young men carried off to Exile by the Babylonians, this Azariah was re-named Abednego by his captors. See ABEDNEGO. DANIEL 1:6—2:17

AZARIAHU

1 One of the six sons of King Jehoshaphat who was given lavish presents as an inheritance by his father, Azariahu was slaughtered by his older brother Jehoram when their father Jehoshaphat died. II CHRONICLES 21:2

2 This Azariahu was one of the five military leaders enlisted by the High Priest Jehoiada to participate in a carefully prepared coup, depose the cruel Queen Athaliah, and crown Joash. II CHRONICLES 23:1

AZAZ

A chieftain of the tribe of Reuben, Azaz was the father of Bela, and was mentioned in the genealogies by the Chronicler. I CHRONICLES 5:8

AZAZIAH

1 One of the Levites who served as a musician during the proceedings when David brought the Ark to Jerusalem, Azaziah led the procession playing a lyre. I CHRONICLES 15:21

2 This Azaziah was the father of Hoshea, a chief in the tribe of Ephraim who was listed in David's census. I CHRONICLES 27:20

3 A Levite, this man had the heavy responsibility of guarding and overseeing the offerings dedicated in the Temple in Hezekiah's time. II CHRONICLES 31:13

AZBUK

Azbuk was the father of Nehemiah, the man who supervised the rebuilding of Jerusalem's walls after the Exile of Babylon. NEHEMIAH 3:16

AZEL

One of Saul's descendants through Jonathan, and a member of the tribe of Benjamin, Azel fathered six sons, and was a stalwart member of the branch of the tribe living near Gibeon. I CHRONICLES 8:37—38; 9:43—44

AZGAD

Azgad was the head of a large clan that returned from Exile in Babylon and joined in rebuilding Jerusalem and signing the covenant to keep the Law. EZRA 2:12; 8:12; NEHEMIAH 7:17; 10:15

AZIEL

A Levite who was a talented psaltery player, Aziel participated in the celebrations when David brought the Ark to Jerusalem. I CHRONICLES 15:20.

AZIZA

One of the clan of Zattu who married a non-Jewish woman during the Exile, Aziza agreed to observe Ezra's regulation against interfaith marriages and returned to Jerusalem without his wife. EZRA 10:27

AZMAVETH

1 A member of the tribe of Benjamin who belonged to Saul's family, Azmaveth was listed in the roll of the clan by the Chronicler. I CHRONICLES 8:36; 9:42

2 This Azmaveth, was a valiant soldier who earned a place in "The Thirty," David's elite corps of heroes Like many of David's men he was or iginally on the side of Saul, a fellow-Benjaminite, but later joined David. Azmaveth and his two sons were so skilled with the bow and the sling that they could use either with deadly effect with either hand. Azmaveth came to David at Ziglag, and was commissioned as a company commander in David's army. Later, in David's kingdom, Azmaveth was appointed to the important position of superintendent of the royal treasury. II SAMUEL 23:31; I CHRONICLES 11:33; 12:3; 27:25

AZOR One of Jesus' ancestors, Azor was listed in Matthew's genealogy as a grandson of Zerubbabel. MATTHEW 1:13—14.

AZRIEL
1 The head of a family listed in the rolls of the half-tribe of Manasseh, Azriel was assigned territory east of the Jordan during the conquest of Canaan. His family, like so many members of the tribes of Manasseh, Reuben, and Gad, drifted into the idolatrous cults of the Canaanites, and were later overrun by the Assyrians. I CHRONICLES 5:24
2 This Azriel was the father of Jeremoth, who was the governor of the tribe of Naphtali according to David's census. I CHRONICLES 27:19
3 This Azriel was the father of Seraiah, one of the guards sent by the angry king to arrest Jeremiah's secretary, Baruch. JEREMIAH 36:26

AZRIKAM
1 One of the sons of Neraiah, Azrikam was a descendant of David listed in the Chronicler's family tree of the royal family of Judah. I CHRONICLES 3:23
2 One of the sons of Azel, this Azrikam was a descendant of Saul and Jonathan, and was listed in the Chronicler's family tree of Saul's descendants. I CHRONICLES 8:38; 9:44
3 This third Azrikam was the grandfather of Shemaiah, one of the Levites who volunteered to settle in devastated Jerusalem after the Exile in Babylon. I CHRONICLES 9:14; NEHEMIAH 11:15
4 Commander of King Asa's royal palace in Judah, this Azrikam was guilty of condoning his monarch's idolatry, luxury, and injustice. When Pekah of Israel invaded Judah, an Ephraimite hero named Zichri killed Azrikam and many of the royal staff of Judah. II CHRONICLES 28:7

AZUBAH
1 This Azubah was Caleb's first wife and mother of three of his children. I CHRONICLES 2:18—19
2 A daughter of Shilhi, this Azubah was remembered as the mother of King Jehoshaphat. I KINGS 22:42; II CHRONICLES 20: 31

AZUR See AZZUR

AZZAN A member of the tribe of Issachar, Azzan was the father of Paltiel, the man chosen from Issachar to work with the committee of representatives of the other tribes in allocating the Promised Land equitably among the various tribes and their clans. NUMBERS 34:26

AZZUR

1 One of those who assisted Nehemiah to rebuild the walls of Jerusalem after the Exile, this Azzur joined in signing the covenant promising to keep the Law. NEHEMIAH 10:17

2 A Gibeonite, this Azzur was remembered as the father of the false prophet Hananiah, who broke the yoke from Jeremiah's neck and derided his gloomy message. JEREMIAH 28

3 This Azzur was the father of Jaazaniah, one of the twenty-five leaders who pretended to be so wise against whom the prophet Ezekiel thundered. EZEKIEL 11:1

B

BAAL-HANAN
1 A descendant of Esau listed in the genealogical tables of his family, Baal-hanan became the seventh king of Edom. GENESIS 36:38—39; I CHRON-ICLES 1:49—50
2 A Gederite in David's service, this Baal-hanan was made superintendent of David's orchards. I CHRONICLES 27:28

BAALIS A wily chief of the fierce Ammonites, Baalis stirred the troubled international waters in 586 B.C. by sending an assassin to kill Gedeliah, the Jew appointed by the Babylonians as governor of the occupied country. JEREMIAH 40

BAANA
1 This Baana, son of Ahilud, was one of twelve men appointed by Solomon to get provisions for Solomon's family, household, and staff for one month each year, and was assigned to forage the territory in the vicinity of Megiddo. I KINGS 4:12
2 Another Baana who had the same heavy and unpopular responsibility as 1, this man was a son of Hushai, and was assigned to forage in Asher and Bealoth. I KINGS 4:16
3 The father of Zadok, who returned from Exile in Babylonia and helped Nehemiah rebuild the walls of Jerusalem. NEHEMIAH 3:4

BAANAH
1 One of two fierce sons of Rimmon, Baanah became chief of the raider bands in kinsman Saul's army and fought under Saul's son, Ishbosheth. Later, he and his brother treacherously murdered Ishbosheth in bed, and brought Ishbosheth's head to David for a reward. Distrusting them for their sneaky killing of Ishbosheth, David ordered them executed and their dismembered bodies exhibited in disgrace. II SAMUEL 4

53

2 The father of Heleb, who was one of David's bravest soldiers and a member of the elite corps of "The Thirty." II SAMUEL 23:29; I CHRONICLES 11:30

3 This Baanah was one of the heads of families that returned with Zerubbabel to Jerusalem after the Exile in Babylon. EZRA 2:2; NEHEMIAH 7:7; 10:27

BAARA The wife of Shahariam, one of the tribe of Benjamin, Baara and another wife were sent away by their husband. I CHRONICLES 8:8

BAASEIAH A Levite of the clan of Kohath, Baaseiah was an ancestor of Asaph, the tabernacle musician in David's time. I CHRONICLES 6:40

BAASHA Although of humble origin in the tribe of Issachar, Baasha made his mark in the northern kingdom of Israel by bringing off a conspiracy against King Nadab, Jeroboam's son, in which he not only killed Nadab but murdered all the family. Baasha as king was little better than his predecessor. His twenty-four year reign was a dreary succession of bloody, expensive raids and counter-raids against Judah and Syria, and a continuation of the cult of calf worship. I KINGS 15—16; 21:22; II KINGS 9:9; II CHRONICLES 16; JEREMIAH 41:9

BAKBAKKAR One of the Levites who returned from the Exile in Babylon to Jerusalem. I CHRONICLES 9:15

BAKBUK Bakbuk was the father of Temple servants who returned from Exile in Babylon to Jerusalem with Zerubbabel. EZRA 2:51; NEHEMIAH 7:53

BAKBUKIAH
1 A Levite who returned to Jerusalem with Zerubbabel after the Exile in Babylon, this Bakbukiah was number two leader in the Temple worship. NEHEMIAH 11:17; 12:9

2 Another Bakbukiah, also a Levite, was a guard who had a post at the storehouse by the city gates at the time of Ezra and Nehemiah. NEHEMIAH 12:25

BALAAM A soothsayer who lived in Pethor, Balaam was hired by King Balak of Moab to pronounce a curse on the Israelites, then wandering from Egypt to the Promised Land. The angel of the Lord intervened, causing Balaam's jackass to speak to Balaam. Instead of a curse, Balaam gave a blessing, and was promptly fired by Balak. Later, Balaam persuaded many Israelites to adopt the immoral ceremonies pertaining to the cults of the heathen tribes. When the Israelites overcame the Midianites and Moabites, they slaughtered Balaam along with the leaders of the defeated tribes. NUMBERS 22, 23, 24, 31; DEUTERONOMY 23:4, 5; JOSHUA 13:22; 24:9—10; NEHEMIAH 13:2; MICAH 6:5; II PETER 2:15; JUDE 11; REVELATION 2:14

BALAC See BALAK

BALADAN The father of the king of Babylon, Berodach-baladan, who was the contemporary of Hezekiah, about 700 B.C. II KINGS 20:12; ISAIAH 39:1

BALAK Son of Zippor, Balak was a king of Moab who is best remembered for unsuccessfully trying to hire the soothsayer Balaam to pronounce a curse on the tribes of Israelites when they were wandering in the wilderness. NUMBERS 22, 23, 24; JOSHUA 24:9; JUDGES 11:25; MICAH 6:5

BANI
1 A famous warrior from the tribe of Gad, this Bani was a member of David's elite corps of "The Thirty." II SAMUEL 23:36
2 Another Bani, this one is a Levite who is listed as the ancestor of Ethan, one of David's leaders of worship in the house of the Lord. I CHRONICLES 6:46
3 This Bani was one of the tribe of Judah who was the ancestor of Uthai, one of the first to return from Exile in Babylon to Jerusalem. I CHRONICLES 9:4
4 Probably another by the same name, this Bani (called "Binnui" in Nehemiah) was the head of a clan of 642 people who returned with Zerubbabel from Exile in Babylon to Jerusalem. EZRA 2:10; 10:29
5 This Bani was remembered as the father and grandfather of several men who had married non-Jewish women during the Exile. EZRA 10:34; 38
6 A prominent Levite at the time of Nehemiah, this Bani and his family helped rebuild the wall of Jerusalem after the Exile, and signed the covenant with Nehemiah to keep the Law. This Bani's son became chief of the Levites in Jerusalem. NEHEMIAH 3:17; 8:7; 9:4—5; 10:13—14; 11:22

BARABBAS The prisoner released by Pilate in place of Jesus, Barabbas is mentioned by name in all four gospel accounts as a well-known revolutionary and brigand. Matthew adds the ironic fact that Barabbas also was called "Jesus." When Pilate wished to get Jesus Christ off his hands by releasing Him in honor of the Passover, the crowd, at the urging of the authorities cried instead for the release of Jesus Barabbas and the crucifixion of Jesus Christ. MATTHEW 27; MARK 15; LUKE 23; JOHN 18

BARACHEL The father of Elihu, who was one of those who tried to reason with Job. JOB 32:2, 6

BARACHIAH Father of the prophet Zechariah, who prophesied after the return from Exile. ZECHARIAH 1:1, 7; MATTHEW 23:35

BARACHIAS See BARACHIAH

BARAK A member of the tribe of Naphtali, Barak was summoned by Deborah, one of the Judges or rulers of the tribes after they entered Canaan, and ordered to head a punitive raid against Sisera, an obnoxious and dangerous Canaanite chief. Barak's successful exploits were celebrated in a famous song or ode in Judges 5. JUDGES 4, 5; HEBREWS 11:32

BARIAH The son of Shemaiah, one of David's descendants, Bariah is listed by the Chronicler in the roll of David's family. I CHRONICLES 3:22

BARJESUS Also known as Elymas, Barjesus was a clever Oriental magician and soothsayer who was kept on the staff of the Roman proconsul at Cyprus, Sergius Paulus. When Paul and Barnabas preached the gospel to

Sergius Paulus and won a sympathetic ear, Barjesus tried to undermine them. He was beaten at his own game, however, when Paul struck him blind. ACTS 13

BARJONAH See PETER

BARKOS An ancestor of some Temple servants who returned to Jerusalem with Zerubbabel from Exile in Babylon. EZRA 2:53; NEHEMIAH 7:55

BARNABAS Friend and companion of Paul, Barnabas was named Joseph, and was a Levite whose home was Cyprus. Highly respected by Christian leaders, Barnabas was instrumental in bringing the newly converted Saul from Tarsus to Antioch, and influential in having Saul received by the apostles in Jerusalem. Later, the two were commissioned by the church at Antioch to conduct a missionary tour. After returning and reporting to Antioch and Jerusalem, Barnabas and Paul planned a second trip, but separated after arguing whether or not to take along Mark, Barnabas' nephew, who had deserted them on the first journey. The friendship, however, continued. Paul speaks warmly of Barnabas in his letters. There are no reliable accounts of Barnabas' subsequent career or death. ACTS 4, 9, 11—15; I CORINTHIANS 9:6; GALATIANS 2; COLOSSIANS 4:10

BARSABBAS
1 The man who almost became one of the Twelve, Barsabbas was nominated with Matthias to be Judas' successor. The lot, however, fell on Mat-

thias. This Barsabbas is sometimes known as Joseph Barsabbas. ACTS 1:23
2 This Barsabbas, also known as Judas Barsabbas, was sent with Silas by the apostles in Jerusalem to carry a letter to Antioch. This letter told of the decision of the General Assembly at Jerusalem that it would not be necessary to circumcise non-Jewish converts to the church. ACTS 15:22—29

BARTHOLOMEW One of the Twelve Apostles, Bartholomew was also known as Nathanael. A native of Cana in Galilee, a neighboring village to Nazareth, Bartholomew was skeptical of any messiah ever hailing from Nazareth—until he met Jesus. He was not as prominent as others of the Twelve, but is carried in all the lists of the disciple band. Tradition has it that Bartholomew later preached the gospel in India and was martyred. MATTHEW 10:3; MARK 3:18; LUKE 6:14; JOHN 1:45—49; 21:2; under the name, NATHANAEL: ACTS 1:13

BARTIMAEUS The blind beggar who was a well-known nuisance at the entrance to Jericho, Bartimaeus was given both his sight and a new dignity when Jesus healed him. MARK 10:46

BARUCH
1 A son of Zabbai, this Baruch helped Nehemiah rebuild the wall of Jerusalem after the Exile in Babylon. NEHEMIAH 3:20, 10:6
2 This Baruch was the father of Maaseiah, one of those who volunteered to move to Jerusalem after the Exile. NEHEMIAH 11:5
3 The most famous of those bearing

the name, this Baruch was the loyal secretary to the prophet Jeremiah. Although he was from a famous family in Jerusalem, Baruch faithfully wrote down the stern words against Jerusalem dictated by Jeremiah, read them to the king, and took the abuse of the court for daring to read such words. Even after the fall of Jerusalem in 586 B.C., Baruch stuck by Jeremiah. JEREMIAH 32, 36, 43, 45

BARZILLAI

1 A wealthy man in Gilead, Barzillai showed kindness to David when David was fleeing from Absalom during Absalom's revolt. David did not forget Barzillai's aid; he invited him to live in his court in Jerusalem after Absalom's defeat. Barzillai declined to go because of his age, but sent his son instead. David, in appreciation of Barzillai's goodness later helped Barzillai's son to go into business in Bethlehem by buying him an inn. II SAMUEL 17:27; 19:31—39; I KINGS 2:7; EZRA 2:61; NEHEMIAH 7:63

2 This Barzillai was the father of Adriel, the man who married Saul's oldest daughter, Merab. II SAMUEL 21:8

3 This Barzillai was one of those who could not trace his ancestry, so took the name of his wife's family, Barzillai of Gilead (see 1). His descendants were among those who returned after the Exile in Babylon, and were mentioned specifically in the lists compiled. EZRA 2:61; NEHEMIAH 7:63

BASEMATH

1 This woman named Basemath became one of Esau's wives and the mother of his son, Reuel. Esau's domestic affairs were apparently far from peaceful. Genesis remarks that Basemath also made life bitter for her in-laws, Isaac and Rebekah. GENESIS 26:34—35; 36:3—17

2 The daughter of King Solomon, this Basemath married Ahimaaz, one of twelve key men responsible for supplying Solomon's household with provisions for one month each year. I KINGS 4:15

BASHEMATH See BASEMATH

BASMATH See BASEMATH

BATHSHEBA The adulterous wife of Uriah the Hittite, one of David's bravest captains, Bathsheba had an affair with David which culminated when David treacherously arranged her husband's death. After her marriage to David, she schemed to gain prominence for herself and her child by David, Solomon. She even contrived to have David name Solomon as his successor. II SAMUEL 11:3; 12:24; I KINGS 1—2; PSALM 51 (title)

BATHSHUA See BATHSHEBA

BAVAI See BAVVAI

BAVVAI The son of Henadad, a governmental official, Bavvai helped repair the walls on the southeast of Jerusalem under Nehemiah's leadership, after the return from Exile in Babylon. NEHEMIAH 3:18

BAZLITH The ancestor of a group of temple servants who returned to Jerusalem with Zerubbabel after Exile in Babylon. EZRA 2:52; NEHEMIAH 7:54

BAZLUTH See BAZLITH

BEALAH One of the tribe of Benjamin, Bealah was one of the group of doughty warriors who grew disgusted with their kinsman, Saul, and joined David at Ziglag. Like the others in his battalion, Bealah could use a bow or slingshot to deadly effect with either his right or left hand. I CHRONICLES 12:5

BEBAI The leader of a clan that returned with Zerubbabel to Jerusalem after the Exile in Babylon, Bebai was one of those who signed the covenant with Nehemiah to keep the Law. EZRA 2:11; 8:11; NEHEMIAH 7:16; 10:15, 28

BECHER
1 One of Benjamin's sons, listed in the rolls of the tribes in Genesis and Chronicles. GENESIS 46:21; I CHRONICLES 7:6—8
2 One of Ephraim's sons, listed in the rolls of the tribes in the census by Moses, this Becher is called "Bered" by the Chronicler. NUMBERS 26:35, I CHRONICLES 7:20 (called BERED)

BECHORATH Grandson of Becher, the son of Benjamin, Bechorath was remembered primarily as the great-great grandfather of Saul, first king of Israel. I SAMUEL 9:1

BECORATH See BECHORATH

BEDAD The father of a powerful king of Edom, Hadad, who subdued the neighboring tribes and made

Edom a stronghold before the Israelites crossed into Canaan. GENESIS 36:35; I CHRONICLES 1:46

BEDAN
1 Along with Jerubaal (that is, Gideon), Jephthah, and Samuel, Bedan was remembered as one of the great heroes and deliverers of Israel in the period following the conquest of Canaan and before the crowning of Saul. Although his name is not included specifically in the Book of Judges, he was undoubtedly one of the "judges" or chieftains that emerged as a strongman and wise leader among the tribes. I SAMUEL 12:11
2 One of the descendants of Manassah through Manassah's son, Machir, this Bedan is mentioned in the roll of the tribes by the Chronicler. I CHRONICLES 7:17

BEDAIAH Like many others of the family of Bani, Bedaiah married a non-Jewish woman during the Exile and disobeyed the Law. EZRA 10:35

BEELIADA See ELIADA

BEERA One of the sons of Zophah, listed in the genealogy of the tribe of Asher by the Chronicler. I CHRONICLES 7:37

BEERAH The son of a chief in the tribe of Reuben, Beerah was captured by Tiglath-Pileser, the Assyrian dictator, and carried away to Assyria. I CHRONICLES 5:6

BEERI
1 A Hittite, Beeri was the father of a woman named Judith, who became

one of Esau's numerous wives. GENE-SIS 26:34

2 This Beeri was the father of the great prophet, Hosea. HOSEA 1:1

BELA
1 A strong desert chief who became the first king of Edom, Bela ruled the area east of the Jordan commanding important caravan routes. GENESIS 36:32—33; I CHRONICLES 1:43—44

2 Benjamin's oldest son, this Bela was the head of a large and prolific clan which became distinguished for its fighting men. GENESIS 46:21; NUMBERS 26:38—40; I CHRONICLES 7:6—7; 8:1—3

3 A son of Azaz in the tribe of Reuben, this Bela was a minor chieftain in the tribe and lived as a desert nomad east of the Jordan. I CHRONICLES 5:8

BELSHAZZAR Son of mighty King Nebuchadnezzar, Belshazzar was the last king of Babylon before it fell to the Persians under Cyrus, about 550 B.C. On the last night of his reign, at a great banquet, mysterious handwriting appeared on the wall which no one could decipher. Belshazzar sent for Daniel the prophet, and learned the ominous meaning of the message. DANIEL 5, 7:1; 8:1

BELTESHAZZAR The Babylonian name given to the prophet Daniel by Belshazzar's court. See DANIEL DANIEL 1:7; 2:26; 5:12

BENAIAH
1 A brawny champion and loyal follower of David, Benaiah was the son of Jehoiada, a priest from a village in southern Judah. He distinguished himself on numerous occasions by defeating selected champions from the enemy camp in fight-to-the-finish contests. Once he even descended into a pit to kill a lion. These feats earned Benaiah a place even ahead of "The Thirty," the elite corps of David's top fighters. After serving as David's chief bodyguard, he was assigned the same responsibility under Solomon, and carried out his rulers' orders to execute various men of questionable loyalty. He later succeeded Joab as chief of staff. II SAMUEL 8:18; 20:23; 23:20; 22; I KINGS 1—2; 4:4; I CHRONICLES 11:22—24; 18:17; 27:5—6

2 From Pirathon in Ephraim, this Benaiah was one of David's army officers who served as a division commander and went on active duty during the eleventh month of each year. II SAMUEL 23:30; I CHRONICLES 11:31; 27:14

3 Another Benaiah, this individual was a chieftain in the tribe of Simeon, and was one of those who pushed out the native shepherds in the lush valley of Gedor to get pasture land for his flocks. I CHRONICLES 4:36

4 This Benaiah was a Levite singer who was appointed to play a harp in the worship services in David's House of the Lord. I CHRONICLES 15:18—20; 16:5

5 Another musician, this Banaiah was a priest who played one of the trumpets before the Ark of the Covenant in David's House of the Lord. I CHRONICLES 15:24; 16:6

6 This Benaiah was the father of Jehoiada, one of David's most trusted advisors. I CHRONICLES 27:34

7 Another Benaiah, a Levite, was the grandfather of the prophet Jahaziel who counselled King Jehoshaphat. II CHRONICLES 20:14

8 A Levite also, this Benaiah lived in Hezekiah's time and was given the important position of overseeing the offerings presented in the Temple. II CHRONICLES 31:13

9 One of the family of Parosh at the time of the Exile in Babylon, this Benaiah took a non-Jewish woman as a wife. EZRA 10:25

10 A son of Pahath-moab, this Benaiah also married outside the faith, breaking the Law. EZRA 10:30

11 One of Bani's many sons who wed a non-Jewish girl, this Benaiah also thus deviated from the requirements of his faith. EZRA 10:35

12 This Benaiah, a son of Nebo, was another on the long list of those who married outside the faith during the time of the Exile. EZRA 10:43

13 This man named Benaiah was the father of Pelatiah, one of the evil counsellors in the nation of Judah who were condemned by Ezekiel. EZEKIEL 11:1, 13

BENAMMI The product of the incestuous relationship between Lot's daughter and the drunken Lot, Benammi was traditionally said to be the founder of the tribe of Ammonites, a cruel, crafty desert horde loathed by the Israelites. GENESIS 19:38

BENHADAD

1 Benhadad I, king of Damascus, was bribed by Asa of Judah to attack Baasha of Israel while Baasha was building the fort at Ramah. Although Benhadad's father and Asa's father had signed a pact, Benhadad shrewdly insisted on gold to induce him to attack Israel. During his diversionary campaign, Asa razed Ramah and used the materials to fortify his own border. I CHRONICLES 15; 16

2 Son and successor to **1**, Benhadad II made two ill-advised sieges of King Ahab's capital, Samaria. His prestige and territory shrank after these failures. When he later became ill, Benhadad sent his servant Hazael to ask the prophet Elisha whether or not he would recover. When Hazael returned, he smothered Benhadad and crowned himself king. I KINGS 20; II KINGS 6:24; 8:7—9

3 Benhadad III was the name given to the son of Hazael, who usurped the throne from Benhadad II. Benhadad III lacked his father Hazael's acumen, however, and lost most of the gains made by his father. Joash, king of Israel, invaded Benhadad's country three times, recovering much territory. II KINGS 13

BENHAIL A prominent leader in Judah, Benhail was one of those sent by King Jehoshaphat to explain the Law in the towns and villages of Judah during Jehoshaphat's reform program. II CHRONICLES 17:7

BENHANAN One of Shimon's sons listed in the genealogy of the tribe of Judah by the Chronicler. I CHRONICLES 4:20

BENHESED One of Solomon's commissary officers, Benhesed was assigned one of twelve districts and was given the onerous responsibility of collecting provisions during one month each year for Solomon's huge household and staff. I KINGS 4:10

BENINU A Levite, Beninu was one of those who signed the covenant with Nehemiah promising to observe the Law. NEHEMIAH 10:13

BENJAMIN
1 Named "son of my sorrow," or Ben-oni, by his mother, who died shortly after he was born, this boy, the youngest son of Jacob, was renamed "son of the right hand," or Benjamin, by his father. When his full-brother, Joseph, was prime minister of Egypt during the severe famine, Jacob reluctantly sent Benjamin and his half-brothers to buy grain. After loading Benjamin with gifts and recalling him and his brothers to Egypt, Joseph revealed himself as their brother and moved Benjamin and the rest of the family to Goshen. Benjamin's descendants made up one of the twelve tribes which eventually settled in the Promised Land of Canaan. GENESIS 35, 42—46; 49:27; EXODUS 1:3; DEUTERONOMY 33:12; I CHRONICLES 2:2; 7:6
2 A great-grandson of Benjamin 1, this man was a mighty fighter and head of a large family. I CHRONICLES 7:10
3 One of the sons of Harim who had married outside the faith during the Exile, this Benjamin was listed by Ezra as one of those who had broken the Law. EZRA 10:32
4 Perhaps the same as 3, a man named Benjamin is included in the lists of those who worked with Nehemiah in rebuilding the wall of Jerusalem after the Exile in Babylon. This Benjamin also participated in the services of purifying the wall. NEHEMIAH 3:23; 12:34

BENO One of the descendants of Merari, Beno is included in the list of minor Levites who served in the House of the Lord in David's time. I CHRONICLES 24:26—27

BEN-ONI The name Rachel gave Benjamin. See BENJAMIN. GENESIS 36:18

BENZOHETH One of the sons of Ishi, Benzoheth was carried in the rolls of the tribe of Judah as a descendant of Caleb, son of Jephunneh. I CHRONICLES 4:20

BEOR
1 The father of Bela, the first king of Edom. GENESIS 36:32; I CHRONICLES 1:43
2 The father of the seer, Balaam. NUMBERS 22:5; 24:3,15; 31:8; DEUTERONOMY 23:4; JOSHUA 13:22; 24:9; MICAH 6:5

BERA A king of Sodom at the time of Abraham, Bera was defeated in a fierce battle near the Dead Sea. Sodom was plundered, and Lot, Abraham's nephew, was carried off as a captive. GENESIS 14

BERACAH One of the fierce fighters from the tribe of Benjamin who could use the bow and slingshot with deadly effect with either hand, Beracah and the other members of his troop grew disillusioned with their kinsman Saul, and came over to David's side at Ziglag. I CHRONICLES 12:3

BERACHAH See BERACAH

BERAIAH A son of Shimei, Beraiah was a member of the tribe of Benjamin, and was listed in the genealogy of that tribe by the Chronicler. I CHRONICLES 8:21

BERECHIAH

1 One of the descendants of King Jehoiakim of Judah, Berechiah is mentioned in the genealogy of David's family by the Chronicler. I CHRONICLES 3:20

2 Another Berechiah was the father of Asaph, the great singer in David's worship services. I CHRONICLES 6:39; 15:17

3 A son of Asa, a Levite, this Berechiah was one of the Levites who returned to Palestine after Exile in Babylon. I CHRONICLES 9:16

4 This Berechiah was one of the Levites appointed in David's time to be a gatekeeper for the Ark of the Covenant in the place of worship. I CHRONICLES 15:23

5 A chief in the tribe of Ephraim in the days of Pekah, king of Israel, this man named Berechiah had the courage to oppose his king's plans to enslave prisoners-of-war from Judah. Berechiah and a few others risked disfavor by looking after the prisoners and returning them to their own people in Jericho. II CHRONICLES 28:8—15

6 The father of Meshullam, one of Nehemiah's co-workers who helped rebuild the wall after the return from Exile in Babylon. NEHEMIAH 3:3, 30; 6:18

BERED See BECHER 2

BERI One of the sons of Zophah, Beri was a warrior, head of a prominent clan, and leader in the affairs of the tribe of Asher. I CHRONICLES 7:36

BERIAH

1 One of Asher's sons, Beriah was a powerful chieftain in the tribe of Asher and ancestor of the strong clans of Heber and Malchiel. His name is mentioned in all the rolls of the tribe. GENESIS 46:17; NUMBERS 26:44—45; I CHRONICLES 7:30—31

2 This Beriah was one of Ephraim's sons and the head of a strong clan that bore his name in subsequent years. Hebrew scholars are not able to shed much light on why the Chronicler states that Beriah received his name "because evil had befallen the house." The root of the name is not known. I CHRONICLES 7:23

3 A member of the tribe of Benjamin who lived near Aijalon, this man named Beriah led his powerful clan in a successful raid against the Canaanites at Gath. I CHRONICLES 8:13—16

4 A Levite who served in the sanctuary of the Lord in David's time, this Beriah was included in the roll of the Gershom division of Levites. The list states that Beriah and his brother, Jeush, had so few sons that they were lumped together as one family. I CHRONICLES 23:10—11

BERENICE See BERNICE

BERNICE Oldest daughter of Herod Agrippa I, Bernice was born in 28 A.D. and showed all the family characteristics of immoral living and a dilettante interest in religion. She and her brother, Herod Agrippa II, were visiting the Roman procurator, Festus, at Caesarea when the Apostle Paul was given his hearing. After the outbreak of the Jewish insurrection, Bernice allied herself with her Roman friends, and for a time caused scandal in Rome by living with the Emperor Titus. ACTS 25—26

BERODACH-BALADAN
See MERODACH-BALADAN

BESAI An ancestor of temple singers who returned with Zerubbabel to Jerusalem after the Exile in Babylon. EZRA 2:49; NEHEMIAH 7:52

BESODEIAH A man whose son, Meshullam, helped repair the Old Gate of Jerusalem when Nehemiah rebuilt the wall of Jerusalem after the Exile in Babylon. NEHEMIAH 3:6

BETHUEL Abraham's nephew, Bethuel, was the son of Nahor and the father of Laban and Rebekah. Although he was mentioned in connection with Isaac's suit to marry Rebekah, his son Laban was the one who arranged the marriage. GENESIS 22, 24, 25, 28

BEZAI The head of a numerous clan, 323 of whom returned to Jerusalem from Exile in Babylon, Bezai was one of those who signed the covenant with Nehemiah to keep the Law. EZRA 2:17; NEHEMIAH 7:23; 10:18

BEZALEEL See BEZALEL

BEZALEL
1 An artist designer, Bezalel took Moses' inspired ideas about the tabernacle and produced the finished product. Bezalel not only drew up the plans, but supervised construction. He was an expert craftsman in wood, metal, and precious stones, as well as an architect, engineer, and foreman. EXODUS 31, 35—38; I CHRONICLES 2: 20; II CHRONICLES 1:5
2 One of Pahath-moab's sons who married outside the faith during the Exile, this Bezalel was one of those who broke the Law. EZRA 10:30

BEZER A chieftain listed in the roll of the tribe of Asher, Bezer was renowned as a powerful warrior and head of a strong clan. I CHRONICLES 7:20

BICHRI The ancestor of Sheba, the leader of a revolt against David. II SAMUEL 20

BIDKAR One of Ahab's army officers, Bidkar served with Jehu on King Ahab's staff. When Jehu led a successful palace revolt against Ahab's son, Joram, Bidkar became Jehu's aide and disposed of Joram's body in Naboth's field. II KINGS 9:25

BIGTHA One of seven attendants to Persian King Ahasuerus, Bigtha was ordered by the drunken king to bring the unwilling Queen Vashti to his wild party. ESTHER 1:10

BIGTHAN, BIGTHANA One of two attendants in the Persian court who plotted to kill King Ahasuerus, Big-

63

than would have carried out his plan had he not been discovered by Mordecai, Esther's uncle. Mordecai had been marked for the gallows by the scheming Haman, and his discovery of Bigthan's plot not only saved his own life, but averted a bloodbath against all the Jews. ESTHER 2:21; 6:2

BIGVAI

1 A companion of Zerubbabel, Bigvai and his clan returned to Jerusalem from Babylon with a large contingent of exiles. EZRA 2:2, 14; 8:14; NEHEMIAH 7:7, 19

2 Another Bigvai, this man was one of those faithful Jews who joined with Nehemiah, after rebuilding the wall of Jerusalem following the Exile, to sign the covenant to keep the Law. NEHEMIAH 10:16

BILDAD One of the three friends who came to visit and philosophize with Job, Bildad took a position somewhere between the rambling, elderly Eliphaz and the curt, coarse Zophar. All three, however, were convinced that Job's suffering was caused by Job's sin, and did not hesitate to tell Job so. JOB 2; 8; 18; 25; 42

BILGAH

1 A priest who served in David's sanctuary, Bilgah was the head priest of the fifteenth team appointed for sanctuary service. I CHRONICLES 24:14

2 Another priest named Bilgah, or Bilgai, this man was one of those who returned with Zerubbabel to Jerusalem from Exile in Babylon. After helping Nehemiah rebuild the wall, he

joined in signing the covenant to observe the Law. NEHEMIAH 10:8

BILGAI See **BILGAH 2**

BILHAH The servant girl whom Laban gave to Rachel, Jacob's wife, Bilhah was later given by the childless Rachel to her husband, Jacob, to provide him with some heirs. Bilhah was the mother of two of Jacob's sons, Dan and Naphtali. Later she was guilty of an illicit affair with another of Jacob's sons, Reuben. GENESIS 29:29; 30:35; 37:2; 46:25; I CHRONICLES 7:13

BILHAN

1 A son of Ezer and grandson of Seir, Bilhan was a king or chief of the land of Hor, and is listed in the genealogy of Esau's extensive family. GENESIS 36:27; I CHRONICLES 1:42

2 A son of Jediael of the tribe of Benjamin, this Bilhan was a strong clan chieftain and an able warrior, and the father of seven sons who were prominent family heads in the tribe. I CHRONICLES 7:10

BILSHAN A nobleman-official, Bilshan was one of those who chose to return to Jerusalem with Zerubbabel from Exile in Babylon. Bilshan was a man of some importance, and was listed as one of Zerubbabel's closest companions. EZRA 2:2; NEHEMIAH 7:7

BIMHAL One of Japhlet's sons, Bimhal is listed in the rolls of the tribe of Asher by the Chronicler. He was the chief of a large clan and a strong warrior. I CHRONICLES 7:33

BINEA One of Saul's descendants through Saul's son Jonathan, Binea is named in the genealogy of the tribe of Benjamin by the Chronicler. I CHRONICLES 8:37; 9:43

BINNUI

1 This Binnui was a man whose descendants were part of the contingent of exiles that returned to Jerusalem with Zerubbabel. In Ezra 2:10 he is referred to as BANI. EZRA 2:10; NEHEMIAH 7:15

2 Another Binnui, this man was a well-known and illustrious Levite who returned to Jerusalem with Zerubbabel and the exiles from Babylon. His son, Noadiah, was one of those appointed to weigh and count the gold and silver brought for the rebuilt Temple. EZRA 8:33; NEHEMIAH 8:7 (called *Bani* here); 9:4 (called *Bunni* in this place); 12:8

3 One of several sons of Pahathmoab who married non-Jewish wives during the Exile, this Binnui and thirteen of his sons, who also married outside the faith, were all guilty of breaking the Law. EZRA 10:30, 38

4 Another Binnui, this man was a Levite and a son of Henadad. He worked with Nehemiah rebuilding the wall of Jerusalem after the Exile, overseeing the construction of the section from Azariah's house "to the Angle and the corner." NEHEMIAH 3:24; 10:9

BIRSHA The king of Gomorrah, a city near the Dead Sea, Birsha and four other rulers were defeated in a battle in the Valley of Siddim, in the region near the Dead Sea. Birsha and the king of Sodom both died horrible deaths in the hot pits nearby, and their cities were plundered. Lot, Abraham's nephew, was one of those carried off captive from Sodom. Abraham partially avenged Birsha's death by defeating his attackers. GENESIS 14

BIRZAITH The head of a clan and a noted warrior, Birzaith was listed in the family tree of the tribe of Asher. I CHRONICLES 7:31

BIRZAVITH See BIRZAITH

BISHLAM An officer in the Persian King Artaxerxes's service, Bishlam and several of his associates wrote from Palestine protesting the rebuilding of Jerusalem and warning Artaxerxes that he was asking for trouble if he allowed the work to continue. The letter caused an order to be sent, temporarily restraining the exiles from working. EZRA 4

BITHIAH The daughter of the Egyptian pharaoh, Bithiah became one of the wives of Mered, a descendant of Judah, during the Israelites sojourn in Egypt. I CHRONICLES 4:17

BLASTUS An official in the court of King Herod Agrippa I, Blastus intervened (probably because he was bribed) for the inhabitants of Tyre and Sidon to get them an audience with Agrippa. The stormy scene between Agrippa and the delegation from the unfortunate cities resulted in Agrippa's final illness and death. ACTS 12:20—23

BOANERGES See JAMES, SON OF ZEBEDEE and JOHN, SON OF ZEBEDEE

BOAZ A well-to-do landowner of the tribe of Judah near Bethlehem,

Boaz took pity on a young Moabite widow named Ruth who was working in his fields. The tender story of Boaz's kindness and Ruth's loyalty is the plot of the Book of Ruth. Boaz and Ruth married. Their son, Obed, was David's grandfather. RUTH, I CHRONICLES 2:11 —12; Matthew 1:5; Luke 3:32

BOCHERU One of six sons of Azel, Bocheru was a member of the tribe of Benjamin who claimed descent from Saul through Jonathan. He and his family are listed among those who returned from Exile in Babylon. I CHRONICLES 8:38; 9:44

BOHAN One of Reuben's sons, Bohan is remembered principally because a stone marker named for him was the boundary between the lands of the tribe of Benjamin and the tribe of Judah. JOSHUA 15:6; 18:17

BUKKI
1 Fifth high priest after Aaron, Bukki came from an illustrious family of Levites. Bukki's son, Uzzi, carried on the priestly tradition. I CHRONICLES 6:5, 51; EZRA 7:4
2 This Bukki was a son of Jogli of the tribe of Dan. He was one of twelve outstanding leaders elected to represent the twelve tribes and assist Moses in dividing the Promised Land fairly among them. NEHEMIAH 34:22

BUKKIAH A musician like his famous father, Heman, Bukkiah was a Levite who was allotted the leadership of the sixth group of singers in the House of the Lord during David's time. I CHRONICLES 25:4, 13

BUNAH One of the descendants of Judah, Bunah was a son of Jerahmeel and was carried in the list of the tribe of Judah by the Chronicler. I CHRONICLES 2:25

BUNNI
1 A Levite who lived at the time of Ezra, after the Exile, Bunni had a prominent part in the great worship service in Jerusalem when the exiles publicly confessed their sins and separated themselves from all non-Jews. Later he joined with Nehemiah in signing the covenant to keep the Law. NEHEMIAH 9:4; 10:15
2 A different Bunni, this man is listed as the ancestor of Shemaiah, one of the Levites who volunteered to move to Jerusalem after the Exile. NEHEMIAH 11:15

BUZ
1 Abraham's nephew, Buz was the son of Nahor, Abraham's brother. His descendants made up a tribe located in the Arabian desert. GENESIS 22:21
2 Another man named Buz is mentioned by the Chronicler as a member of the tribe of Gad. I CHRONICLES 5:14

BUZI A member of an old priestly family tracing its ancestry to Zadok, Buzi is best remembered as the father of the great prophet Ezekiel. EZEKIEL 1:3

C

CAIAPHAS The high priest who presided at the ecclesiastical hearing of Jesus, Caiaphas succeeded his wily father-in-law, Annas, to the high office when Annas was deposed, 14 A.D. Disregarding justice, Caiaphas engineered Jesus' speedy trial and execution, first on the grounds that Jesus was stirring up the population to a dangerous state, and then on the grounds that Jesus was guilty of blasphemy. Thus he had Jesus crucified because of patriotism and religion. The death sentence was ratified by the Sanhedrin, and Jesus was passed on to Pilate. Caiaphas was an arch-enemy of the church, was present at the trial of Peter and John, and did whatever he could to persecute Christians. He was finally removed from office by the Roman procurator Vitellius in 37 A.D. MATTHEW 36; LUKE 3:2; JOHN 11:49; 18:13—28; ACTS 4:6; 5:17; 5:21; 5:27; 7:1; 9:1

CAIN The oldest son of Adam and Eve, Cain was the first murderer, the first farmer, and the first city-dweller. Annoyed because his brother Abel's offering was more acceptable to God, Cain killed Abel. He tried to hide his guilt, but could not, and was forced to face up to God for what he had done. Condemned to be a restless wanderer, Cain, the murderer, later built the first city, Enoch. GENESIS 4; HEBREWS 11:4; I JOHN 3:12; JUDE 11

CAINAN
1 Enos' son and Seth's grandson (See KENAN). GENESIS 5; I CHRONICLES 1:2; LUKE 3:37
2 The son of Arphaxad, according to the family genealogy of Joseph, Jesus' father, which Luke records. LUKE 3:36

CALCOL Zerha's son and Judah's grandson, Calcol was renowned for his wisdom. He was remembered in subsequent years as one of the four wisest men of the nation, surpassed only by Solomon. I CHRONICLES 2:6; I KINGS 4:31

CALEB

1 The son of Jephunneh, this Caleb was one of the twelve spies sent by Moses to scout the Promised Land of Canaan. Caleb and Joshua were the only two who did not allow the difficulties to minimize God, and presented an unpopular minority report urging the tribes to move at once to take the land. As a reward for their faith and courage, Caleb and Joshua were the only two original members of the tribes permitted to go into the Promised Land. Caleb was awarded the area surrounding Hebron, and drove out the giant sons of Anak. NUMBERS 13, 14, 26, 32, 34; DEUTERONOMY 1:36; JOSHUA 14, 15, 21; JUDGES 1, 3; I SAMUEL 25:3; 30:14; I CHRONICLES 2; 4:15; 6:56

2 Another Caleb, the son of Hezron, is included in the tribal list under Judah's tribe, Perez's clan. He was probably the grandfather of Caleb 1. I CHRONICLES 2:18, 19, 42

CANAAN

The son of Ham and grandson of Noah, Canaan carried the curse that was inflicted on his father for peering at the drunken Noah, and was condemned to be a lackey for his uncles, Shem and Japheth. His descendants came to be called Canaanites, and were the inhabitants of the land which was later won from them by Shem's descendants, the Israelites. GENESIS 9, 10; I CHRONICLES 1

CANDACE

A title held by all the queens of Ethiopia. The "Candace" mentioned in the Bible was the wealthy dowager queen whose royal treasurer was baptized by Philip near Gaza. ACTS 8:27

CARCAS

One of seven important servants in Persian King Ahasuerus's court, Carcas was ordered by his drunken king to bring the unwilling Queen Vashti to a wild party in progress in the royal banquet hall. ESTHER 1:10

CARKAS See CARCAS

CAREAH See KAREAH

CARMI

1 Carmi, a member of the tribe of Judah, was the father of Achan, whose deceit and greed cost Joshua a defeat in his first attempt to capture Ai. JOSHUA 7; I CHRONICLES 2:7; 4:1

2 Another Carmi, this one was a son of Reuben and head of a clan which came to be called Carmites. GENESIS 46:9; EXODUS 6:14; NUMBERS 26:6; I CHRONICLES 5:3

CARPUS

A Christian who lived at Troas in Asia Minor, Carpus entertained Paul on this last journey. Paul forgot his cloak at Carpus' house and mentioned it in his second letter to Timothy. Tradition insists that Carpus was one of the seventy disciples, and that he later became bishop of Berea. II TIMOTHY 4:13

CEPHAS See PETER

CHALCOL See CALCOL

CHELAL

One of Pahath-moab's sons

who married outside the faith during the Exile, Chelal thus broke the Law. EZRA 10:30

CHELLUH See CHELUHI

CHELUB
1 One of the members of the tribe of Judah, Chelub is included in the list of the family by the Chronicler. I CHRONICLES 4:11
2 This Chelub was the father of Ezri, one of David's farm superintendents. I CHRONICLES 27:26

CHELUBAI See CALEB 2

CHELUHI One of the many sons of Bani who took non-Jewish girls for wives during the Exile, Cheluhi transgressed the Law. EZRA 10:35

CHENAANAH
1 This Chenaanah was the father of Zedekiah, the false prophet who slapped Micaiah for prophesying that King Ahab would be killed at Ramoth-Gilead. I KINGS 22:11; II CHRONICLES 18:10
2 A son of Bilhan, and the head of a family in the tribe of Benjamin, Chenaanah was a tribal leader and an able warrior. I CHRONICLES 7:10

CHENANI A Levite in Ezra's time, Chenani was one of those who took an active part in the great national service at which the returned exiles publicly confessed their sin. NEHEMIAH 9:4

CHENANIAH
1 A Levite musician, Chenaniah led the choirs in the festivities when David brought the Ark of the Covenant up to Jerusalem. I CHRONICLES 15:22—28
2 Another Chenaniah was a Levite from the Izharite clan who, with his sons, was appointed as a civil servant under David to look after legal and judicial matters. I CHRONICLES 26:29

CHERAN A son of Dishon of the clan of Seir, Cheran's name was carried in the list of Edomite first families. GENESIS 36:26; I CHRONICLES 1:41

CHESED Abraham's nephew, Chesed was a son of Abraham's brother Nahor. He was a chieftain in the Mesopotamian plain, and founder of a desert tribe that later became known as the Chaldeans. GENESIS 22:22

CHILEAB David's second son by Abigail, Chileab was also sometimes known as Daniel. Two of his younger brothers, Absalom and Adonijah, stirred up revolts against their father. Chileab never distinguished himself, and sank into obscurity. II SAMUEL 3:3

CHILION A son of Naomi, Chilion and his brother, Mahlon, left their mother's home near Bethlehem and moved to Moab during a famine, and married girls from Moab—Orpah and Ruth. After ten years in Moab, both Chilion and Mahlon died. Their widows went to Bethlehem to live with Naomi, where, later, Ruth married Boaz. RUTH

CHIMHAM The son of Barzillai, the man from Gilead who showed kindness to David when David had to flee because of Absalom's revolt, Chimham was brought to Jerusalem by David.

David wanted to repay Barzillai for his kindness and by bringing him to Jerusalem, but the old man asked that his son be invited instead. Later David set Chimham up in the hotel business in Bethlehem. It was perhaps at that inn some thousand years later that Joseph and Mary tried to find accommodations. II SAMUEL 19; JEREMIAH 41:17

CHISLON A prominent member of the tribe of Benjamin, Chislon was the father of Elidad, one of those elected as representatives of the twelve tribes to help Moses parcel out the land fairly to the tribes after their planned move into Canaan. NUMBERS 34:21

CHLOE A woman whose slaves reported the troubles in the Corinthian Church to the Apostle Paul, Chloe perhaps lived in the city from which Paul was writing, Ephesus, or perhaps at Corinth itself. Although it is not specifically stated in the Bible, many scholars believe that Chloe herself was a Christian. I CORINTHIANS 1:11

CHUSAN RISH-A-THAIM See CUSHAN RISH-A-THAIM

CHUZA The steward in the court of Herod Antipas, Chuza is best remembered as the husband of Joanna, one of the women who helped Jesus and His disciples. LUKE 8:3

CLAUDIA One of Paul's friends who lived at Rome, Claudia was probably connected with the Emperor Claudius' household, perhaps as a slave or a relative. She was probably the wife of Pudens and the mother of Linus, mentioned also in II Timothy 4:21. Claudia's family was part of the circle of loyal friends who ministered to Paul during his imprisonment in Rome. II TIMOTHY 4:21

CLAUDIUS The fourth emperor of Rome and successor to the notorious Caligula, Tiberius Claudius Drusus Nero Germanicus (or Claudius, as he was usually called) was the nephew of the great Augustus and was brought to power unexpectedly by a brief uprising of the Praetorian Guard in 41 A.D. He was weak and pliable, dominated by his wives, and finally murdered by his wife, Agrippiana, in 54 A.D. In the New Testament, he was remembered for his decree expelling all Jews from Rome. ACTS 11:28; 18:2

CLAUDIUS LYSIAS A Roman army officer responsible for keeping the peace in volatile Jerusalem, Claudius Lysias rushed in with his squads to put down the uproar that the Apostle Paul had stirred up. Claudius Lysias nervously jumped to the conclusion that Paul was an agitator for an underground organization that had recently been terrorizing the area, and prepared to scourge him. But when he heard that Paul was a Roman citizen, Claudius took him into protective custody and passed him on to the procurator, Felix. Claudius Lysias, who had bought his citizenship, was impressed that Paul was born a Roman citizen. ACTS 23

CLEMENT A co-worker and friend

of Paul, Clement was one of the Christians who lived at Philippi. The name is fairly common (the historian Tacitus mentions five men named Clement) and nothing certain is known about this Clement beyond what Paul writes in his letter to Philippi. PHILIPPIANS 4:3

CLEOPAS A disheartened and disillusioned follower of the crucified Jesus, Cleopas was one of two men who were trudging to Emmaeus when the Risen Lord joined them. They did not recognize Him, however, until He broke bread with them that evening. They immediately rushed back to Jerusalem through the dusk to share the news with the other disciples. LUKE 24:18

CLEOPHAS See CLOPAS

CLOPAS Clopas was the husband of a woman named Mary, who was herself a sister of Mary, mother of Jesus, and one of the women who stayed with Jesus' mother at the Cross. JOHN 19:25

COL-HOZEH A member of the tribe of Judah, Col-Hozeh was the father of Shallum, a district leader among those who returned from Exile in Babylon and the superintendent of construction of the Fountain Gate on the wall of Jerusalem. Other members of Col-Hozeh's family were also prominent during the time Nehemiah rebuilt Jerusalem. NEHEMIAH 3:15; 11:5

CONANIAH
1 A Levite who lived during the days

of King Hezekiah's reform, Conaniah was given the heavy responsibility of being the treasurer of all Temple funds. II CHRONICLES 31:12—13
2 Another Levite, this Conaniah lived in King Josiah's time. As a prominent citizen and Temple leader, Conaniah joined his king and other leaders in making substantial gifts at the Passover during Josiah's reform. II CHRONICLES 35:9

CONIAH See JEHOIACHIN

CONONIAH See CONANIAH 1

CORNELIUS The Roman centurion in the Italian cohort stationed at Caesare, Cornelius sent for Peter and asked to be received as a convert to the Christian faith. Peter had been opposed to receiving anyone into the Church who did not first go through the ceremony of becoming a Jew, but at the time of Cornelius' request, Peter had a vision which revealed that God has no compunction about associating with non-Jews. Cornelius was baptized, Peter's first Gentile convert. One tradition about Cornelius' later life speaks of him as founding a church at Caesare; another holds that he became the bishop of Scamandros. ACTS 10

COSAM An ancestor of Jesus through Joseph, Cosam is listed in Luke's geneology of Joseph's ancestors as a son of Elmodan. LUKE 3:28

COZ A member of the tribe of Judah who traced his ancestry back through Caleb the son of Hur, Coz was a tribal chieftain listed in the family genealogy of Judah. I CHRONICLES 4:8

COZBI An immoral Midianite woman who lived during Moses' time, Cozbi, like a number of her sisters from Midian and Moab, caused many men of Israel to forget their loyalty to God. Cozbi and a man from the tribe of Simeon were surprised and speared to death by Phineas, one of Moses' lieutenants, after brazenly and publicly disregarding Moses' injunction against intimacies between his men and Midianite or Moabite women. NUMBERS 25

CRESCENS One of the Apostle Paul's staunchest friends, Crescens stayed with Paul during his prison sentence at Rome. Later he was sent by Paul to visit the churches at Galatia. Some legends have him founding churches in Europe in such cities as Vienna; others have him serving as bishop of Chalcedon. II TIMOTHY 4:10

CRISPUS Once a prominent Jew and head of the synagogue in Corinth, Crispus was converted by Paul's preaching to accept Jesus as the Christ. Crispus and his family had the distinction of being among the few people that Paul personally baptized. There is a legend that Crispus subsequently became the bishop of Aegina. ACTS 18:8; I CORINTHIANS 1:14

CUSH
1 A son of Ham and grandson of Noah, Cush was regarded as the ancestor of the Cushites, the Negro tribes south of Egypt. GENESIS 10; I CHRONICLES 1

2 Referred to only in the title of Psalm 7, this man named Cush was apparently a member of the tribe of Benjamin who was part of Saul's forces fighting David. PSALM 7

CUSHAN-RISHATHAIM A powerful desert king, Cushan forced the tribes of Israel to pay tribute to him for eight years during the days of the judges, after the conquest of Canaan. Cushan's victory and iron grip were interpreted as God's punishment for the tribes' unfaithfulness to God. Othniel, one of the judges, finally broke Cushan's hold over Israel. HABAKKUK 3:7

CUSHI
1 A fleet-footed soldier in Joab's division, Cushi was ordered to run to David and tell the sad news of Absalom's death after Joab had put down Absalom's rebellion. II SAMUEL 18
2 Another Cushi was an ancestor of Jehudi, King Jehoiakim's messenger who summoned Jeremiah's secretary, Baruch, to read Jeremiah's prophecy to the court. JEREMIAH 36:14
3 Another Cushi, this man was the father of Zephaniah, the prophet who was a contemporary of King Josiah. ZEPHANIAH 1:1

CUTH See CUTHAH

CUTHA See CUTHAH

CUTHAH The father of a group of temple singers who returned from Exile to Jerusalem with Zerubbabel, Cuthah may also have been the name of a town in Babylon. The lists in Ezra and Nehemiah of those who returned from Exile do not carry this name. II KINGS 17:24, 30

CYRENIUS See QUIRINIUS

CYRUS The founder of the Persian Empire, Cyrus took over the decayed Babylonian Empire with the help of a revolt in southern Babylonia in 538 B.C. Realizing how difficult it was to keep restless uprooted populations subjugated, Cyrus sent home the peoples who had been deported from their homelands and sent to Babylonia by the Assyrians and Babylonians. Thus to the Jews, who had been in exile in Babylon for over half a century, Cyrus was a great deliverer. His empire stretched from the passes of what is now Afghanistan to the shores of the Mediterranean. II CHRONICLES 36; EZRA 1, 3, 4, 5, 6; ISAIAH 44:28; 45:1; DANIEL 1:21; 6:28; 10:1

D

DALAIAH   See DELAIAH

DALPHON   One of the ten wicked sons of the infamous Haman, Dalphon joined his father and brothers in a plot to persecute the Jews in Persia. The plan was stopped in time by the intervention of Queen Esther, and Dalphon and the other conspirators were hung. ESTHER 9:7

DAMARIS   A woman who lived in Athens, Damaris was one of the few who were converted by Paul on his visit to the great Greek city. Some scholars believe that the fact that she was able to listen to Paul on the Areopagus—something no woman of a good family could have done—and the fact that there is no mention of her social standing, indicate that Damaris was one of the *Hetairai* or companions of ancient Greece, a group of women who were given an education similar to that of today's Japanese geishas. ACTS 17:34

DAN   One of Jacob's sons by Rachel's servant girl, Bilhah, Dan was the ancestor of the tribe called Dan. This was a small, one-clan family that eventually settled in the extreme north of Canaan and built the city of Dan. GENESIS 30:6; 35:25; 46:23; 49:16—17; EXODUS 1:4; NUMBERS 26:42; JOSHUA 19:47; I CHRONICLES 2:2

DANIEL
1   David's son, also called Chileab. (See CHILEAB) I CHRONICLES 3:1
2   A priest from the family of Ithamar, this Daniel returned with Ezra from Exile in Babylon, helped Nehemiah rebuild Jerusalem, and joined in signing the covenant to keep the Law. EZRA 8:2; NEHEMIAH 10:6
3   The great prophet, this Daniel was the most famous of those carry-

75

ing the name. A blueblood who was one of the outstanding youths of Judah in the time of King Jehoiakim, Daniel, together with the cream of the nation's leadership, was carried off to Babylon as a captive of the Babylonian king, Nebuchadnezzar. Daniel and his companions withstood the Babylonians' intensive efforts to indoctrinate them as members of the Babylonian court (Nebuchadnezzar even gave Daniel a Babylonian name, and trained him and three companions to serve the royal throne). When other wise men could not interpret Nebuchadnezzar's dreams, Daniel succeeded, and thus proved himself to be wiser than the Babylonian astrologers and magicians. Later, at the feast of the decadent emperor Belshazzar, Nebuchadnezzar's successor, Daniel correctly interpreted the handwriting on the wall as a warning of Belshazzar's downfall. When the Persians took over the Babylonian Empire, Daniel held a prominent position under the Persian ruler, Cyrus. Jealous Persians had Daniel arrested for refusing to bow to the emperor and acknowledge him divine. Thrown into a den of lions, Daniel emerged unharmed, and wrote a series of striking visions about the future of Israel which are now contained in the Book of Daniel. EZE-KIEL 14:14—20, 28:3; DANIEL; MATTHEW 24:15; MARK 13:14

DARA A son of Zerah and a grandson of Judah, Dara is listed in the Chronicler's genealogy of the tribe of Judah. I CHRONICLES 2:6

DARDA One of the wisest men of all time in Israel, Darda is mentioned in the list of the great men whose wisdom was not surpassed by anyone except Solomon. I CHRONICLES 2:6

DARIUS
1 The great reorganizer of the Persian Empire after Cyrus' sudden death and the revolts that followed, Darius vanquished the other claimants to the throne and put Persia on the map permanently. He eventually became master of all the territory from India to eastern Europe, and organized an efficient and ruthless government. His only set-back was at Marathon where he was defeated by the Athenians in 491 B.C. During his reign, the Jews, returned from Exile, completed the new Temple in Jerusalem which replaced the earlier one destroyed by the Babylonians. Darius even contributed funds for the project. He was succeeded by his son Xerxes when he died in 486 B.C. EZRA 4, 5, 6; HAGGAI 1:1, 15; 2:10; ZECHARIAH 1:1, 7; 7:1
2 Another Persian King by the same name, mentioned by Nehemiah (Nehemiah 12:22), this was either Darius II (423—404 B.C.), or Darius III (336—330 B.C.) who lived at the same time as the high priest Jaddua, mentioned by Nehemiah in the same verse. If the Darius referred to was Darius III, he was toppled from power by Alexander the Great.
3 Darius "the Mede" was one of Cyrus the Persian's top aides and administrators. This Darius was the person who actually captured Babylon and ruled it during Cyrus' absences. This was the Darius who appointed the prophet Daniel as one of three in

charge of one hundred and twenty satraps who ruled the provinces. DAN-IEL 5, 6, 9, 11

DARKON A servant of Solomon, Darkon was the ancestor of a contingent of his family that returned from Exile in Babylon to Jerusalem with Zerubbabel. EZRA 2:56; NEHEMIAH 7:58

DATHAN One of the tribe of Reuben, Dathan plotted with Korah, Abiram, and On to overthrow Moses. They took advantage of the dissatisfaction among the tribes and were ready to lead a revolt when they were killed by a sudden earthquake. NUMBERS 16, 26; DEUTERONOMY 11:6; PSALM 106:17

DAVID Israel's most famous king, David was considered to be the ideal ruler and the prototype for the promised Messiah, in Jewish thinking. David was Jesse's youngest son, born at Bethlehem as one of the tribe of Judah, and early noted for his musical ability. Sent to soothe the emotionally ill King Saul with his music, David rapidly advanced in Saul's court until his popularity made Saul insanely jealous. David fled for his life, and became leader of a band of outlaws. After Saul's death on Mount Gilboa, David returned home, was made the king of Hebron and waged a long but successful war against the Philistines. He ultimately won over the supporters of the house of Saul, was recognized as king of the entire nation, and moved his capital to a point midway between Israel and Judah, changing the name of this Jebusite city to Jerusalem. Following this move, David made Jerusalem the religious center of the new nation by bringing the Ark of the Covenant into the capital. His magnanimity to former enemies won him the respect of nearly everyone. At the same time, David showed himself to be a good organizer and general. He extended the nation's borders in all directions, and brought prosperity and prominence to his people. His later years were marred by a sordid affair with Bathsheba. David's bad example undermined his own sons. Incest, murder, rebellion, and plots within David's own household turned his final days into ones of deep trial. One son, Absalom, nearly succeeded in his revolt. Nevertheless, David's deep trust in God, his sense of justice, and his personal attractiveness were apparent until nearly the end of his life. The nation fondly remembered his reign as its golden age. I and II SAMUEL; I and II KINGS; I and II CHRONICLES; RUTH; EZRA; NEHEMIAH; PSALMS; PROVERBS; ECCLESIASTES; SONG OF SOLOMON; ISAIAH; JEREMIAH; EZEKIEL; HOSEA; AMOS; ZECHARIAH; MATTHEW; MARK; LUKE; JOHN; ACTS; ROMANS; II TIMOTHY; HEBREWS; REVELATION

DEBIR A king in the Amorite city of Eglon, Debir joined with four other kings to march against Joshua's allies, the Gibeonites. Heeding the Gibeonites' call for help, Joshua marched all night and surprised Debir and his allies in a dawn attack. Debir was executed afterwards. JOSHUA 10

DEBORAH

DEBORAH

1 Rebekah's nurse, Deborah was like a member of the family. She died following Jacob's return to Canaan after twenty years—accompanied by his family this time—and she was buried in a prominent place under an oak in Bethel. GENESIS 35:8

2 The militant heroine in Israel in the days of the judges, Deborah, aided by Barak, rallied the tribes of Israel to unite in an attack on Sisera and the Canaanites, who had been raiding the tribes for several years. In the great battle at Kishon, a violent storm helped the tribes defeat the Canaanites. Deborah and Barak immortalized the victory in a famous ode or song. Deborah was looked up to as one of the great leaders and judges of the tribes in the period before the kingdom. JUDGES 4—5

DEDAN

1 A son of Raamah and a grandson of Cush, this Dedan was a descendant of Noah through Ham. GENESIS 10:7; I CHRONICLES 1:9

2 This man named Dedan was one of Jokshan's sons, and a grandson of Abraham. He was the progenitor of a tribe called the Dedanites who were energetic traders in the ancient world, working the caravan routes across the desert to Damascus and Tyre. GENESIS 25:3; I CHRONICLES 1:32

DEKAR The father of the man called Ben-deker or "son of Dekar" who was one of Solomon's twelve commissary officers responsible for providing supplies for the palace for one month each year. I KINGS 4:9

DELAIAH

1 One of the sons of Elioenai, this man named Delaiah was a descendant of David and Solomon and was listed in the Chronicler's family tree of David's descendants. I CHRONICLES 3:24

2 A priest in David's house of the Lord, this Delaiah picked the lot to be twenty-third officer of the sanctuary. I CHRONICLES 24:18

3 The son of Shemaiah, this Delaiah was a nobleman in the court of King Jerhoiakim of Judah in the time of the prophet Jeremiah. He and a few others urged the irate king not to burn the scroll of Jeremiah's dire prophecies about Judah, but their plea was disregarded. JEREMIAH 36:25

4 This Delaiah was the father of the Shemaiah who was bribed to intimidate Nehemiah and stop him from building the wall of Jerusalem. NEHEMIAH 6:10

5 Another Delaiah, this man was the head of a family that returned to Jerusalem with Zerubbabel from the Exile in Babylon. Tragically, however, his genealogy had been lost, and he could not trace his ancestry as other Jews were proud to be able to do. EZRA 2:60; NEHEMIAH 7:62

DELILAH A Philistine woman who lived in Sorek, Delilah used her wiles on the great Israelite hero, Samson. Delilah charmed Samson into revealing the secret of his great strength—his Nazirite vow never to cut his hair—and then betrayed him by turning him over to the Philistines, who tortured and blinded the hapless lover. JUDGES 16

DEMAS One of the Apostle Paul's co-workers and esteemed friends for a time, Demas shared Paul's hardships during the first part of his prison term in Rome. Demas even joined Paul in sending personal greetings to fellow Christians at Colossae and to Philemon's family. Later, "in love with the present world," (II Timothy 4:10) Demas forsook Paul. It would seem either that Demas was lured away from the faith by some enticement or that he found the going too hard. There is no word about Demas' subsequent career, and no tradition that he ever returned to the faith. COLOSSIANS 4:14; PHILEMON 24; II TIMOTHY 4:10

DEMETRIUS
1 A silversmith in Ephesus, Demetrius stirred up a riot in Ephesus because Paul's preaching was hurting the business of making and selling models of the town goddess, Artemis. Demetrius cloaked his attack on Paul by appealing to the religion and patriotism of his townspeople. Paul narrowly escaped being seized, and hurriedly left Ephesus. ACTS 19:23—38
2 A Christian convert who lived at Ephesus, this Demetrius was highly respected among the Christian believers. Because the names are identical, and because both lived in Ephesus, there is a faint possibility that this Demetrius was the same as Demetrius 1, which would mean that the ringleader of the opposition later became a mainstay of the Church. III JOHN 12

DEUEL A member of the tribe of Gad, Deuel was the father of Elia-saph, the chief of Gad who helped Moses in the census of the tribes and played a prominent part in tribal leadership. NUMBERS 1:14; 2:14; 7:42, 47; 10:20

DIBLAIM The father of Gomer, Hosea's faithless wife, whom the prophet took back with him. HOSEA 1:3

DIBRI A member of the tribe of Dan, Dibri was the father of a daughter who married an Egyptian. This daughter's son, Dibri's grandson, was stoned to death for blasphemy. LEVITICUS 24:11

DIDYMUS See THOMAS

DIKLAH One of Joktan's sons and a descendant of Noah through Shem, Diklah was the head of a tribe that lived in the Arabian desert. GENESIS 10:27; I CHRONICLES 1:21

DINAH The daughter of Jacob and Leah, Dinah was seduced by Shechem, the son of the chief of a tribe in Canaan. Although Shechem wanted to marry Dinah, and offered to pay the marriage dowry, Dinah's brothers, Simeon and Levi, were determined to avenge the dishonor. After tricking Shechem and all his men into consenting to circumcision, Simeon and Levi then massacred the convalescing Canaanites. GENESIS 30; 34; 46:15

DIONYSIUS A man of Athens, Dionysius was one of the few in the Greek city converted to Christ by the Apostle Paul. He was a distinguished citizen, and served on the council of Areopagus. Some think that Dionysius might have taken down Paul's speech on Mar's Hill in Athens and given it to Luke. Ancient traditions claim that Dionysius became the first bishop in Athens, and died a martyr's death in the Domitian persecution. ACTS 17:34

DIOTREPHES A pushy member of a Christian congregation who loved the limelight, Diotrephes was a trouble-maker for John the elder, the author of Third John. Diotrephes challenged John's authority by refusing to receive messengers from John and putting out of the church anyone who showed these messengers any hospitality. III JOHN 9—10

DISHAN One of the sons of Seir the Horite, Dishan was a desert tribal chieftain in the genealogy of the Edomites. GENESIS 36:21

DISHON
1 Another son of Seir the Horite, Dishon was a brother of Dishan. As in the case of all the others in this list, Dishon was also the name of a desert clan of Horites. GENESIS 36:21
2 A relative of **1**, this Dishan was the son of Anah, the nomad shepherd who found the hot springs in the desert. GENESIS 36:25; I CHRONICLES 1:38—41

DIVES See LAZARUS

DODAI An officer in David's army, Dodai was an Ahohite who was a division commander on active duty the second month of every year. I CHRONICLES 27:4

DODAVAH See DODAVAHU

DODAVAHU A man of Judah who lived in Mareshah, Dodavahu was the father of Eliezer, the prophet who foretold dire consequences for King Jehoshaphat because of his naval alliance with Shaziah. II CHRONICLES 20:37

DODO
1 A member of the tribe of Issachar after the Israelites had invaded Canaan, this Dodo was the grandfather of the great judge and hero of the tribe, Tola. JUDGES 10:1
2 An Aholite, this individual was the father of Eleazar, the great warrior and officer of "The Thirty," David's elite corps of guards. II SAMUEL 23:9; I CHRONICLES 11:12
3 A man of Bethlehem, this Dodo was the father of Elhanan, one of the great fighters under David who won a place on the roll of "The Thirty," David's most trusted and valiant soldiers. II SAMUEL 23:24; I CHRONICLES 11:26

DOEG An Edomite who was chief herdsman for King Saul, Doeg saw that Ahimelech, the priest at Nob, had given aid to David, then an outlaw with a price on his head. Doeg reported this to Saul, then carried out Saul's order to kill Ahimelech and the other priests at Nob in reprisal. The cruel Doeg went even further, and massacred everyone in Nob. I SAMUEL 21—22; PSALM 52

DORCAS A woman of some means who became a Christian, Dorcas was much loved for her acts of charity in Joppa. In addition to giving money to the needy, she sewed clothes for the poor. When she died suddenly, the members of her congregation sent an urgent appeal to Peter in nearby Lydda. Peter raised her to life again. ACTS 9:36—41

DRUSILLA The youngest of Herod Agrippa I's three daughters, Drusilla was a beautiful and amoral princess who scandalized pious Jews by deserting her husband, Azizus, and marrying the Gentile Roman governor of Judea, Felix. Drusilla and Felix were living at Caesarea when Paul was arrested. Drusilla listened in at the hearing before Felix when Paul preached and presented his case. ACTS 24

DUMAH A son of Ishmael, Dumah was a descendant of Abraham and the founder of an Arab tribe in the desert. GENESIS 25:14; I CHRONICLES 1:30

E

EBAL

1 A son of Shobal, this Ebal was a grandson of Seir the Horite, and was head of a clan of Arabs in the desert. GENESIS 36:23; I CHRONICLES 1:40

2 Another clan head, this man named Ebal was a son of Joktan and a descendant of Shem and Noah. I CHRONICLES 1:22

EBED

1 One of the tribe of Ephraim, this Ebed was the father of Gaal, the ringleader of the unsuccessful revolt against King Abimelech of the city of Shechem. JUDGES 9

2 The son of a man named Jonathan in the time of the Exile, this Ebed was one of the heads of a family who returned to Jerusalem from Babylon with Ezra. EZRA 8:6

EBED MELECH An Ethiopian servant of Zedekiah, the ruler of Judah just before the Babylonian occupation, Ebed Melech was the man who interceded to have the prophet Jeremiah released from the underground cistern in which his enemies had put him. With the king's permission, Ebed Melech lowered a rope, hauled Jeremiah out of the mire of the hole, and thus saved the prophet's life. As a reward, Jeremiah promised him that he would not be slaughtered when the Babylonians sacked Jerusalem. JEREMIAH 38—39

EBER

1 A descendant of Noah through Shem, Eber is the man from whom the Hebrews got their name. He is included in the genealogies of the ancestors of the tribes of Israel. GENESIS 10—11; I CHRONICLES 1:18—25

2 One of the tribe of Gad, this Eber was the head of a family in that tribe and was included in the rolls of the

83

important men of Gad. I CHRONICLES 5:13

3 A member of the tribe of Benjamin, this Eber was a son of Elpaal, and was one of the group that invaded and settled Canaan. He, like the others listed, headed a family that grew into a clan. I CHRONICLES 8:12

4 Another Benjaminite, this Eber was one of Shaskak's sons and is listed with the others of his tribe in the roll of the first families of the tribe of Benjamin. I CHRONICLES 8:22

5 A priest in the time of Joiakim, this Eber was the son of Amok and was the head of a family. NEHEMIAH 12:20

EBIASAPH Korah's great-grandson, Ebiasaph was descended from a long line of distinguished Levites. He was the ancestor of the great singer Heman and the famous gatekeeper Shallum. I CHRONICLES 6:23, 37; 9:19

EDAR See EDER

EDDIAS See IZZIAH

EDEN A Gershonite in the tribe of Levi who was the son of Joah, Eden was a Temple official in Hezekiah's time who was appointed to assist in the Temple treasury department. II CHRONICLES 29:12; 31:15

EDER

1 A descendant of Merari, Levi's son, Eder was the respected head of a family in David's time and a Levite serving in the sanctuary. I CHRONICLES 23:23; 24:30

2 One of the sons of Beriah, this Eder was a member of the tribe of Benjamin and was carried in the lists of that tribe by the Chronicler. I CHRONICLES 8:15

EDOM "Edom" or "Red" was the nickname given to Isaac's son, Esau, because of the red color of the pottage for which he sold his birthright to his brother Jacob. The name stuck, and became the title of a powerful tribe of Esau's descendants, which later became a kingdom in the area of Petra, the city in the red rocks east of the Dead Sea. GENESIS 25, 36

EGLAH One of David's wives, Eglah was mother of David's sixth son, the undistinguished Ithream. II SAMUEL 3:5; I CHRONICLES 3:3

EGLON An energetic king of Moab, Eglon joined with two other desert tribes, the Amalekites and the Ammonites, and crossed the Jordan and seized Jericho during a period of decline among the Israelites after the death of Othniel. For the next eighteen years Eglon oppressed the tribes of Israel. This was interpreted by the prophets as divine punishment for Israel's faithlessness to the Lord. Eglon was stabbed to death by Ehud, a Benjaminite, and his people were forced out of the country during the uprising among the Israelites that followed his death. JUDGES 3

EHI One of Benjamin's sons, Ehi is listed in the Genesis family tree of Jacob's sons' families. Like the others listed, Ehi was the head of a family. GENESIS 46:21

EHUD

1 A great-grandson of Benjamin, this

Ehud is listed in the tribal rolls by the Chronicler as one of Bilhan's sons, and the father of some of those who were carried away into exile in Manahath. I CHRONICLES 7:6; 8:6

2 The bold, left-handed murderer of King Eglon, this Ehud was also a member of the tribe of Benjamin, and was a son of Gera. After eighteen years of Eglon's oppression in Jericho, Ehud organized a party of steel-nerved men who pretended to bring tribute to the fat dictator. Returning alone afterwards, Ehud asked to meet Eglon to pass on a secret with no others present, and shoved his dagger so far into Eglon's belly that the fat covered even the handle. Ehud escaped safely and organized his countrymen to throw out the Moabites. He became one of Israel's greatest judges. JUDGES 3

EKER A descendant of Judah through Jerahmeel, Eker was carried in the roll of the tribe of Judah as one of Ram's sons. I CHRONICLES 2:27

ELA See ELAH 3

ELADAH See ELEADAH

ELAH

1 One of chiefs of Edom, this Elah is number five on the list of the great tribal leaders. Elah, like other Edomites, claimed descent from Esau. GENESIS 36:41; I CHRONICLES 1:52

2 Another Elah, this man was a member of the tribe of Benjamin who was best remembered as the father of Shimmei, one of Solomon's twelve commissary officers. I KINGS 4:18

3 A son of Baasha, king of Israel,

this Elah was a careless drunk who stayed behind to carouse and drink while his army fought at Gibbethon. His reign had lasted only a year when he and his family were cut down by Zimri. His wickedness ended just as Jehu had prophesied. I KINGS 16

4 This Elah was noted only because he was the father of Hoshea, the last king of Israel before that nation was overrun by the Assyrians in 731 B.C. II KINGS 15:30; 17:1; 18:1—9

5 The son of Caleb, the great spy sent into the Promised Land, this Elah was listed in the roll-call of the heads of clans in the tribe of Judah. I CHRONICLES 4:15

6 A member of the tribe of Benjamin in Nehemiah's time, this man named Elah was one of the first to resettle in Jerusalem after the Exile in Babylonia. I CHRONICLES 9:8

ELAM

1 Shem's son and Noah's grandson, this Elam became the ancestor of a proud and powerful tribe, the Elamites, who held extensive areas east of Persia. GENESIS 10:22; I CHRONICLES 1:17

2 A son of Shashak of the tribe of Benjamin, this Elam is mentioned in the Chronicler's genealogical table of the tribes. I CHRONICLES 8:24

3 A Levite of the Korah clan, this Elam was the fifth son of Meshelemiah, a famous gatekeeper in David's house of worship. I CHRONICLES 26:3

4 The patriarch of a large family that returned to Jerusalem with Ezra after the Exile in Babylon, this Elam was remembered also as the head of a clan who joined Nehemiah in signing the covenant. One of Elam's descendants pushed Ezra to insist that all good Jews cast off their non-Jewish wives, which action forced six others from the family to break off their marriages with outsiders. EZRA 2:7; 8:7; 10:2, 26; NEHEMIAH 7:12; 10:14

5 One bearing the same name and living at the same time as **4,** this Elam also was the head of one of the families that left Babylon after the Exile and went back to rebuild Jerusalem. EZRA 2:31; NEHEMIAH 7:34

6 This Elam was a priest who participated in the elaborate ceremonies with which Nehemiah dedicated the rebuilt wall of Jerusalem after the return from Exile. NEHEMIAH 12:42

ELASAH

1 The son of a priest, Elasah was one of those who married a non-Jewish woman during the Exile and, following Ezra's orders, left her after the return from Babylon to Jerusalem. EZRA 10:22

2 A messenger who carried communiques from vassal King Zedekiah of Judah to his superior, Nebuchadnezzar of Babylon, this Elasah and his fellow-messenger, Gemariah, once carried a note from the prophet Jeremiah to those in Exile in Babylon. The note urged the exiles to plan a long stay in Babylon, but promised them that God would eventually deliver them. JEREMIAH 3

ELDAAH A son of Midian, Abraham's son, and thus a grandson of Abraham, Eldaah was sent with his father to live in the desert to the east. He became the head of a clan in the tribe his father founded, the Midianites. GENESIS 25:4; I CHRONICLES 1:33

ELDAD One of the seventy elders selected to help Moses govern the tribes, Eldad and another elder, Medad, were on one occasion apart from the elders and Moses, and began to prophesy. Although Joshua tried to stop them because they were somewhat out of order, Moses chided Joshua, telling him that he wished the Lord would inspire more men like Eldad and Medad. NUMBERS 11

ELEAD One of Ephraim's sons, Elead was killed when he and his brothers went on a cattle raid to Gath. I CHRONICLES 7:21

ELEADAH One of the sons of Ephraim, Eleadah is named in the genealogy of the tribe of Ephraim, and became the head of a clan of that tribe. I CHRONICLES 7:20

ELEASAH

1 A member of the tribe of Judah, this Eleasah was mentioned as a son of Helez in the clan of Hezron. I CHRONICLES 2:39—40

2 One of Saul's descendants, this other Eleasah was a son of Raphah, and was listed as one of the tribe of Benjamin. I CHRONICLES 8:37

ELEAZAR

1 One of Aaron's sons and Moses' nephews, Eleazar was, like his three brothers and his father, a commissioned priest. After his brothers, Abihu and Nadab, suddenly died for their disobedience to God, Eleazar and his surviving brother, Ithamar, moved up to be chief assistants to Aaron. Later, on Aaron's death, Eleazar became chief priest. He helped Moses in his census and Joshua in dividing the land of Canaan among the conquering tribes. Eleazar was the ancestor of all high priests until 168 B.C. except for a brief period in the time of Eli and Solomon. EXODUS 6:23—25; 28:1; LEVITICUS 10; NUMBERS 3; 4:16; 16:37—39; 19:3—4; 20:25—26; 25:7—11; NUMBERS 26, 27, 31, 32, 34; DEUTERONOMY 10:6; JOSHUA 14:1; 17:4; 19:51; 21:1; 22: 13—32; 24:33; JUDGES 20:28; I CHRONICLES 6, 9, 24; EZRA 7:5

2 This Eleazar, a son of Abinadab, was commissioned to look after the Ark of the Covenant when it was returned by the Philistines, and kept in Abinadab's house at Kiriath-Jearim before David moved it to Jerusalem. I SAMUEL 7:1

3 One of David's three greatest heroes, this Eleazar was the son of Dodo, the Ahohite. He won his place among David's immortals by his one-man stand in a barley field which turned panic into a victory over the Philistines. Fighting with David through all of his campaigns, Eleazar was second only to Jashobeam the Hachmonite in honor and accomplishments. II SAMUEL 23:9; I CHRONICLES 11:12

4 A Levite in David's time who was descended from Merari, this Eleazar had the misfortune according to the Hebrews, of having no sons. His daughters were married to their three cousins. I CHRONICLES 23:21, 22; 24:28

5 A son of Phineas living at the time of Ezra, this Eleazar was a priest who returned with Ezra from Exile in Babylon to Jerusalem. He assisted in bringing the expensive Temple utensils and other valuable equipment. EZRA 8:33

6 Perhaps the same as 5, perhaps a different Eleazar, this man took part in the elaborate dedication ceremonies when Nehemiah completed rebuilding the wall of Jerusalem after the return from Exile in Babylon. NEHEMIAH 12:42

7 A member of the family of Parosh, this Eleazar was one of the many who married a non-Jewish wife during the Exile and was forced by Ezra to dissolve his marriage. EZRA 10:25

8 A last Eleazar mentioned in the Bible, this one was listed in Jesus' family tree by Matthew as a son of Eliud, and Joseph's great-grandfather. MATTHEW 1:15

ELHANAN

1 A son of Jair and a hero of Bethlehem in the wars against the Philistines, Elhanan was the warrior who killed Lahmi, the brother of the giant Goliath. I CHRONICLES 20:5; II SAMUEL 21:19

2 One of David's mightiest fighters, this Elhanan was a son of Dodo of Bethlehem. He won a place in David's elite corps of great warriors called "The Thirty," and served as an officer in David's troops. II SAMUEL 23:24; II CHRONICLES 11:26

ELI A high priest of Israel at Shiloh

in the days before the monarchy, Eli was one of the few high priests descended from Aaron's son Ithamar, and was the first man to serve both as priest and judge. Eli took Hannah's young son, Samuel, under his wing and tutored him in the ways of God. Later he had to hear the youthful Samuel's prophesy against him because of Eli's worthless sons. In spite of the warning, Eli could not bring himself to crack down on his sons. When the news came that his two surviving sons had been killed by the Philistines, Eli collapsed and died of a broken neck. I SAMUEL 1—4; 14:3; I KINGS 2:27

ELIAB

1 A son of Helon of the tribe of Zebulun, this Eliab was one of the leaders of all the tribes at the time of Moses. He was elected to represent his tribe when Moses conducted the census, and served as one of the twelve representatives of tribes in assisting Moses during the journey from Egypt to Canaan. NUMBERS 1:9; 2:7; 7:24—29; 10:16

2 A disgruntled member of the tribe of Reuben, this Eliab was the father of Dathan and Abiram, two of the ringleaders of the revolt against Moses in the wilderness. NUMBERS 16, 26; DEUTERONOMY 11:6

3 David's oldest brother, this Eliab was one of Jesse's stalwart sons who joined Saul's army to fight the aggressive neighboring Philistines. When his young brother David visited the camp at the time Goliath was taunting Israel's forces, Eliab spoke belittlingly to David. Eliab was such a strong, handsome soldier that the old prophet Samuel at first assumed that Eliab must be the man chosen to follow Saul as king. Also known as Elihu, he later became governor of Judah. I SAMUEL 16; 17; I CHRONICLES 2:13; II CHRONICLES 11:18; 27:18

4 One of the ancestors of the great prophet Samuel, this Eliab was a Levite of Kohath's branch of the tribe. I CHRONICLES 6:27

5 A fleet mountain fighter from the tribe of Gad, this Eliab originally was a member of one of King Saul's crack brigades. He and his fellows, disillusioned with Saul, deserted to David and fought valiantly for David. I CHRONICLES 12:8—15

6 A Levite musician at the time of David, this Eliab was appointed to play the harp in David's worship services. He participated in the festive celebrations when David brought the Ark up to Jerusalem. I CHRONICLES 15:18—20; 16:5

ELIADA

1 One of nine sons born to David in Jerusalem, Eliada never distinguished himself in any way, and earned no honors except for mention of his name in the family records. II SAMUEL 5:16; I CHRONICLES 3:8

2 A desert chieftain of the Aramites, Eliada was the father of Rezon, a marauder who was a nuisance to Solomon. I KINGS 11:23

3 A military leader from the tribe of Benjamin, this Eliada was one of King Jehoshaphat's division commanders. His troops were tough Benjaminites, skilled with both bow and shields. II CHRONICLES 17:17

ELIADAH See ELIADA 2

ELIAH See ELIJAH 3 and 4

ELIAHBA A man from Shaalbon, Eliahba was one of David's fiercest fighting men. He was so outstanding that he won a place in the crack corps called "The Thirty," and served as an officer in David's army. II SAMUEL 23:32; I CHRONICLES 11:33

ELIAKIM
1 A son of Hilkiah, this Eliakim was Isaiah's staunch supporter and a top man in King Hezekiah's government. After the Assyrian seige against Jerusalem fell apart as Isaiah predicted, Eliakim replaced Shebnah as Hezekiah's prime minister. II KINGS 18—19; ISAIAH 22:20; 36—37
2 The name King Jehoiakim originally was known by. This Eliakim was King Josiah's son and was one of the last kings of Judah. His new name, Jehoiakim, was bestowed by Pharaoh Necho of Egypt. II KINGS 23:34; II CHRONICLES 36:4
3 A priest in the period after the exiles returned from Babylon to Jerusalem, this Eliakim participated in the impressive service when Nehemiah dedicated the rebuilt wall of Jerusalem. NEHEMIAH 12:41
4 An ancestor of Jesus, this Eliakim is included in Jesus' family tree by both Matthew and Luke. MATTHEW 1:13; LUKE 3:30

ELIAM
1 The father of Bathsheba, the woman whom David married after an adulterous affair, Eliam might have been a foreigner, since he married his daughter originally to a Hittite named Uriah. II SAMUEL 11:30
2 A son of Ahithophel the Gilonite, this Eliam was one of David's greatest soldiers. He won undying fame by being named to the rolls of "The Thirty," David's most elite regiment, and served as an army officer. II SAMUEL 23:34

ELIASAPH
1 A son of Deuel of the tribe of Gad, this Eliasaph served as chief of his tribe at the time Moses conducted his census of the tribes. NUMBERS 1:14; 2:14; 7:42—47; 10:20
2 A son of Lael, this Eliasaph was headman of a clan of Gershonites at the time of Moses' census. NUMBERS 3:24

ELIASHIB
1 A Levite in David's time, this Eliashib served in David's sanctuary. He picked the eleventh lot, or turn to serve. I CHRONICLES 24:12
2 A descendant of David, this Eliashib was a son of Elioenai, and was carried in the genealogy of the royal family of Judah. I CHRONICLES 3:24
3 The best known of all who carried the name Eliashib, this man was a high priest at the time of Nehemiah, and came from one of the first families of Judah. Although Eliashib helped rebuild the walls of Jerusalem with Nehemiah after the Exile in Babylon, he was not in accord with Nehemiah's policy of Jewish exclusivism. Eliashib, in fact, ignored Nehemiah's rulings,

permitted his own family to marry outside the faith, and entertained the non-Jew Tobiah in the rebuilt Temple while Nehemiah was away. Nehemiah's angry reaction later must have chilled the relationship between Eliashib and himself. NEHEMIAH 3, 12, 13; EZRA 10:6

4 Another with the same name who was a Levite during the Exile, this Eliashib was a temple singer, and was one of the many who married outside the faith. EZRA 10:24

5 A member of the family Zattu, this man named Eliashib was another who took a non-Jewish girl for a wife during the Exile, and later obediently followed Ezra's orders to leave her and his children. EZRA 10:27

6 One of the many men from the family of Bani who married outside the faith during the time of the Exile, this Eliashib also left his wife in order to observe the Law. EZRA 10:36

ELIATHAH One of the sons of the famous Levite singer, Heman. Eliathah and his family were the twentieth team of those serving in the sanctuary of David. I CHRONICLES 25:4, 27

ELIDAD A leader in the tribe of Benjamin at the time of Moses, Elidad was elected by his tribe to represent the Benjaminites when Moses called for twelve, one representing each tribe, to assist him in dividing the land of Canaan fairly among the tribes after they should complete the conquest. NUMBERS 34:21

ELIEHOENAI
1 A Levite of the Korah branch of the tribe, this Eliehoenai was a gatekeeper who served in David's sanctuary. I CHRONICLES 26:3

2 The head of a family that returned with Ezra from Exile in Babylon to Jerusalem, this Eliehoenai was a descendant of Pahath-moab. EZRA 8:4

ELIEL
1 The prophet Samuel's great grandfather, this Eliel was listed as one of the ancestors of Heman, David's great singer in the sanctuary. I CHRONICLES 6:34

2 The head of a family of the tribe of Manassah, this Eliel was one of the many from his tribe who turned away from the Lord and joined the local Canaanite cults. I CHRONICLES 5:24

3 One of Shimei's sons of the tribe of Benjamin, this third Eliel was the head of a large clan in the tribe. I CHRONICLES 8:20

4 Another by the same name in the same tribe, this Eliel was the son of Shashak, and was also chieftain of a family in the tribe. I CHRONICLES 8:22

5 An outstanding soldier in David's service, this Eliel was one of three great fighters given particular mention in David's army. This man was one of "The Thirty," David's elite corps of the strongest and the bravest. He was distinguished from the others by being identified as "the Mahavite." I CHRONICLES 11:46

6 Another member of David's superheroes, "The Thirty," this Eliel was also a valiant fighter and an officer in David's army. I CHRONICLES 11:47

7 Another illustrious soldier, this Eliel came from the tribe of Gad and first served under Saul. Disillusioned with Saul, he and other officers finally deserted and joined David, then an outlaw. Like others in his outfit, Eliel was a fleet-footed mountain fighter. I CHRONICLES 12:11

8 One of Hebron's sons who was also a Levite priest, this Eliel was one of those chosen by David to assist in bringing the Ark of the Covenant up to Jerusalem from Kiriath-jearim. I CHRONICLES 15:9—11

9 Another Levite, this man with the name Eliel lived in Hezekiah's time. He bore the responsibility for assisting Conaniah and Shimei in the Temple treasury. II CHRONICLES 31:13

ELIENAI One of Shimei's sons of the tribe of Benjamin, Elienai was the chieftain of a clan listed in the tribe's genealogy. I CHRONICLES 8:20

ELIEZER

1 Abraham's trusted servant, this Eliezer, one of some dozen in the Bible, was connected with Damascus in some unknown way. Until Isaac's birth, Abraham's possessions were willed to this servant. Undoubtedly Eliezer was "the servant" mentioned in Genesis 24 who is sent to Abraham's own people to get a wife for Isaac. GENESIS 15:2

2 Moses' second son, this Eliezer was given his name (meaning "God is help" in Hebrew) by Moses to express his thanks for God's deliverance from the pharaoh. EXODUS 18:4; I CHRONICLES 23; 26:25

3 Another Eliezer was a grandson of Benjamin through Becher, Benjamin's son, and a chieftain in the tribe. I CHRONICLES 7:8

4 A priest and musician in David's time, this Eliezer played his trumpet in the ceremonies when David brought the Ark of the Covenant to Jerusalem. I CHRONICLES 15:24

5 A Levite in David's sanctuary, this man named Eliezer and his sons were assigned responsibilities in the treasury offices of the House of the Lord. I CHRONICLES 26:25

6 One of the tribe of Reuben in David's day, this Eliezer, the son of Zichri, was the head man in his tribe when David made his census. I CHRONICLES 27:16

7 A bold, outspoken prophet at the time of King Jehoshaphat of Judah, this Eliezer denounced his king for joining Ahaziah, king of Israel, in a foolish and costly shipping venture. As Eliezer predicted, Jehoshaphat lost heavily when the ships were all wrecked before their first voyage. II CHRONICLES 20:37

8 One of the opinion-makers among the Exiles in Babylon, this Eliezer was sent by Ezra to Casiphia in Babylonia to try to talk former priests and temple attendants into returning with Ezra to Jerusalem. EZRA 8:16

9 One of the priests who had married an outsider during the Exile in Babylon, this Eliezer at first broke the Law, but finally obeyed Ezra and put away his non-Jewish wife. EZRA 10:18

10 Another who had married outside the faith, this Eliezer was one of the Levites who left his foreign wife in obedience to Ezra's instructions to keep the Law. EZRA 10:23

11 This man, like **9** and **10**, married a non-Jew and later repented.

He was one of the sons of Harim.
EZRA 10:31
12 One of Jesus' ancestors, this Eliezer is included in Luke's genealogy. LUKE 3:29

ELIHOENAI See ELIEHOENAI

ELIHOREPH One of the sons of Shisha, Elihoreph and his brother Ahijah were cabinet officers in Solomon's government. Their title was "secretary," meaning that Elihoreph was one of Solomon's top officials. I KINGS 4:3

ELIHU

1 Samuel's great-grandfather, this Elihu was also known as Eliel. See ELIEL 1. I SAMUEL 1:1
2 One of the tribe of Manasseh, Elihu was a man of valor in battle. He was originally on the side of Saul, but grew disillusioned and joined David, then an outlaw. Eliel became one of David's officers. I CHRONICLES 12:20
3 A Levite who was from the Korah branch of the tribe, this man served in David's house of the Lord as a doorkeeper. I CHRONICLES 26:7
4 David's oldest brother, this man named Elihu was also known by the name Eliab. See ELIAB 3.
5 A descendant of Abraham's brother, Nahor the Elihu, "the son of Barachel the Buzite of the family of Ram," appears in the book of Job as the moderator of the discussion after Job's three friends, Bilded, Zophar, and Eliphaz, prove unable to win their argument that Job is being punished by God. JOB

ELIJAH

1 The greatest prophet of the Old Testament, Elijah was one of the most colorful and outspoken men in history. Born and raised in an obscure village in Gilead, Elijah's entire career was a protest against the idolatry and corruption into which the northern kingdom, Israel, had declined. He clashed repeatedly with Ahab, the morally weak, vain king, and Jezebel, Ahab's domineering, prophet-persecuting wife. A patriot as well as a prophet, Elijah saved his nation from going the way of Ahab and Jezebel by serving as the conscience of his country. Elijah's human qualities of fear and despair are also shown in the Bible. After his brief victory over the false prophets on Mount Carmel, Elijah had to flee for his life, and dejectedly hid in a cave on Sinai until God lifted him and sent him back to serve. He passed on his mantle to the young Elisha, but his zeal for justice and obedience to God he imparted to all subsequent prophets. Elijah's end was mysterious: he and Enoch are the only two men in the Bible who were "translated," or did not taste death. He was referred to repeatedly by Jesus' contemporaries, and even thought by some to have reappeared in the person of Jesus. Among Orthodox Jews to this day Elijah's return is expected at every Passover. I KINGS 17—19, 21; II KINGS 1—3, 9—10; MALACHI 4:5; MATTHEW 11:14; 16:14; 17:3; MARK 9:4; LUKE 1:17; 9:8, 19, 30; JOHN 1:21
2 A son of Jehoram of the tribe of Benjamin, this man also named Elijah

was a chieftain of a clan within his tribe, according to the genealogy. I CHRONICLES 8:27

3 A son of Harim in Ezra's time, this Elijah was one of the many priests who married outside the faith during the Exile, thus breaking the Law. EZRA 10:21

4 A son of Elam, this Elijah was a Levite who lived during the Exile in Babylonia, and who took a non-Jewish bride. Later, obeying Ezra, Elijah left her to keep the faith and people pure. EZRA 10:26

ELIKA A man of Harod who was one of David's toughest battle veterans, Elika won a place in David's exclusive corps of "The Thirty," and served as a distinguished officer in David's army. II SAMUEL 23:25

ELIMELECH A man of Judah, Elimelech married Naomi and became the father of Mahlon and Chilion. Elimelech and his family were forced by a famine to emigrate to Moab, where Elimelech died. His sons married Moabite women, Orpah and Ruth. After the death of Elimelech's sons, Ruth insisted on following her mother-in-law Naomi back to Judah. RUTH 1, 2, 4

ELIOENAI

1 A descendant of David who lived after the time of the Babylonian Exile, this Elioenai was a son of Neariah, and is listed in the genealogy of the royal family of Judah. I CHRONICLES 3:23—24

2 A member of the tribe of Simeon, this Elioenai was a well-known chieftain and clan head in the tribe. I CHRONICLES 4:36

3 One of Benjamin's grandsons, this Elioenai was a son of Becher, and the head of a prominent family in the tribe of Benjamin. I CHRONICLES 7:8

4 A priest at the time of the Exile in Babylon who married outside the faith, this Elioenai, a son of Pashur, later repented and forsook his non-Jewish wife as Ezra demanded. EZRA 10:22

5 A Levite who went through the same experiences as **4,** this Elioenai was one of Zattu's sons. EZRA 10:27

6 Possibly the same as **4,** a priest named Elioenai is mentioned as one of those who took part in the dedication service after Nehemiah rebuilt the wall of Jerusalem following the return from Babylon. NEHEMIAH 12:41

7 For the Elioenai mentioned in some translations of I CHRONICLES 26:3, see ELIEHOENAI **1.**

8 For the Elioenai mentioned in some translations of Ezra 8:4, see ELIEHOENAI **2.**

ELIPHAL One of David's hardy veterans, Eliphal's valor on the battlefield earned him a place in the elite corps of heroes, "The Thirty," and a commission as an officer in David's army. I CHRONICLES 11:35; II SAMUEL 23:34, as ELIPHELET

ELIPHALAT See ELIPHELET

ELIPHAZ

1 A son of Esau, Eliphaz was the father of a group of Arab desert chiefs who lived in the land of Edom. GENESIS 36; I CHRONICLES 1:35—36

2 One of Job's three friends, this Eliphaz was the oldest and gravest of the trio. More tactfully than the others, Eliphaz tried to persuade Job that his sufferings were God's punishment for his sin. JOB 2, 4, 15, 22, 42

ELIPHELEH See ELIPHELEHU

ELIPHELEHU A Levite in David's time, Eliphelehu was a doorkeeper and musician in the sanctuary. When David brought the Ark of the Covenant up from Kireath-jearim to Jerusalem, Eliphelehu was one of those who led the procession playing lyres. I CHRONICLES 15:18, 21

ELIPHELET

1 One of David's thirteen sons, Eliphelet was born in Jerusalem, well after David was securely established as king of the united kingdom. His name is carried in the lists of David's family and their descendants under various similar spellings. II SAMUEL 5:16; I CHRONICLES 3:6,8; 14:7

2 The man named Eliphelet listed in II Samuel 23:34 was the same as Eliphal. See ELIPHAL

3 A descendant of King Saul, through Saul's son Jonathan, this Eliphelet was listed in the genealogy of the tribe of Benjamin. I CHRONICLES 8:39

4 One of Adonikam's sons at the time of the Exile in Babylon, this Eliphelet and his family were among those who returned to Jerusalem with Ezra. EZRA 8:13

5 Another by the same name who lived at the same time, this Eliphelet, a son of Hashum, married a non-Jewish woman, thereby breaking the Law. EZRA 10:33

ELISABETH See ELIZABETH

ELISHA The disciple of, and successor to, the great prophet Elijah, Elisha was plowing when Elijah threw his mantle on the youth, adopting him as his son and calling him as a prophet. After about six years, Elijah was "translated," and Elisha became the chief prophet in the northern kingdom of Israel. Elisha continued in his ministry for fifty-five years. Most of his work was a continuation of the reforms begun by Elijah. A patriot with a concern for justice and morality in his nation, Elisha intervened in national affairs and had a hand in overthrowing the house of Omri. More than any other prophet in the Old Testament, Elisha was a miracle worker and adviser of kings. I KINGS 19; II KINGS 2—9, 13

ELISHAH A descendant of Noah, Elishah was the ancestor of a people who lived near the Mediterranean and were producers of an expensive purple dye valued by the ancient world. GENESIS 10:4; I CHRONICLES 1:7; EZEKIEL 27:7

ELISHAMA

1 Joshua's grandfather, this Elishama was a chief of the tribe of Ephraim at the time Moses conducted his census in the wilderness. NUMBERS 1:10; 2:18; 7:48—53; 10:22; I CHRONICLES 7:26

2 One of David's thirteen sons, this

Elishama was born in Jerusalem after David became king of the united kingdom. Elishama is listed in all the genealogies of the royal house of Judah. He was sometimes called Elishua. II SAMUEL 5:16; I CHRONICLES 3:6, 8; 14:5, 7

3 Another Elishama was the son of Jekamiah, who was carried on the roll of chieftains of clans in the tribe of Judah. I CHRONICLES 2:41

4 Perhaps another by the same name, perhaps the same as **3,** this Elishama was the grandfather of Ishmael, the man who assassinated the traitor, Gedaliah, who had been appointed governor of Judah by the Babylonians. II KINGS 25:25; JEREMIAH 41:1

5 An important official in King Jehoiakim's court in Judah, this Elishama handled the correspondence from the prophet Jeremiah to the king. JEREMIAH 36

6 A priest in King Jehoshaphat's time, this Elishama was one of those sent to conduct an intensive adult-education program on the Law in the cities of Judah. II CHRONICLES 17:8

ELISHAPHAT An important army officer in Judah in the reign of the brutal Queen Athaliah, Elishaphat was brought in on the plot to replace Athaliah with young Joash which the high priest Jehoiada was hatching. Elishaphat cooperated by bringing key leaders to the carefully pre-arranged coronation of Joash. The coup was successful; Joash became king and Athaliah was murdered. II CHRONICLES 23:1

ELISHEBA Aaron's wife, Elisheba was a daughter of Amminadab and a sister of Nahshon, a chieftain in the tribe of Judah. EXODUS 6:23

ELISHUA See ELISHAMA 2

ELIUD One of Jesus' ancestors, Eliud is listed in the genealogy of Joseph by Matthew. MATTHEW 1:14—15

ELIZABETH The mother of John the Baptist, Elizabeth was descended from Aaron and related to Mary, Jesus' mother. Although Elizabeth and her husband Zechariah were devout Jews, they suffered the disgrace of being childless for many years, until they were promised a son by the angel Gabriel. In her sixth month of pregnancy, Elizabeth was visited by her young cousin Mary, who had been awed and frightened by the angelic announcement that she, too, would bear a son. Elizabeth gave Mary the comfort and understanding she needed at that time. LUKE 1

ELIZAPHAN

1 A son of Uzziel of the family of Kohath of the tribe of Leir, Elizaphan was a clan chieftain during the time of Moses whose responsibility it was to look after the Ark and various articles of worship in the tabernacle. NUMBERS 3:30; I CHRONICLES 15:8; II CHRONICLES 29:13

2 Another Elizaphan who lived in Moses' day, this man was a chief of the tribe of Zebulun, and the son of Parnach. He was one of twelve elected—one man representing each tribe—to help Moses portion out the Promised Land to the tribes. NUMBERS 34:25

ELIZUR A leader from the tribe of Reuben, Elizur was one of twelve men —one representative from each tribe —who assisted Moses when he divided Canaan among the tribes. NUMBERS 1:5; 2:10; 7:30, 36; 10:18

ELKANAH
1 One of the sons of Korah, the ringleader of the revolt against Moses, Elkanah apparently had no part in his father's plot; we assume this, since his life was spared when Korah and the others died. EXODUS 6:24; I CHRONICLES 6:23
2 A descendant of **1**, this Elkanah was Samuel's father. Elkanah's wife, Hannah, was childless for many years and felt the disgrace keenly. Elkanah however, comforted her, and later, when Samuel was small, joined Hannah in presenting the boy to the Lord by leaving him with Eli the priest. I SAMUEL 1, 2; I CHRONICLES 6:27, 34
3 A nephew of **1** and an ancestor of **2**, this Elkanah was a son of Assir, one of Korah's sons. He is listed among the ancestors of the Levites who were important men in David's sanctuary. I CHRONICLES 6:25, 36
4 Related to all the three mentioned above, this Elkanah was the father of Zophai or Zuph, and was the great-grandson of **3**. He, too, was noted in the genealogy of Levites who were among David's famous men, and was an ancestor of Heman the singer. I CHRONICLES 6:26, 35

5 Grandfather of Berechiah, one of the first to return to Jerusalem from Babylon after the Exile, this Elkanah was also a Levite and an ancestor of those who lived in the villages of the Netophathites. I CHRONICLES 9:15
6 A Korahite who was a skilled, experienced fighting man, this Elkanah was one of those who fought originally for Saul, but later grew disgusted with Saul and went over to David. Elkanah belonged to a battalion of Benjaminites who could fight with either hand, using both the deadly sling and bow. I CHRONICLES 12:6
7 A Levite in David's time, this Elkanah and another Levite, Berechiah, were appointed doorkeepers for the Ark, a position of great prestige in David's sanctuary. I CHRONICLES 15:23
8 Prime minister of Judah under wicked King Ahaz, this Elkanah was marked to die when King Pekah of Israel overran Judah. Zichri, a soldier from Ephraim, slaughtered Elkanah along with others of the royal family. II CHRONICLES 28:7

ELMADAM One of Jesus' ancestors, Elmadam, a son of Er, is listed by Luke in the family tree of Joseph. LUKE 3:28

ELMODAM See ELMADAM

ELNAAM The father of Jeribai and Joshaviah, two of David's mightiest soldiers, both members of the crack guards brigade, "The Thirty." I CHRONICLES 11:46

ELNATHAN
1 Elnathan was the father of Queen

Nehushta, and thus the grandfather of her son, who was the weak playboy, King Jehoiachin. II KINGS 24:8

2 A son of Achbor, this Elnathan was an adviser, crony, and hatchet-man of King Jehoiakim in the days of the prophet Jeremiah. Elnathan headed the party of assassins sent to find and execute Uriah, the prophet who had shaken King Jehoiakim with a stern warning and then had gone into hiding. Elnathan was also one of those present when Jeremiah's grim prophecies were read to the irate king. Although he tried to keep Jehoiakim from slashing and burning the letter from Jeremiah, Elnathan was not much moved by the warnings. JEREMIAH 26, 36

3 A chieftain who lived at the time of the Exile at Babylon, this man named Elnathan accompanied Ezra from Babylon to Jerusalem. Elnathan joined Ezra in his three-day conference near Ahava. EZRA 8:16

4 Another chieftain who was a contemporary of Ezra, this Elnathan also traveled with Ezra from Babylon to Jerusalem and participated in the conference at Ahava. EZRA 8:16

5 This Elnathan, a teacher, was one of Ezra's party going from Babylon to Jerusalem. This Elnathan also took part in the Ahava conference. EZRA 8:16

ELON

1 Esau's father-in-law, this Elon was a Hittite chieftain. GENESIS 26:34; 36:2

2 One of Zebulun's three sons, this Elon was the head man of a clan in the tribe. GENESIS 46:13; NUMBERS 26:26

3 Another of the tribe of Zebulun, this Elon was one of the minor judges of Israel in the days betwen the conquest of Canaan and the start of the kingdom. Elon served as arbitrator of disputes and advisor to the tribal leaders for ten years, and was buried in the town of Elon. JUDGES 12:11—12

ELPAAL A son of Shaharaim of the tribe of Benjamin, Elpaal was the chieftain of a prominent family in the tribe. His sons were outstanding for building several towns and conquering Gath. I CHRONICLES 8:11, 12, 18

ELPALET See ELIPHELET 1

ELPELET See ELIPHELET 1

ELPHALET See ELIPHELET 1

ELUZAI One of a fierce group of Benjaminites who finally had their fill of Saul's madness and joined up with David, then an outlaw, Eluzai was able to wield a dangerous bow or sling with either his left or right hand. Eluzai became an officer in David's army. I CHRONICLES 12:5

ELYMAS See BAR-JESUS

ELZABAD

1 A fleet-footed mountain fighter, Elzabad was one of the shaggy men from the tribe of Gad who were so dissatisfied with Saul that they finally crossed the Jordan and joined David, then a fugitive from Saul. A fierce warrior, Elzabad was commissioned an officer in David's army. I CHRONICLES 12:2

2 A Levite from the Korahite branch of the tribe, this Elzabad, son of Shemaiah, served in David's sanctuary as a doorkeeper, and was respected as the head of a family and model citizen. I CHRONICLES 26:7

ELZAPHAN

1 One of Levi's grandsons and Uzziel's sons, Elzaphan was a cousin of Moses, Aaron, and Miriam. When Nadab and Abihu died for offering unholy fire to the Lord, Elzaphan was one of those assigned the job of removing the bodies. EXODUS 6:22; LEVITICUS 10:4

2 Another Elzaphan, this man was a leader from Zebulun who was also known as Elizaphan. See ELIZAPHAN **2**

ENAN A chieftain in the tribe of Naphtali at the time of Moses' census in the wilderness, Enan was best remembered as the father of Ahira, one of those who assisted in taking the census. NUMBERS 1:15; 2:22; 7:78—83; 10:27

ENEAS See AENEAS

ENOCH

1 Cain's oldest son, this Enoch was the ancestor of an ancient tribe and the one for whom Cain named the earliest city. GENESIS 4:17—18

2 A son of Jared and a descendant of Adam through Seth, this Enoch was the father of Methuseleh, and one of two men in the Old Testament who did not taste death (Elijah was the other) because they were such godly, humble men. GENESIS 5; I CHRONICLES 1:3; LUKE 3:37; HEBREWS 11:5; JUDE 14

ENOS See ENOSH

ENOSH Seth's son and Adam's grandson, Enosh lived at the time when "men began to call upon the name of the Lord," or started to pray to God, instead of trying to placate unknown gods with sacrifices. GENESIS 4:26; 5:6—11; I CHRONICLES 1:1; LUKE 3:38

EPAENETUS A Christian believer living in Rome at the time Paul the Apostle wrote his letter to the Church at Rome, Epaenetus is one of those singled out at the end for a special word of greeting. Epaenetus, according to the same reference in the letter, was originally from Asia (now called Asia Minor), and was one of the first converts. There are inscriptions in which the name "Epaenetus" occurs, one of which states that one by that name hailed from the Asian city of Ephesus. ROMANS 16:5

EPAPHRAS One of the Apostle Paul's friends and co-workers, Epaphras was from Colossae, and founded the church in his home town. He was looked up to as a leader in the church in Asia, and came to visit Paul in prison in Rome to report on the church in his area. Seized by the Romans, he was thrown into prison with Paul. Some of Paul's deepest tributes are applied to Epaphras: "fellow prisoner," "faithful minister." COLOSSIANS 1:7; 4:12; PHILEMON 23

EPAPHRODITUS A Christian believer from Philippi, Epaphroditus was sent by his home congregation to carry collected money for Paul during the apostle's imprisonment in Rome. Epaphroditus stayed with Paul, helping until he took seriously ill and nearly died. Recovering, he asked to return home to Philippi. Paul sent his touching letter to the Philippians back with Epaphroditus, and referred to the faithful messenger in glowing terms as "my brother and fellow-worker and fellow soldier." PHILIPPIANS 2:25; 4:18

EPHAH
1 A grandson of Abraham and a son of Midian, Ephah was the founder and patriarch of a tribe that roamed the desert in Arabia and sent caravans of gold and frankincense from Sheba (Yemen). GENESIS 25:4; I CHRONICLES 1:33; ISAIAH 60:6
2 One of Caleb's concubines, this Ephah was the mother of some of his children. I CHRONICLES 2:46
3 One of Jahdai's sons, this Ephah was a chieftain of a clan in the tribe of Judah, and was remembered in the genealogy of the tribe by the Chronicler. I CHRONICLES 2:47

EPHAI A man who lived at the beginning of the time of the Exile but was allowed to stay in Judah, Ephai was the father of some who were murdered by the patriot Ishmael for co-operating with Gedeliah, the Jew appointed by the Babylonians as governor of occupied Judah. JEREMIAH 40:8

EPHER
1 One of Abraham's grandsons and one of Midian's sons, Epher was listed in the family genealogy as an ancestor of a desert tribe in Arabia. GENESIS 25:4; I CHRONICLES 1:33
2 Another named Epher, this man was a clan headman of one of the branches of the tribe of Judah. I CHRONICLES 4:17
3 A warrior and clan chieftain in the tribe of Manasseh, this Epher was one of those who forsook the Lord and took up the local cults of the conquered Canaanites. I CHRONICLES 5:24

EPHLAL A descendant of Judah through Perez and Jerahmeel, Ephlal was a tribal leader who is mentioned in the roll of Judah's heads of families. I CHRONICLES 2:37

EPHOD One of the tribe of Manasseh, Ephod was the father of Hanniel, the representative of his tribe who helped Joshua divide the land. NUMBERS 34:23

EPHRAIM Joseph's younger son, Ephraim, like his older son Manasseh, was born in Egypt. Both boys were adopted by Jacob, who wanted to show special favor toward Joseph, his own favorite son. At this same ceremony, over Joseph's protests, Jacob insisted in giving the younger brother, Ephraim, preeminence over his older brother, Manasseh. The tribe which sprang from Ephraim eventually became the strongest in Israel, holding the wooded hill-country near Samaria. GENESIS 41:52; 46:20; 48:1—20; 50:23; NUMBERS 26:28; I CHRONICLES

7:20—22. Other references to the tribe of Ephraim, include: NUMBERS 1, 7, 10, 13, 26, 34; DEUTERONOMY 33, 34; JOSHUA 14, 16, 17, 21; JUDGES 1, 5, 7, 8, 10, 12; II SAMUEL 2; I CHRONICLES 6, 9, 12, 27; II CHRONICLES 15, 17, 25, 28, 30, 31, 34; PSALMS 60, 78, 80, 108; ISAIAH 7, 9, 11, 17, 28; JEREMIAH 7, 31; EZEKIEL 37, 48; HOSEA 4—14; OBADIAH 19; ZECHARIAH 9 and 10

EPHRATAH See EPHRATHAH

EPHRATH See EPHRATHAH

EPHRATHAH The second wife of Caleb, son of Hezron, Ephrathah was the mother of Hur, and later the grandmother of the famous spy, Caleb, son of Jephunneh. I CHRONICLES 2:19,50; 4:4

EPHRON A Hittite who was a son of Zohar, Ephron was a landowner in Palestine at the time Abraham journeyed from Ur. When Sarah, Abraham's wife, died, Ephron courteously sold Abraham a plot near Hebron with a cave which Abraham made into a family burial place. GENESIS 23; 25: 9; 49:29—30; 50:13

ER
1 Judah's oldest son by Shua's daughter, the Canaanite girl, Er married Tamar, but died because of some undescribed wickedness. GENESIS 38; 46:12; NUMBERS 26:19; I CHRONICLES 2:3
2 A grandson of Judah and a son of Shelah, this Er is named in the family tree as one of the earliest clan chieftains in the tribe of Judah. I CHRONICLES 4:21

3 One of Jesus' ancestors, this Er appears, from Luke's genealogy, to have lived betwen the times of David and Zerubbabel. LUKE 3:28

ERAN A grandson of Ephraim, Eran was the ancestor of the Eranites, a family or clan in the tribe, and lived at the time of Moses' census. NUMBERS 26:36

ERASTUS
1 A co-worker and friend of Paul the Apostle, this Christian named Erastus helped Paul in his ministry in Ephesus, and was later sent with Timothy into Macedonia (now northern Greece). Apparently Erastus was a troubleshooter and messenger for Paul; he is next heard of in Corinth. ACTS 19:22; I TIMOTHY 4:20
2 We cannot be certain whether or not this Erastus is a different man from 1. We know that this Erastus was the city treasurer of the unknown town from which Paul was writing Romans, and was an esteemed member of the church. If he were city treasurer of Corinth or Ephesus, he would probably not have been able to travel about as freely as 1 apparently did. On the other hand, if 1 had settled in either Corinth or Ephesus— both of which we know he visited— and one of these towns was the place from which Paul wrote Romans, then 1 and 2 might have been the same man. ROMANS 16:23

ERI A son of Gad, Eri was one of those in Gad's family who went into Egypt during the famine in Joseph's time. He was the patriarch of a well-known clan in the tribe of Gad known as Erites. GENESIS 46:16; NUMBERS 26:16

ESARHADDON Grandson of the mighty Sargon of Assyria and son of the powerful Sennacherib, Esarhaddon succeeded Shalmaneser as king of Assyria after a brief but bloody war with his brothers. He was a skillful strategist and able organizer; his powerful armies continued to make Assyria's name feared and hated by everyone from Egypt to the nomads of western Asia. Judah, under King Manasseh, was forced to pay tribute and be a satellite nation to Assyria. Esarhaddon died on a campaign in 668 B.C. II KINGS 19:37; EZRA 4:2; ISAIAH 37:32

ESAU The elder of Isaac's twin sons, Esau was "the hairy one," nicknamed "Edom" or "Red," and was said to have struggled with his brother, Jacob, even while they were being born. He was an outdoorsman, and his father's favorite because he brought in wild game. He was tricked out of his birthright, or inheritance, and his standing as Isaac's elder son, by his scheming brother Jacob, who offered a bowl of pottage when he was hungry and faint. Later, when Isaac was on his deathbed, Esau was tricked again by the wily Jacob—this time out of his father's final blessing. Furious, Esau swore he would kill Jacob, but was frustrated by Jacob's flight out of the country. Twenty years later the two met peaceably. Esau subsequently moved his great tribe to the area called Edom, east of the Dead Sea

area. However, his descendants, the Edomites, and Jacob's descendants, the Israelites, had little but contempt for one another. GENESIS 25—28; 32 —33; 35—36; JOSHUA 24:4; I CHRONICLES 1:34—35; MALACHI 1:2—3. References to the tribe of Esau: DEUTERONOMY; JEREMIAH; OBADIAH

ESHBAAL See ISHBOSHETH

ESHBAN Eshban was one of Dishon's sons of the family of Seir, part of the group related to Esau, and was a desert chieftain of the Edomites. GENESIS 36:26; I CHRONICLES 1:41

ESHCOL An Amorite chief who lived near Hebron at the time Abraham came to Palestine, Eshcol and his brothers, Mamre and Aner, teamed up with Abraham to pursue the five chieftains who had conquered Sodom and Gomorrah and captured Lot, Abraham's nephew. GENESIS 14

ESHEK A descendant of Saul through Jonathan, Eshek is listed in the genealogical list of the tribe of Benjamin. I CHRONICLES 8:39

ESHTEMOA A son of Ishbah, Eshtemoa was from the city-state of Maacah, and was an important chieftain in the tribe of Judah. His descendants in the village named for Eshtemoa were on David's side during David's fugitive days. I CHRONICLES 4:17, 19

ESHTEMOH See ESHTEMOA

ESHTON A chieftain in the tribe of Judah, Eshton's name was carried in the roll of the tribe by the Chronicler. I CHRONICLES 4:11—12

ESLI An ancestor of Jesus, according to Luke, Esli's name appears in the family tree of Joseph. LUKE 3:25

ESROM See HEZRON

ESTHER An orphaned Jewish girl who was raised in Persia by her cousin Mordecai, Esther (originally named "Hadassah") was chosen because of her beauty to take the place of the fickle and obstinate queen Vashti at a state banquet, and then to reign beside King Ahasuerus as his queen. Ahasuerus' prime minister, Haman, angry because Mordecai would not bow down to Haman, claimed that all Jews were subversive, and planned to annihilate them all. Esther, risking her position and her very life, interceded for her people. Ahasuerus countermanded Haman's orders, and had Haman and his sons hanged. The Jews still commemorate this great occasion at the Feast of Purim each year. ESTHER

ETHAN
1 One of the wisest men of Israel, Ethan was said to be surpassed in sagacity only by King Solomon. He was often called Ethan the Ezrahite. I KINGS 4:31; PSALM 89
2 This Ethan was a son of Zerah, and was listed as one of the chieftains of a clan in the genealogy of the tribe of Judah. I CHRONICLES 2:6—8
3 One of the ancestors of the great Levite singer, Heman, this Ethan, a son of Zimmah, was a blueblood tracing his ancestry back to Gershom, Levi's son. I CHRONICLES 6:42

4 A renowned musician in David's time, this Ethan, son of Kishi or Kishaiah, was a Levite tracing his ancestry back to Merari. Ethan belonged to the exclusive group of singers in David's sanctuary. At the time the Ark of the Covenant was brought up to Jerusalem, Ethan had a prominent part in the festivities as a cymbal player. I CHRONICLES 6:44; 15:17—19

ETHBAAL Queen Jezebel's father, Ethbaal was king of Tyre and Sidon, and patron of the heathen cults that were so popular in ancient Palestine. His daughter Jezebel took his paganism with her when she married King Ahab and corrupted Israel. Many historians, such as Josephus, state that Ethbaal was originally a priest of Astarte who murdered to grab the throne of Tyre and Sidon. I KINGS 16:31

ETHNAN One of the sons of Helah of the tribe of Judah, Ethnan was a clan head whose name was listed in the family tree of the tribe of Judah by the Chronicler. I CHRONICLES 4:7

ETHNI Related to a famous group of musicians and an ancestor of the great singer in David's sanctuary, Heman, Ethni was part of a long line of illustrious Levites who traced their lineage back to Gershom, Levi's son. I CHRONICLES 6:41

EUBULUS A Christian believer who lived at Rome at the time that the Apostle Paul was held prisoner there, Eubulus was a friend of Paul, Timothy, and other members of the early church. He joined Paul in sending personal greetings to Timothy when Paul wrote his second letter to his "son" Timothy. II TIMOTHY 4:21

EUNICE A Jewish woman who lived at Lystra in Asia Minor, Eunice was married to a non-Jewish husband. Their son, Timothy, was never circumcised, perhaps out of respect for Eunice's husband. However, Eunice and her mother, Lois, carefully taught the youngster the Old Testament. Probably converted to Jesus Christ by Paul's first trip through Lystra, she was a Christian by the time Paul visited Lystra a second time. ACTS 16:1; II TIMOTHY 1:5; 3:15

EUODIA One of the members of the church at Philippi, Euodia and another woman of the congregation, Syntyche, disagreed on some unknown subject to such an extent that Paul asked them "to agree in the Lord." Euodia and Syntyche had both worked closely with Paul, and perhaps were charter members of the congregation at Philippi. Possibly they were deaconesses, and possibly they held some of the worship services in their homes. PHILIPPIANS 4:2

EUTYCHUS A young member of the Christian congregation at Troas who fell asleep while perched on a third-floor windowsill, during the Apostle Paul's preaching one night, Eutychus tumbled to the ground below and was thought to be dead. Paul revived him, took him upstairs again, broke bread, and resumed his sermon. ACTS 20:9

EVE Adam's wife, Eve was the first woman. Her name in Hebrew means "life-giving," and she was named "Eve" because she was the mother of all living men. Like her husband Adam, Eve rebelled against God and put her own plans and wisdom ahead of God's. Her disobedience triggered Adam's, and produced the chain reaction of anxiety and guilt in every person, and the estrangement between man and God, man and woman, brothers, nations and races, that continues to this day. GENESIS 3:20; 4:1; II CORINTHIANS 11:3; I TIMOTHY 2:13

EVI One of five desert chiefs from the tribe of Midian who had been harassing Moses and the Israelites, Evi and his four allies were killed in a fierce battle with the tribes of Israel. His territory in the land of Moab was assigned later to the tribe of Reuben. NUMBERS 31:8; JOSHUA 13:21

EVIL-MERODACH Nebuchadnezzar's son and successor as king of Babylon, Evil-Merodach reigned only two years, and was a wastrel and a fool. He was remembered in the Bible because he released King Jehoiachin of Judah from prison, where he had been confined for thirty-seven years, and treated him to a place at the royal table. II KINGS 25:27; JEREMIAH 52:31

EZBAI The father of Naari, one of the elite troop of "The Thirty," David's top fighters, Ezbai's name and identity are somewhat uncertain since the parallel account of the names of "The Thirty" in II Samuel 23:35 sub-

stitutes the name: "Paari the Arbite."
I CHRONICLES 11:37

EZBON
1 One of Gad's sons, Ezbon was a chieftain in the tribe of Gad. The genealogy of the tribe in Numbers lists Ezbon's name as "Ozni." GENESIS 46:16; NUMBERS 26:16
2 A grandson of Benjamin and a son of Bela, this man Ezbon was a warrior chieftain in the tribe of Benjamin, and the head of a clan. I CHRONICLES 7:7

EZEKIAS See HEZEKIAH 1

EZEKIEL The temple priest who was carried into captivity in Babylon with the cream of Judah's leadership, Ezekiel began ministering to the group of exiled Jews living near him in Tel Avib. His complaints against his own people were that they were stubborn, self-righteous, and rebellious against God. After word came to the captives that Jerusalem had been destroyed, Ezekiel was accorded more serious attention by the Jews in Babylon. Ezekiel, in turn, prophesied a new Israel. His book is a series of prophecies over a period of twenty-two years, from 592—570 B.C. EZEKIEL

EZAR See EZER 1

EZER
1 One of Seir's sons, this Ezer was a chieftain of a clan of Horites in the desert, and is mentioned in the genealogy of the ancestors of the various tribes. GENESIS 36; I CHRONICLES 1:38, 42
2 One of Ephraim's sons, this Ezer and his brother Elead were killed on a cattle raid at Gath. His name is carried in the roll of the tribe by the Chronicler. I CHRONICLES 7:21
3 A chieftain of a family in the tribe of Judah, this Ezer is given a place in the family tree as a descendant of Caleb, son of Hur. I CHRONICLES 4:4
4 One of the shaggy, fleet-footed mountain men from the tribe of Gad who were such formidable fighters, this Ezer and his comrades from Gad grew fed up with Saul. They joined the outlaw David's forces and fought valiantly for David. Ezer became an officer in David's army. I CHRONICLES 12:9
5 A Levite who was a son of Joshua, this Ezer worked with Nehemiah in repairing the walls of Jerusalem after the Exile in Babylon. NEHEMIAH 3:19
6 Still another Ezer was a priest in Nehemiah's time who took a prominent part in the service of dedication for the rebuilt walls of Jerusalem. NEHEMIAH 12:42

EZRA
1 Ezra was a strong-minded leader-priest-scribe in the period after the fall of Babylon who won permission in 458 B.C. to lead a group of ex-patriot priests and other Jews back to Jerusalem. Ezra insisted on a rigid obedience to the Law, especially in regard to the purity of the Jewish community. Against great opposition, he rammed through a decree forcing all Jews to divorce their foreign mates. EZRA; NEHEMIAH 8, 12
2 Another Ezra who lived at about the same time as Ezra 1 was also a priest and the head of an illustrious family of priests. He was part of the

contingent of Jews that returned from Exile in Babylon to Jerusalem with Zerubbabel. NEHEMIAH 12:1

EZRAH A clan chieftain in the tribe of Judah, Ezrah was a descendant of the famous spy, Caleb. Ezrah's name appears in the genealogy of the tribe of Judah. I CHRONICLES 4:17

EZRI The son of Chelub, Ezri was appointed to superintend all of those who worked at raising crops on David's farms. I CHRONICLES 27:26

F

FELIX The greedy, unscrupulous, and cruel procurator, or governor, of Judea when the Apostle Paul was arrested in Jerusalem, Felix was appointed by the Emperor Claudius to succeed Cumanus, and served from 52 to 60 A.D. The historian Josephus claimed that Felix broke his word to Jewish groups, and once brutally killed 400 men suspected of terrorist activity without giving them a trial or checking on facts. He was such an incompetent that the Emperor Nero finally recalled him to Rome. Even in Rome, a Jewish delegation from Palestine tried to bring charges against Felix for malfeasance in office. Felix, however, managed to evade trial. The New Testament describes how he conducted a hearing in Paul's case. Instead of dispensing justice to Paul, a Roman citizen, Felix allowed Paul's case to drag on for two years, and even tried to extort bribe money from Paul. Felix sent for the Apostle many times to talk, but obviously never intended to take the claims of the gospel seriously. ACTS 23—25

FESTUS The successor to Felix as procurator of Judea, Porcius Festus served two stormy years in the office, 60 to 62 A.D. A series of riots between Jews and pagans and the terrorist activities of the *Sicarii* ("wielders of small swords") kept Festus busy, and he put down the troubles with a heavy hand. Paul's case landed in Festus' hands after Felix was recalled. Festus held another hearing at which Paul, weary after two years of confinement, dramatically appealed to Caesar, which was a privilege any Roman citizen could invoke. A few days later when King Agrippa visited Festus, Festus mentioned Paul's case, and Agrippa asked to hear Paul speak. Paul's stirring testimony about the meaning of Christ in his life prompted Festus to decide that Paul was mad, but did not deserve death or imprisonment. ACTS 24—26

FORTUNATUS A prominent member of the Christian church at Corinth, Fortunatus was a companion, for a time, of the Apostle Paul, and a courier for some of Paul's correspondence with the Corinthian church. He was in Ephesus when Paul had to write to Corinth—probably the famous "angry" letter referred to in I Corinthians 5:9—11. Fortunatus and his two companions from Corinth, Stephanas and Achaicus who were also with Paul in Ephesus, were sent back to Corinth to carry the letter and to act on Paul's behalf in straightening out the trouble in the church. Probably Fortunatus returned with the reply from Corinth, which caused I Corinthians to be written. I CORINTHIANS 16:17

G

GAAL A son of Ebed who moved to Shechem, Gaal skillfully played on the dislike of the Shechemites toward King Abimelech, Gideon's son, and whipped them to revolt. He died in the battle when Abimelech ambushed Shechem to quell the rebellion. JUDGES 9:26—41

GABBAI A member of the tribe of Benjamin, Gabbai was one of those elected to repopulate Jerusalem after the return from Exile in Babylonia. NEHEMIAH 11:8

GABRIEL The angel or special agent of God, Gabriel is mentioned by both Daniel and Luke. Daniel states that Gabriel interpreted Daniel's vision of the ram and the he-goat and also Jeremiah's prophecy. Luke writes that Gabriel announced to Zechariah that he would become the father of John the Baptist. In Jewish mythology, Gabriel was always God's messenger and is portrayed as resembling a man. DANIEL 8:16; 9:21; LUKE 1:9, 26

GAD
1 The seventh of Jacob's twelve sons, Gad was a full brother to Asher because they were both Jacob's sons through Leah's maid, Zilpah. He was the ancestor of a large clan which ultimately joined Moses in the trip from Egypt to the Promised Land. The tribe of Gad was awarded territory east of the Jordan on the condition that it would help the other tribes in the conquest of Canaan. GENESIS 30: 11; 35:26; 46:16; 49:19; EXODUS 1:4
2 A prophet who was an advisor and close associate to David, this Gad was best remembered for his stern denunciation of David's census, and his instructions to David to build an altar on Mount Moriah as penance. Later in David's reign, Gad was eclipsed by Nathan as the outstanding

prophet. There is a line in I Chronicles (29:29) referring to an account of David's reign written by Gad; this account unfortunately, has been lost. I SAMUEL 22:5; II SAMUEL 24:11—18; I CHRONICLES 21:9—19; 29:29; II CHRONICLES 29:25

GADDI A son of Susi and a member of the tribe of Manasseh, Gaddi was one of the twelve men sent by Moses to spy in the Promised Land. Gaddi was among those who were so awed by the size and strength of the Canaanites that they advised against invading the land. NUMBERS 13:11

GADDIEL A son of Sodi of the tribe of Zebulun, Gaddiel was another of Moses' twelve spies sent to reconnoiter the land of Canaan. Gaddiel was part of the majority of ten who were so frightened by the Canaanites that they returned warning that the conquest of Canaan was impossible. NUMBERS 13:10

GADI Gadi was the father of Menahem, the man who assassinated Shallum and made himself king of Israel. II KINGS 15:14—17

GAHAM Abraham's nephew, Gaham is listed among the offspring of Nahor, Abraham's brother, and was the head of a desert clan. GENESIS 22:24

GAHAR A temple servant around the time of the Exile, Gahar was the head of a family which returned from Babylon to Jerusalem with Zerubbabel. EZRA 2:47; NEHEMIAH 7:49

GAIUS

1 A man of Corinth who was converted by the Apostle Paul, this Gaius had the distinction of being one of the very few to be baptized by Paul in person. Gaius was a leader in the Christian congregation at Corinth and a prominent person in the community. Paul was among those entertained in Gaius' home, and was grateful for Gaius' hospitality. I CORINTHIANS 1:14; ROMANS 16:23

2 Another Christian carrying the common first name, Gaius, this man was also a close friend and trusted companion of Paul. This Gaius is best remembered as one of Paul's party arrested in the riot at Ephesus. He and Aristarchus, another companion seized that day, were distinguished from others named Gaius by being identified as "men of Macedonia." ACTS 19:29

3 Still another named Gaius who was one of Paul's associates, this man was identified as the Gaius who was from the town of Derbe. He accompanied Paul when Paul went from Philippi to Troas after his riot-ridden tour of Asia Minor and Greece. ACTS 20:4

4 An altogether different Gaius from any of the others was the man to whom Third John was addressed. This Gaius was a close friend of the author, who called him "the beloved" and thanked him for his gracious hospitality. III JOHN 1

GALAL

1 A Levite who lived at the time of the Exile, Galal was one of the first to return to Jerusalem when the Jews were allowed to leave Babylon. I CHRONICLES 9:15

2 Another Levite, this man named Galal was the ancestor of a prominent Levite, Obadiah, who returned to Jerusalem after the Exile. I CHRONICLES 9:16; NEHEMIAH 11:17

GALLIO A member of a prominent Roman family (his brother was the famous philosopher, Seneca, his nephew, the poet, Lucan), Gallio was a witty, urbane man whose good connections with Nero won him the position of proconsul of Achaia. He took office in Corinth at the time of Paul's first missionary trip to that city, and met Paul briefly when some disgruntled members of the synagogue tried to bring charges against Paul. Gallio tossed the case out of court, and ignored the ruckus which broke out immediately afterwards when some Greeks beat up the head of the synagogue. ACTS 18:12—17

GAMALIEL
1 A leader in the tribe of Manasseh, this Gamaliel was elected to assist Moses in the census of the tribes. NUMBERS 1:10; 2:20; 7:54, 59; 10:23
2 The great Jewish teacher, this Gamaliel was renowned for his wisdom and humane interpretations of the Law. Grandson of the famous Rabbi Hillel, Gamaliel led the more liberal wing of the Pharisees. He is remembered in the New Testament as the member of the Sanhedrin who warned his colleagues not to kill Peter and the other apostles, and as the teacher of Saul of Tarsus, later Paul. ACTS 5:34; 22:3

GAMUL A Levite who lived at the time of David, Gamul was a prominent citizen and priest who headed the twenty-second group of priests in the service in the House of the Lord. I CHRONICLES 24:17

GAREB A close associate of David during David's outlaw days, Gareb was a fighter from Judah who won himself a place in "The Thirty," David's elite corps, and served as an officer in David's army. II SAMUEL 23:38; I CHRONICLES 11:40

GASHMU See GESHEM

GATAM A descendant of Esau, Gatam is listed in the family genealogies as Eliphaz's son. GENESIS 36:11,16; I CHRONICLES 1:36

GAZEZ
1 One of Caleb's sons, Gazez is named in the family tree by the Chronicler. I CHRONICLES 2:46
2 A grandson of Caleb, this Gazez is carried in the Chronicler's list as a son of Haran. I CHRONICLES 2:46

GAZZAM A Levite at the time of the Exile, Gazzam was the father of a group of temple servants that returned to Jerusalem from Babylon. EZRA 2:48; NEHEMIAH 7:51

GEBER One of Solomon's twelve commissary officials, Geber had the heavy responsibility of getting provisions for Solomon's enormous staff and household for one month each

111

year. Geber was given a large but sparsely populated and mountainous territory, and would have found his assignment an onerous one. I KINGS 4:19

GEDALIAH

1 The son of Ahikam, the man who saved the prophet Jeremiah from being killed by super-patriots, Gedaliah was appointed governor of the devastated, depopulated country after Nebuchadnezzar conquered Judah. Gedaliah tried to preserve what was left of his nation, but was treacherously murdered in a plot hatched by the king of the Ammonites. II KINGS 25; JEREMIAH 39—43

2 A Levite who was one of Jeduthun's sons, this Gedaliah was a musician who joined others in his family in serving in worship services in David's House of the Lord. I CHRONICLES 25: 3, 9

3 A priest at the time of the Exile who had married outside of the faith, this Gedaliah was forced by Ezra to leave his wife and promise to keep the Law in every detail. EZRA 10:18

4 The grandfather of the prophet Zephaniah. ZEPHANIAH 1:1

5 A hot-headed nobleman who was one of those who resented Jeremiah's prophecies, this Gedaliah and his henchmen got King Zedekiah's permission to throw Jeremiah into an empty cistern to silence him for good. The prophet, however, was saved by a servant. Gedaliah was probably among those later deported to Babylon. JEREMIAH 38:1

GEDOR A member of the tribe of Benjamin, Gedor was the head of a clan and one of King Saul's ancestors. I CHRONICLES 8:31; 9:37

GEHAZI The insensitive but shrewd servant of the Prophet Elisha, Gehazi understood better than Elisha how the Shunamite woman might be rewarded for her kindness to Elisha, and advised Elisha that she really wanted a son more than anything. Later, however, when the son died, Gehazi roughly tried to keep her from seeing Elisha, and unsucessfully tried to revive the boy himself. Elisha, however, did grant her an audience, and raised her son to life again. Gehazi's greed got the best of him when the Syrian King Namaan was cured of leprosy. Although Elisha had declined payment, Gehazi collected in Elisha's name—and came down with leprosy himself as punishment. II KINGS 4, 5, 8

GEMALLI A member of the tribe of Dan, Gemalli was the father of Ammiel, one of the twelve spies sent by Moses into Canaan. NUMBERS 13:12

GEMARIAH

1 A scribe who was a son of Shaphan and a leading citizen of Judah in the nation's last days under King Jehoiakim, Gemariah was present when Jeremiah's secretary, Baruch, read the scroll of Jeremiah's prophecies. He joined with others in trying to dissuade the enraged Jehoiakim from destroying the scroll. Gemariah, however, was not deeply moved by Jeremiah's words. JEREMIAH 36

2 A contemporary of **1**, this Gemariah was a son of Hilkiah, the man whom Zedekiah, Nebuchadnezzar's appointee in captured Jerusalem, sent to Babylon with messages. Gemariah was also a messenger—the bearer of Jeremiah's great letter to the Jews who had been carried away as captives to Babylon. JEREMIAH 29:3

GENUBATH Son of the Edomite prince, Hadad, who had fled to Egypt after David's raid in Edom, Genubath was born and raised in Egypt. I KINGS 11:20

GERA Although mentioned as one of Benjamin's sons in Genesis 46:21, other records all state that Gera was Benjamin's grandson through Benjamin's son, Bela. He was a powerful clan chieftain, and gave his name to a clan in the tribe of Benjamin. Gera was mentioned as the ancestor of such men as Ehud and Shimei. GENESIS 46: 21; JUDGES 3:15; II SAMUEL 16:5; 19: 16, 18; I KINGS 2:8; I CHRONICLES 8:3 —7

GERSHOM
1 Moses' oldest son by Zipporah, Gershom receives surprisingly little mention in the Bible, considering the importance of his father. He was probably the son whom Zipporah circumcised EXODUS 4:25. The only other references are to a few of his descendants. EXODUS 2:22; 18:3; JUDGES 18: 30; I CHRONICLES 23:15—16; 26:24
2 This second Gershom (or Gershon) was the oldest of Levi's three sons, and was born in Palestine before Jacob and his sons migrated to Egypt. Gershom's descendants became an illustrious group of Levites, and were renowned as musicians and singers in the Temple services. GENESIS 46:11; EXODUS 6:16—17; NUMBERS 3, 4, 7, 10, 26; JOSHUA 21:6; I CHRONICLES 15:7; 23:6
3 A descendant of Phinehas, this person named Gershom was one of those who returned from the Exile in Babylon to Jerusalem with Ezra. EZRA 8:2

GERSHON See GERSHOM 2

GERSON See GERSHOM 3

GESHAM See GESHAN

GESHAN One of Caleb's many descendants, Geshan's name is carried in the genealogies by the Chronicler. I CHRONICLES 2:47

GESHEM An Arab chieftain living in the neighborhood of Jerusalem when the Jews were beginning to return home after the Exile in Babylon, Geshem made things difficult for Nehemiah. Geshem jeered when Nehemiah announced his plan to rebuild the walls of Jerusalem, but spread the rumor that Nehemiah was going to revolt when the walls were nearly finished. This wily adversary allied with others who hated the Jews to plot against Nehemiah's life. NEHEMIAH 2:19; 6:1—6

GETHER Noah's great-grandson and one of Aram's sons, Gether is listed in the family tree as one descended through Shem, Aram's father. GENESIS 10:23; I CHRONICLES 1:17

GEUEL One of the leaders from the tribe of Gad, Geuel was his tribe's representative in the group of twelve spies sent by Moses to reconnoiter the

113

Promised Land. Geuel joined with the majority of spies in reporting that the Canaanites were too huge and powerful for the tribes ever to conquer them. NUMBERS 13:15

GIBBAR A man who lived during the Exile, Gibbar and his family were among those who returned from Babylon to Jerusalem with Zerubbabel. EZRA 2:20

GIBEA One of Caleb's grandsons listed in the genealogy of the tribe of Judah, Gibea is believed by some scholars to refer to the name of the village of Gibeah, south of Hebron. I CHRONICLES 2:49

GIDDALTI A Levite who was one of the great singer Heman's sons, Giddalti was also a famous musician. He was one of those assigned to blow the horns in David's sanctuary, and was in charge of the twenty-second detachment of sanctuary servants. I CHRONICLES 25:4, 29

GIDDEL
1 One who lived at the time of the Exile, Giddel and his family were among the group of temple servants that returned from Babylon to Jerusalem with Zerubbabel. EZRA 2:47; NEHEMIAH 7:49
2 This Giddel was one of Solomon's servants. He was the ancestor of another family that carried the name, "sons of Giddel," that returned from Babylon with Zerubbabel. EZRA 2:56; NEHEMIAH 7:58

GIDEON The plucky deliverer of Israel from the marauding Midian-ites, Gideon and his hand-picked crew of three hundred commandos threw the Midianites into panic by a sudden night attack. The Ephraimites belatedly joined Gideon in mopping up the Midianite remnants the next day, but peevishly complained that they should have been allowed a more prominent part in the operation. Gideon proved his diplomatic skills by soothing the Ephraimites with a flattering speech. He also punished the villagers of Penuel and Succoth who had sneered and refused food to Gideon's men. Established as the strongman of the region, Gideon ruled as "judge" over the tribes and their clans for forty years, until his death. He was also known by the names of Jerubbaal and Jerubbesheth. JUDGES 6—8; II SAMUEL 11:21

GIDEONI A member of the tribe of Benjamin, Gideoni was the father of Abidan, one of those selected to help Moses in his census of the tribes. NUMBERS 1:11; 2:22; 7:60—65; 10:24

GILALAI A Levite musician in Nehemiah's time, Gilalai participated in the service of dedication when the walls of Jerusalem were rebuilt after the return from the Exile. Gilalai played one of the old instruments used in David's time. NEHEMIAH 12:36

GILEAD
1 Grandson of Manasseh and son of Machir, Gilead gave his name to the district and the clan of Gilead, located in the lush Jordan valley. NUMBERS 26:29—30; 27:1; 36:1; JOSHUA 17:1—3; I CHRONICLES 2:21—23; 7:14—17

2 Another Gilead, this man was the father of the famous judge of Israel, Jephthah. JUDGES 11:1—2

3 A son of Michael, a member of the tribe of Gad, this individual named Gilead was included in the tribal genealogy by the Chronicler. I CHRONICLES 5:14

GINATH This man is remembered only as the father of Tibni, the man who lost out to Omri in the struggle for the throne of Israel after Zimri's death. I KINGS 16:21—22

GINNETHO See GINNETHOI

GINNETHOI A priest and leading citizen among those who returned to Jerusalem after the Exile in Babylon, Ginnethoi participated with Nehemiah in the service rededicating the walls of rebuilt Jerusalem, and signed the covenant promising to keep the Law. NEHEMIAH 10:6; 12:4, 16

GINNETHON See GINNETHOI

GISHPA A Levite who came to live in Jerusalem after the return from Exile in Babylon, Gishpa was a supervisor over other temple servants and resided on the hill called Ophal, opposite the Temple. NEHEMIAH 11:21

GISPA See GISHPA

GOG

1 A member of the tribe of Reuben and the grandson of Joel, this man named Gog was listed in the tribal family tree by the Chronicler. I CHRONICLES 5:4

2 The dreaded leader of the savage hordes that swept out of central Asia and terrorized the ancient world, Gog was probably the person known as Gyges of Lyda, or what is now Armenia, the first king of that area who was known to the Assyrians. The name "Gog" was given as a title to subsequent rulers of Magog. Gog's invasion of western Asia Minor caused great numbers to be uprooted and displaced, earning Gog the title "prince of Rosh, Meshech, and Tubal" from the areas he grabbed. His name became a synonym for terror, bloodshed, and homelessness among the ancients, including the Bible writers of Ezekiel and Revelation. EZEKIEL 38—39; REVELATION 20:8

GOLIATH The giant of the Philistine armies from Gath who singlehandedly cowed the armies of Israel, Goliath stood ten and one half feet tall. He repeatedly challenged the Israelites to man-to-man combat, and taunted them for refusing. He suffered an ignominious death when a then-unknown shepherd boy named David stepped forward one day and with a rock from his sling, felled the mighty Goliath. I SAMUEL 17; 21:9; 22:10

GOMER

1 The son of Japheth and the grandson of Noah, Gomer was believed to be an ancestor of the half-civilized tribes that roamed Central Asia and were called Cimmerians by the Greeks. GENESIS 10:2—3; I CHRONICLES 1:5—6

2 This Gomer was a woman, the faithless wife of the great prophet Hosea. In spite of her infidelity, Hosea forgave her and took her back, and used the incident as an illustration of love of God toward the faithless nation of Israel. HOSEA 1:3

GUNI

1 One of Naphtali's sons, Guni was a chieftain in the tribe and founder of the clan know as Gunites. GENESIS 46:24; NUMBERS 26:48; I CHRONICLES 7:13

2 A member of the tribe of Gad, this Guni was remembered as the father of a chieftain in the tribe named Abdiel. I CHRONICLES 5:15

H

HAAHASHTARI A descendant of Judah, Haahashtari was one of Ashhur's sons, and was listed in the family records of the tribe of Judah. I CHRONICLES 4:6

HABAIAH One of the Temple servants who brought his family back to Jerusalem from the Exile in Babylon alongside Zerubbabel, Habaiah suffered the misfortune of not being able to trace his ancestry among the genealogies of the tribes of Israel. This meant that he was not able to serve as a priest in the Temple. EZRA 2:61; NEHEMIAH 7:63

HABAKKUK One of the eight minor prophets in the Old Testament, Habakkuk's writings close with the words, "on my stringed instrument," indicating that Habakkuk was perhaps a Levite and a Temple musician. Habakkuk wrote shortly before the Baby-lonian invasion of Judah, at the time when Babylon was crushing all nations. His brief book is a dialogue between God and prophet in which he asks God why the tyrant, Babylon, is allowed to flourish. Although legends about Habakkuk's life were numerous in later Jewish history and throughout the Middle Ages, there are no additional personal details about him in the Bible. HABAKKUK

HABZINIAH A Rechabite (one who took a vow never to drink wine), Habziniah's grandson is mentioned as one who was tested by Jeremiah. JEREMIAH 35:3

HACHALIAH The father of Nehemiah, the man who rebuilt the walls of Jerusalem. NEHEMIAH 1:1; 10:1

HACHMONI The father of Jehiel, chum of David's sons. I CHRONICLES 27:32

117

HADAD

HADAD

1 One of Ishmael's sons, and thus one of Abraham's grandsons, this Hadad is listed in the genealogies of Abraham's family. GENESIS 25:15; I CHRONICLES 1:30

2 A king of the powerful desert kingdom of Edom who was a son of Bedad, this Hadad came from the city of Avith. His fame rested on his victory over the Midianites in a all-but-forgotten battle in Moab. GENESIS 36:35; I CHRONICLES 1:46

3 Another king of Edom, this Hadad ruled from the city of Pai with his queen, Mehetabel. In Genesis 36:39, he is called Hadar. I CHRONICLES 1:50—51

4 Another Edomite, this Hadad was one of the few to escape the bloodbath when Joab killed most of the Edomite royal family during David's invasion of Edom. Hadad was taken to Egypt as a child, and later married into the pharaoh's family. After David and Joab died, Hadad returned to Edom and annoyed Solomon with his raids from his mountain fastnesses. I KINGS 11

HADADEZER King of a strong desert nation in northern Syria called Zobah, Hadadezer persistently stirred up trouble against David. Including the Syrians, the Ammonites, and the Arameans in his schemes to smash David, Hadadezer suffered a series of defeats which permanently ruined his country, Zobah. II SAMUEL 8; 10; I KINGS 11:23; I CHRONICLES 18:19

HADAR See HADAD

HADAREZER See HADADEZER

HADASSAH Mordecai's cousin, the Persian queen who was better known by the name Esther. See ESTHER

HADLAI A chief of the tribe of Ephraim, Hadlai held sway during the reign of Pekah. He was recorded as the father of Amasa in the Chronicler's list. II CHRONICLES 28:12

HADORAM

1 One of Joktan's sons, this Hadoram was a tribal chieftain who was mentioned in the family tree of Shem, Noah's son. GENESIS 10:27; I CHRONICLES 1:21

2 Son of Tou, the king of Hamath in northern Syria, this Hadoram was sent by his father with gifts and congratulatory messages to David after David wiped out the forces of Tou's arch-enemy, Hadadezer. I CHRONICLES 18:10

3 The man in charge of the forced-labor gangs at the time of Rehoboam, this Hadoram was sent by the high-handed Rehoboam to impose plans to continue the labor levies on the restive nation. The act sparked a rebellion which killed Hadoram, split the kingdom, and left Rehoboam as king only of the smaller southern half, Judah. II CHRONICLES 10:18

HAGAB A Levite, Hagab was remembered as the ancestor of a group of temple singers who returned with Zerubbabel from Exile in Babylon to Jerusalem. EZRA 2:46

HAGABA See HAGABAH

118

HAGABAH This man was also the head of a family of temple musicians who returned from Exile in Babylon to Jerusalem with Zerubbabel's party. EZRA 2:45; NEHEMIAH 7:48

HAGAR Sarah's Egyptian servant girl, Hagar was sent by the childless Sarah to Abraham to produce an heir for Abraham. Hagar became the mother of Abraham's son, Ishmael. The two women inevitably were jealous of one another, and Hagar's insults to Sarah and Sarah's harshness toward Hagar led Hagar to run away temporarily. A few years later, when God's promise was unexpectedly fulfilled and Sarah gave birth to Abraham's son, Isaac, Hagar was forced to flee permanently with her young son. God, however, heard the boy's cries and delivered Hagar and Ishmael from death by thirst and starvation in the wilderness. GENESIS 16, 21, 25

HAGGAI One of the minor prophets, Haggai lived in the tumultuous era after the defeat of Babylon and rise of Persia, about 520 B.C. Reading the signs of the times and noting the slow progress of the Jews who had returned from Exile in rebuilding the Temple in Jerusalem, Haggai made a strong patriotic and religious appeal to the leaders of the Jewish community to rebuild the Temple immediately—and thus receive God's blessings again. His vigorous book galvanized the returned exiles into action; within four years the Temple was rededicated. EZRA 5:1; 6:14; HAGGAI

HAGGERI See HAGRI

HAGGI Gad's second son, Haggi was a chieftain in the tribe of Gad and the founder of the clan known as Haggites. GENESIS 46:16; NUMBERS 26:15

HAGGIAH A member of the tribe of Levi, Haggiah was descended from Levi's son, Merari, and is mentioned in the tribal family tree by the Chronicler. I CHRONICLES 6:30

HAGGITH One of David's wives, Haggith was received into the royal harem in Hebron just before David became king of the united kingdom. She is remembered primarily because she was the mother of David's son, Adonijah. II SAMUEL 3:4; I KINGS 1:5, 11; 2:13; I CHRONICLES 3:2

HAGRI The father of Mibhar, one of David's great fighters who was a member of "The Thirty."

HAKKATAN Father of Johanan, one of the clan chieftains who accompanied Ezra from Babylon to Jerusalem after the Exile. EZRA 8:12

HAKKOZ
1 A chieftain in the tribe of Judah, Hakkoz (or Coz or Koz as he is also called by some translators) is listed in the genealogy of Judah. I CHRONICLES 4:8
2 A priest who was appointed to head the seventh turn in the worship services in David's sanctuary, this Hakkoz was the head of a well-known family of Levites in Jerusalem, many of whom, years later, returned to help

rebuild the Temple after the Exile in Babylon. I CHRONICLES 24:10; EZRA 2:61; NEHEMIAH 3:4; 21

HALLOHESH One of the Jews that returned to Jerusalem after the Exile in Babylon, Hallohesh and his family helped Nehemiah rebuild the walls and participated in the covenant-signing whereby they promised to keep the Law. NEHEMIAH 3:12; 10:24

HALOHESH See HALLOHESH

HAM Noah's youngest son, Ham was the founder of one branch of the human family according to the ancient Hebrews. This branch was thought to have settled in Egypt. The earliest Egyptian name for Egypt was "Ham." GENESIS 5:32; 6:10; 7:13; 9:18—22; 10:1, 6, 20; I CHRONICLES 1:4, 8

HAMAN The arch-villain in the Book of Esther, Haman was instigator of one of the first pogroms against the Jews. As prime minister of Persia under Ahasuerus, Haman and his sons, annoyed because Mordecai, the Jew, refused to bow down to Haman, plotted a massacre of all the Jews. This bloodbath was prevented only by the timely intervention of beautiful Queen Esther, who took the risk of disclosing that she, too, was Jewish. Haman and his sons were hanged. Jews to this day observe the joyous deliverance at Purim. ESTHER

HAMMEDATHA The Persian father of Haman, Ahasuerus' Prime Minister, who was hanged for plotting to kill all Jews. ESTHER 3, 8, 9

HAMMOLECHETH The granddaughter of Manasseh, Hammolecheth was Machair's daughter and Gilead's sister and an ancestor of the great warrior-judge, Gideon. I CHRONICLES 7:18

**HAMMOLEKETH
  See HAMMOLECHETH**

HAMMUEL A chieftain of the tribe of Simeon, Hammuel had his name included in the roll by the Chronicler. I CHRONICLES 4:26

HAMOR Head of a powerful Canaanite clan, Hamor was the father of Shechem, the man who got Dinah, the Israelite girl, in trouble. Shechem sent Hamor to ask to marry Dinah, thus and proposing intermarriage between his tribe and the Israelites. Instead, Dinah's brothers, Simon and Levi, vengefully plotted retaliation, and slaughtered Hamor, Shechem, and the men of the tribe. GENESIS 33:19; 34; JOSHUA 24:32; JUDGES 9:28

HAMRAN See HEMDAN

HAMUEL See HAMMUEL

HAMUL One of Judah's descendants through Pharez, Hamul was the progenitor of a clan called Hamulites. GENESIS 46:12; NUMBERS 26:21; I CHRONICLES 2:5

HAMUTAL One of King Josiah's wives, Hamutal was the mother of two mediocrities on the throne of Judah, Kings Jehoahaz and Zedekiah. I KINGS 23:31; 24:18; JEREMIAH 52:1

HANAMEEL The cousin of Jeremiah, Hanameel sold a plot of land to Jeremiah at a time when land values were plummeting because of the threat of the Babylonian invasion. Jeremiah bought the field to demonstrate his confidence that he would live to see peace in the land again. JEREMIAH 32

HANAN

1 A member of the tribe of Benjamin, this Hanan was a son of Shashak, and was listed as one of the clan sheiks in the tribal records. I CHRONICLES 8:23

2 Another Benjaminite, this Hanan was a descendant of Saul, and one of Azel's six sons. I CHRONICLES 8:38; 9:44

3 The son of Maacah, this Hanan was one of David's greatest warriors. His bravery and exploits won him a place in the exclusive corps known as "The Thirty," and a commission in David's army. I CHRONICLES 11:43

4 A Temple servant who lived during the Exile in Babylon, this Hanan and his family were members of the party which returned to Jerusalem with Zerubbabel. EZRA 2:46; NEHEMIAH 7:49

5 A Levite who was one of those determined to bring the Jews back to a strict observance of the Law, this Hanan joined Ezra in the intensive adult education program of teaching the people the Law. Later he joined with Nehemiah in signing the covenant. NEHEMIAH 8:7; 10:10

6 The son of Zaccur, this Hanan was also a Levite who lived in Nehemiah's time. He was appointed assistant treasurer in the Temple storehouses by Nehemiah. NEHEMIAH 13:13

7 The head of a prominent family in Jerusalem after the Exile when Nehemiah rebuilt the city wall, this Hanan joined in signing the covenant promising to keep the Law. NEHEMIAH 10:22

8 Another Hanan who lived in Nehemiah's Jerusalem, this man also was the head of a family and participated in the solemn service of signing the covenant. NEHEMIAH 10:26

9 A son of Igdaliah, this Hanan was a respected Levite who served in the Temple. In Jeremiah's time, this Hanan's son had quarters in the Temple. JEREMIAH 35:4

HANANEEL See HANANEL

HANANEL Some think that this was the name of the builder of a large tower in Jerusalem in Nehemiah's time; others maintain that the name refers simply to the name of the tower, which in Hebrew means "God is gracious." NEHEMIAH 3:1; 12:39; JEREMIAH 31:38; ZECHARIAH 14:10

HANANI

1 A son of the great musician Heman, Hanani also was a Levite who played and sang in David's sanctuary. I CHRONICLES 25:4, 25

2 A bold holy man and seer who told off King Asa for trying to buy off Syria by entering into an expensive and dangerous alliance with Syria's Benhadad, Hanani was slapped into prison by the angry King Asa. Later, Hanani's son, Jehu, carried on the family tradition by appearing before Baasha and Jehoshaphat to denounce their schemes. II CHRONICLES 16:7; 19:2; 20:34; I KINGS 16:1, 7

3 Another Hanani, this man was a priest who married a non-Jewish girl during the Exile in Babylon, but who obeyed Ezra's strict rules against marrying outside the faith and sent his wife away. EZRA 10:20

4 Nehemiah's brother, this Hanani went back from Jerusalem to the city of Susa to report on the desperate plight of the Jews who had returned to Jerusalem after the Exile. Later, Hanani was appointed one of the governors of Jerusalem by Nehemiah. NEHEMIAH 1:2; 7:2

5 A Levite who was a well-known musician, this Hanani lived in Nehemiah's time and took an active part in the impressive service when the rebuilt wall of Jerusalem was dedicated. NEHEMIAH 12:36

HANANIAH

1 This Hananiah was one of the sons of the great Levite musician, Heman. Like the rest of his family, Hananiah was a talented singer and instrumentalist, and was given a prominent part in David's worship services. Hananiah headed the sixteenth group of sanctuary musicians. I CHRONICLES 25:4, 23

2 Chief of Staff of King Uzziah's army, this Hananiah had charge of equipping, training, and organizing Uzziah's strong military machine in Israel in the late ninth century B.C. II CHRONICLES 26:11

3 Another Hananiah, this man was mentioned only because he happened to be the father of Zedekiah, one of King Jehoiakim's advisors and a lead-ing citizen of Judah at the time of Jeremiah. JEREMIAH 36:12

4 The priest-prophet who claimed so confidently that he spoke for God and that Jeremiah did not, this Hananiah smashed Jeremiah's yoke (symbolizing the captivity of Judah under Babylon that Jeremiah was certain would come soon). Using the same religious vocabulary as Jeremiah, this false prophet dramatically insisted that God would never permit Babylon to conquer Judah, but would smash the king of Babylon. Jeremiah predicted death for this lying prophet —and within two months, Hananiah died. JEREMIAH 28

5 Grandfather of Irijah, this Hananiah was remembered chiefly because he was related to the guard who arrested the prophet Jeremiah on charges of deserting to the enemy. JEREMIAH 37:13

6 One of the tribe of Benjamin, this Hananiah was one of Shashak's sons and a clan chieftain in the tribe. I CHRONICLES 8:24

7 One of Daniel's three companions who shared his perils and trials, this Hananiah was better known as Shadrach. Shadrach, or Hananiah, was a young Jerusalem blueblood who was carried off to the Babylon court, but who refused to adopt Babylonian culture or faith. After the miraculous deliverance from the fiery furnace, he and his companions rose to the top administrative posts in the province. DANIEL 1, 2

8 One of Zerubbabel's sons, this Hananiah returned with his illustrious father to Jerusalem in one of the first groups to go from Babylon after the Exile. I CHRONICLES 3:19, 21

9 A son of Bebai, this Hananiah was recorded as one of the large number who married outside the faith during the Exile in Babylon, thus breaking the Law. EZRA 10:28

10 A druggist and priest, this man by the same name returned to Jerusalem after the Exile and worked hard at rebuilding the city wall under Nehemiah's direction. NEHEMIAH 3:8

11 A son of Shelemiah, this Hananiah may be the same as **10**. He, too, joined Nehemiah's work battalion and rebuilt the wall of Jerusalem after the Exile. NEHEMIAH 3:30

12 One of the two military commanders of Jerusalem in Nehemiah's time, this Hananiah won high praise from Nehemiah for his faithfulness and piety. He resided in the fortress on the north side of the Temple. NEHEMIAH 7:2

13 Another Hananiah, not identified with any of the others with the same name who lived in Nehemiah's time, this Hananiah and his family were among those who joined Nehemiah in signing the solemn covenant, promising to keep the Law. NEHEMIAH 10:23

14 A priest who took important parts in the Temple services in the era of the high priest Jehoiakim, this Hananiah was mentioned also as one of those who participated in the impressive service when Nehemiah rededicated the rebuilt wall of Jerusalem. NEHEMIAH 12:12, 41

HANNAH The devout mother of the prophet-leader, Samuel, Hannah was one of two wives of Elkanah. Her trust in God was rewarded when she finally bore a child. Fulfilling her promise that the youngster would be raised in the service of the Lord, Hannah brought Samuel to the aged priest, Eli. Each year she wove the boy a coat and brought it when she came annually to Shiloh to make her sacrifice. Later Hannah became the mother of five other youngsters, and was regarded as a prophetess. I SAMUEL 1, 2

HANNIEL

1 A chieftain in the tribe of Manasseh in Moses' time, this Hanniel, a son of Ephod, was his tribe's representative when Moses chose men from each of the twelve tribes to assist him in dividing up the Promised Land. GENESIS 25:4; I CHRONICLES 1:33

2 A chieftain of a clan in the tribe of Asher, this Hanniel was one of Ulla's three sons, and was renowned as a tough fighter, according to the Chronicler. I CHRONICLES 7:39

HANOCH

1 Abraham's grandson, this Hanoch is carried in the genealogies of Abraham's offspring, and was listed as one of Midian's children. GENESIS 25:4; I CHRONICLES 1:33

2 Another Hanoch, this individual was one of Reuben's sons and the founder of the clan in the tribe of Reuben called Hanochites. GENESIS 46:9; EXODUS 6:14; NUMBERS 26:5; I CHRONICLES 5:3

HANUN

1 The insolent son of the Ammonite King Nahash, Hanun deliberately insulted David's messengers when David sent his condolences upon the death of Nahash. Hanun's rash act touched off a war which ruined the Ammonites. II SAMUEL 10; I CHRONICLES 19

2 A son of Zalaph, this Hanun worked hard at repairing the ravine gate in the rebuilding program in Jerusalem under Nehemiah after the Exile. NEHEMIAH 3:13, 30

HAPPIZZEZ A Levite who served in the sanctuary in David's time, Happizzez headed the eighteenth group of sanctuary priests. He was also known as Aphses. I CHRONICLES 24:15

HARAN

1 Abraham's youngest brother and Terah's son, this Haran was the father of Lot who accompanied Abraham from Ur to Canaan. GENESIS 11

2 A Levite of the Gershonite branch of the tribe, this Haran and his brothers, Shimei's sons, all served in the sanctuary in David's time. I CHRONICLES 23:9

3 One of the sons of Caleb, Moses' great spy, this Haran is named in the long genealogical list of the descendants of Judah. I CHRONICLES 2:46

HARBONA An attendant who served Persian King Ahasuerus at the time Haman plotted to massacre all the Jews, Harbona was one of those sent to summon Queen Vashti to Ahasuerus' wild party. Later, when Haman's evil plot was uncovered, Harbona suggested that Haman be strung upon the gallows which Haman had built for the Jew Mordecai. ESTHER 1:10; 7:9

HAREPH Son of Caleb, the son of Hur, Hareph was a chieftain in the tribe of Judah, and listed in the family records by the Chronicler. I CHRONICLES 2:51

HARHAIAH A goldsmith, Harhaiah was principally remembered because his craftman son, Uzziel, helped rebuild the wall of Jerusalem after the return from Exile. NEHEMIAH 3:8

HARHAS Harhas was recorded as the grandfather of Shallum, who was the husband of Huldah the prophetess. II KINGS 22:14

HARHUR A Levite, Harhur was the head of a large family of temple servants who returned to Jerusalem after the Exile in Babylon. EZRA 2:51; NEHEMIAH 7:53

HARIM

1 A prominent priest in David's time, this Harim was in charge of the third group in the services in the sanctuary. His descendants were among those who returned with Zerubbabel to Jerusalem after the Exile. I CHRONICLES 24:8; EZRA 2:39; 10:21; NEHEMIAH 3:11; 7:42

2 Another Harim, apparently a layman and not a priest, this man was the forebear of a large group that returned from Exile to Jerusalem. Many of his descendants had married outside the faith, and were made to renounce their marriages. EZRA 2:32; 10:31; NEHEMIAH 7:35

3 Perhaps related to one of the preceding, this Harim was a priest who lived in Jerusalem after the return from Exile, and who joined Nehemiah in signing the covenant promising to keep the Law after the wall had been rebuilt. NEHEMIAH 10:5; 12:15

4 Another Harim, possibly a kinsman of the others by the same name mentioned above, this person also participated as the head of a household in the solemn service of the signing of the covenant with Nehemiah, promising to keep the Law. NEHEMIAH 10:27

HARIPH This man's family was among the party that returned to Jerusalem from Exile in Babylon and later joined Nehemiah in signing the covenant promising to observe the Law. NEHEMIAH 7:24; 10:19

HARNEPHER A member of the tribe of Asher, Harnepher was a clan chieftain, and was recorded in the tribe's genealogy as a son of Zopher. I CHRONICLES 7:36

HAROEH A member of the tribe of Judah, Haroeh's name occurs in the tribal list as one of Shobal's sons. I CHRONICLES 2:52

HARSHA A Temple servant, Harsha's family was among those returned to Jerusalem with Zerubbabel after the Exile. EZRA 2:52; NEHEMIAH 7:54

HARUM A member of the tribe of Judah, Harum is another of those men who are simply remembered as a name in the genealogies. Harum was listed as the father of Aharhel and as a descendant of Caleb, son of Hur. I CHRONICLES 4:8

HARUMAPH The father of Jedaiah, one of those who helped Nehemiah rebuild the wall of Jerusalem. NEHEMIAH 3:10

HARUZ King Manasseh's father-in-law, Haruz was remembered as the father of Queen Meshullemeth, and grandfather of King Amon of Judah. II KINGS 21:19

HASADIAH Son of the patriot-leader Zerubbabel who led a large group from Exile in Babylon to Jerusalem, Hasadiah had royal blood in his veins because of his ancestor, King Jehoiakim. I CHRONICLES 3:20

HASENUAH See HASSENUAH

HASHABIAH

1 A Levite of the Merari branch of the tribe, this Hashabiah was an ancestor of Ethan, one of the renowned musicians in David's sanctuary. I CHRONICLES 6:45

2 Another Levite, also of the Merari branch, this Hashabiah was recorded as the great grandfather of Shemaiah, one of the first Levites to return to Jerusalem after the Exile. I CHRONICLES 9:14

3 One of the six sons of the great Levite musician, Jeduthun, this Hashabiah and his brothers played the lyre and sang in the sanctuary in David's time. I CHRONICLES 25:3

4 A Levite who descended from Hebron of the Kohath branch of the tribe, this Hashabiah and his clan carried the responsibility of overseeing civic and religious affairs in Israel westward from the Jordan in David's kingdom. I CHRONICLES 26:30

5 The chief officer of all Levites at the time of David's census, this Hashabiah was a son of Kemuel. I CHRONICLES 27:17

6 Still another Levite who was also a chief of his tribe, this man by the same name played a key role in King Josiah's great observance of Passover after the reform movement and Temple repair program. II CHRONICLES 35:9

7 Another Levite, this Hashabiah was, like so many others of the name, part of the Merari branch of the tribe. He lived during the Exile in Babylon and returned to Jerusalem with Ezra. EZRA 8:19

8 One of the leading priests in Ezra's party of exiles returning to Jerusalem from Babylon, this Levite named Hashabiah, one of the Kohath branch of the tribe, was one of twelve entrusted with the sacred Temple utensils. EZRA 8:24

9 Another Levite by the same name, this Hashabiah was a prominent priest after the Exile. He worked with Nehemiah in repairing the wall of Jerusalem, participated in the services of rededicating the wall, and joined in signing the covenant promising to keep the Law. NEHEMIAH 3:17; 10:11; 12:24, 26

10 A son of Bunni, this Hashabiah was a contemporary of others of the same name in Nehemiah's time, and was a Levite who volunteered to settle in Jerusalem after the Exile to help rebuild the holy city. NEHEMIAH 11:15

11 Son of Mattaniah, this Hashabiah was a priest who was remembered as the grandfather of Uzzi, leader of the Jerusalem Levites in Nehemiah's time. NEHEMIAH 11:22

12 Perhaps the same as one of the preceding Hashabiahs who lived in Jerusalem after the Exile (scholars are not certain), perhaps another bearer of the popular name, this Hashabiah was noted as the priest who was head of the family of Hilkiah in the days when Jehoiakim was high priest. NEHEMIAH 12:21

HASHABNAH A head of a well-known family in Jerusalem after Nehemiah rebuilt the wall following the Exile, Hashabnah was one of the leading citizens who signed the covenant with Nehemiah promising to observe the Law. NEHEMIAH 10:25

HASHABNEIAH

1 This Hashabneiah by the name was the father of Hattush, one of those who helped rebuild the wall of Jerusalem after the Exile in Babylon. NEHEMIAH 3:10

2 A leading Levite in Jerusalem after the Exile, this Hashabneiah had a prominent part in the ceremonies when the wall was rededicated and the covenant was signed under Nehemiah. Some scholars identify this Hashabneiah with Hashabiah **9**. NEHEMIAH 9:5

HASHABNIAH
  See HASHABNEIAH

HASHBADANA
  See HASHBADDANAH

HASHBADDANA
  See HASHBADDANAH

HASHBADDANAH A prominent Levite in Jerusalem after the Exile, Hashbaddanah was one of the seven who stood at Ezra's left when Ezra gathered the population for a great national meeting to hear the Law. NEHEMIAH 8:4

HASHEM A proud father of several sons who were made members of "The Thirty," David's elite corps of guardsmen and fighters. I CHRONICLES 11:34

HASHUB See HASSHUB

HASHUBAH Son of the illustrious Zerubbabel, the leader who brought the first contingent of exiles home to Jerusalem from Babylon, Hashubah accompanied his family on the journey and resettled in Jerusalem. I CHRONICLES 3:20

HASHUM
1 One of those who was the head of a large family at the time of the Exile, Hashum returned to Jerusalem with Zerubbabel. After the wall was rebuilt, Hashum was one of those who joined Nehemiah in the signing of the covenant, promising to keep the Law. EZRA 2:19; 10:33; NEHEMIAH 7:22; 10:18
2 Another Hashum, this man, probably a Levite, was one of the outstanding men of Jerusalem, and was selected to stand with Ezra at the great national assembly when Ezra read the Law to the people in rebuilt Jerusalem after the Exile. NEHEMIAH 8:4

HASRAH See HARHAS

HASSENAAH The father of the men who rebuilt the Fish Gate in the wall of Jerusalem in Nehemiah's time, Hassenaah was probably the Hassenuah who was mentioned in the list of those from the tribe of Benjamin who resided in Jerusalem after the Exile. NEHEMIAH 3:3

HASSENUAH Probably the same man as the Hassenaah mentioned above, Hassenuah is named at the head of a family in the list of those from the tribe of Benjamin living in Jerusalem after the return from the Exile in Babylon. I CHRONICLES 9:7; NEHEMIAH 11:9

HASSHUB
1 A son of Pahath-moab, this Hasshub helped Nehemiah rebuild the wall of Jerusalem after the return from Exile in Babylon. He was recorded as working on the Tower of the Ovens. NEHEMIAH 3:11
2 Another of the same name who lived at the same time and also worked to repair Jerusalem, this Hasshub rebuilt the section of the city wall opposite his house. NEHEMIAH 3:23
3 Probably a different Hasshub, this man was a leading citizen and head of a family in Jerusalem who joined Nehemiah in signing the covenant to keep the Law. NEHEMAH 10:23
4 A Levite of the Merari branch of the tribe, this Hasshub was the father of Shemaiah, one of those who volunteered to settle in devastated Jerusalem when the exiles returned from Babylon. I CHRONICLES 9:14; NEHEMIAH 11:15

HASUPHA A Levite, Hasupha was the head of a family of Temple servants that returned from exile in Baby-

127

lon to Jerusalem with Zerubbabel. EZRA 2:43; NEHEMIAH 7:46

HASHUPHA See HASUPHA

HATACH See HATHACH

HATHACH An official of the Persian court appointed by King Ahasuerus to be a servant to Queen Esther, Hathach was instrumental in getting the news of Haman's plot to massacre the Jews to Esther. ESTHER 4

HATHATH One of the sons of Othniel, the judge of Israel, Hathath's name is one of the many in the lengthy genealogy of the tribe of Judah. I CHRONICLES 4:13

HATIPHA A Levite, Hatipha was the head of a family of Temple servants that returned from the Exile in Babylon to Jerusalem. EZRA 2:54; NEHEMIAH 7:56

HATITA A gate keeper or porter in the Temple, Hatita was the ancestor of a family group that went back to Jerusalem after the Exile in Babylon. EZRA 2:42; NEHEMIAH 7:45

HATTIL A slave or servant of Solomon's, Hattil was the ancestor of a family that resettled in Jerusalem after the Exile in Babylon. EZRA 2:57; NEHEMIAH 7:59

HATTUSH
1 A well-known Levite, this Hattush returned with Zerubbabel from the Exile in Babylon to Jerusalem. He was listed with other priests who joined Nehemiah in signing the covenant to keep the Law. NEHEMIAH 10:4; 12:2
2 A descendant of David and son of Schechaniah, this Hattush of royal blood was among the party of exiles that returned to Jerusalem with Ezra. I CHRONICLES 3:22; EZRA 8:2
3 Son of Hashabneiah, this Hattush was active in the rebuilding program after the Exile. He repaired the wall of Jerusalem opposite his house. NEHEMIAH 3:10

HAVILAH
1 A descendant of Noah through Noah's son, Ham, this Havilah was a son of Cush. To the ancients, Havilah was the founder of one of the oldest tribes on earth. GENESIS 10:7; I CHRONICLES 1:9
2 Another descendant of Noah, this Havilah traced his lineage through Noah's son, Shem. This Havilah's father was Joktan. As in the case of other early characters, Joktan and Havilah founded tribes inhabiting certain areas in the Arabian peninsula. GENESIS 10:29; I CHRONICLES 1:23

HAZAEL The ruler of Damascus who became the powerful and fearful king of Syria, Hazael shook all the nations in the ninth century B.C. by his victories. He came to power when sent by King Benhadad to Elisha to ask what Benhadad's chances of recovering from illness were. Seeing an opportunity to bring haughty, irreligious Israel to heel by being humbled by Syria, Elisha secretly anointed Hazael king. Hazael took the cue, murdered Benhadad, and embarked on a long period of raking Israel, Judah, and other kingdoms with a series of invasions. I KINGS 19; II KINGS 8—13; I CHRONICLES 22; AMOS 1:4

HAZAIAH A member of the tribe of Judah, Hazaiah was remembered as the ancestor of Maaseiah, a chief of a province who volunteered to live in Jerusalem after the return from the Exile in Babylon. NEHEMIAH 11:5

HAZELELPONI
See **HAZZELELPONI**

HAZIEL A Levite from the Gershom branch of the tribe, Haziel was a prominent member of the tribe at the time of Solomon. I CHRONICLES 23:9

HAZZELELPONI A daughter of Etam, Hazzelelponi was listed in the family tree of the tribe of Judah by the Chronicler. I CHRONICLES 4:3

HEBER
1 A member of the tribe of Asher, this Heber was a son of Beriah. He was the ancestor and founder of the strongest clan of his tribe, the Heberites. GENESIS 46:17; NUMBERS 26:45; I CHRONICLES 7:31, 32; LUKE 3:35
2 A Kenite blacksmith who married the Hebrew girl, Jael, the heroine who boldly killed Sisera, the cruel Amalakite, in her tent with a tent-peg. JUDGES 4:11—17; 5:24
3 A member of the tribe of Judah, this otherwise undistinguished man named Heber is carried in the rolls of his tribe as a son of Mered and the father of Soco. I CHRONICLES 4:18
4 One of the tribe of Benjamin, this Heber was one of Elpaal's sons. The Chronicler indicates that he was a pure-blooded Hebrew, as contrasted to others of the tribe that had some Moabite ancestry. I CHRONICLES 8:17

HEBRON
1 Levi's grandson and Kohath's third son, Hebron is a shadowy figure in early Hebrew history who gave his name to a clan known as Hebronites. EXODUS 6:18; NUMBERS 3:19; I CHRONICLES 6:2, 18; 23:12,19
2 One of Mareshah's sons and the father of Korah, this man named Hebron is listed in the genealogy of Caleb, son of Hezron, among the records of the tribe of Judah. I CHRONICLES 2:42, 43; 15:9

HEGAI One of the head servants in the household of the Persian despot, Ahasuerus, Hegai was a eunuch who supervised the royal harem. ESTHER 2

HEGE See **HEGAI**

HELAH One of the two wives of Asher, a man of the tribe of Judah, Helah was the mother of Tekoa. I CHRONICLES 4:5,7

HELDAI
1 A captain of the sanctuary guards in David's time, this Heldai was appointed to head the detachment for the twelfth monthly tour of duty. He was also known in some records by the names Heled and Heleb. I CHRONICLES 27:15
2 A deeply respected man, this Heldai and a group of companions came back from Exile in Babylon to Jerusalem bringing a morale-booster in the form of gold and silver to the exiles that had returned earlier with Zerubbabel. Heldai's gifts were fashioned into a crown for the high priest, Joshua, and kept in the rebuilt Tem-

ple as a memorial to Heldai. ZECHARIAH 6:10,14

HELEB The same person as Heldai 1, Heleb was the name of an officer in David's service. II SAMUEL 23:29

HELED Another name of Heldai 1, this spelling was the version used by the Chronicler. I CHRONICLES 11:30

HELEK A descendant of Joseph's son, Manasseh, through Gilead, Helek was a powerful early chieftain in the tribe of Manasseh, and the founder of the clan known as Helekites. NUMBERS 26:30; JOSHUA 17:2

HELEM

1 A member of the tribe of Asher, Helem is the name of a clan chieftain who fathered four sons who are also in the tribal roll. I CHRONICLES 7:35

2 The misspelling for Heldai 2 in some translations of ZECHARIAH 6:14

HELEZ

1 A hero in David's army, this Helez hailed from Ephraim and was known as "the Pelonite." He was such an outstanding fighter in the days when David was an outlaw that he was later made a member of the exclusive corps called "The Thirty." Later he was commissioned a captain in David's sanctuary guards, and appointed to take charge of the seventh monthly group on duty. II SAMUEL 23:26; I CHRONICLES 11:27; 27:10

2 A member of the tribe of Judah with illustrious ancestry (Hezron, Jerahmeel, and others), this Helez was a son of Azariah 8, and a clan chieftain named in the tribe's family tree. I CHRONICLES 2:39

HELI The father of Joseph, who was the husband of Mary the mother of Jesus, Heli was also believed to be an uncle of Mary. LUKE 3:23

HELKAI A Levite in Jerusalem a generation after the return from Exile under Zerubbabel, Helkai served as a priest representing the Meraioth family. NEHEMIAH 12:15

HELON A member of the tribe of Zebulun, Helon was the father of Eliab, who represented his tribe in Moses' census of the tribes in the wilderness. NUMBERS 1:9; 2:7; 7:24, 29; 10:16

HEMAM See HOMAM

HEMAN

1 For the HEMAN mentioned in GENESIS 36:22, see HOMAM.

2 Renowned for his wisdom, this Heman was a son of Zerah and was remembered fondly through the ages as one of the four wisest men of the ancient tribes who were surpassed only by Solomon. I KINGS 4:31; I CHRONICLES 2:6

3 The famous musician in David's sanctuary, this Heman won a name for himself and his family by his singing and playing. Heman was a grandson of the prophet Samuel. He was honored by being picked to serve as one of three leading Levites in the impressive worship services, and became the head of a guild of vocalists and instrumentalists. I CHRONICLES 6:33; 15:17, 19; 16:41—42; 25:1—6; II CHRONICLES 5:12; 29:14; 35:15; PSALM 88, title

HEMDAN The son of Dishon, an

Edomite desert chief, Hemdan is listed in the Genesis 36:26 genealogy, but somehow his name in the parallel list of the family names in I Chronicles 1:41 got changed to HAMRAN. The correct form is Hemdan. GENESIS 36:26; I CHRONICLES 1:41

HEPHER
1 The son of Gilead of the tribe of Manasseh, Hepher was the chieftain in the tribe whose family became known as Hepherites. His granddaughters—who had no brothers—were the first to raise the question of property rights for women without brothers. NUMBERS 26:32; 27:1; JOSHUA 17:2,3
2 A member of the tribe of Judah, this Hepher was the son of Asshur, and stepbrother of Tekoa, according to the Chronicler's genealogy of the tribe. I CHRONICLES 4:6
3 A Mecherathite, this Hepher was renowned as a daring and fierce warrior, and won a place as a member of "The Thirty," David's elite corps of guardsmen-heroes. I CHRONICLES 11:36

HEPHZIBAH The wife of King Hezekiah of Judah, Hephzibah was the mother of the infamous King Manasseh. II KINGS 21:1

HERESH One of the first to return to Jerusalem from the Exile in Babylon, Heresh was the head of a family and a prominent person on the staff of the Temple servers. I CHRONICLES 9:15

HERMAS A man to whom Paul sent his greeting in the letter to the Romans, Hermas is simply a name to us today. So many slaves were called Hermas that it is impossible to single out anyone as the Hermas to whom Paul was alluding. Tradition says that Hermas became the bishop of Philipololis. The non-canonical writing known was "The Shepherd of Hermas" could not possibly have been written before the second century, and has relationship to the Hermas of Paul's day. ROMANS 16:14

HERMES Another whom Paul remembered fondly in his list of those whom he wanted to send special greetings, Hermes (not to be confused with Hermas) was probably also a Greek Christian living in Rome. The name was as common as John is to us, and there is nothing more known about Hermes. Legend holds that he was one of the Seventy, and served as Bishop of Salona. ROMANS 16:14

HERMOGENES An early Christian who was one of Paul's helpers, Hermogenes was one of those in Asia who deserted Paul during the apostle's final imprisonment. Paul did not elaborate to Timothy on exactly what Hermogenes had done, but implied that Hermogenes was afraid that he might be considered guilty by his association with the apostle. Phygelus and all the others from Asia joined Hermogenes' defection. II TIMOTHY 1:15

HEROD
1 First of those of the name "Herod" in the Bible is Herod the Great, the talented, unscrupulous tyrant who was appointed to rule Judea by the Romans, Anthony, Octavius,

and the Senate following his father's assassination. Herod used craft and brutality to consolidate his position, and was unquestioned dictator from 37 B.C. to 4 B.C. Incredibly suspicious and jealous, Herod even executed members of his immediate family, including his wife, Mariamne, and favorite son and heir, Antipater, as well as all the male babies in Bethlehem, according to Matthew. In spite of his cruelty and lust, he promoted an elaborate building program throughout Judea, including the Temple at Jerusalem, which impressed Jesus' disciples on their visit to the capital. In his old age, Herod turned into a maniac, his peculiarities probably accentuated by the unnamed horrid disease that caused him an agonizing death. MATTHEW 2; LUKE 1:5

2 Son of Herod the Great, this Herod was called Herod Antipas or Herod the Tetrarch, and was given the territory of Galilee and Perea to rule. A builder like his father, Herod Antipas built Tiberius along the Sea of Galilee for his capital. His notorious affair and marriage with Herodias was his eventual downfall. It affronted his devout subjects, and enraged his first wife, daughter of Aretas, the Nabatean king. Later, Aretas marched against Antipas and humiliatingly defeated him. When John the Baptist thundered against the marriage, Antipas slapped him into prison and later, at Herodias' insistence, beheaded him. Rumor had it that Jesus was next on Antipas' list, and Jesus temporarily left Antipas' territory. Interestingly, the only person that Jesus ever called by the name of an animal was Herod Antipas, whom Jesus dubbed "that fox." Antipas met Jesus briefly: Jesus was sent for an informal hearing when Pilate tried to get Jesus off his hands early in Jesus' trial. Herod Antipas' ambitious wife prodded him to demand the title of king from the emperor, but the emperor had had enough of this reckless playboy-tyrant. Herod Antipas was removed in 39 A.D. and banished to Gaul, where he died. MATTHEW 14; MARK 6, 8; LUKE 3, 8, 9, 13, 23; ACTS 13:27; 13:1

3 Grandson of Herod the Great **1**, this Herod was better known as Herod Agrippa I. Sent to Rome to be raised after his father, Aristobulus, was killed by grandfather Herod the Great, Herod Agrippa I was raised as a Roman dandy. The Emperor Caligula in 37 A.D. finally appointed him king of the territories that tetrarchs Philip and Lysanias had ruled. When his nephew, Herod Antipas, demanded the title of king also, Herod Agrippa I brought charges which caused Herod Antipas' dismissal, and Herod Agrippa I was awarded Antipas' tetrarchy as well. As inheritor of his grandfather's kingdom, Herod Agrippa I agreeably surprised his Jewish subjects by living as a strict Jew and protecting all Jewish customs. However, he ruthlessly persecuted the early church, arresting Peter and John and beheading James, brother of John. He was stricken in office in 44 A.D. of an unnamed disease, and died within a few days. ACTS 12, 23

HERODIAS Granddaughter of Herod the Great and daughter of Aristobulus, Herodias was an ambitious princess whose incestuous marriages shocked the Jews and brought her husbands to ruin. The ancient historian, Josephus, reports that she was wed first to a step-brother (by whom she had Salome), next to an uncle, Philip, and finally to Herod Antipas. Furious that her scandals had provoked some biting sermons by John the Baptist, Herodias hounded her husband to clap John into jail, and eventually engineered John's execution one night after Salome, her daughter, danced for Antipas. Her ambition proved to be her husband's undoing. Jealous that newly-crowned Herod Agrippa I was called "king" and her husband was not, Herodias prodded Antipas to demand the same title. Agrippa got to the emperor first, however, and brought charges which led to Antipas' dismissal and exile. Herodias went with her husband, and stayed with him until his death in Gaul. MATTHEW 14; MARK 6; LUKE 3:19

HERODION Herodian was one of the Christians living in Rome whom Paul greeted by name in his letter to the church at Rome. Paul calls Herodion "my kinsman," meaning probably that Herodion was also born and raised as a Jew. There is no way of knowing what connection Herodion had with the family of kings named Herod. Perhaps he was a servant or an ex-slave in the service of one of the royal family, and had been taken to Rome on one of the many sojourns in the capital by members of the families of the Herods. ROMANS 16:11

HESED The father of one of the commissary officials who had to gather provisions for one month annually for Solomon's enormous entourage. I KINGS 4:10

HETH Canaan's second son, Heth was an ancient chieftain whose family-clan became known as Hittites. These Hittites were inhabitants of the mountains in Judah, and later became adversaries of the Israelites. Abraham dealt with some of Heth's family when he bought the cave of Machpelah. GENESIS 10:15; 23:7; 25:10

HEZEKI See HIZKI

HEZEKIAH

1 The famous reform-minded king of Judah, Hezekiah succeeded his weak, pagan-minded father, Ahaz, and successfully led his country through the frightening days when Assyria was sweeping over the world in the eighth century B.C. In spite of the fact that Samaria, capital of the northern kingdom of Israel, had fallen, and that many in Judah advised surrendering to the Assyrian host or entering into dangerous foreign alliances, Hezekiah heeded the prophet Isaiah's advice and stood fast. The Assyrian King Sennacherib's seige of Jerusalem suddenly and miraculously ended when a plague decimated the Assyrian army. Even today, visitors to Jerusalem can see Hezekiah's tunnel, the conduit through the rock which brought water into the city during the seige—one of the many projects initiated by the energetic king. After the glorious deliverance from seige, Hezekiah launched a long-needed reform of morals and religion in the nation. The Canaanite cults were stamped out and their shrines destroyed, and worship was centralized in Jerusalem. His reign was long remembered as one of the peaks in the history of Judah. Unfortunately, his son and successor, Manasseh did not continue his work. II KINGS 16, 18—21; I CHRONICLES 3:13; 4:41; II CHRONICLES 28:27, 29—33; PROVERBS 25:1; ISAIAH 1:1; 36—39; JEREMIAH 15:4; 26:18,19; HOSEA 1:1; MICAH 1:1

2 Possibly the same as **1**, a man named Hezekiah is named as one of the ancestors of the prophet Zephaniah. ZEPHANIAH 1:1

3 The head of a large family who lived at the time of the Exile in Babylon, this Hezekiah brought his family back to Jerusalem to live when the exiles were permitted to return. EZRA 2:16; NEHEMIAH 7:21

HEZION The grandfather of King Benhadad of Syria, whom Asa, king of Judah, persuaded to make an alliance against King Baasha of Israel. I KINGS 15:18

HEZIR
1 A priest in David's sanctuary, Hezir was appointed to head the seventeenth division of priests in the rotating groups which served in David's house of worship. I CHRONICLES 24:15
2 A layman who was the head of a household of returned exiles, this Hezir lived in Jerusalem in Hezekiah's time, and joined with other responsible citizens in signing the covenant with Nehemiah promising to keep the Law. NEHEMIAH 10:20

HEZRAI See HEZRO

HEZRO A staunch fighting man from Carmel in the mountains of northern Judah, Hezro won imperishable fame by being elected to "The Thirty," David's elite corps of heroes. This also meant that Hezro was a commissioned officer in David's army. II SAMUEL 23:35; I CHRONICLES 11:37

HEZRON
1 Reuben's son and Jacob's grandson, this Hezron was a tribal chieftain whose offspring became known as the clan of Hezronites. Like others in early Bible times, nothing is known of the man beyond his name and family connection. GENESIS 46:9; EXODUS 6:14; NUMBERS 26:6; I CHRONICLES 5:3
2 Another by the same name and living at nearly the same time as **1**, this Hezron was a grandson of Judah and a son of Perez, and, according to the genealogies of both Matthew and Luke, an ancestor of Jesus. Hezron's distinguished descendants also included King David. GENESIS 46:12; NUMBERS 26:21; RUTH 4:18—19; I CHRONICLES 2:5, 9, 18, 21, 24, 25; 4:1

HIDDAI A staunch supporter and fearless fighter for David, Hiddai, from Gaash in Ephraim's mountains, was rewarded with a place in David's Hall of Fame for his best soldiers, "The Thirty," and a commission in David's royal army. He was also known by the name Hurai. II SAMUEL 23:30; I CHRONICLES 11:32

HIEL The builder from Bethel who in King Ahab's time was sent to rebuild Jericho, Hiel carried out the horrible custom then prevalent in pagan circles of sacrificing two of his children to guarantee success in carrying out a building program. Hiel thus fulfilled the curse of Joshua centuries earlier on the one who would rebuild Jericho. I KINGS 16:34

HILKIAH
1 Remembered because of his son's position in the royal court of King Hezekiah, this Hilkiah was father of Eliakim, superintendent of Hezekiah's household. II KINGS 18:18, 26, 37
2 The best known of those who were named Hilkiah, this individual was the high priest at the time of Josiah's reign in Judah. Hilkiah was the man who discovered the document we know as Deuteronomy in the Temple while the building was undergoing renovation in 621 B.C. The scroll was rushed to Josiah, and triggered an intensive reform in the worship and morals of the nation. No one knows how the scroll was hidden in the Temple for so many years, or who wrote it. II KINGS 22:4—14; 23:4, 24; I CHRONICLES 6:13; 9:11; II CHRONICLES 34:9—22; EZRA 7:1; JEREMIAH 29:3
3 A member of an ancient and respected family of priests in the village of Anathoth, this Hilkiah was best remembered through his famous son, Jeremiah, the great prophet of Judah in its last days. JEREMIAH 1:1
4 A near-contemporary of 3, this

Hilkiah was also the father of a better-known son, Gemariah, one of the men sent to carry Zedekiah's message from Jerusalem to King Nebuchadnezzar in Babylon. JEREMIAH 29:3
5 A Levite of the Merari branch of the tribe, this Hilkiah was the ancestor of Ethan, one of the prominent musicians in David's sanctuary. I CHRONICLES 6:45
6 Another Levite, also of the Merari side of the tribe, this Hilkiah was one of Hosah's sons who were appointed gatekeepers in David's sanctuary. I CHRONICLES 26:11
7 A well-known priest in Jerusalem after the return from Exile in Babylon, this Hilkiah took a prominent part in the solemn national gathering when Ezra assembled the population and read the Law to all the people. NEHEMIAH 8:4

HILLEL A man who lived in Ephraim shortly after the conquest of Canaan by the tribes of Israel, Hillel was the father of Abdon, one of the judges of Israel. JUDGES 12:13, 15

HINNOM The man whose name was attached to the deep ravine outside Jerusalem called the Valley of Hinnom, which was the place of human sacrifice and the garbage dump of the royal city, Hinnom is only a name in the Bible. Nothing whatsoever is known about the man, not even his parentage or tribe. JOSHUA 15:8; 18:16; II KINGS 23:10; II CHRONICLES 28:3; 33:6; NEHEMIAH 11:30; JEREMIAH 7: 31, 32; 19:2, 6; 32:35

HIRAH The Adullamite shepherd

who was the great friend and sheep-herding partner of Judah, son of Jacob, Hirah served as Judah's messenger to pay Tamar after she had tricked Judah into using her as a prostitute. GENESIS 38

HIRAM

1 The wealthy and powerful king of Tyre, and the good friend of David and Solomon, King Hiram provided skilled workmen and quantities of cedar planks for building the Temple in Jerusalem. In return, Solomon sent Hiram great quantities of wheat, barley, oil, and wine. Hiram and Solomon also joined forces on a highly profitable shipping venture, and brought back fortunes in gold, silver, ivory, apes, and peacocks. Although his other achievements are not mentioned in the Bible, we know that Hiram was a great builder and effective ruler, fortifying and beautifying Tyre and campaigning against Cyprus, one of his restless provinces. II SAMUEL 5:11; I KINGS 5:1—18; 9:11—27; 10: 11—22; I CHRONICLES 14:1; II CHRONICLES 2:13; 8:2—18; 9:10, 21

2 The creative genius who designed and fashioned the furnishings in Solomon's Temple, this Hiram was the son of a woman from the tribe of Naphtali and a brassworker from Tyre. He was sent by King Hiram (no relation) to work for Solomon, and in addition to serving as architect for the great structure, this artistic Phoenician cast the two great brass pillars, the enormous basin known as "the molten sea" and the elaborate base supporting it, the twelve oxen, and all the exquisite utensils used in the Temple services. Hiram was skilled at working with metals, wood, stone, precious stones, and fabrics. I KINGS 7

HIZKI A member of the tribe of Benjamin, Hizki was listed in the roll of other chieftains and important men of his illustrious tribe. In some translations his name is "Hezeki." I CHRONICLES 8:17

HIZKIAH

1 For the Hizkiah in Zephaniah 1:1, see HEZEKIAH **2**.
2 Another Hizkiah, this man was a descendant of David and Solomon through his father, Neariah. His name is listed in the genealogy of the royal family. I CHRONICLES 3:23

HOBAB One of Moses' in-laws, Hobab was the man whom God used to guide the children of Egypt through the wilderness after they fled from Egypt. Hobab was a member of that early monotheistic tribe known as the Kenites. His exact relationship to Moses is unclear. Some scholars are inclined to identify Hobab as Jethro, Moses' father-in-law; others, as a brother of Zipporah, Moses' wife. For generations the Israelites remembered Hobab's kindness, and because of him Saul once even spared his tribe from slaughter. I SAMUEL 15:6; NUMBERS 10:29; JUDGES 4:11

HOBAIAH See HABAIAH

HOD A member of the tribe of Asher, Hod was a powerful clan chieftain whose name was carried in the roll of great men through the long history of the tribe. I CHRONICLES 7:37

HODAIAH See **HODAVIAH**

HODAVIAH

1 One of David's descendants, this Hodaviah was remembered as a member of the royal family of Judah many generations after David. I CHRONICLES 3:24

2 A head man of a strong clan in the tribe of Manasseh, this Hodaviah and his fellow tribesmen settled on the east side of the Jordan River after the tribes had wandered in the wilderness. Like others in the tribe, Hodaviah adopted the cults of those he conquered, and deserted God. The Assyrian King Pul invaded and carried away Hodaviah's entire clan. I CHRONICLES 5:24

3 A Benjaminite, this Hodaviah was remembered as an ancestor of Sallu, one of the first to return from Exile in Babylon to Jerusalem. I CHRONICLES 9:7

4 A Levite, this Hodaviah was the head of one of the families which came from Exile in Babylon to Jerusalem. Hodaviah was active in Nehemiah's Jerusalem, and was also called Hodevah. EZRA 2:40; NEHEMIAH 7:43

HODESH The wife of Shaharaim, a member of the tribe of Benjamin, Hodesh bore Shaharaim several sons after he dismissed two other wives. I CHRONICLES 8:9

HODEVAH See **HODAVIAH 4**

HODIAH

1 A head of a family in the tribe of Judah, this Hodiah is listed in the tribal genealogy by the Chronicler. The King James Version erroneously translates this section to identify Hodiah as the wife of a man named Ezra. Actually Hodiah was a man, an ancestor of Keilah the Garmite and Eshtemoa the Maacathite. I CHRONICLES 4:19

2 A well-known Levite leader in Jerusalem after the Exile, this Hodiah was selected as one of the teachers to instruct the people in the meaning of the Law when Ezra assembled the population in a great national gathering. Not only was Hodiah given a prominent role in these impressive services, but he was one of those mentioned by name who joined Nehemiah in signing the covenant to keep the Law. NEHEMIAH 8:7, 9:5; 10:10

3 Another Levite named Hodiah who lived in Jerusalem in Nehemiah's time, this man also participated in Nehemiah's service of covenant signing following the rebuilding of the walls after the Exile. NEHEMIAH 10:13

4 Since Hodiah was a common name in the period following the Exile, this Hodiah was one of three by that name who signed the covenant with Nehemiah. NEHEMIAH 10:18

HODIJAH See **HODIAH**

HOGLAH One of the family of daughters of Zelophehad, a member of the tribe of Manasseh at the time of Moses, Hoglah and her sisters pointed out to Moses and the other leaders how unjust the existing inheritance rules were for women like themselves who had no brothers. The protest carried; the rules were changed to allow property to pass to daughters when there were no male heirs. Hoglah and her sisters were later married to others in the tribe of Manasseh. NUMBERS 26:33; 27:1; 36:11; JOSHUA 17:3

HOHAM One of the original inhabitants of Canaan when Joshua and the Israelites invaded the land, Hoham was a ruler of the fierce tribe of Amorites at Hebron. Hoham persuaded four other chiefs to join him in ganging up on the tribe of Gibeon, with whom Joshua had an alliance. Joshua came to Gibeon's aid, smashed the oppressors, and killed Hoham and the other four kings in the cave of Makkedah. JOSHUA 10

HOMAM Also written as Hemam, Homam was a descendant of Seir, one of the ancient Edomites. GENESIS 36: 22; I CHRONICLES 1:39

HOPHNI The greedy, unprincipled sons of the pious Eli, Hophni and his brother Phinehas were a scandal to the priesthood. They persisted in taking advantage of their position as priests by grabbing exorbitant amounts of the sacrifices to the Lord, and causing some women to compromise themselves. When their priest-father Eli failed to curb them, an unknown prophet and the boy-prophet Samuel predicted a grisly downfall to Eli's house. As predicted, Hophni and Phinehas died in battle. I SAMUEL 1, 2, 4

HORAM The king of the city-state of Gezer in southwestern Canaan at the time of Joshua's conquest, Horam made the mistake of coming to the aid of Lachish when Joshua was beseiging that city. Joshua turned and subdued Horam's force and killed Horam. JOSHUA 10

HORI
1 One of the sons of Seir, the ancient desert chieftain in Edom, Hori was another clan head of the early Edomites and the ancestor of the Horites. GENESIS 36:22; I CHRONICLES 1:39
2 A member of the tribe of Simeon, this Hori was remembered as the father of Shaphat, one of the twelve spies sent by Moses to reconnoiter the Promised Land. NUMBERS 13:5

HOSAH A Levite, Hosah was selected by David to be one of the first doorkeepers in the sanctuary when the Ark of the Covenant was brought up to Jerusalem shortly after David became king. I CHRONICLES 16:38; 26:10, 11, 16

HOSEA This is the prophet who, in blunt but poignant imagery, described Israel's unfaithfulness to God in terms of a wife's infidelity to her husband. Hosea spoke from personal experience: he had gone through the anguish of taking back his own wayward wife, Gomer. Living in the northern kingdom of Israel during the chaotic days following King Jeroboam II's death, Hosea was sensitive to the situation in his society, and perceptive to the conditions in the government. His writings cover the period from approximately 745 to 735 B.C. His book is a somewhat disjointed monologue in which he indicts his countrymen for deserting the Lord. To underscore God's displeasure with Israel, Hosea named his children "Jezreel," "Loruhamah," and "Loammi," which meant "God soweth," "not pitied," and "not my people." At the same time, however, Hosea showed a depth of tenderness as he described the patience and forgiveness of God. Hosea is called the first of the "minor prophets." HOSEA

HOSHAIAH

1 One who had an active part in Nehemiah's impressive service dedicating the rebuilt walls of Jerusalem after the return from Exile, this Hoshaiah headed one part of the procession of leading men from Judah at the ceremonies. NEHEMIAH 12:32

2 The father of Azariah **24** or Jezeniah, a leading citizen of Jerusalem at the time the Babylonians began to deport the Jews. JEREMIAH 42:1; 43:2

HOSHAMA One of the royal family of Judah and a descendant of David, Hoshama was a son of Jeconiah, the next-to-last king of Judah. I CHRONICLES 3:18

HOSHEA

1 Hoshea was the name that Joshua, the son of Nun, originally carried until Moses renamed him "Joshua." See JOSHUA, SON OF NUN. DEUTERONOMY 32:44, some translations; NUMBERS 13:8

2 The chief officer of the tribe of Ephraim, this Hoshea was a well-known leader in David's time. I CHRONICLES 27:20

3 The last king of the northern kingdom, Israel, this Hoshea tried to steer a perilous course between the two mightiest nations of his day, Assyria and Egypt. Hoshea began as a satellite ruler under Assyria, but secretly

arranged for Egyptian protection and withheld his tribute to Assyria. Sargon of Assyria then beseiged Hoshea's Samaria, but the Egyptian promises of help were never kept. Samaria fell in 722 B.C., and the ten tribes of the northern kingdom were deported. Hoshea was probably either horribly tortured or carried off as a captive. II KINGS 15:30; 17:1—6; 18:1—10

4 A leading citizen in Jerusalem after the Exile, this Hoshea was one of those who is mentioned by name as joining with Nehemiah in the signing of the covenant to keep the Law. NEHEMIAH 10:23

HOTHAM

1 A member of the tribe of Asher, this Hotham, a son of Heber, was a powerful warrior and clan chief who was remembered in the tribal roll-call of heroes. I CHRONICLES 7:32

2 This second Hotham, an Aroeite, was the proud father of Shama and Jehiel, two of David's greatest fighters and members of "The Thirty," David's elite corps. I CHRONICLES 11:44

HOTHIR A Levite of the Kohath group, Hothir was one of the famous musician Heman's sons. Like his father, Hothir had a prominent part in David's worship services. Hothir headed the twenty-first group of those who served in the sanctuary. He and his family were renowned for their skill as composers, vocalists, and instrumentalists. I CHRONICLES 25:4

HUL Great-grandson of Noah, grandson of Shem, and son of Aram, Hul was the ancestor of an Aramean tribe

that took his name. GENESIS 10:23; I
CHRONICLES 1:17

HULDAH Renowned as a prophetess,
Huldah was the wife of Shallum,
keeper of the wardrobe in Jerusalem
in King Josiah's reign in Judah. When
the scroll containing what we call
Deuteronomy was found by the high
priest Hilkiah during the repairs of
the Temple and taken to King Josiah,
Josiah immediately had it sent to Huldah. Huldah returned the book with
the dire warning that God's day of
reckoning for the nation was fast approaching, but would be temporarily
delayed because of King Josiah's piety
and desire for reform. II KINGS 22:14;
II CHRONICLES 34:22

HUPHAM See HUPPIM

HUPPAH A priest in David's time,
Huppah played a prominent role in
David's worship services. He was appointed to be in charge of the thir-
teenth course of the groups serving in
the sanctuary. I CHRONICLES 24:13

HUPPIM A strongman and family
chieftain in the tribe of Benjamin,
Huppim was the founder of the clan
called Huphamites. Some of the genealogies list him as a son of Benjamin
(Genesis and Numbers), the Chronicler lists Huppim as a grandson of
Benjamin. GENESIS 46:21; NUMBERS
26:39; I CHRONICLES 7:12, 15

HUR
1 The companion of Moses and
Aaron, Hur helped prop up Moses'
arms during the fierce battle with the
Amalekites so that the Israelites could

win. He stayed with Aaron when
Moses ascended Mount Sinai and was
deputized by Moses to join with
Aaron in hearing problems and settling disputes during Moses' absence.
Jewish tradition holds that Hur was
the husband of Moses' sister Miriam.
EXODUS 17:10, 12; 24:14
2 Perhaps the same as 1, this Hur,
the grandfather of Bezalel, was the
designer of the tabernacle, the place
of worship of the tribes under Moses.
This Hur's family lineage made him
a member of the tribe of Judah, and
a descendant of Hezron and Perez.
EXODUS 31:2; 35:30; 38:22; I CHRON-
ICLES 2:19, 20, 50; 4:1—4; II CHRON-
ICLES 1:5
3 This Hur was a Midianite chief
who consented to go along with
Balaam's treachery against Moses and
the Israelites. Moses sent Phinehas
and an armed horde to punish the
Midianites. Hur, four other Midianite
chiefs, and Balaam were all slaughtered, and the Israelites seized great
quantities of loot. NUMBERS 31:8;
JOSHUA 13:21
4 Another Hur, this one was remembered as the father of one of Solomon's twelve commissary officers who
had to procure supplies for the royal
staff. I KINGS 4:8
5 This Hur was also the father of a
son better known than himself—Rephaiah, ruler of half of Jerusalem in Nehemiah's time. NEHEMIAH 3:9

HURAI See HIDDAI

HURAM
1 Benjamin's grandson and Bela's
son, this Huram was a clan chieftain

in the tribe of Benjamin whose name was carried in the tribal roll call years later. I CHRONICLES 8:5

2 The name used by some translators for both Hiram, the king of Tyre, and Hiram the artist-designer of the Temple. See HIRAM

HURI A member of the tribe of Gad, Huri was the father of Abihail and grandfather of a group of Gadite chieftains who settled their families in the territory east of the Jordan. I CHRONICLES 5:14

HUSHAH Grandson of Hur **2** and son of Ezer, Hushah was an early member of the tribe of Judah. He was identified with a place in Judah that is now forgotten. I CHRONICLES 4:4

HUSHAI A staunch friend of David, Hushai agreed to feign support of Absalom when Absalom plotted against David. Hushai not only kept David informed of the developments of the revolt, but successfully foiled the well-laid plans of Ahithrophel, Absalom's advisor. An Archite from the country west of Bethel north of Jerusalem, Hushai was also remembered as the father of Baana, one of Solomon's twelve commissary officers responsible for procuring supplies for Solomon's staff and household for one month each year. II SAMUEL 15:32, 37; 16:16 —18; 17:5—15; I KINGS 4:16; I CHRONICLES 27:33

HUSHAM A desert chief from the land of Temani, Husham became one of the early kings of Edom, a powerful state in the Arabian peninsula. GENESIS 36:34—35; I CHRONICLES 1:45 —46

HUSHIM
1 Also known in Numbers as Shuhum, Hushim was one of the sons of Dan, Jacob's son. Hushim was an ancient clan patriarch whose family became known as Shuhamites, a large clan within the tribe of Dan. GENESIS 46:23; NUMBERS 26:42

2 An early clan headman of the tribe of Benjamin, this man named Hushim was a grandson of Benjamin and son of Aher. Like others living in the early days of Hebrew history, nothing is known of the man besides his name and family relationship. I CHRONICLES 7:12

3 Married to Shaharaim, this woman named Hushim was one of the two wives of Shaharaim whom he sent away. She is recorded as the mother of two sons, Abitub and Elpaal, and is one of few women to be listed by name in the tribal genealogies. I CHRONICLES 8:8, 11

HYMENAEUS A heretic who was undermining the faith of many of Paul's weaker converts, Hymenaeus was mentioned twice by Paul in his correspondence to Timothy. Hymenaeus had slipped into the error of teaching that the resurrection was simply an allegorical way of saying that one's soul was released from sin. This distortion of the gospel was appealing to many who had gnostic leanings or Greek backgrounds. Paul recognized the dangers of Hymenaeus' claims and finally excommunicated him. I TIMO- THY 1:20; II TIMOTHY 2:17

I

IBHAR One of David's sons, Ibhar was born in Jerusalem after David's coronation as king of the united kingdom. Although his mother was a wife of David and not a concubine—which meant that Ibhar was reckoned a legal son and heir of David—and although his name was carried in all three lists of the royal family, Ibhar never distinguished himself in any way except that he had David as one of his parents. II SAMUEL 5:15; I CHRONICLES 3:6; 14:5

IBNEIAH A member of the tribe of Benjamin, Ibneiah was one of the first to bring his family back from Babylon after the Exile and settle in Jerusalem. He was head man of the tribe of Benjamin at the time. I CHRONICLES 9:8

IBNIJAH A Benjaminite, Ibnijah was remembered as the ancestor of one of the first brave families to venture back

from Babylon to Jerusalem after the Exile. I CHRONICLES 9:8

IBRI A Levite of the Merari branch of the tribe, Ibri was one of the servants in the sanctuary of the Lord in David's Jerusalem. I CHRONICLES 24:27

IBSAM Grandson of Issachar and son of Tola, Ibsam was a mighty warrior and head of a well-known clan in the tribe of Issachar. I CHRONICLES 7:2

IBZAN A native of the Bethlehem of Zebulun (north of Nazareth), Ibzan succeeded Jephthah as a judge of Israel, and served as strongman and rallying point for the confederation of tribes for seven years, until his death. Ibzan was exceptionally affluent, and was able to afford enough wives to produce thirty sons and thirty daughters. The only other mention of his exploits was that he managed to

143

ICHABOD

marry off each of the sixty children. JUDGES 12:8, 10

ICHABOD The grandson of old Eli, the pious priest, and the son of Phinehas, the unprincipled priest, Ichabod was born amidst the tragedies of his father's death in battle and his grandfather's death from a fall caused by the shock of the news. Ichabod's mother, stunned by the double tragedy, named the newborn infant Ichabod ("inglorious"), and collapsed in death herself. I SAMUEL 4:21; 14:3

IDBASH An early clan chieftain in the tribe of Judah, Idbash was listed in the tribal genealogy as a son of Etam. I CHRONICLES 4:3

IDDO
1 This Iddo was the father of Abinadab, commissary officer for King Solomon's household and staff for one month each year. I KINGS 4:14
2 A Levite of the Gershom side of the family, this Iddo is included in the tribe's genealogy. In the parallel list of names in I CHRONICLES 6:43, Iddo is listed as Adaiah. I CHRONICLES 6:21
3 This Iddo was the son of Zechariah, and served the chief of the tribe of Manasseh in the area east of the Jordan at the time of David. I CHRONICLES 27:21
4 The prophet-seer who pronounced God's displeasure against four kings —Solomon, Rehoboam, Jeroboam, and Abijah—this Iddo was respected as a knowledgeable source of information on the ways of God and men. The Chronicler counted on Iddo for historical information on the reigns of

many of the tenth century B.C. rulers, and referred to him by name. II CHRONICLES 9:29; 12:15; 13:22
5 The grandfather of the prophet Zechariah (or his father, according to Ezra), this Iddo was a Levite who might have been related to Iddo **2**. EZRA 5:1; 6:14; ZECHARIAH 1:1, 7
6 Perhaps the most famous by the name, this Iddo was a Levite who gathered a large number of temple servants in Babylon and trained them at a place called Casiphia. Iddo's school provided Ezra with a large number of the recruits of Levite singers and servants for the worship in the Temple in Jerusalem. EZRA 8:17
7 One of those who had married outside the faith during the Exile in Babylon, this Iddo agreed to leave his non-Jewish wife during Ezra's rigid reform. EZRA 10:43
8 A priest who returned from Babylon with Zerubbabel after the Exile, this Iddo served in Jerusalem in Nehemiah's time. NEHEMIAH 12:4, 16

IEDDIAS See IZZIAH

IEZER See ABIEZER 1

IGAL
1 The son of Joseph of the tribe of Issachar, this Igal was one of the twelve spies sent by Moses to reconnoiter the Promised Land. Igal was one of the ten who were cowed by the size and strength of the inhabitants of Canaan and brought back the majority report advising Moses and the Israelites not to attempt an invasion. NUMBERS 13:7
2 The son of Nathan of Zobah, this Igal was one of David's boldest, toughest fighters. He won imperishable fame

144

by being elected to "The Thirty," David's elite corps of guards, and held a commission in David's army. He was also known by the name Joel. II SAMUEL 23:36; I CHRONICLES 11:38

3 This Igal was a son of Shemaiah, a descendant of David. As a member of the royal family he was remembered in the genealogy of the house of David. I CHRONICLES 3:23

IGEAL See IGAL 3

IGDALIAH A priest, Igdaliah was remembered as the father of Hanan, the man in whose Temple chambers the prophet Jeremiah met with the Rechabites. JEREMIAH 35:4

IKKESH A man in Tekoa, Ikkesh was best known as the father of Ira, the great man of valor in David's army and one of "The Thirty," David's top fighters. II SAMUEL 23:26; I CHRONICLES 11:28; 27:9

ILAI The Ahohite who also was known as Zalmon, Ilai was such an outstanding soldier in David's service that he was elected to "The Thirty," David's honor roll of greatest heroes, and given a commission in David's army. II SAMUEL 23:28; I CHRONICLES 11:29

IMLA The father of Micaiah, who was the prophet consulted by Kings Ahab and Jehoshaphat before their ill-fated campaign. Micaiah refused to echo the words of the false prophets who had encouraged the kings. I KINGS 22:8, 9; II CHRONICLES 18:7, 8

IMLAH See IMLA

IMMER

1 The head of a famous family of priests in David's time, Immer, like his sons and descendants, took a prominent and responsible position in the worship services in Jerusalem. Immer picked the lot to head the sixteenth contingent of priests in the sanctuary. I CHRONICLES 9:12; 24:14; EZRA 2:37; 10:20; NEHEMIAH 3:29; 7:40; 11:13

2 Another priest, this Immer lived at the time of the prophet Jeremiah. His son, the priest Pashhur, was guilty of assaulting Jeremiah and imprisoning the prophet in stocks. JEREMIAH 20:1

IMNA A member of the tribe of Asher, Imna was a son of Helem, a clan chieftain and strong warrior in the tribe. I CHRONICLES 7:35

IMNAH

1 The oldest son of Asher, Imnah, also known as Jumnah, was a powerful chief in the tribe and was remembered in the tribal genealogy. GENESIS 46:17; NUMBERS 26:44; I CHRONICLES 7:30

2 A Levite, this Imnah was the father of Kore, a prominent official in Jerusalem in Nehemiah's time. II CHRONICLES 31:14

IMRAH A member of the tribe of Asher, Imrah was a son of Zophah, and an early clan chieftain in the tribe. I CHRONICLES 7:36

IMRI

1 A member of the tribe of Judah, this Imri was remembered as the ancestor of Uthai, one of the first from his tribe to return from Exile in Babylon to Jerusalem. I CHRONICLES 9:4

2 This Imri was remembered because he was the father of Zaccur, who was active in helping Nehemiah get the walls of Jerusalem rebuilt after the Exile. NEHEMIAH 3:2

IOB A son of Issachar and a grandson of Jacob, Iob was one of Jacob's family who emigrated from Canaan during the famine when Joseph invited his father and brothers to move to Egypt. In Numbers 26:24 and I Chronicles 7:1; Iob is called Jashub. GENESIS 46:13

IPHDEIAH One of Shashak's sons in the tribe of Benjamin, Iphdeiah was a chief of the tribe who settled in Jerusalem. I CHRONICLES 8:25

IR A grandson of Benjamin and a son of Bela, Ir was listed in the tribal genealogy as the father of Shuppim and Huppim. I CHRONICLES 7:7, 12

IRA

1 A priest in David's time, Ira was a "Jairite," that is, from Jair, a clan in Gilead. "Ira, the Jairite" is called "David's priest" in the one list of important court officials in which his name appears. Strangely, his name is omitted in parallel lists in other places, such as II Samuel 8:15 and I Chronicles 18:14. II SAMUEL 20:26

2 The "Ithrite," this second Ira hailed from Jattir, in the hills of Judah, and was such a staunch fighter that he won undying fame by being elected to "The Thirty," David's elite corps of guardsmen. He also was a commissioned officer in David's royal army. II SAMUEL 23:38; I CHRONICLES 11:40

3 This Ira was a son of Ikkesh of Tekoa, and was also one of the great heroes in David's service, and a member of that indomitable band called "The Thirty." Later, as an officer in David's service, this Ira commanded the guard in the sixth course of service for one month in the sanctuary. II SAMUEL 23:26; I CHRONICLES 11:28; 27:9

IRAD Enoch's son and Cain's grandson, Irad is listed in the genealogy of the first descendants of Adam. GENESIS 4:18

IRAM A descendant of Esau, Iram was an early chief of the tribe of Edom, a powerful desert people in the area east of the Jordan. GENESIS 36:43; I CHRONICLES 1:54

IRI See IR

IRIJAH A suspicious sentry on duty in Jerusalem during the siege by the Babylonians, Irijah arrested Jeremiah on trumped-up charges of trying to desert to the enemy. In spite of Jeremiah's denials, the prophet was severely beaten and thrown into prison because of Irijah's unsupported accusation. JEREMIAH 37:13—14

IRNAHASH An early member of the tribe of Judah, Irnahash is a name in the tribal genealogy. Some scholars suspect that Irnahash may have actually been the name of a town in ancient times. I CHRONICLES 4:12

IRU The oldest son of Caleb, son of Jephunneh, the great spy for Moses in Canaan, Iru was remembered in the roll call of famous men in the tribe of Judah. I CHRONICLES 4:15

ISAAC Born so late in the lives of Abraham and Sarah that they laughed in disbelief when God promised them a son, Isaac's name in Hebrew means "laughter." As a boy, he accompanied his father to Mount Moriah in obedience to the Divine command to Abraham to sacrifice his son. Isaac's life was spared when God intervened at the last minute. Isaac accepted Rebekah as his wife after a trusted family servant brought her from Abraham's home country to be his bride, and became the father of the twins, Esau and Jacob. During a famine he took his family to Gerar. Isaac became wealthy during his sojourn with the Philistines, and they became jealous. After a series of incidents over water rights, Isaac and the Philistines reached an understanding: Isaac and his herds stayed in the area of Beersheba. Isaac in his old age, blind and feeble, was tricked by Jacob into bestowing his final blessing on Jacob, the younger son, instead of Esau, the older and Isaac's favorite. Isaac was buried with his parents at Hebron. GENESIS 17—35

ISAIAH The greatest of the Old Testament prophets, Isaiah's long career spanned the turbulent period from King Uzziah's death, about 740 B.C. to the end of Sennacherib's seige of Jerusalem in 701 B.C. or later. Judah's kings, especially timid and shaky Ahaz, persistently wanted to rely on political deals with foreign powers, usually Assyria or Egypt, to save the country. Luxury and vice were ruining the nation's vitality. With insight into the workings of God in history, Isaiah stated that Assyria was God's instrument to chastise His disobedient people. At the same time, he announced that there were limits to what any earthly power, even Assyria and other superpowers, could do. A remnant, Isaiah predicted, would be spared to continue God's work, and, ultimately, a God-sent Deliverer would inaugurate a new age of justice and peace. Judah's gravest crisis came in Hezekiah's reign. Strong pressures were brought to bear on the king to join the revolt against Assyria and enter into intrigue with Egypt. Isaiah, master statesman and spokesman for God, pointed out the politicians' lack of trust in God, their desire to break an agreement with Assyria, and their foolishness in relying on Egypt. Isaiah's advice was ignored. Inevitably, Assyria invaded. Isaiah alone was calm. Miraculously, a plague decimated the Assyrian armies and Jerusalem was spared. Apart from the information that Isaiah was the son of Amoz (*not* the prophet, Amos), lived in Jerusalem, married a prophetess, and had two children (named, significantly, "a remnant shall return" and "the spoil speeds, the prey hastes"), and always managed to get the ear of the reigning king, we know nothing of Isaiah's personal life. His public career closed after Sennacherib's ill-fated seige of Jerusalem. II KINGS 19—20; II CHRONICLES 26:22; 32:20, 32; ISAIAH 1—39

ISCAH Abraham's niece, Iscah was the daughter of Abraham's brother, Haran, and is mentioned in the family tree of Terah, Abraham's father. GENESIS 11:29

ISHBAH A member of the tribe of Judah, Ishbah was remembered as one who had the blood of Egyptian royalty in his veins through his father Mered's marriage to the Egyptian princess, Bithiah. Ishbah's paternal grandfather was the famous spy, Caleb, and his name is carried in Caleb's genealogy. I CHRONICLES 4:17

ISHBAK One of Abraham's sons by his concubine, Keturah, Ishbak was a desert chieftain and founder of a desert clan. GENESIS 25:2; I CHRONICLES 1:32

ISHBI-BENOB A gigantic Philistine, Ishbi-benob was one of the four enormous warriors who were eventually killed in battles by David's men. Ishbi-benob nearly succeeded in killing the weary David before Abishai intervened and saved David's life. II SAMUEL 21:16

ISHBOSHETH The sole surviving son of King Saul after Saul's defeat and death on Mount Gilboa, Ishbosheth was proclaimed king of Israel by his able general, Abner. Ishbosheth, however, made the mistake of accusing his chief supporter, Abner, of disloyalty after discovering Abner in an affair with Saul's concubine, Rizpah. Abner went over to David; Ishbosheth was shortly afterward murdered by two of his officers. The house of Saul came to an end, and David was invited to rule the ten northern tribes as well as the two southern ones. II SAMUEL 2—4

ISHHOD See ISHOD

ISHI
1 A member of the tribe of Judah through the branch of the family headed by Jerahmeel, Hezron's son, this first named Ishi is listed in the Chronicler's record of the tribe as one of the clan heads. I CHRONICLES 2:31
2 Another chief in the tribe of Judah, this Ishi was descended from the great spy for Moses in Canaan, Caleb, the son of Jephunneh. I CHRONICLES 4:20
3 A member of the tribe of Simeon at the time of the conquest of Canaan, this Ishi was the father of some stalwart sons who led a contingent of their tribesmen against the Amalekites at Mount Seir and settled in the area. I CHRONICLES 4:42
4 A chief in the tribe of Manasseh, this Ishi was an arrogant leader who settled in the area east of the Jordan, then forsook his loyalty to the Lord who had brought him and the others out of Egypt and the wilderness to the Promised Land. Ishi, like many others, dabbled in the cults of the Canaanites. The Chronicler reminds all readers that the Assyrians were God's agents of punishment, and carried Ishi's clan to captivity. I CHRONICLES 5:24

ISHIAH See ISSHIAH

ISHIJAH See ISSHIAH OR ISSHIJAH

ISHMA A son of Etam in the tribe of Judah, Ishma was a descendant of Caleb, son of Hur in the tribal rolls. I CHRONICLES 4:3

ISHMAEL

1 Abraham's son by Hagar, Sarah's Egyptian servant girl, Ishmael was taken as an infant into the desert when his mother fled from Abraham's camp after animosity flared between Hagar and Sarah. The Lord heard Hagar's cry for help and gave Ishmael his name ("I have heard"); He then ordered Hagar to return to Sarah and Abraham. Ishmael was circumcised with the rest of the males in Abraham's camp, and was a favorite of Abraham because he was Abraham's oldest son. Jealousy between Hagar and Sarah drove Hagar and Ishmael into the wilderness a second time. Again God intervened and saved the boy from death by thirst, promising Hagar that Ishmael would be the father of twelve princes. Ishmael grew up to be a wild nomad roaming the desert stretches in southern Canaan, famous as an archer. He married an Egyptian girl and fathered twelve sons who, as promised, became the ancestors of powerful tribes in the area east of the Arabah. When Abraham died, Ishmael returned to help Isaac bury their father. GENESIS 16, 17, 25, 28; 36:3; I CHRONICLES 1:28—31

2 One of Saul's descendants, this Ishmael was one of Azel's six sons, and is carried in the roll of prominent men in the tribe of Benjamin. I CHRONICLES 8:38; 9:44

3 This Ishmael was the father of Zebadiah, King Jehoshaphat's number one man in the kingdom of Judah. II CHRONICLES 19:11

4 A son of Jehohanan, this Ishmael was one of the army officers who brought off the coup that deposed the ruthless queen mother Athaliah, and put Joash on the throne in the ninth century B.C. II CHRONICLES 23:1

5 One of Passhur's sons, this Ishmael was a priest who married outside the faith during the Exile in Babylon. At Ezra's bidding, he put away his foreign wife and promised to observe the Law rigidly. EZRA 10:22

6 A descendant of David and a member of the royal house of Judah, this Ishmael was a ruthless superpatriot who commanded a body of Jewish irregulars after the fall of Jerusalem in 586 B.C. Fanatically opposed to anyone who cooperated in any way with the Babylonians, Ishmael murdered Gedaliah, the Babylonian-appointed ruler, and took over Mizpeh. Shortly after, he compounded his crimes by senselessly butchering seventy religious pilgrims whom he had tricked into coming to Mizpeh. The Jewish leaders, knowing what the reaction would be in Babylon to Ishmael's bloody exploits, moved swiftly to cut him down. Ishmael, however, escaped to join the Ammonites. The prophet, Jeremiah, was one of Ishmael's many prisoners for a time. Ishmael's orgy of murder brought swift reprisals upon all the Jews left in Palestine by the Babylonians. A vast contingent of Jews was taken captive to Babylon shortly after Ishmael's escape. II KINGS 25:23—25; JEREMIAH 40—41

ISHMAIAH

1 The chief of the tribe of Zebulun in David's time, Ishmaiah was mentioned in the records of David's census and the list of leaders in his kingdom. Ishmaiah was recorded as the son of one named Obadiah. I CHRON-ICLES 27:19

2 One of the greatest warriors of the entire Bible, Ishmaiah, a native of Gibeon, began his career as a member of Saul's army. He was a crack marksman with either his right or left hand, and an expert with both the bow and the sling. Ishmaiah, like many others of his kinsmen, grew disillusioned with Saul as Saul grew increasingly psychotic, and finally joined David at Ziglag. Ishmaiah's exploits as a fearless fighter not only won him a place in "The Thirty," David's elite corps of all-time heroes, but also recognition as a leader of that valiant band. I CHRONICLES 12:4

ISHMERAI One of the sons of Elpaal in the tribe of Benjamin, Ishmerai was a chieftain in the tribe as well as a descendant of Benjamin. I CHRONICLES 8:18

ISHOD Related through his mother, Hammolecheth, to Manasseh, one of the twelve tribes' founders, Ishod enjoyed considerable power in the tribe of Manasseh. His uncle, Gilead, the tribe's chief, was a grandson of Manasseh. Ishod and the others of his tribe settled east of the Jordan. I CHRONICLES 7:18

ISHPAH One of the tribe of Benjamin, Ishpah was a son of Beriah, and a leader and chieftain in the tribe. His name was carried in the roll of tribal notables by the Chronicler. I CHRONICLES 8:16

ISHPAN One of Shashak's sons in the tribe of Benjamin, Ishpan was a clan chieftain in the tribe by virtue of his descent from Benjamin. I CHRONICLES 8:22

ISHUA See ISHVAH

ISHUAI See ISHVI

ISHUI See ISHVI

ISHVAH Asher's second son, Ishvah was a clan head and a powerful warrior who was remembered as one of the heroes of the tribe of Asher. GENESIS 46:17; I CHRONICLES 7:30

ISHVI

1 Asher's third son, Ishvi was another strong chieftain in the tribe of Asher. His family became known as the Ishvites in the tribe. GENESIS 46:17; NUMBERS 26:44; I CHRONICLES 7:30

2 This Ishvi was one of Saul's sons by his wife Ahinoam. Ishvi's full blood-brother, Jonathan, was the better known of this group of Saul's sons. I SAMUEL 14:49

ISMACHIAH A Levite official during the reign of King Hezekiah, Ismachiah was appointed as one of the assistants in the receiving department of the Temple treasury. The position was one of deep responsibility as well as high privilege. II CHRONICLES 31:13

ISMAIAH See ISHMAIAH 2

ISPAH See ISHPAH

ISRAEL See JACOB

ISSACHAR

1 The ninth son of Jacob, his fifth by Leah, Issachar was the head of one of the twelve families that became known as the tribes of Israel. Little personal data is available on Issachar besides the records of his birth and his children. Like others of his time, he was undoubtedly a nomad desert sheik. When his offspring, the tribe of Issachar, came into Canaan, they were assigned the fertile plain of Esdraelon in southern Galilee. GENESIS 30:18; 35:23; 46:13; 49:14; EXODUS 1:3; I CHRONICLES 2:1; 7:1

2 A Levite who was a son of Obededom, this Issachar was a gatekeeper in David's sanctuary by virtue of his relationship through his father as a Levite of the Korah side of the tribe. I CHRONICLES 26:5

ISSHIAH

1 The youngest of five sons of Izrahiah, this Isshiah was a great-great-grandson of Issachar, and a powerful chief of the tribe in David's time. I CHRONICLES 7:3

2 A valiant fighter, this Isshiah was one of the clan of Korah who decided to throw in his lot with David during the time David was hounded as an outlaw by Saul. Isshiah and the others who joined David at Ziglag were doughty warriors, and helped turn the tide in David's favor. I CHRONICLES 12:6

3 A Levite in David's time, this Isshiah, as a son of Uzziel, was a leader in the Kohath branch of the tribe, and served in David's sanctuary under another Levite named Micah. I CHRONICLES 23:20; 24:25

4 Another Levite, this Isshiah was a son of Rehabiah. He lived in David's time, and is mentioned by name as the head of a family. He, too, served in the sanctuary. I CHRONICLES 24:21

5 For the name given in some translations of Ezra 10:31, see ISSHIJAH.

ISSHIJAH One of the sons of Harim who married outside the faith during the Exile in Babylon, Isshijah finally obeyed Ezra's strict orders and put aside his non-Jewish wife. EZRA 10:31

ISUAH See ISHVAH

ISUI See ISHVI

ITHAI One of David's mightiest soldiers and most famous heroes, Ithai won deathless fame as a member of "The Thirty," David's roll of outstanding fighters, and won a commission as an officer in David's army. Ithai was a member of the tribe of Benjamin, which meant that as a kinsman of Saul, David's adversary, Ithai might originally have been a supporter of Saul. I CHRONICLES 11:31; II SAMUEL 23:29

ITHAMAR Aaron's youngest son by Elisheba, Ithamar and his two brothers, Nadab and Abihu, were appointed priests by Moses at the same time that Aaron was appointed. After Nadab and Abihu died from dabbling in strange cults, Ithamar was responsible for the tabernacle during the wilderness wanderings. In succeeding generations Ithamar's descendants played key parts in Israel's history as guardians of the Ark, high priests, and priests in the Temple. EXODUS 6:23; 28:1; 38:21; LEVITICUS 10:6, 16; NUMBERS 3:2, 4; 4:28, 33; 7:8; 26:60; I CHRONICLES 6:3; 24:1—6

ITHIEL

1 A Benjaminite, this Ithiel was the ancestor of Sallu, who volunteered to live in Jerusalem after the Exile in Babylon. NEHEMIAH 11:7

2 An unknown person, this Ithiel was the name of one of those to whom Agur delivered his wise sayings in the Book of Proverbs. PROVERBS 30:1

ITHMAH One of the tribe of Moab, and thus originally an outsider among those descended from the twelve tribes of Israel, Ithmah became a trusted insider by his bravery and prowess as one of David's greatest warriors. He is listed among "The Thirty," David's elite corps, and was an officer in the royal army. I CHRONICLES 11:46

ITHRA David's brother-in-law through his marriage to David's sister Abigail, Ithra was also known as Jether, the Ishmaelite. Ithra or Jether was best remembered as the father of Amasa, one of the restless young army men who joined David's son, Absalom, in the ill-fated revolt. II SAMUEL 17:25; I KINGS 2:5, 32; I CHRONICLES 2:17

ITHRAN

1 A son of Dishon and a grandson of Seir, this Ithran was an early Horite desert chieftain whose clan took his name and became known as Thranites. GENESIS 36:26; I CHRONICLES 1:41

2 The son of Zophah of the tribe of Asher, this Ithran was a chieftain, and was remembered in the tribe's roll of strong leaders. I CHRONICLES 7:37

ITHREAM David's sixth son by Eglah (also known as Michal), Ithream lost his mother at the time of his birth in Hebron, lived under the shadow of more illustrious brothers, and is remembered only as an obscure name in the genealogy of the royal family of Judah. II SAMUEL 3:5; I CHRONICLES 3:3

ITTAI

1 Although he was from Gath, and a Philistine, Ittai was one of David's most loyal supporters and ablest generals. Probably expelled from Gath along with his followers, Ittai joined David shortly before Absalom's revolt broke out. At the time when David's outlook was bleakest, Ittai insisted on staying with David, in spite of David's warnings that the cause seemed hopeless. Ittai was one of three generals who quashed Absalom and saved David's kingdom. II SAMUEL 15:19—22; 18:2—12

2 For the Ittai mentioned in II SAMUEL 23:29, see ITHAI.

IZHAR Grandson of Levi and son of Kohath, Izhar was an early clan chieftain whose family was known as Izharites. Izhar is named in the various genealogies of the tribe of Levi. EXODUS 6:18—21; NUMBERS 3:19; 16:1; I CHRONICLES 6:2, 18, 38; 23:12, 18

IZLIAH One of Elpaal's sons in the tribe of Benjamin, Izliah was a clan head in the tribe who lived in Jerusalem at the time of David's census. I CHRONICLES 8:18

IZRAHIAH Great grandson of Issachar, Izrahiah was the son of Uzzi and the father of five stalwart sons who, with Izrahiah, were leaders in the tribe of Issachar. I CHRONICLES 7:3

IZRI Also known by the name of Zeri, Izri was an important Levite in David's time who presided over one of the sanctuary choirs because of his musical ability. I CHRONICLES 25:11

IZZIAH One of the many in the family of Parosh who married outside the faith during the Exile in Babylon, Izziah agreed to Ezra's rigid insistence that the faith be kept pure, and separated from his non-Jewish wife. EZRA 10:25

J

JAAKAN One of Ezer's sons, and one of Seir the Horite's grandsons, Jaakan was an ancient desert chief in the area of Edom. His descendants made up a tribe or clan carrying his name. GENESIS 36:27 (where he was called AKAN.) DEUTERONOMY 10:6; I CHRONICLES 1:42

JAAKOBAH A powerful chief in the tribe of Simeon, Jaakobah, together with other chieftains from that tribe, expelled the Canaanites dwelling in the rich pasturelands of Gedor and took over their lands. I CHRONICLES 4:36

JAALA One of Solomon's servants, Jaala was best remembered as the ancestor of a family which returned from Exile in Babylon to Jerusalem with Zerubbabel. EZRA 2:56; NEHEMIAH 7:58

JAALAH See JAALA

JAALAM One of Esau's sons by his marriage to Aholibamah, Jaalam was born in Canaan before his father emigrated to Edom. He was a desert chieftain in Edom, and was remembered in the genealogies of Esau's family. GENESIS 36:5, 14, 18; I CHRONICLES 1:35

JAANAI A powerful chieftain in the tribe of Gad, Jaanai lived at Bashan in the area east of the Jordan. I CHRONICLES 5:12

JAARESHIAH See JARESIAH

JAARE-OREGIM A man of Bethlehem, Jaare-oregim was the father of the bold warrior Elhanan, who dared to take on one of the Philistine giants in man-to-man combat, and mortally wounded him. II SAMUEL 21:19

JAASAU See JAASU

JAASIEL

1 The Mezobaite hero who was one of David's most valiant soldiers, Jaasiel won imperishable glory by being

155

chosen as one of "The Thirty," David's corps of top fighters. He also held a commission in the royal army. I CHRONICLES 11:47

2 A son of Abner, this Jaasiel was appointed as the chief of the tribe of Benjamin in David's time. He was a cousin of Saul. Some scholars think that Jaasiel **1** and **2** may be the same person. I CHRONICLES 27:21

JAASU One of the many sons of Bani who married non-Jewish brides during the Exile, Jaasu agreed to accept Ezra's rigid orders to separate himself from his mate and thus keep the faith pure. EZRA 10:37

JAAZANIAH

1 A Maacathite from Judea who was a leading patriot at the time of the Babylonian conquest, Jaazaniah pledged his allegiance to the Babylonian-appointed king, Gedeliah, and after Gedeliah's foul murder by Ishmael, pursued Ishmael. Frightened because Ishmael got away, Jaazaniah and other leaders—against the advice of the prophet Jeremiah—decided to seek refuge in Egypt. II KINGS 25:23; JEREMIAH 40:8; 41:1—42:22

2 A Rechabite, this Jaazaniah carefully remained true to his tribal vow not to touch wine. Jaazaniah's faithfulness to his ancestors' command was used by the prophet Jeremiah as an example to the entire nation of Judah at a time when most were disobedient to God's commands. JEREMIAH 34:3ff

3 One of those seen in a vision by the prophet Ezekiel, this Jaazaniah, son of Shaphan, was singled out as the instigator of idolatrous revelry

among seventy of the elders in the sacred precincts of the Temple in Jerusalem. EZEKIEL 8:11

4 Another by the same name who was glimpsed in a vision by the prophet Ezekiel, this Jaazaniah, the son of Azur, was condemned by Ezekiel for his evil counsel to the leaders of the land. EZEKIEL 11:1

JAAZIAH A Levite of the Merari branch of the tribe, Jaaziah was a chieftain who was listed in the tribal roll in David's time. I CHRONICLES 24: 26, 27

JAAZIEL A Levite who was also known as Aziel, Jaaziel was a gifted musician who was appointed to be one of the instrumentalists in the worship services in David's sanctuary. I CHRONICLES 15:18, 20

JABAL One of the sons of Lamech by his marriage to Adah, Jabal was the first man to take up the life of a nomad tent-dweller and herdsman. GENESIS 4:20

JABESH The father of Shallum, the conspirator who killed King Zechariah of Israel after a brief but wicked six-month reign, and ruled in his stead. II KINGS 15:10—14

JABEZ A member of the tribe of Judah, this clan head was respected for being "more honorable than his brothers," and being deeply dependent on the Lord. I CHRONICLES 4:9—10

JABIN

1 A King of Hazor in northern Palestine, Jabin organized a powerful con-

156

federation of tribes to attack the Israelites and throw them out of Canaan. Instead, Jabin suffered a humiliating defeat when Joshua suddenly attacked first. JOSHUA 11:1—15

2 Another king of Hazor by the same name, this powerful ruler and his general, Sisera, oppressed the tribes of Israel for twenty years. Deborah the prophetess and Barak the judge finally rallied the dispirited Israelites, raised an army, and defeated Jabin so conclusively that the northern Canaanites never bothered Israel again. JUDGES 4; PSALM 83:9

JACAN A member of the tribe of Gad, Jacan was one of the tribe's chieftains, and lived in Bashan east of the Jordan when the Israelites settled there after the years of wandering. I CHRONICLES 5:13

JACHAN See JACAN

JACHIN

1 One of Simeon's sons, Jachin left Palestine with his family and the other descendants of Jacob during the famine when Joseph invited them to move to Egypt. Jachin became a clan head in the tribe of Simeon. GENESIS 46:10; EXODUS 6:15; NUMBERS 26:1—12

2 A dedicated priest, this Jachin was one of those who returned from the Exile in Babylon to ravaged Jerusalem, and worked hard under Nehemiah to rebuild the Temple. I CHRONICLES 9:10; NEHEMIAH 11:10

3 A priest in the time of David, this Jachin proudly traced his ancestry back to Aaron. He served as the head of the twenty-first contingent of the priests appointed to serve in worship services in David's sanctuary. I CHRONICLES 24:17

JACOB The younger twin brother of Esau and the son of Isaac and Rebekah, Jacob—known later as Israel —was the father of the twelve sons whose families became known as the tribes of Israel. Jacob's name means "supplanter," and literally from his birth onward he tried to supplant his older brother, Esau. He first took advantage of Esau's hunger and made Esau trade his birthright for a tasty stew; later he deceived his aging, blind father into granting him the father's final blessing, which Isaac had meant for Esau. Esau, of course, was furious at his scheming brother, and Jacob fled for his life. During his flight, at Bethel one night, Jacob experienced the vision of God's angels descending on steps to him—his first awareness of God's plans for him. He proceeded to Haran, the ancestral home, and lived with his uncle Laban for twenty years. There Jacob met his match in craftiness; Laban by a series of ruses married off both his daughters, Leah and Rachel, to Jacob, and kept Jacob in servitude longer than they had agreed on. Finally outwitting Laban, Jacob, with the many members of his family and his large flocks, journeyed toward Palestine. Jacob, however, remembered his past injustices to Esau and worried about the reception Esau would give him. After dividing his following into two forces, so that one at least might escape if Esau attacked, Jacob found himself alone. That night he dreamed that he wrestled with an angel. For the first time Jacob found himself conquered; he refused, however, to let his antagonist go until he received a blessing. Jacob was not only given a blessing but a new name, "Israel," meaning that he was one who had persevered with the Lord. Shortly after, Jacob met his brother Esau, and was relieved to find that Esau held no grudge. Jacob then settled down to the quiet life of a family patriarch in Palestine, which was interrupted in his old age by a severe famine and the emigration to Egypt at the urging of his son, Joseph. Jacob died in Egypt, but was buried in the family burial cave at Hebron. GENESIS 25, 27 —37, 42, 45—50

JADA A member of the tribe of Judah who traced his ancestry back through Jerahmeel and Hezron, Jada was a clan chieftain mentioned in the tribal chronicles. I CHRONICLES 2:28, 32

JADAU See JADDAI

JADDAI One of the sons of Nebo who had married outside the faith during the Exile in Babylon, Jaddai agreed to Ezra's strict interpretation of the Law whereby marriages with outsiders were nullified. EZRA 10:43

JADDUA

1 A Levite who lived in Jerusalem after the return from Exile in Babylon, this Jaddua was a leading citizen who joined Nehemiah in the impressive service signing the covenant promising to keep the Law. NEHEMIAH 10:21

2 A descendant of Jeshua, the high priest in Jerusalem at the time the Jews returned from Exile in Babylon, this Jaddua was also a high priest and a contemporary of Darius III, the Persian. NEHEMIAH 12:11, 22

JADON A Meronothite, Jadon returned to the ruins of Jerusalem after the Exile in Babylon, and was one of the dogged group that worked to rebuild the walls under Nehemiah's guidance and inspiration. NEHEMIAH 3:7

JAEL A brave but treacherous woman, Jael skewered Sisera, general of the Canaanite forces, with a tent peg after the uprising of the tribes of Israel against the Canaanites led by Barak and Deborah. Jael was the wife of Heber the Kenite. When Sisera escaped after a battle, Jael showed hospitality to the exhausted Sisera, then smashed his skull. JUDGES 4:17—22; 5:6, 24

JAHATH

1 One of Judah's grandsons, this Jahath was an early clan chieftain of the tribe whose name was remembered in the tribal annals. I CHRONICLES 4:2

2 One of Levi's great-grandsons, this Jahath was descended from Gershom, and was an ancestor of Asaph, a leading Levite musician in the time of David. I CHRONICLES 6:20, 43

3 Another Levite descended from Gershom, Levi's son, this Jahath was the head of the Shimei family of Levites and an important man in David's sanctuary. I CHRONICLES 23:10, 11

4 Still another Levite, this Jahath was part of the Kohath branch of the tribe. He also was a leader in the sanctuary worship services in David's time. I CHRONICLES 24:22

5 A Levite of the Merari side of the tribe, this man named Jahath lived in the reign of King Josiah. When the high priest Hilkiah secured funds to renovate the Temple, Jahath was one of the supervisors of repairs. During this renovation program, the scroll which we call Deuteronomy was discovered. II CHRONICLES 34:12

JAHAZIAH See JAHZERAH

JAHAZIEL

1 One of the group of Benjaminites who grew so disenchanted with Saul that they joined David at Ziglag, this Jahaziel was a famous warrior. Like his cohorts, he could fight with either hand and was an expert marksman with both the sling and the bow. I CHRONICLES 12:4

2 A priest, this Jahaziel took part in the festivities when the Ark of the Covenant was brought to Jerusalem shortly after David's coronation as king of the twelve tribes and the selection of Jerusalem as his national capital. I CHRONICLES 16:6

3 A Levite who could point with pride to an illustrious family tree, this Jahaziel was listed in David's census among the distinguished families of the kingdom. I CHRONICLES 23:19, 24:23

4 The fearless Levite who averted panic when the Moabites and Ammo-nites swarmed across the borders of King Jehoshaphat's Judah, this Jahaziel encouraged the frightened king and people, and spurred them to a stunning victory. II CHRONICLES 20

5 A member of a clan known as the Sons of Zattu, this Jahaziel was the father of Shecaniah, one of those who returned with Ezra from Exile in Babylon to Jerusalem. EZRA 8:5

JAHDAI A member of the tribe of Judah whose name appears in the lengthy family genealogy kept by the Chronicler, Jahdai was the father of six sons and a descendant of Caleb, the great spy. I CHRONICLES 2:47

JAHDIEL A powerful chieftain of a clan in the tribe of Manasseh, Jahdiel was one of those who forsook the Lord after the conquest of the tribes, and adopted the local cults. The Chronicler points out that God's judgment on Jahdiel came when the Assyrians eventually carried away the tribe of Manasseh into captivity. I CHRONICLES 5:24

JAHDO A member of the tribe of Gad and a tribal chief who was the son of Buz, Jahdo was remembered as one of the illustrious early leaders of the tribe. I CHRONICLES 5:14

JAHLEEL Zebulun's youngest son, Jahleel was one of the descendants of Jacob who journeyed to Egypt when famine threatened Canaan. Later, Jahleel's family, known as Jahleelites, left Egypt with Moses. GENESIS 46:14; NUMBERS 26:26

JAHMAI

JAHMAI Issachar's grandson and Tola's son, Jahmai was remembered as a fierce fighter and respected clan chieftain in the tribe of Issachar. I CHRONICLES 7:2

JAHZEEL Jacob's grandson and Naphtali's oldest son, Jahzeel was an early chief in the tribe of Naphtali. Like others of Jacob's sons' families, Jahzeel emigrated to Egypt at Joseph's urging when a famine seared Canaan. His family, which came to be known as Jahzeelites, joined Moses in the Exodus. GENESIS 46:24; NUMBERS 26:48; I CHRONICLES 7:13

JAHZIEL See JAHZEEL

JAHZERAH A priest, Jahzerah was the ancestor of Maasai, one of the priests who returned after the Exile to live in Jerusalem. I CHRONICLES 9: 12

JAIR
1 A bold leader in the tribe of Manasseh at the time of the conquest of Canaan by tribes of Israel, Jair was assigned by Moses to capture the strong towns in the area east of the Jordan river. NUMBERS 32:41; DEUTERONOMY 3:14; JOSHUA 13:30; I KINGS 4:13; I CHRONICLES 2:22
2 One of the strong men, known as judges, who dispensed justice and rallied the tribes of Israel in an emergency, this Jair hailed from Gilead, and fathered thirty sons who assisted their father in governing the villages of Gilead. He succeeded Tola, and ruled as a judge for twenty-three years. JUDGES 10:3—5
3 The father of Elhanan, this Jair was also known as JAARE-ORIGIM (which see). II SAMUEL 21:19; I CHRONICLES 20:5
4 A member of the tribe of Benjamin, this Jair was remembered as the father of Mordecai, the saintly Jew who raised his young cousin Esther. ESTHER 2:5

JAIRUS The president of the Jewish synagogue and an important man in the large Galilee fishing town of Capernaum, Jairus came to Jesus as the distraught parent of a dying daughter. Jesus compassionately came to Jairus' house and found that the girl had already been pronounced dead. The tender scene where Jesus raised Jairus' little girl is recorded by the writers of the Synoptic Gospels. MATTHEW 9: 8ff; MARK 5:21ff; LUKE 8:40ff

JAKAN See AKAN

JAKEH The father of Agur, the author of the sayings in the thirtieth chapter of Proverbs. PROVERBS 30:1

JAKIM
1 One of Shimei's sons of the tribe of Benjamin, Jakim was a chieftain of a family in the tribe and a respected leader, according to the tribal records. I CHRONICLES 8:19
2 A priest at the time of David who could trace his family back to Aaron, this Jakim was appointed to head the twelfth contingent of sanctuary priests. I CHRONICLES 24:12

JALAM See JAALAM

JALON A member of the tribe of Judah who was one of Ezrah's sons, Jalon was a descendant of the great spy, Caleb, and a chieftain in the tribe of Judah whose name was carried in the tribal genealogy. I CHRONICLES 4:17

JAMBRES The name tradition gave to one of the magicians in the court of Pharaoh when Moses and Aaron appeared to beg release for the Israelites, Jambres is named in the Bible only by Paul. Jambres and Jannes, who were not mentioned by name in the accounts in Exodus, opposed Moses and matched Aaron miracle for miracle before the pharaoh. II TIMOTHY 3:8

JAMES
1 The son of Zebedee and the brother of John, this James was one of the twelve disciples of Jesus. He was fishing when called by Jesus to be a fisherman of men, but probably had known Jesus for some time. Many scholars think that James' mother, Salome, was a sister of Mary, Jesus' mother (see Matthew 27:56, Mark 15:40, and John 19:25), which would have meant that James and Jesus were cousins. James was one of the "inner circle" of the Twelve, is mentioned in all lists among the first four, and accompanied Jesus on occasions when Jesus invited a few to be with Him, such as at the transfiguration, the raising of Jairus' daughter, and Gethsemane. Jesus nicknamed James and his brother, John, "Sons of Thunder." James' stormy temper was shown when he demanded that Jesus send down fire to destroy an inhospitable Samaritan village, and when he imperiously asked Jesus for the places of prominence in the Kingdom. James, in spite of his weaknesses, was such an effective witness to the Resurrected Lord that he was the first of the Twelve to die for the gospel. Herod Agrippa, about 44 A.D., had James put to death by the sword. Although he is the patron saint of Spain, and although there are fanciful traditions galore about James' miracles before and after his death in that country, it is highly improbable that James ever left Palestine. MATTHEW 4:21; 10:2; 17:1; MARK 1:19,29; 3:17; 5:37; 9:2; 10:35,41; 13:3; 14:33; LUKE 5:10; 6:14; 8:51; 9:28, 54; ACTS 1:13; 12:2; GALATIANS 2:12

2 The son of Alphaeus, this James was also one of the Twelve. Since both this James and Matthew are called "the son of Alphaeus," it is likely that they were brothers. James, son of Alphaeus, heads the third group of the Twelve in the lists by the gospel writers. Nothing else is known of this quiet man who was chosen by Jesus to be one of His closest friends. Some scholars identify James, son of Alphaeus, with the man known as James "the Little" or "the Less," but the evidence seems to indicate that the two were separate individuals. MATTHEW 10:3; MARK 3:18; LUKE 6:15; ACTS 1:13

3 James "the Less" or James "the Little" was a third man carrying the name James who is mentioned in the New Testament. (Strangely, no one is named James in the Old.) His mother was a devout woman named Mary, who was undoubtedly the wife of Clopas, the mother of another son, Jo-

seph, and one of the four women present at the crucifixion. James' nickname "the Less" could mean either James "the Short" or James "the Younger"; the original Greek word could be interpreted either way. Although some scholars maintain that this James and the one who was the son of Alphaeus were the same person, this is unlikely, since Mark apparently distinguished between the two by giving each one the name by which he was most commonly known. James "the Less" is another of those unknown and unsung heroes of the faith who were part of the group of Jesus' early followers. MATTHEW 27:56; MARK 15:40; LUKE 24:10

4 One of four brothers of Jesus, this James was at first unconvinced of Jesus' claims. James, his brothers, and his mother, Mary, at one point even tried to persuade Jesus to drop His controversial ministry because they thought that Jesus was mad. It was not until the resurrection that James was committed as one of Jesus' followers. From that point on, James was identified with the disciple group in Jerusalem. He was part of the group waiting in the Upper Room before the ascension and Pentecost, and within ten years became the leader in Jerusalem of those who acknowledged Jesus as Lord. As a symbol of the respect he enjoyed in Jerusalem, James became known as "the Just." The Apostle Paul, shortly after his dramatic conversion, came to Jerusalem and called on James. When Peter escaped from prison and fled to the house of Mary, Mark's mother, he asked that word be sent to James. Later, when the conservative followers of Jesus were uneasy because Paul was preaching to Gentiles, James was one of those who presided at the conference at Jerusalem and issued the agreement whereby Paul was approved as the apostle to the non-Jews. A few years later, when the tensions over the question of whether a man could be a Christian without first being circumcised as a Jew made a second conference necessary, James was looked to as the president of the council or assembly. James proposed the solution which vindicated Paul. Paul reported to James after his third missionary journey, and was warned by James of the plots against him. James was the author of the Epistle of James, a short letter packed with references to Jesus' teachings and paraphrases of the Sermon on the Mount. Paul's reference in I Corinthians 9:5 indicates that James was married. Josephus and Hegesippus, ancient historians, tell us that James was executed by fanatical Jewish leaders near the time of the revolt and seige of Jerusalem. MATTHEW 13:55; MARK 5:3; ACTS 12:17; 15:13; 21:18; I CORINTHIANS 15:7; GALATIANS 1:19; 2:9; JAMES 1:1; JUDE 1

5 A fifth James, this man was remembered as the father of the Apostle Thaddeus, or Judas, (not Iscariot, the one who betrayed Jesus), one of the Twelve. Nothing whatsoever is known of him. LUKE 6:16

JAMIN

1 One of the sons of Simeon, Jamin

and the other descendants of Jacob dwelling in Palestine emigrated to Egypt at the invitation of Joseph, in order to escape the famine. Later, Jamin's family known as Jaminites, joined Moses in the Exodus from Egypt. GENESIS 46:10; EXODUS 6:15; NUMBERS 26:12; I CHRONICLES 4:24

2 A member of the tribe of Judah, this Jamin was a son of Ram, and could trace his ancestry back through Hezron and Perez. He was a tribal clan chieftain in the early days of the tribe. I CHRONICLES 2:27

3 A prominent priest who returned from Exile in Babylon to Jerusalem, this Jamin took an active part in Ezra's crash program to educate the people on the Law. NEHEMIAH 8:7

JAMLECH A powerful clan chieftain in the tribe of Simeon, Jamlech was one of those who invaded the lush valley of Gedor to seize it from the Amalekites for their families during the reign of King Hezekiah of Judah. I CHRONICLES 4:34

JANAI See JAANAI

JANNA See JANNAI

JANNAI One of Jesus' ancestors, according to the genealogical table laid out by Luke, Jannai was a forebear of Joseph. LUKE 3:24

JANNES The name tradition assigned to one of the magicians in the pharaoh's court when Moses and Aaron came to beg for the release of the children of Israel, Jannes is not mentioned by name in the Old Testament at all. Paul supplies the names that Jewish folklore gave the magicians—Jannes and Jambres—who thwarted Moses' and Aaron's plans for some time by matching their wondrous signs before the pharaoh. II TIMOTHY 3:8

JAPHETH One of Noah's three sons, Japheth was the ancestor of many ancient Middle East tribes. He accompanied the rest of the family on the voyage in the ark during the flood, and compassionately covered his father when Noah lay drunk and naked after the wine-making experiment. Japheth's children became the legendary founders of all the peoples to the north and west of the Fertile Crescent. GENESIS 5:3; 6:10; 7:13; 9:18—27; 10:1—21; I CHRONICLES 1:4—5

JAPHIA
1 The head of the powerful city-state of Lachish at the time the Israelites were invading Canaan, Japhia joined four other Amorite rulers in attacking the Gibeonites. Joshua, who had signed a pact promising aid to the Gibeonites if attacked, caught the Amorite city-states completely by surprise in a series of night marches and brilliant maneuvers. Japhia and the four other kings were dragged from hiding in a cave after the defeat, and were swiftly executed. JOSHUA 10:3

2 One of David's sons, this Japhia is mentioned in three genealogical accounts of the royal family of Judah. No biographical details, however, are given. II SAMUEL 5:15; I CHRONICLES 3:7; 14:6

JAPHLET Asher's great grandson,

JARAH

Japhlet was an early chieftain in the tribe of Asher. His ancestors and descendants are mentioned, along with his name, in the family tree by the Chronicler. I CHRONICLES 7:32—33

JARAH One of Saul's descendants, Jarah is included in the genealogy of Saul's descendants by the Chronicler. He was also known as Jehoadah. I CHRONICLES 8:36; 9:42

JAREB There is difference of opinion among scholars over whether Hosea meant "Jareb" as a title or a proper name. Some versions translate "Jareb" as "the great king" (RSV) of Assyria, others as the name of an actual monarch. If Jareb was the name of an Assyrian king, no one is sure which one. Many Assyrian rulers changed their names when they ascended to the throne. HOSEA 5:13; 10:6

JARED One of Seth's descendants, Jared was the father of Enoch and the grandfather of Methuselah, and was listed among the early genealogy of the human family. GENESIS 5:15—20; I CHRONICLES 1:2; LUKE 3:36

JARESIAH One of the sons of Jeroham, a chieftain in the tribe of Benjamin, Jaresiah was also a head man in the tribe. He and his family lived in Jerusalem after the conquest of Canaan by the tribes of Israel. I CHRONICLES 8:27

JARHA The Egyptian slave who married the boss's daughter—in this case because the boss, Sheshan, had no sons to carry on the family name

—Jarha became a member of the tribe of Judah by marriage, and the father of Attai, later a tribal chieftain. I CHRONICLES 2:34, 35

JARIB

1 For the man named "Jarib" in I Chronicles 4:24, see JACHIN.
2 One of the leaders among the deported Jews at the time of the Exile in Babylonia, Jarib was sent by Ezra to Iddo's seminary to get Levites to accompany Ezra back to Jerusalem. EZRA 8:16
3 One of the priests who married outside the faith during the Exile, this unfortunate man named Jarib consented to obey Ezra's strict edict against interfaith marriages, and separated from his non-Jewish wife. EZRA 10:18

JAROAH A member of the tribe of Gad, Jaroah was an obscure chieftain in the early days of the tribe. I CHRONICLES 5:14

JASHEN This ancient worthy is now remembered only because he was an ancestor of Eliahba, one of David's elite corps "The Thirty." II SAMUEL 23:30

JASHIB See IOB

JASHOBEAM David's greatest military hero and the leader of David's guerrilla chieftains while David was an outlaw, Jashobeam was a son of Zabdiel and Hachmonite. Like other disaffected followers of Saul, Jashobeam joined the outlawed David. He won his fame by slaughtering three hundred in one battle. After David

164

was established as king of the united kingdom, Jashobeam was appointed commander of the leading division in David's army. I CHRONICLES 11:11; 12:6; 27:2

JASHUB
1 For the Jashub listed among Issachar's sons. NUMBERS 26:24; I CHRONICLES 7:1, see IOB.
2 One of Bani's many sons who married outside the faith during the Exile, this Jashub complied with Ezra's strict rules against interfaith marriages and left his Babylonian wife. EZRA 10:29

JASON A Jewish convert to Christianity who lived in Thessalonica, Jason was Paul's host when the riot broke out over Paul's teachings. Jason's house was searched and Jason was hailed before the city officials. He paid bail and was freed after promising not to disturb the peace any more. Paul got away and left for Beroea with Silas. In the Letter to the Romans, Paul includes greetings from Jason, one of "his kinsmen," meaning probably that Jason was a fellow-Jew, and perhaps a fellow countryman. The name "Jason" was frequently the Greek name adopted by Jews named "Joshua." ACTS 17:5—9; ROMANS 16: 21

JATHNIEL A Levite who was a son of Meshelmiah, Jathniel was one of the gatekeepers in David's sanctuary because of his illustrious family background. I CHRONICLES 26:2

JAVAN Noah's grandson and Japheth's son, Javan in the ancient genealogies was said to be the ancestor of those who lived in the Greek Islands, northern Greece, and Cyprus. Like nearly all of these shadowy figures in the era before historical records were kept, Javan is little more than a name and a traditional founder of early nations. GENESIS 10:2, 4; I CHRONICLES 1:5, 7

JAZIZ An employee of David, Jaziz the Hagerite was in charge of David's flocks, superintending all the shepherds and overseeing the wool production. I CHRONICLES 27:30

JEATERAI See JEATHERAI

JEATHERAI A Levite descended from Levi's son Gershom, Jeatherai (also known as Ethni) was an ancestor of Asaph, the great musician in David's sanctuary. I CHRONICLES 6:21

JEBERECHIAH The father of Zechariah, the friend who served as a witness for Isaiah. ISAIAH 8:2

JECAMIAH See JEKAMIAH 2

JECHILIAH The wife of King Amaziah of Judah, Jechiliah was the mother of Uzziah or Azariah, king of Judah for fifty-two years. Jechiliah is mentioned as a native of Jerusalem. Her son's long, useful reign undoubtedly reflected the qualities of this woman. II KINGS 15:2; II CHRONICLES 26:3

JECHOLIAH See JECHILIAH

JECHONIAH See JEHOIACHIN

JECHONIAS See JEHOIACHIN

JECOLIAH See JECHILIAH

165

JECONIAH

JECONIAH See **JEHOIACHIN**

JECONIAS See **CONANIAH**

JEDAIAH
1 A highly respected priest who served in David's sanctuary in Jerusalem, Jedaiah was the forbear of a distinguished family that, years later, returned to Jerusalem after the Exile and helped rebuild the city. I CHRONICLES 9:10; 24:7; EZRA 2:36; NEHEMIAH 7:39; 11:10; 12:6, 7, 19, 21
2 Another Jedaiah, this man was one of those who were entrusted to carry the expensive gold and silver articles from Babylon to Jerusalem after the Exile when the Temple was being rebuilt. ZECHARIAH 6:10, 14
3 A clan chieftain in the tribe of Simeon, this Jedaiah was an ancestor of Ziza, one of the Simeonites who wrested the vale of Gedor from the Amalekites. I CHRONICLES 4:37
4 The son of Harumaph, this Jedaiah took an active part in rebuilding Jerusalem under Nehemiah's leadership after the Exile. NEHEMIAH 3:10

JEDIAEL
1 One of Benjamin's sons, Jediael was a powerful clan head in the early days of the tribe of Benjamin. His descendants were a strong and respected family. I CHRONICLES 7:6, 10, 11
2 The son of Shimri, this Jediael was one of David's staunchest friends and boldest fighters. Originally from the tribe of Manasseh, Jediael left Saul and joined David at Ziglag. He won immortality in Judah by being appointed as one of "The Thirty," of David's troops. I CHRONICLES 11:45; 12:20
3 A Levite of the Korah branch of the tribe, this Jediael was one of Meshelemiah's sons who served as a gatekeeper in David's sanctuary because of his family background. I CHRONICLES 26:2

JEDIDAH The daughter of Adaiah of Bozkath, Jedidah was the wife of Amon, one of Judah's worst kings, but she was also the mother of Josiah, one of the best. She was left a widow when Josiah was only eight, and much of the credit for Josiah's character must go to this godly woman. II KINGS 22:1

JEDIDIAH Meaning "beloved of the Lord," this was the nickname assigned Solomon by Nathan, the prophet. II SAMUEL 12:25

JEDUTHUN One of the great musicians in David's sanctuary services, Jeduthun was a talented vocalist and instrumentalist whose sons were also elevated to positions of honor in the Jerusalem worship. Jeduthun, Heman, and Asaph were the heads of three great guilds of singers and musicians. Because Ethan's name is listed in place of Jeduthun's in some records of the three guilds, scholars have suggested that Jeduthun and Ethan may be variant names for the same man. I CHRONICLES 9:16; 16:38—42; 25:1—3; II CHRONICLES 5:12; 29:14; 35:15; NEHEMIAH 11:17; TITLES OF PSALMS 39, 62, 77

JEEZER The grandson of Manasseh and the son of Gilead, Jeezer was also known as IEZER (which see). NUM-BERS 26:30

JEHALELEEL See JEHALLELEL

JEHALLELEL

1 One of the tribe of Judah, this Jehallelel was descended from Moses' great spy, Caleb, and was remembered in the tribal genealogy by the Chronicler. I CHRONICLES 4:16

2 Another Jehallelel, this man was a Levite of the Merari branch of the tribe who lived at the time of Hezekiah and was remembered primarily because he was the father of the priest, Azaraiah, who cleansed the Temple during Hezekiah's reform. II CHRONICLES 29:12

JEHDEIAH

1 A Levite, Jehdeiah was a son of Shubael, a descendant of Levi through Amram, who ministered in David's sanctuary in Jerusalem. I CHRONICLES 24:20

2 One of David's business agents responsible for managing the royal estates, this Jehdeiah was overseer of the large flocks of she-asses. I CHRONICLES 27:30

JEHEZEKEL See JEHEZKEL

JEHEZKEL One of the priests in David's sanctuary in Jerusalem, Jehezkel chose the lot to head the twentieth contingent of priests. I CHRONICLES 24:16

JEHIAH A Levite in David's time, Jehiah was one of those who took part in the ceremonies when David brought the Ark of the Covenant to Jerusalem shortly after his coronation.

Jehiah was one of the two gatekeepers for the Ark. I CHRONICLES 15:24

JEHIEL

1 A famous and talented musician in David's day, this Jehiel was a Levite who played the harp and lyre in David's sanctuary. He had a prominent part in the worship services and was mentioned by name by the Chronicler three times. I CHRONICLES 15:18, 20; 16:5

2 Another Levite in David's time, this Jehiel was a clan head in the tribe at the time of David's census of the tribes. Jehiel, proud to trace his ancestry through his father, Ladan, back to Gershom, was given the honor and task of serving as treasurer of the building fund when David collected from the people to finance the Temple. I CHRONICLES 23:8; 29:8

3 A son of Hachmoni, this third Jehiel assisted David's uncle, Jonathan, as tutor and companion of David's sons. I CHRONICLES 27:32

4 This Jehiel was one of the sons of King Jehoshaphat of Judah. When Jehoshaphat died, Jehoram, Jehiel's brother, succeeded to the throne. Jehiel, who like his other brothers had been given generous portions of Jehoshaphat's estate, was suddenly murdered along with the other princes and leaders by his brother Jehoram, who was apparently taking no chances that any of his brothers would try to displace him. II CHRONICLES 21:2

5 An important Levite official in King Hezekiah's treasury department, this Jehiel assisted in receiving and tabulating the offerings and taxes paid by the people. II CHRONICLES 31:13

6 One of the chief priests in King Josiah's time, this man named Jehiel and the other two chief priests donated liberally to make possible a successful observance of Passover—the first in years—during Josiah's great reform in Judah. II CHRONICLES 35:8
7 A Jew who lived in Babylon at the time of the Exile, this Jehiel was the father of Obadiah, one of those who returned to Jerusalem with Ezra. EZRA 8:9
8 This Jehiel was remembered as the father of Shecaniah, the returned exile who proposed to Ezra and his countrymen that they put away their non-Jewish wives in order to purify the faith. EZRA 10:2
9 One of the descendants of Harim, this Jehiel was a priest who had married outside the faith during the Exile in Babylon, but obeyed Ezra's strict command to leave his mate in order to keep the faith pure. EZRA 10:21
10 A descendant of Elam, this man by the same name also took a non-Jewish bride during the Exile, breaking the Law. EZRA 10:26

JEHIELI A Levite of the Gershom branch of the tribe, Jehieli was a son of Ladan, and was assigned a post in the sanctuary treasury in Jerusalem during David's time. I CHRONICLES 26:21

JEHIZKIAH A powerful chief from the tribe of Ephraim, Jehizkiah supported his king, Ahaz of Israel, in the war against Judah. After victory, however, Jehizkiah and a few other bold souls took the risk of opposing Ahaz's plan to sell the captives from the defeated tribes into slavery. Jehizkiah magnanimously fed and clothed his captive brothers and returned them to their homes. II CHRONICLES 28:8—15

JEHOADAH See JARAH

JEHOADDAH See JARAH

JEHOADDAN The wife of Joash, king of Judah, Jehoaddan was widowed when Joash was assassinated. Her son, Amaziah, succeeded his father to the throne of Judah. II KINGS 14:2; II CHRONICLES 25:1

JEHOAHAZ
1 Jehu's son, Jehoahaz became king of Israel, the northern kingdom, inheriting a tottering state. The neighboring kings of Damascus and Syria had already seized large chunks of Israel's territory, and the nation had deserted God for pagan-cults. Jehoahaz was so ineffective a ruler that Israel was repeatedly invaded. He finally turned to the Lord, and was promised deliverance from the Syrians in due time. He died, however, before seeing the Syrians put out of Israel. II KINGS 10:35; 13:1—25; 14:1, 8, 17; II CHRONICLES 25:17, 25
2 One of King Josiah's younger sons, Jehoahaz succeeded Josiah after the fiasco against the Egyptians at Megiddo, where Josiah died. The people by-passed Jehoahaz's older brothers, and insisted on having Jehoahaz anointed ruler of Judah. His three-month reign in Jerusalem was distinguished only by the usual royal tolerance of evil. Neco, the Egyptian pharaoh, descended on Jerusalem and carried Jehoahaz to Egypt, where he eventually died. II KINGS 23:30—34; II CHRONICLES 36:1—4

3 The son of Jehoram, king of Judah, this third Jehoahaz was made a king of Judah because he was the only royal heir to survive an attack by the Philistines and Arabs. Also known as Ahaziah, this Jehoahaz permitted the same scandalous conditions in the nation as his father had. His death came at the hands of Jehu, the conspirator who cut down Jehoahaz at the same time he killed King Joram of Israel, when the two kings tried an ill-planned sortie to recapture Ramoth-Gilead. II CHRONICLES 21:17; 25:23

JEHOASH

1 King Ahaziah's son, Jehoash or Joash succeeded to the throne of Judah when a lad of seven. His grandmother, queen mother Athaliah, brutally wiped out every other member of his family when Jehoash was an infant, and would have murdered him, too, had he not been hidden by an aunt and raised in secret. Thanks to an outstanding high priest, Jehoiada, who masterminded the revolution that deposed Athaliah and crowned young Jehoash, and who then acted as regent during the boy's youth, Judah revived. In spite of a promising start, Jehoash's character deteriorated gradually. He permitted some of the nation's leaders to continue to dabble with idols. Following a humiliating invasion by Syria, two disgusted servants murdered Jehoash in his bed at his fortress in Jerusalem. II KINGS 11:21; 12:1—20; 14:1—23; I CHRONICLES 3:11; II CHRONICLES 22:11; 24:1—24; 25:23—25

2 A king of Israel, this Jehoash followed his father Jehoahaz, who had ended his dismal reign without seeing the promised deliverance from the Syrians. Jehoash was more energetic than his father, and raised an army which stopped the Syrian menace. When Amaziah, king of Judah, persistently taunted him, Jehoash of Israel finally marched, broke into Jerusalem, and looted it after defeating Amaziah. Although Jehoash was not renowned for his piety, he recognized the strength of Israel was its trust in the Lord, and he wept when the mighty prophet Elisha died. Jehoash, also known as Joash, was succeeded by his son, the infamous Jeroboam. II KINGS 13:9—25; 14:1—27; I CHRONICLES 25:17—25; HOSEA 1:1; AMOS 1:1

JEHOHANAN

1 A Levite of the Korah branch of the tribe, this Jehohanan served as a gatekeeper in the sanctuary in Jerusalem in David's time. I CHRONICLES 26:3

2 One of King Jehoshaphat's top military leaders, this Jehohanan was one of five commanders of armies, and was assigned one of Jehoshaphat's key fortresses in Judah. II CHRONICLES 17:15

3 Possibly the same as **2**, Jehohanan is mentioned as the father of Ishmael, one of those who conspired with the great high priest Jehoiada to depose the wicked Queen Athaliah and crown young Joash as king of Judah. II CHRONICLES 23:1

4 The son of Eliashib, this man named Jehohanan was high priest in Jerusalem at the time Ezra returned from Exile in Babylon. Ezra retired to

Jehohanan's rooms after the decision to keep the faith pure by insisting that all marriages with non-believers be terminated. Jehohanan the high priest was also known as Johanan and Jonathan. EZRA 10:6; NEHEMIAH 12:11, 22, 23

5 One of the descendants of Bebai who married outside the faith during the Exile, this Jehohanan obeyed the injunction to keep the faith pure by leaving his foreign wife. EZRA 10:28

6 The son of Tobiah, the half-Jewish Ammonite who hindered Nehemiah in his efforts to rebuild Jerusalem, this Jehohanan married the daughter of Meshullam, a member of the prominent families in Jerusalem. Jehohanan was part of the faction that continued to plague Nehemiah. NEHEMIAH 6:18

7 A priest who returned from Exile in Babylon to Jerusalem with Zerubbabel, this man named Jehohanan served in the rebuilt Temple at the time Joiakim was high priest. Jehohanan was part of the contingent of priests who were descended from Amariah. NEHEMIAH 12:13

8 Another priest in Jerusalem after the return from Exile, this Jehohanan participated in Nehemiah's service in which the rebuilt walls were dedicated. NEHEMIAH 12:42

JEHOIACHIN The son of King Jehoiakim of Judah, Jehoiachin was the last king of Judah before Nebuchadnezzar snuffed out the valiant but faithless little nation. Succeeding a father who left the kingdom in a hopeless condition, eighteen-year-old Jehoiachin ruled only three months. The Babylonians under Nebuchadnezzar sacked Jerusalem, removing not only all the treasures but the cream of the population, including Jehoiachin. Jehoiachin, unlike other Jews in Babylon who were allowed considerable freedom, was imprisoned during Nebuchadnezzar's entire reign. He was finally released when Evil-Merodach replaced Nebuchadnezzar, and was kept under house arrest in Babylon for the rest of his life. Jehoiachin was also known as JECONIAH, CONIAH, JOAKIM, JECHONIAS and JECHONIAH. II KINGS 24:6—15; 25:27; II CHRONICLES 36:8—9; JEREMIAH 22: 24, 28; 24:1; 37:1; 52:31; EZEKIEL 1:2

JEHOIADA

1 A native of the southern Judean village of Kabzeel, this Jehoiada was a priest who was remembered chiefly because he was the father of the mighty Benaiah, one of David's greatest fighters, a member of "The Thirty" and the head of David's bodyguards. II SAMUEL 8:18; 20:23; 23:20—22; I KINGS 1:8—44; 2:25—46; 4:4; I CHRONICLES 11:22—24; 18:17; 27:5, 34

2 The great high priest and patriot, this Jehoiada kept Judah from foundering during the grim days of the mad Queen Athaliah and the childhood days of her young grandson, Jehoash. After King Ahaziah's death, a ruthless reign of terror by the maniac queen mother, Athaliah, followed, during which all members of the royal family were murdered by her order—except for one infant prince, Jehoash, who was hidden. Jehoiada carefully masterminded a revolution which deposed Athaliah and crowned young Jehoash. During the years when Jehoash was growing up, Jehoiada held the reins of government. He was so highly esteemed that when he died he was given the signal honor of burial in the royal tombs. I KINGS 11, 12; II CHRONICLES 22—24

3 A chief of the Aaronites, this Jehoiada and his followers joined David at Hebron and pledged their allegiance to him as king of the united kingdom. I CHRONICLES 12:27

4 For the name given as "Jehoiada" in some translations of Nehemiah 3:6, see JOIADA.

5 A priest in Jerusalem before the Babylonian invasion, this Jehoiada was mentioned by Jeremiah as a priest who was replaced by Zephaniah, the son of Maaseiah. JEREMIAH 29:26

JEHOIAKIM The depraved king of Judah during its final decay, Jehoiakim was put on the throne by Pharaoh Neco, the Egyptian who killed Jehoiakim's father, Josiah, and removed Jehoiakim's popular younger brother, Jehoahaz. Even Jehoiakim's name, originally Eliakim, was assigned by Neco. Jehoiakim's corruption and cruelty speeded the decline of Judah. He encouraged atrocities, such as child sacrifice, that were part of the heathen cults. Critics were silenced with imprisonment or murder; the prophet Uriah was executed, and Jeremiah was forced into hiding. When the international political scene suddenly shifted after the Babylonian ruler,

Nebuchadnezzar, defeated the Egyptian Pharaoh, Neco, Jehoiakim was reduced to a puppet-king under Babylon. He rashly rebelled, and Nebuchadnezzar eventually returned to seize Jerusalem. It is not clear whether Jehoiakim was assassinated by his own subjects, executed by Nebuchadnezzar, or carried off to Babylon. II KINGS 23:34—36; 24:1—19; I CHRONICLES 3:15—16; II CHRONICLES 36:4—8; JEREMIAH 1:3; 22:18—24; 25:1; 26:1 —23; 27:1, 20; 28:4; 35:1; 36:1—32; 37:1; 45:1; 46:2; 52:2; DANIEL 1:1—2

JEHOIARIB The priest in Jerusalem who was the head of a large clan of priests, Jehoiarib was the leader of the first of the twenty-four contingents of priests to serve in David's sanctuary. His descendants, however, were seventeenth in order years later, in Zerubbabel's time. I CHRONICLES 9:10; 24:7

JEHONADAB

1 David's nephew, Jehonadab or Jonadab was a companion of David's son, Amnon, and helped Amnon scheme to molest his half-sister, Tamar. After Amnon's death at the hands of Tamar's outraged brother, Absalom, a wild rumor reached David that Absalom had massacred the rest of the royal family. Jehonadab put the grief-stricken David's mind at rest by telling him that Amnon alone had been killed. II SAMUEL 13:3—6; 30—35

2 The son of the strict teetotaler, Rechab, a Kenite, this Jehonadab carried on his father's desert nomad tradition of refusing to drink wine and refusing to settle down in one place to

JEHONATHAN

raise crops. Jehonadab supported Jehu in his revolt against the corrupt King Ahab of Israel, and personally accompanied Jehu when Jehu's men killed Ahab's family and massacred the leading Baal-worshippers in Samaria. Jehonadab, also known as Jenadab, was held up as an example of faithfulness by Jeremiah, to rebuke the Israelites for their faithlessness to the Lord. II KINGS 10:15—23; JEREMIAH 35

JEHONATHAN
1 For the Jehonathan mentioned in I Chronicles 27:25, see JONATHAN 7.
2 A Levite in King Jehoshaphat's time who was one of the leading citizens of Judah, this Jehonathan was one of those sent throughout Judah by Jehoshaphat to conduct an intensive training program on the meaning of the Law. II CHRONICLES 17:8
3 Head of the distinguished family of priests descended from Shemaiah in the days after the Exile when Nehemiah was struggling to rebuild Jerusalem, this Jehonathan served under the high priest Joiakim, son of Jeshua. NEHEMIAH 12:18

JEHORAM
1 Son of the vicious Queen Jezebel and King Ahab of Israel, this Jehoram followed his brother to the throne. Although he made some pretense at suppressing some of the infamous cults imported by his mother, Jehoram did not promote any real reform among his people. He was an able organizer; he persuaded Jehoshaphat of Judah to join him in quelling the Mo-

abites. Like nearly all the kings of Israel, Jehoram tangled with the prophets, especially Elisha. He died unmourned when Jehu brought off a successful coup, killing both Jehoram and his nephew, King Ahaziah of Judah, and establishing Jehu as king of Israel. I KINGS 8:9; II KINGS 1:17; 3:1—6; 9:24; II CHRONICLES 22; 5—7
2 This second Jehoram was the son and successor of King Jehoshaphat of Judah, and a contemporary of **1**. To seal an alliance between his father and Ahab, king of Israel, Jehoram was given the daughter of Ahab and Jezebel, Athaliah, as his bride. Athaliah dominated her husband, persuading him to reintroduce and encourage Baal worship in Judah. Jehoram even stooped to murdering his six brothers when he was crowned king. During his sorry reign, Libnah and Edom broke away from Judah. He was so loathed by his subjects that when he died they refused him burial in the royal tombs. I KINGS 22:50; II KINGS 1:17; 8:16—29; 12:18; I CHRONICLES 3:11; II CHRONICLES 21:1—16; 22:1—11
3 A priest and leading citizen of Judah at the time of King Jehoshaphat, this man named Jehoram was one of those sent by Jehoshaphat throughout the nation to give intensive instruction in the meaning of the Law to the people. II CHRONICLES 17:8

JEHOSHABEATH
See JEHOSHEBA

JEHOSHAPHAT
1 The king of Judah who was the son and successor of Asa, Jehoshaphat

172

tried to be a model of piety and a guardian of the faith by sending teachers of the Law throughout the kingdom and closing down Baal shrines. Probably his biggest contribution was to stop the long-running feud between Judah and the northern kingdom of Israel. However, when Jehoshaphat married his son to Athaliah, daughter of Israel's notorious Jezebel and Ahab, he unwittingly brought trouble. Athaliah later sent Judah on a downward spiral of degradation. Jehoshaphat's alliance with Israel meant cooperating on some ventures which were more helpful to the kings of Israel than to himself, and which sometimes ended in disaster—like the grandiose maritime scheme which collapsed when a storm wrecked Jehoshaphat's ships. Nonetheless, Jehoshaphat kept the Edomites, Philistines, and Arabs as his vassals. His twenty-five year reign was considered a high point in Judah's history. I KINGS 15:24; 22:1—51; II KINGS 1:17; 3:1—14; 8:16; 12:18; I CHRONICLES 3:10; II CHRONICLES 17—22

2 The son of Alihud, this Jehoshaphat served as chief record keeper for David and Solomon, and enjoyed a privileged position on David's staff. II SAMUEL 8:16; 20:24; I KINGS 4:3; I CHRONICLES 18:15

3 One of Solomon's twelve commissary officers, this Jehoshaphat was the son of Paruah. He was responsible for scraping enough provisions from the territory of Issachar to feed Solomon's enormous entourage for one month each year. I KINGS 4:17

4 The son of Nimshi, this man was the father of Jehu, the bold general who successfully brought off the conspiracy against the house of Ahab which killed King Jehoram of Israel and installed Jehu as the new ruler. II KINGS 9:2—14

5 For the men whose names are translated "Jehoshaphat" in some translations of I CHRONICLES 11:43 and 15:24, see JOSHAPHAT 1 and 2.

JEHOSHEBA Sometimes known as Jehoshabeath, this brave, resourceful woman was the daughter of King Jehoram of Judah. When her depraved stepmother, Athaliah, determined to wipe out all male members of the royal family, Jehosheba managed to conceal her infant nephew, Joash, who was the only surviving heir to the throne. II KINGS 11:2; II CHRONICLES 22:11

JEHOSHUA See JOSHUA, SON OF NUN

JEHOSHUAH See JOSHUA, SON OF NUN

JEHOZABAD
1 The son of Shomer or Shimrith, a Moabitess, Jehozabad was on the royal staff of King Joash of Judah. Apparently disgusted with his master's spinelessness during the Syrian invasion, Jehozabad and other servants conspired to murder Joash in his bed. Jehozabad, in turn, was put to death by Joash's son, Amaziah. II KINGS 12:21; II CHRONICLES 24:26

2 The second son of Obededom, a Levite of the Korah branch of the tribe, this Jehozabad was one of the

173

family which served as gatekeepers in the Temple. I CHRONICLES 26:4

3 A prominent officer in Jehoshaphat's army, this Jehozadab was second-in-command in the division of fighters from the tribe of Benjamin. II CHRONICLES 17:18

JEHOZADAK A priest who traced his lineage to Zadok, Jehozadak was a blueblood in Judah whose grandfather, Hilkiah, was high priest at the time the Exile in Babylon began, and whose grandson, Jeshua, was a high priest who accompanied Zerubbabel when the first group of Jews returned to Jerusalem from the Exile. I CHRONICLES 6:14, 15

JEHU

1 The general in King Jehoram's service who plotted the downfall of the House of Ahab and made himself king of Israel, this Jehu was designated the man of destiny by the great prophet, Elijah. With a series of lightning moves, Jehu killed Jehoram the king of Judah, and Jehoram's nephew, Ahaziah, wiped out the survivors of Ahab's family, including Jezebel, then trapped and slaughtered the most zealous Baal-worshippers. According to the prophets, Jehu was a ruthless, tricky person who grabbed the throne without any real attempt to clean up the corruption in Israel. On the black obelisk of Shalmanezer III, the Assyrian, Jehu is mentioned as one who paid tribute to Assyria, indicating that for a time Israel was a vassal state to Assyria. Later, Syria became the chief threat and tore large pieces of territory from Jehu's Israel. In spite of these humiliations, however, Jehu was deeply respected as an able king. I KINGS 19; II KINGS 9, 10, 12—15; II CHRONICLES 22; 25:17; HOSEA 1:4

2 An outspoken spokesman for the Lord, Jehu, who was the son of another bold prophet, Hanani, denounced King Jehoshaphat of Judah for his alliance with the evil Ahab of Israel and wrote a history of Jehoshaphat's reign that was used by the Chronicler as source material. This Jehu also forecast doom for Baasha, king of Israel, for his disobedience to the Lord. I KINGS 16; II CHRONICLES 19:2; 20:34

3 A member of the tribe of Judah, this Jehu is listed in the tribal records as a descendant of Judah through Hezron. He was the son of Obed and the father of Azariah. All these men were chieftains of clans. I CHRONICLES 2:38

4 Another Jehu, this man was a son of Joshibiah and a clan chieftain of the tribe of Simeon who, in Hezekiah's time, joined others from his tribe to drive the Amalekites out of the lush valley of Gedor so they could pasture there themselves. I CHRONICLES 4:34—43

5 A native of the village of Anathoth, this Jehu was one of David's greatest warrior-heroes. He was an expert with the bow and the sling, and could shoot either with either hand. Although related to Saul, and originally on Saul's side, Jehu and most of his kinsmen joined David at Ziglag. I CHRONICLES 12:3

JEHUBBAH One of Shemer's sons

in the tribe of Asher, Jehubbah was an early clan chieftain mentioned in the tribe's genealogy. I CHRONICLES 7:34

JEHUCAL Shelemiah's son, Jehucal was one of King Zedekiah's personal staff. During the seige of Jerusalem, Jehucal carried Zedekiah's plea to the prophet Jeremiah to be remembered in his prayers. JEREMIAH 37:3; 38:1

JEHUDI A member of the staff of King Jehoiakim of Judah, Jehudi was sent to bring Baruch, Jeremiah's secretary, to read Jeremiah's prophecies to the king and some of the leading men. Later, Jehudi himself was forced to read the scrolls written by Jeremiah. As Jehudi finished reading each sheet, the angry Jehoiakim slashed it with his knife, then threw it into the fire. JEREMIAH 36

JEHUDIJAH The name given in some translations for the name of Ezra's Jewish wife, Jehudijah means simply "the Jewess." I CHRONICLES 4:18

JEHUEL A Levite who belonged to the guild of Temple musicians founded by Heman, Jehuel took a prominent part in cleaning up the Temple and inaugurating a much-needed reform in Judah during Hezekiah's reign. II CHRONICLES 29:14

JEHUSH See JEUSH 3

JEHIEL See JEIEL

JEIEL
1 One of the early chiefs of the tribe of Reuben, this Jeiel is listed in the tribal roll by the Chronicler. I CHRONICLES 5:7

2 The father of Gibeon and an ancestor of Saul, this Jeiel was a member of the tribe of Benjamin whose name is listed in the genealogy of the house of Saul. I CHRONICLES 8:29; 9:35

3 One of the two sons of Hotham the Aroerite, Jeiel, like his brother Shama, was one of David's mightiest heroes and is listed in the roll call of David's elite corps. I CHRONICLES 11:44

4 A Levite noted for his musical ability on the harp and lyre, this Jeiel was one of those who participated in the worship services in David's sanctuary in Jerusalem. I CHRONICLES 15:18, 21; 16:5; II CHRONICLES 20:14

5 One of King Uzziah's staff, this Jeiel kept the records of Judah's manpower strength. II CHRONICLES 26:11

6 Another Levite, this man named Jeiel lived in King Josiah's time. He donated generously so that a proper Passover could be observed in Jerusalem after the start of Josiah's reform. II CHRONICLES 35:9

7 One of the sons of Nebo who married outside the faith during the Exile in Babylon, this Jeiel obeyed Ezra's stringent regulations against interfaith marriages, and put away his wife. EZRA 10:43

8 For the name translated as Jeiel in some versions of II CHRONICLES 29:13, see JEUEL 2.

9 For the name translated as Jeiel in some versions of EZRA 8:13, see JEUEL 3

JEKAMEAM Levi's grandson and

Hebron's son, Jekameam was the head of a clan of Levites. I CHRONICLES 23:19; 24:23

JEKAMIAH

1 A son of Shallum and a descendant of Jerahmeel, this Jekamiah is listed with other notables of the tribe of Judah in the tribal roll. I CHRONICLES 2:41

2 One of David's descendants, this member of the royal family of Judah was Jeconiah's son. He was also known as Jecamiah. I CHRONICLES 3:18

JEKUTHIEL A clan chieftain in the tribe of Judah, Jekuthiel traced his ancestry back through Moses' famous spy, Caleb, son of Jephunneh. I CHRONICLES 4:18

JEMIMA See JEMIMAH

JEMIMAH One of Job's daughters, Jemimah was the eldest of the three girls born to Job after his terrible troubles and the return of his prosperity and health. JOB 42:14

JEMUEL Also known as Nemuel, Jemuel was the oldest of Simeon's sons. He went with the rest of his grandfather Jacob's descendants to Egypt when the famine struck Canaan. Like other sons of the twelve sons of Jacob, Jemuel was a clan head. His descendants accompanied Moses to the Promised Land. GENESIS 46:10; EXODUS 6:15; as "Nemuel": NUMBERS 26:12; I CHRONICLES 4:24.

JEPHTHAE See JEPHTHAH

JEPHTHAH Son of a prostitute in Gilead, Jephthah was thrown out of his home community by his more respectable relatives. He attracted a group of restless outlaws and acted as leader on their raids. When the Ammonite invasions threatened Israel, Jephthah was called home to command Israel's forces. Rashly vowing to sacrifice the first person to meet him if the Lord should send him home victorious, Jephthah defeated the Ammonites, then returned home. The first to meet him was his daughter, who, after deep lamenting, was sacrificed —although human sacrifice was expressly forbidden by the Law. When the tribe of Ephraim peevishly made trouble because it had not been asked to fight the Ammonites, Jephthah battled and subdued it. He ruled as one of the judges for six years. JUDGES 11, 12; I SAMUEL 12:11

JEPHUNNEH

1 One of the early members of the tribe of Judah, Jephunneh was the father of Caleb, the great spy who reconnoitered the Promised Land. Caleb was not cowed by the inhabitants, and brought back the unpopular minority report that the Israelites would be able to conquer the Canaanites. NUMBERS 13:6

2 Another and lesser-known Jephunneh, this man was a son of Jether and a chieftain of a strong clan in the tribe of Asher. I CHRONICLES 7:38

JERAH A descendant of Noah through his son Shem, Jerah was a son of Joktan, and was popularly believed to be the ancestor of one of the early desert tribes of the East. GENESIS 10:26; I CHRONICLES 1:20

JERAHMEEL

1 The great-grandson of Judah, this Jerahmeel was Hezron's oldest son. His clan, the Jerahmeelites, settled in the Negev in southern Judah, but was later absorbed into the tribe of Judah. I CHRONICLES 2

2 A Levite of the Merari side of the tribe, this Jerahmeel was appointed to represent his family by serving in the sanctuary in David's Jerusalem. I CHRONICLES 24:29

3 One of King Jehoiakim's sons, this Jerahmeel and two other court officials were ordered to arrest the prophet Jeremiah and his faithful secretary, Baruch, after Jehoiakim was enraged by the prophecies Jeremiah had written. Jeremiah and Baruch managed to hide from Jerahmeel and his henchmen. JEREMIAH 36:26

JERED One of the tribe of Judah and a descendant of Caleb the spy, Jered was the ancestor of the group that invaded and lived on at Gedor. I CHRONICLES 4:18

JEREMAI One of Hashum's family who married outside the faith during the Exile in Babylon, Jeremai agreed to Ezra's strict orders, and put away his non-Jewish wife. EZRA 10:33

JEREMIAH

1 The great prophet from a long and distinguished line of priests of Anathoth, a village northeast of Jerusalem, Jeremiah had to speak for the Lord during the heartbreaking final days of his beloved nation, Judah. Although a profound patriot, he was in opposition to nearly everything his king did, and was called a traitor, ar rested, hounded, and threatened throughout his career. Jeremiah seeing more clearly than most men the domestic implications of the corruption in Judah and the political implications of the rise of Babylon, urged his government to cease its flirtation with Egypt. Repeatedly disregarding Jeremiah's advice, King Jehoiakim, King Jehoiachin, and later, King Zedekiah tried uprisings against Babylon and entered into secret alliance with Egypt. Jeremiah's pleas were interpreted as treason. At one point he was left to die in an unused cistern, but was rescued by a friendly Ethiopian. As Jeremiah predicted, Jerusalem was captured and the flower of Judah's population deported. A misunderstood, lonely, sensitive man, Jeremiah's deeply emotional writings have given him the title: "the weeping prophet." He wanted to remain in Judah after the fall of Jerusalem, but was taken forcibly to Egypt by a gang of super-patriots. No one knows how he died, but the hint is that he was killed by some of his own countrymen. II CHRONICLES 35:25; 36:12—22; EZRA 1:1; JEREMIAH; DANIEL 9:2

2 The father-in-law of King Josiah, this Jeremiah was a man from Libnah whose daughter, Hamutal, married into the royal family of Judah. Since Libnah had been allocated to the Levites, this Jeremiah most likely was a priest. Through his daughter, Jeremiah probably influenced King Josiah to push for a reform in the nation. His grandsons, Jehoahaz and Zedekiah, when they in turn came to the throne, were among the worst of Judah's kings. II KINGS 23:31; 24:18; JEREMIAH 52:1

3 A powerful clan head in the tribe of Manasseh, this Jeremiah settled with many of his tribe in the area east of the Jordan after the Israelites' wanderings. Like many others of his tribe, Jeremiah deserted the Lord for the exotic cults of the new land. The Assyrian, Tiglath-Pileser, later deported most of these clans. I CHRONICLES 5:24

4 An expert with the deadly bow and sling with either his left hand or his right, this Jeremiah was a warrior from the tribe of Benjamin who, disenchanted with Saul, deserted with most of his cohorts to David at Ziglag. I CHRONICLES 12:4

5 Another superb fighter, this Jeremiah was one of the cream of the tribe of Gad and was part of the detachment that joined David in the wilderness. Like his fellows, this Jeremiah was a shaggy-faced, light-footed mountain man. I CHRONICLES 12:10

6 Another of the tribe of Gad who joined David, this man named Jeremiah was also a formidable warrior. His reputation put him tenth on the list of those in his tribe's forces. I CHRONICLES 12:13

7 A priest at the time of the Exile in Babylon, this Jeremiah returned to devastated Jerusalem with Zerubbabel. He helped rebuild the city walls, had a prominent part in the impressive service rededicating the walls, and joined Nehemiah in the covenant to keep the Law. A few scholars think that there were actually two priests named Jeremiah who lived after the Exile and were mentioned by Nehemiah. NEHEMIAH 10:2; 12:1, 12, 34

8 The father of Jaazaniah, the man held up as an example of faithfulness to Judah by the prophet Jeremiah, this Jeremiah was a Rechabite. As one of that clan, he had vowed to be a total abstainer and shepherd-nomad in an attempt to pull the nation back to purer ways. JEREMIAH 35:3

JEREMOTH

1 One of Benjamin's grandsons, this first Jeremoth was the son of Becher, and an early clan chief in the tribe of Benjamin. I CHRONICLES 7:8

2 Another member of the tribe of Benjamin, this Jeremoth was also a clan chieftain who was remembered in the roll of tribal notables. I CHRONICLES 8:14

3 One of Levi's great-grandsons, this Jeremoth was descended from Merari and Mushi, and was an early clan leader in the tribe of Levi. I CHRONICLES 23:23; 24:30

4 Another Levite by the same name, this Jeremoth was a great musician in David's sanctuary services. By lot, he was selected to head the fifteenth contingent of singers and instrumentalists in the worship. I CHRONICLES 25:22

5 The head of the tribe of Naphtali in David's time, this Jeremoth, son of Azriel, was noted in the records of the census made by David. I CHRONICLES 27:19

6 One of the descendants of Elam who married outside the faith during the Exile, this man named Jeremoth was forced to leave his non-Jewish mate to keep the faith pure. EZRA 10:26

7 One of the family of Zattu who married a non-Jewish woman during the Exile, this Jeremoth also went along with Ezra's strict rules against interfaith marriages, and left his wife. EZRA 10:27

8 Still another who broke the Law by marrying a non-believer during the Exile, this Jeremoth was one of the family of Bani. EZRA 10:29

JERIAH Hebron's son and an early clan chieftain in the tribe of Levi, Jeriah was the ancestor of one group of Temple Levites who were given a prominent part in worship services after David's time. I CHRONICLES 23: 19; 24:23; 26:31

JERIBAI One of David's greatest warriors, Jeribai earned himself a place in the exclusive company of "The Thirty," David's elite corps of all-time great heroes. I CHRONICLES 11:46

JERIEL Issachar's grandson and Tola's son, Jeriel was an early clan chieftain in the tribe of Issachar. I CHRONICLES 7:2

JERIJAH See JERIAH

JERIMOTH
1 Benjamin's grandson and Bela's son, Jerimoth was a mighty warrior and clan chieftain in the early days of the tribe of Benjamin. I CHRONICLES 7:7
2 One of the deadly warriors from the tribe of Benjamin who left Saul to join David at Ziglag, this Jerimoth was equally proficient with the left hand or the right at shooting the bow

or the deadly sling. I CHRONICLES 12:5
3 One of the sons of the great Levite musician Heman, this Jerimoth was also skilled with the harp, cymbals, and lyre, and, as a Levite, served in David's sanctuary in Jerusalem. I CHRONICLES 24:5
4 One of David's sons who is not mentioned in any other list, this Jerimoth was recorded as the father of the woman who married King Rehoboam of Judah. II CHRONICLES 11:18
5 A prominent Levite in King Hezekiah's time, this Jerimoth was assigned to assist in receiving and counting the offerings in the Temple. II CHRONICLES 31:13
6 Some versions translate "Jerimoth" as "Jeremoth" in certain places. See also JEREMOTH

JERIOTH The Hebrew text is difficult to figure out in this passage, but Jerioth was probably either the wife or the concubine of Caleb, son of Hezron. I CHRONICLES 2:8

JEROBOAM
1 The first king of the northern ten tribes after the kingdom split following Solomon's death, Jeroboam was an ambitious, shrewd, and capable Ephraimite. Solomon recognized his abilities and appointed him to take charge of the contingent of forced-laborers from the tribe of Joseph who were working on the fortifications in Jerusalem. Jeroboam, at the urging of the prophet Ahijah, tried to organize a revolt against Solomon, but when it fizzled, Jeroboam fled to Egypt until Solomon's death. Appointing himself as spokesman for the discontented

masses who were tired of heavy taxes and forced labor gangs, Jeroboam urged Solomon's son and successor, Rehoboam, to ease the burdens on his subjects. Rehoboam imperiously refused. Jeroboam led the northern tribes into seceding from the kingdom, and was crowned king of Israel. He soon brought down the wrath of the prophets by erecting golden calves at the old-time shrines at Bethel and Dan, so that he could keep his people from going back to Jerusalem to worship at the Temple. The cults at Bethel and Dan undermined the worship and morals of Israel, and earned Jeroboam the title, "who made Israel to sin." Although he showed immense promise in his younger days, most of his twenty-two years as king were disappointing. Egypt overran his nation at least once, and Judah skirmished almost continually with his troops. He died unmourned. I KINGS 11:26—40; 12:1—32; 13:1—33; 14:1—30; 15:1—34; 16:1—31; 21:22; 22:52; II KINGS 3:3; 9:9; 10:29, 31; 13:2—11; 14:24; 15:9—28; 17:21, 22; 23:15; II CHRONICLES 9:29; 10:2—15; 11:4, 14; 12:15; 13:1—20

2 The son of Jehoash, Jeroboam II, fourth king of the house of Jehu, ruled Israel for forty-one years (790—749 B.C.). Noting that Israel's old enemy, Syria, was distracted by a war with the Assyrians, Jeroboam II recovered most of the territory held by King David centuries earlier, and brought Israel to its last pinnacle of prestige and prosperity. At the same time, social conditions during the reign of Jeroboam II were horrible: the poor were oppressed, justice ignored, luxury worshipped, morality flouted. During Jeroboam II's reign, the prophets Amos and Hosea repeatedly warned the nation of the judgment and doom that would inevitably come. II KINGS 13:13; 14:16—29; 15:1, 8; I CHRONICLES 5:17; HOSEA 1:1; AMOS 1:1; 7:9—11

JEROHAM

1 The grandfather of the prophet Samuel, this Jeroham was a Levite who lived in the hill country of Ephraim. I SAMUEL 1:1; I CHRONICLES 6: 27, 34

2 A well-known warrior and clan chieftain in the tribe of Benjamin, this Jeroham was also remembered as the ancestor of Ibneiah, one of the first to return to Jerusalem after the Exile in Babylon. I CHRONICLES 8:27; 9:8

3 A priest who lived at the time of the Exile in Babylon, this Jeroham was the father of Adaiah, who was one of the first priests to return to Jerusalem when the Jews were permitted to come home. I CHRONICLES 9:12; 11:12

4 A member of the tribe of Benjamin who lived in Gedor, this Jeroham was the father of Joelah and Zebadiah, two doughty, ambidextrous fighters who joined David when he was an outlaw at Ziglag. I CHRONICLES 12:7

5 A member of the tribe of Dan, this Jeroham was the father of Azarel, chief of the tribe at the time of David's census of the nation. I CHRONICLES 27:22

6 Another Jeroham, this man was

remembered as the father of the bold army commander, Azariah, who joined the conspiracy headed by the high priest Jehoiada to depose the vicious Queen Athaliah and crown young Joash as king of Judah. II CHRONICLES 23:1

JERUBAAL See GIDEON

JERUSHA King Uzziah's wife, Jerusha was the daughter of Zadok and the mother of Jotham, son and successor of Uzziah as king of Judah. II KINGS 15:33; II CHRONICLES 27:1

JERUSHAH See JERUSHA

JESAIAH See JESHAIAH

JESHAIAH
1 A descendant of David, this Jeshaiah is listed in the records of the royal family of Judah as a grandson of Zerubbabel, leader of the first contingent of Jews from Babylon to Jerusalem after the Exile. I CHRONICLES 3:21
2 One of the sons of Jeduthun, the Levite musician in David's sanctuary, this Jeshaiah also played the lyre and prophesied in the worship services in Jerusalem. I CHRONICLES 25:3, 15
3 Another Levite, this Jeshaiah was the ancestor of Shelomoth, one of David's most trusted and important officials in the treasury office of the sanctuary. This Jeshaiah could trace his ancestry to Moses. I CHRONICLES 26:25
4 The son of Athaliah and a descendant of Elam, this Jeshaiah was one of those brave souls who accompanied Ezra from Babylon to devas-

tated Jerusalem after the Exile. EZRA 8:7
5 The head of the Merarite branch of the Levites in Ezra's time, this Jeshaiah was one of those specially recruited from the Levite seminary near Babylon to return with Ezra after the Exile and restore the worship in the Temple in Jerusalem. EZRA 8:19
6 A Benjaminite, this Jeshaiah was remembered as the ancestor of Shallu, one of those elected to live in Jerusalem and help rebuild the ruined city after the Jews returned from Exile in Babylon. NEHEMIAH 11:7

JESHARELAH A prominent Levite musician in David's sanctuary, Jesharelah was picked by lot to head up the seventh contingent of those presiding in the musical worship services. I CHRONICLES 25:14

JESHEBEAB A prominent musician from the tribe of Levite, Jeshebeab selected the lot to preside over the fourteenth course of musicians in the services in David's sanctuary. I CHRONICLES 24:13

JESHER A son of Caleb, Hezron's son, of the tribe of Judah, Jesher was an early clan chieftain in the tribe whose name was preserved in the tribe's genealogy. I CHRONICLES 2:18

JESHISHAI An early clan chieftain in the tribe of Gad, Jeshishai was the ancestor of the sons of Abihail, members of the tribe who settled in Palestine after the tribe's wanderings with Moses. I CHRONICLES 5:14

JESHOHAIAH One of the powerful

181

JESHUA

clan chieftains in the tribe of Simeon, Jeshohaiah, with others of his tribe, threw the Amalekites out of the rich valley of Gedor and settled there themselves during the reign of King Hezekiah. I CHRONICLES 4:36

JESHUA

1 In Nehemiah 8:17 this refers to JOSHUA, SON OF NUN (which see).

2 A prominent Levite, this Jeshua was a priest who headed the ninth detachment of priests in the services in David's sanctuary. I CHRONICLES 24:11

3 Another Levite, this Jeshua lived in King Hezekiah's time in Judah, and was assigned a key position, distributing the offerings in the treasurer's office in the Temple. II CHRONICLES 31:15

4 The ancestor of a group that returned from the Exile in Babylon to Jerusalem with Zerubbabel, this Jeshua was a member of the family of Pahath-moab. EZRA 2:6; NEHEMIAH 7:11

5 A Levite who was the head of a prominent family which helped Nehemiah rebuild the Temple after the return from the Exile in Babylon, Jeshua assisted in teaching the Law to the people and joined Nehemiah in sealing the covenant. EZRA 2:40; 3:9; 8:33; NEHEMIAH 8:7; 9:4; 10:9; 12:8, 24

6 The most famous of those named Jeshua at the time of the return from Exile in Babylon, this man was high priest when the first contingent returned to Jerusalem with Zerubbabel. His grandfather, Seriah, had been high priest fifty years earlier when Jerusalem fell, and Jeshua's father, Jehozadak, was taken as a captive to Babylon. When he arrived in Jerusalem, Jeshua started work on rebuilding the altar, and spurred his countrymen to rebuild the ruined Temple. The prophets Haggai and Zechariah referred to Jeshua as "Joshua." EZRA 3:2—9; 4:3; 5:2; 10:18; NEHEMIAH 7:7; 12:1, 7, 10, 26; HAGGAI 1:1, 12, 14; ZECHARIAH 3:1; 6:10, 11

JESHUAH See JESHUA

JESIAH See ISHHIAH

JESIMIEL A chieftain in the tribe of Simeon at the time of King Hezekiah of Judah, Jesimiel, with many other warriors who were also heads of families, chased the Amalekites out of the rich vale of Gedor and settled there with his family and flocks. I CHRONICLES 4:36

JESSE The grandson of Ruth and Boaz, Jesse is best remembered as the father of the great King David. He was a prominent man, perhaps the leader, at Bethlehem, and the father of eight sons. During David's outlaw days, Jesse and his wife were sent to relatives at Moab for safety. He was undoubtedly elderly by that time, and probably did not live to see his youngest son crowned as king of the united monarchy. Although in David's day the term "son of Jesse" was spoken with a sneer, to call attention to David's humble origins, in time it came to be used as a synonym for the expected Messiah. RUTH 4:17, 22; I SAMUEL 16, 17, 20, 22, 25; II SAMUEL 20:1; 23:1; I KINGS 12:16; I CHRONICLES 2:12; 2: 13; 10:14; 12:18; 29:26; II CHRONICLES 10:16; 11:18; ISAIAH 11:1, 10

JESUS

1 Born at Bethlehem during the last years of Herod the Great (MATTHEW 1:18—25; LUKE 2:1—7), Jesus, at His birth, was acclaimed God's Chosen One by shepherds (LUKE 2:8—20). As an infant, Jesus was circumcised and presented in the Temple at Jerusalem, in keeping with Jewish tradition (LUKE 2:21—39). Shortly afterward, star-studying wise men from the East presented Him with gifts of gold, frankincense, and myrrh. (MATTHEW 2:1—12). Warned that King Herod, jealous of the appearance of a newborn rival at Bethlehem, had ordered a massacre of male infants, Joseph and Mary rushed young Jesus to safety in Egypt. (MATTHEW 2:13 —23). Jesus' family remained in Egypt until Herod's death, then went to live at Nazareth in Galilee. Apart from mention of a visit to Jerusalem when He was twelve (LUKE 2:41— 50), there are no other Biblical records of Jesus' boyhood at Nazareth.

When John the Baptist began his ministry, Jesus, then a young man, presented Himself for baptism. Waving aside John the Baptist's protests that he was unworthy to baptize Jesus, Jesus insisted on being baptized (MATTHEW 3:13—17; MARK 1:9—11; LUKE 3:21—23), then withdrew to the wilderness to think and pray about His mission. During this sojourn in the desert, He struggled with temptations (MATTHEW 4:1—11; MARK 1:12 —13; LUKE 4:1—13).

Jesus' public ministry began in His home province of Galilee. Calling for repentance, He announced the imminence of the Kingdom of God (MATTHEW 4:12—17; MARK 1:14—15; LUKE 4:14—15). Rejected in His hometown, Nazareth (LUKE 4:16— 30), Jesus went to the area near the Sea of Galilee (MATTHEW 4:13—16; LUKE 4:31) and called the first of His disciples from His audiences of fishermen near Capernaum (MATTHEW 4: 18—22; MARK 1:16—20; LUKE 5:1 —11; JOHN 1:35—51). These followers accompanied Jesus on His highly successful preaching and healing tour through villages in Galilee. At this point in His career, Jesus enjoyed great popularity among the common people. He began to encounter hostility, however, among the religious leaders, especially when He seemed to treat the Law casually by "working" (healing the sick and plucking grain) on the Sabbath (MATTHEW 12: 1—14; MARK 2:23—28; 3:1—6; LUKE 6:1—11).

Aware that the hostility of the authorities would harden into opposition and persecution, Jesus taught His followers the responsibilities of citizenship in His Kingdom in the Sermon on the Mount (MATTHEW 5, 6, 7) and in parables of the Kingdom (MATTHEW 13). Choosing twelve disciples for special duties (MATTHEW 10:2—

183

JESUS

4; MARK 3:13—19; LUKE 6:12—19), He instructed them and sent them on a quick tour to announce the Kingdom's coming (MATTHEW 9:35—10: 4; MARK 6:6; LUKE 9:1—2).

Shortly afterward, John the Baptist was arrested and beheaded. John's execution made it advisable for Jesus to leave Galilee for a time. Withdrawing to the "pagan" or Gentile areas to the northeast, Jesus, certain that it was only a matter of time until He would be seized and killed, tried to make His disciples aware of His unique mission. On the road to Caesarea-Philippi, He asked them point-blank, "Who do you say that I am?" (MATTHEW 16:13—20; MARK 8:27—30; LUKE 9:18—20). After Peter recognized Jesus' messiahship, Jesus pointed out to the incredulous disciples that this messiahship entailed suffering, death, and resurrection (MATTHEW 16:21—23; MARK 8:31—33; LUKE 9: 21—22). The meaning of Jesus' person, mission, and message was further disclosed to three disciples, Peter, James, and John, when Jesus was transfigured on the slopes of Mount Hermon (MATTHEW 17:1—13; MARK 9:2—13; LUKE 9:28—36).

In the autumn, Jesus paid a visit to Jerusalem during the Feast of Tabernacles. Even though He went to the feast privately, He encountered deep personal hostility from the nation's religious leaders (JOHN 7:1—52). His debates with the authorities in the Temple on His claim that He was the Light of the World (JOHN 8:12—30) provoked His enemies to conspire to silence Him. He did attend the Feast, however, and managed to leave Jerusalem safely (JOHN 10:22—42).

Aware of His impending arrest and death, Jesus instructed a larger group of followers, the Seventy, and sent them on a mission tour (LUKE 10:1—24). In the spring, Jesus approached Jerusalem again. When He arrived at Bethany, He learned to His sorrow that His beloved friend Lazarus, with whom He had often stayed, had died. Jesus astonished everyone by raising Lazarus from the dead (JOHN 11:1—44). The Jerusalem temple authorities, however, were incensed over Jesus' power and popularity. Because of their plots against His life, Jesus withdrew briefly to Ephraim (JOHN 11:45—57).

Knowing that He could easily have stayed in relative safety in Ephraim, Jesus nonetheless chose to fulfill His mission of redemptive suffering. He returned to Jerusalem at Passover time for what was His final visit. His triumphal entry was a public announcement of His messiahship (MATTHEW 21:1—11; MARK 11:1—11; LUKE 19:29—44; JOHN 12:12—19). Boldly carrying His message to the citadel of the opposition, Jesus cleansed the Temple, driving out the moneychangers and animal dealers (MATTHEW 21:12—17; MARK 11:15 —19; LUKE 19:45—48; JOHN 2:13—25).

The chief priests, scribes, and elders challenged Jesus' authority (MATTHEW 21:23—27; MARK 11:27—33; LUKE 20:1—8), and later schemed to trap Jesus with trick questions (MATTHEW 22:15—40; MARK 12:13—34; LUKE 20:20—40). Countering their questions with answers that effectively silenced the interrogators, Jesus denounced the authorities for their hypocrisy (MATTHEW 23:1—39; MARK 12:38—40; LUKE 20:45—47). The disciple Judas joined the conspiracy against Jesus and agreed to lead the authorities to Jesus at a time when they could arrest Jesus in semi-secret. (MATTHEW 26:1—5; 14—16; MARK 14:1—2; 10—11; LUKE 22:1—6).

Thursday was to be Jesus' last day with His disciples. They met together for what was later remembered as the Last Supper (MATTHEW 26:17—30; MARK 14:12—26; LUKE 22:7—30; JOHN 13:1—30). After instituting the Lord's Supper (MATTHEW 26:26—29; MARK 14:22—25; LUKE 22:14—23), Jesus gave His farewell discourse to His contentious disciples (MATTHEW 26:31—35; MARK 14:27—31; LUKE 22:31—38; JOHN 13:31—16:33) and interceded for them in prayer (JOHN 17).

Later, in an olive orchard, known as Gethsemane, outside Jerusalem, Jesus suffered agonies of loneliness and temptation (MATTHEW 26:36—46; MARK 14:32—42; LUKE 22:39—46; JOHN 18:1). That night, betrayed by Judas, Jesus was arrested and marched to the high priest's house for an informal hearing (MATTHEW 26:47 —56; MARK 14:43—52; LUKE 22:47 —53; JOHN 18:1—11). Following the preliminary hearing, Jesus was arraigned before Annas and the high priest Caiaphas and the assembly of the religious authorities, and condemned to death for blasphemy (MATTHEW 26:57; 27:1; MARK 14:53—72; LUKE 22:54—71; JOHN 18:13—27). Because the religious leaders were not empowered to carry out a death sentence without Roman approval, Jesus was remanded to the Roman procurator, Pontius Pilate. The expectation was that Jesus would be speedily executed (MATTHEW 27:2, 11—14; MARK 15:1—5; LUKE 23:1—5; JOHN 18:28 —38). In spite of Pilate's attempts to evade his responsibility by turning Jesus over to Herod (LUKE 23:6—12), and later by trying to release Jesus as a favor to the populace (MATTHEW 27:15—26; MARK 15:6—15; LUKE 23: 13—25; JOHN 18:38—40), Jesus was finally handed over to a squad of soldiers for execution by crucifixion.

After dying on a cross (MATTHEW 27:32—56; MARK 15:21—41; LUKE 23:26—49; JOHN 19:16—37), Jesus' body was buried in a tomb borrowed from Joseph of Arimathea by Joseph and Nicodemus, two members of the Sanhedrin (MATTHEW 27:57—61; MARK 15:42—47; LUKE 23:50—56; JOHN 19:38—42).

On the day following the Sabbath, a group of women visited Jesus tomb, expecting to minister to Jesus' corpse. Finding the tomb empty, they rushed back to Jerusalem and notified the disciples. Before Peter and John reached the tomb, however, Mary Magdalene and others of the women were confronted by Jesus risen from the dead (MATTHEW 28:8—10; JOHN 20:11— 18).

Jesus subsequently appeared to Peter and a companion on the road to Emmaus (MARK 16:12—13; LUKE 24: 13—35), to the disciples in the Upper Room on two occasions (MARK 16:14; LUKE 24:36—43; JOHN 20:19 —29), to seven disciples beside the Sea of Galilee (JOHN 21:1—23), to the eleven on a mountain in Galilee (MATTHEW 28:16—20; MARK 16:15 —18), and to others, including Paul (I CORINTHIANS 15:5—8; ACTS 9:3— 6; 22:6—10; 26:12—18). After a final appearance before the eleven disciples at Jerusalem forty days after the resurrection, Jesus ascended to the Father (MARK 16:19—20; LUKE 24: 44—53; ACTS 1:2—9), and was seen no more except by Paul on the Damascus road (I CORINTHIANS 15:8; ACTS 9:3—6; 22:6—10; 26:12—18). He continues to live, however, and rules as the risen Lord and Saviour of all men. Each of the twenty-seven books in the New Testament carries references to Jesus.

2 A companion of the Apostle Paul, this Jesus was also known by his Greek name, Justus. He was undoubtedly originally a Jew who had acknowledged Jesus as Christ. When Paul was first a prisoner in Rome, Jesus-Justus thoughtfully looked after him. He joined Paul in sending greetings to the Christians at Colossae. Unfortunately, no other details of his life are known. COLOSSIANS 4:11

JESUI See ISHVI

JETHER

1 The name given in Exodus 4:18 for Moses' father-in-law, this Jether was elsewhere always called JETHRO (which see). EXODUS 4:18

2 The great warrior-judge Gideon's oldest son, this Jether appeared briefly in the Biblical narrative when, as a youngster, he was commanded by his father to avenge his uncle's death by killing Zebah and Zalmunna, the two Midianite chieftains. Jether, however, hesitated; Gideon swiftly stepped up and executed them. JUDGES 8:20

3 David's brother-in-law, this Jether was an Ishmaelite who married Abigail, David's sister, and became the father of Amasa. He was known also as ITHRA (which see). I KINGS 2:5, 32; I CHRONICLES 2:17; II SAMUEL 17: 25

4 A son of Jada, a chieftain in the tribe of Judah, this Jether was noted in the tribal genealogy as one who had the misfortune to die childless. I CHRONICLES 2:32

5 Another by the same name in the tribe of Judah, this Jether was one of the sons of Ezrah, a descendant of Moses' great spy, Caleb. This Jether was a clan chieftain in the tribe in the early days. I CHRONICLES 4:17

6 One of the early leaders in the tribe of Asher, this Jether is listed in the family tree of tribal notables by the Chronicler. I CHRONICLES 7:38

JETHETH An obscure chieftain of the Edomites in the early days of the tribe, Jetheth was believed to be a descendant of Esau. GENESIS 36:40; I CHRONICLES 1:51

JETHRO Moses' father-in-law, Jethro was the priest and chief of a clan called Kenites, part of the tribe of Midianites who wandered the desert areas of the northern Sinai peninsula. Moses met Jethro's daughter, Zipporah, after fleeing a murder charge in Egypt, married her, and settled down as one of Jethro's shepherds until the encounter with the Lord at the burning bush. Jethro advised Moses to return to Egypt, and later, during the trying days after the Exodus from Egypt, Jethro joined the wandering Israelite horde. He counseled Moses to delegate responsibilities to others, and acted as a desert guide for a time. He was also known by the names Hobab and Reuel. EXODUS 3:1; 4:18; 18:1—12; NUMBERS 10:29; JUDGES 1:16; 4:11

JETUR Ishmael's son and Hagar's grandson, Jetur was an ancient patriarch whose family became known as the tribe called Jetur. GENESIS 25:15; I CHRONICLES 1:31

JEUEL
1 A descendant of Zerah in the tribe of Judah, this Jeuel was the head of one of the first clans to return after the Exile in Babylon to Jerusalem. I CHRONICLES 9:6
2 A well-known Levite, this Jeuel was the ancestor of a family that took an active part in cleaning up the dilapidated Temple during King Hezekiah's reform in Judah. II CHRONICLES 29:13
3 A Jew who lived in Babylon during the Exile, this Jeuel was one of the brave group that joined Ezra in returning to the homeland to rebuild Jerusalem. EZRA 8:13

JEUSH
1 One of the sons of Esau and his wife Aholibamah, this Jeush became one of the ancient leaders of an Edo-

mite clan. GENESIS 36:5, 14, 18; I CHRONICLES 1:35
2 One of Jediael's sons in the tribe of Benjamin, this Jeush is listed with the other early renowned tribal chieftains by the Chronicler. I CHRONICLES 7:10
3 One of Saul's descendants, this Jeush was a son of Eshek and was mentioned in the family genealogy of the tribe of Benjamin. I CHRONICLES 8:39
4 A Levite of the Gershom side of the tribe, this Jeush was one of Shimei's sons who lived at the time of David's census of the kingdom. Because neither Jeush nor his brother, Beriah, had many sons, the two families were lumped together as one in the lists of families in the tribe. I CHRONICLES 23:10, 11
5 The grandson of Solomon and the son of King Rehoboam by his wife Abihail (one of eighteen wives and sixty concubines), this Jeush was one of eighty-eight children of Rehoboam. He was probably one of those appointed to govern a district in the kingdom. II CHRONICLES 11:19

JEUZ One of Sharharaim's sons in the tribe of Benjamin, Jeuz was an ancient clan chieftain in the tribe. I CHRONICLES 8:10

JEZANIAH See JAAZANIAH 1

JEZEBEL The notoriously evil wife of King Ahab of Israel, Jezebel was the daughter of King Ethbaal of Tyre, and an ardent Baal worshipper. She imported her cult to Israel when she married Ahab, and tried to force it on

187

her subjects. After Ahab built her an elaborate shrine, complete with hundreds of Baal priests, Elijah and the prophets of the Lord forced a showdown at Mount Carmel, and temporarily they won out. Vengeful Jezebel, however, forced Elijah to flee for his life. Jezebel's ruthlessness was legendary. When Ahab yearned to get a vineyard owned by Naboth, Jezebel contrived to have Naboth murdered and the property assigned to Ahab. Elijah boldly predicted that God's judgment would bring the speedy downfall of Ahab's family. Ahab died in battle, but Jezebel reigned for another ten years through her two sons, Ahaziah and Jehoram, both kings of Israel. When Jehu's sudden revolt removed Jehoram, Jezebel was hurled alive from the palace window by her servants. After the victory banquet, when Jehu's men returned to bury her body, they discovered that everything except her hands had been devoured by dogs—a final touch of ignominy. I KINGS 16:31; 18:4—19; 19:1—2; 21: 5—21; II KINGS 9:7—37

JEZER Naphtali's third son, Jezer accompanied his father and the rest of Jacob's family to Egypt when Joseph invited them to settle there after famine struck Canaan. Later, Jezer became known as a chieftain in the tribe of Naphtali. His descendants, known as Jezerites, went with Moses from Egypt. GENESIS 46:24; NUMBERS 46: 29; I CHRONICLES 7:13

JEZIAH See IZZIAH

JEZIEL One of Azmaveth's two sons who joined David at Ziglag, Jeziel and his brother, Pelet, were bold Benjaminites who could fire a sling or shoot a bow with either their right hand or their left. I CHRONICLES 12:3

JEZLIAH See IZLIAH

JEZOAR See IZHAR

JEZRAHIAH The song leader at the great service where Nehemiah rededicated the rebuilt walls of Jerusalem, Jezrahiah was a prominent Levite in charge of the musicians. He was also known as IZRAHIAH in I Chronicles 7:3 (which see). NEHEMIAH 12:42

JEZREEL See page 207

JIBSAM See IBSAM

JIDLAPH Abraham's nephew, Jidlaph was a son of Nahor, Abraham's brother, and the head of an ancient clan in the tribe of the Nahorites. GENESIS 22:22

JIMNA See IMNA

JIMNAH See IMNA

JOAB

1 The son of Zeruiah, David's sister, and therefore the nephew of David, Joab was a ruthless but loyal professional soldier who became commander-in-chief of David's army. He avenged his brother's death by treacherously slaughtering Abner when the latter wanted to surrender to David —thereby also eliminating a possible rival in the army. Joab quickly won a reputation as a competent but brutal general, seizing Jerusalem and conquering the Edomites, Syrians, and Ammonites for his uncle. Unquestioningly obedient—even to the point of becoming an accessory to David's crime—Joab arranged to have Bathsheba's husband, Uriah, killed in action so that David could take Bathsheba. Later, Joab firmly put down Absalom's revolt, even though he had once been a friend of Absalom. He disobeyed David's orders against killing Absalom, however, and was bypassed for a time when Sheba's revolt broke out. When David finally called on Joab to take over the campaign from the faltering Amasa, Joab quickly killed his rival Amasa and successfully quashed the revolt. When David was on his deathbed, Joab backed the wrong man, Adonijah, as David's successor. Solomon, taking no chances with Joab, ordered him put to death. I SAMUEL 26:6; II SAMUEL 2:13—32; 3:22—31; 8:16; 10:7—14; 11:1—25; 12:26—27; 14:1—33; 17:25; 18:2—29; 19:1—13; 20:7—23; 23:18—37; 24:2—9; I KINGS 1:1—41; 2:2—23; 11:15—21; I CHRONICLES 2:16; 11:6 —39; 18:15; 19:8—15; 20:1; 21:3—6; 28:28; 27:7—34

2 A member of the tribe of Judah, this Joab was the son of Seraiah, and the father of a famous family of craftsmen. I CHRONICLES 4:14

3 This man Joab was the head of a family which returned with Zerubbabel from the Exile in Babylon to Jerusalem. EZRA 2:16; 8:19; NEHEMIAH 7:11

JOAH

1 A son of Asaph, keeper of the records in King Hezekiah's court, this first Joah was one of three officials sent by Hezekiah to parley from the city walls with the Assyrian leaders at the time Jerusalem was beseiged. Joah and his two cohorts were frightened by the Assyrians, and tried unsuccessfully to have the conversation conducted in Aramaic so that the people of Jerusalem would not be unnerved by the boasts and threats of the beseigers. II KINGS 18:18—37; ISAIAH 36:3—22

2 A Levite in the early days of the tribe, this Joah was a descendant of Gershom, and head of a family in the tribe. I CHRONICLES 6:21; II CHRONICLES 29:12

3 Another Levite, this Joah was from the Kohath side of the tribe and served as a gatekeeper in David's sanctuary in Jerusalem. I CHRONICLES 26:4

4 Still another Levite, this Joah was a son of Joahaz, recorder in the court of King Josiah. He was one of the most prominent among those assigned to repair the Temple during Josiah's reformation in Judah. II CHRONICLES 34:8

JOAHAZ A well-known Levite at the time of King Josiah of Judah, Joahaz served as chief record-keeper in the court. II CHRONICLES 34:8

JOANAN The grandson of Zerubbabel, Joanan was listed as one of Joseph's ancestors in Luke's genealogy of Jesus' family. LUKE 3:27

JOANNA One of that loyal group of women who were followers of Jesus, Joanna was the wife of Chuza, Herod Antipas' superintendent of royal properties. Healed by Jesus, Joanna grate-

JOASH

fully supplied Jesus and the Twelve with money for their needs, and went to Jerusalem with the group that accompanied Jesus on His last journey. Joanna was with the pathetic handful of women that went to the tomb to embalm Jesus' body and, instead, were surprised by the unexpected news of the resurrection. LUKE 8:3; 24:10

JOASH

1 Father of the great hero and judge of Israel, Gideon, this Joash was headman in his home town among the tribe of Manasseh, and wealthy enough to afford ten servants. Although he looked after the shrine of Baal, he supported his son, Gideon. When Gideon tore down the shrine, Joash not only refused to give in to the enraged townsfolk who wanted to lynch Gideon, but scorned Baal worship in words that later were used by Elijah at Mount Carmel. JUDGES 6—8

2 One of the sons of King Ahab of Israel, this Joash looked after his father's interests at the capital when Ahab was away. Ahab sent the prophet Micaiah to Joash in Samaria, to be imprisoned for predicting defeat for Ahab. I KINGS 22:26; II CHRONICLES 18:25

3 One of Judah's grandsons, this Joash was a son of Shelah, and an ancient clan chief in the tribe. I CHRONICLES 4:22

4 One of Benjamin's grandsons, this Joash was a son of Becher, and an early chieftain in the tribe. I CHRONICLES 7:8

5 A formidable fighter from the tribe of Benjamin who was one of the tough crew that left Saul to join David at Ziglag, this Joash was second-in-command. He could shoot with either hand, and was a deadly marksman with both the bow and sling. I CHRONICLES 12:3

6 A trusted employee of David's, this Joash looked after David's stores of oil. I CHRONICLES 27:28

7 For the king of Judah who in some translations is named Joash, see JEHOASH **1**.

8 For the king of Israel who in some translations is named Joash, see JEHOASH **2**.

JOATHAM One of Joseph's ancestors in Matthew's list of Jesus' forbears, Joatham is listed simply as a son of one Ozias. MATTHEW 1:9

JOB The patient, upright man in the Book of Job whose trust in God could not be shaken, Job was a prosperous, respected family man in the land of Uz who suffered an incredible series of calamities. His wealth suddenly was lost, his children killed. God's adversary, Satan, claimed that Job's piety was superficial, and that Job would forsake God as soon as any setback hit him. When Job's faith remained steadfast, Satan sneered that Job still had his health. Job was next afflicted with a horrid disease. Nonetheless, he refused to listen to his wife's advice to curse God and die. His friends, Eliphaz, Bildad, and Zophar, reflecting the popular viewpoint that all suffering was caused by sin, called upon Job to confess whatever monstrous deeds he had done to bring on such misery. Throughout the ex-

190

perience Job worked his way deeper into the eternal problem of human suffering, and finally was led to understand that God is to be trusted even though life itself should be taken away. Most scholars doubt that Job was actually a historical person. JOB; EZEKIEL 14:14, 20; JAMES 5:11

2 For the name listed in some translations of Genesis 46:13 as Job, see IOB.

JOBAB

1 One of Joktan's sons, and a descendant of Noah's son, Shem, this Jobab was an ancient Semite chieftain whose descendants were connected with the Sabaeans, according to some early Sabaean inscriptions. GENESIS 10:29; I CHRONICLES 1:23

2 An early king of Edom, this Jobab was a son of Zerah of Bosrah. His name is mentioned in the tribal records because the Edomites were descended from Esau, Isaac's son. GENESIS 36:33, 34: I CHRONICLES 1:44, 45

3 The head man of the city-state of Madon in Canaan at the time of Joshua's conquest, this Jobab was pulled into an alliance with most other Canaanite leaders to oppose Joshua. Jobab brought his troops to the meeting place by the waters of Merom and joined the enormous force gathered there. Before this formidable army could move, however, Joshua made a surprise attack and wiped out Jobab and the others. JOSHUA 1:1ff

4 A member of the tribe of Benjamin, this Jobab was a son of Shaharaim by his wife Hodesh, and an

early clan chieftain in the tribe. I CHRONICLES 8:9

5 Another Benjaminite, this Jobab was listed in the tribal genealogy as a son of Elpaal. He, too, was an ancient chieftain in the tribe. I CHRONICLES 8:18

JOCHEBED The wife of Amram, Jochebed is best remembered as the mother of Moses and Aaron. The writer of Exodus states that Jochebed was the daughter of Levi. A resourceful person, Jochebed hid her infant son, Moses, from the Pharoah's squads by putting him in a watertight crib along the Nile near the Princess' walk. The ruse worked when the Princess discovered the baby and hired Jochebed to be the nurse for Moses. Although Moses was raised in the luxury of the Egyptian court, he never forgot that he was a Hebrew. Jochebed obviously counteracted all the corroding forces of the Pharaoh's palace during Moses' formative years, and deserves much credit for molding the character of the great leader. EXODUS 2:1ff; 6:20; NUMBERS 26:59

JODA One of Jesus' ancestors according to one genealogy, Joda is mentioned in the family tree that Luke sets out for Joseph. LUKE 3:26

JOED The father of Meshullam and grandfather of Shallu, one of those who returned to live in Jerusalem after the Exile, Joed was a member of the tribe of Benjamin. NEHEMIAH 11:7

JOEL

1 The son of Pethuel, this Joel was the author of the treatise on God's judgment that is known as the second book of the Minor Prophets. He wrote at a time when plagues of locusts had devastated the country for several years. Although Joel interprets this calamity as God's judgment for the sins of Judah, he promises a new outpouring of God's spirit and the ultimate salvation of Jerusalem. Scholars cannot agree on whether this strange yet fascinating prophet wrote at the time of the Assyrian invasions (eighth century B.C.) or after the Exile in Babylon (sixth, fifth or fourth centuries B.C.), although most now lean toward a later date. JOEL; ACTS 2:16

2 The eldest son of the great prophet Samuel, this Joel was a dishonest, greedy judge at Beersheba. Because Joel and his brother Abijah were so scandalously corrupt, the elders of Israel did not want Samuel's sons to rule, and insisted that Samuel find Israel a king. I SAMUEL 8:2; I CHRONICLES 6:28, 33; 15:17

3 A Levite, this Joel was remembered as one of the great Samuel's ancestors. I CHRONICLES 6:36

4 A chieftain in the tribe of Simeon at the time of King Hezekiah, this Joel was one of those who trekked into the lush valley of Gedor, slaughtered the Amalekites living there, and took it over for himself. I CHRONICLES 4:35

5 An early leader in the tribe of Reuben, this Joel was named in one tribal genealogy. I CHRONICLES 5:4, 8

6 A chief in the tribe of Gad, this Joel probably lived about the time that the tribes were settling down after the wanderings in the desert. I CHRONICLES 5:12

7 An early clan chieftain in the tribe of Issachar, this Joel was listed in the tribal records as one of the sons of Izrahiah. I CHRONICLES 7:3

8 Another Joel, identified as a brother of Nathan, this man was one of David's toughest soldiers. He won immortality by being selected as one of David's roll of heroes, "The Thirty." I CHRONICLES 11:38

9 A Levite of the Gershom branch of the tribe, this Joel was given a prominent part in the festivities when David brought the Ark up to Jerusalem shortly after his coronation. I CHRONICLES 15:7, 11

10 Another well-known Levite in David's time, this Joel was a son of Ladan and was one of those put in charge of the treasury of the House of the Lord in Jerusalem. I CHRONICLES 23:8; 26:22

11 Another Levite who carried the name Joel, this man was a son of Azariah. He was one of those who took an active part in repairing the run-down Temple during King Hezekiah's reform. II CHRONICLES 29:12

12 The son of Pedaiah, this Joel was the headman of the half-tribe of Manasseh at the time of David's census of the tribes. I CHRONICLES 27:20

13 The son of Zichri, this Joel was the overseer of those of his tribe (Benjamin) who returned to Jerusalem after the Exile in Babylon to rebuild the ruined city. NEHEMIAH 11:9

JOELAH One of the sons of Jeroham of Gedor, Joelah and his brother, Zebadiah, were among the group of Benjaminite fighters who left Saul to join David at Ziglag. They were fierce men who could fight with either hand with both the bow and sling. I CHRONICLES 12:7

JOEZER One of the group from the tribe of Benjamin that left Saul to join David at Ziglag, Joezer was a tough fighter who could handle both the bow and sling expertly with either his right hand or his left. I CHRONICLES 12:6

JOGLI One of the tribe of Dan, Jogli was the father of Bukki, the man selected to represent Dan when Moses asked for a representative from each of the tribes to help him divide the Promised Land justly among them. NUMBERS 34:22

JOHA

1 One of the sons of Beriah of the tribe of Benjamin, this Joha was a tribal chieftain who headed a clan in the early days of the tribe. I CHRONICLES 8:16

2 One of the two sons of Shimri who had the honor of being selected as a member of David's elite corps of troopers, this Joha was a mighty warrior. I CHRONICLES 11:45

JOHANAN

1 An officer in the army of the nation of Judah after Jerusalem fell to the Babylonians, Johanan pledged his loyalty to Gedaliah, the Babylon-appointed ruler of the devastated country. Johanan got wind of Ishmael's plot to murder Gedeliah, warned Gedeliah, but was refused permission to kill Ishmael first. After Ishmael managed to kill Gedeliah, Johanan unsuccessfully pursued Ishmael. Johanan realized that the Babylonians would suspect him and his friends of complicity in Gedeliah's death, and decided to flee to Egypt. He forced the prophet Jeremiah to go along with him. II KINGS 25:23; JEREMIAH 40:8—16; 41:11—15; 42:1—8; 43:2—5

2 The oldest son of King Josiah of Judah, Johanan is listed in the genealogy of the royal family of Judah. Because the crown was passed directly to his younger brother, Jehoiakim, and his descendants, some scholars think that this Johanan died young. I CHRONICLES 3:15

3 One of the sons of Elioenai, a member of the royal family of Judah, this Johanan lived after the time of the Exile. His chief claim to fame was being a distant descendant of David. I CHRONICLES 3:24

4 A Levite who was descended from a distinguished line of priests and whose father, Azariah, was high priest under Solomon, this Johanan was a high priest in the Temple, probably in King Rehoboam's time. I CHRONICLES 6:9, 10

5 One of the group of fighters from the tribe of Benjamin that left Saul to join David at Ziglag, this Johanan was a valiant soldier who could fight with either hand with both the bow and the sling. I CHRONICLES 12:4

6 A shaggy mountain man from the tribe of Gad, this Johanan was a fleet-footed warrior who was eighth in reputation among the group from Gad that joined David in the wilderness. I CHRONICLES 12:12

7 A son of Hakkatan, this Johanan was one of the group of brave souls that left Babylon with Ezra to return and rebuild devastated Jerusalem after the Exile. EZRA 8:12

8 A chieftain in the tribe of Ephraim, this Johanan was remembered as the father of Azariah, one of those who showed compassion on captives from Judah after King Ahaz of Judah suffered defeat. II CHRONICLES 28:12

9 For the man named "Johanan" in some translations of Ezra 10:6 and Nehemiah 6:18 see JEHOHANAN **4**.

10 A Levite, this Johanan was a priest at the time of Joiakim, who was high priest in Jerusalem when Nehemiah rebuilt the walls of the ruined city after the Exile. NEHEMIAH 12:22—23

JOHN

1 Called "the Baptist," this John was born when Zechariah and Elizabeth, his parents, were already old. His mother was a relative of Mary, Jesus' mother, making John a cousin of Jesus. Although descended from long lines of priests through both his mother and father, John the Baptist followed the role of the prophet, retreating into the desert (perhaps in response to the death of his aged parents), reflecting on the unfaithfulness of his people, and emerging to preach a compelling message of repentance. He might have had some associations with the Essene community; in any case John, like the Essenes, was ascetic and insisted upon self-immersion to signify cleansing from sin. His manner reminded everyone of the earlier prophets, and stirred the population deeply. Most startling, however, was his announcement that God's message was about to come, and that the hour of judgment was upon the people. Another was to follow him, John announced, who would bring in the new era. John was particularly harsh on the religious authorities for their failure to repent. Great crowds were baptized in the Jordan, among them Jesus. It was not until later, however, that John understood that Jesus was the promised deliverer. He continued his stern preaching until he was arrested by Herod Antipas for daring to denounce the scandalous royal marriage. John the Baptist was beheaded by Antipas, but his influence survived for years. Some of his followers joined Jesus; others continued to revere him. He was the last of the prophets and the forerunner of the Saviour, and, according to Jesus, the greatest man born to woman. MATTHEW 3; 4:12; 9:14; 11:2—18; 14:2—10; 16:14; 17:13; 21:25—32; MARK 1:4—14; 2:18; 6:14—28; 11:27—32; LUKE 1:13—63; 3:2—20; 7:18—33; 9:7—19; 11:1; 16:16; 20:4—6; JOHN 1:6—40; 3:23—27; 4:1; 5:33—36; 10:40—41; ACTS 1:5—22; 10:37; 11:16; 13:24—25; 18:25; 19:3—4

2 The apostle whom Jesus loved, this John was the son of Zebedee and the brother of James the Apostle. With his brother James, John ran a fishing business at Capernaum. He was called by his cousin Jesus to become one of the Twelve, and was always included as one of the inner circle among the disciples. John, with Peter and James, was one of those selected to be with Jesus at the raising of Jairus' daughter, at the transfiguration, and at Gethsemane. He and Peter were selected to prepare the Last Supper, and John was the one to whom Jesus entrusted His mother, Mary, at the cross. John the Apostle had his human side as well. He and his brother James were dubbed "Sons of Thunder." They came storming to Jesus once about a man using Jesus' name to heal, and, on another occasion, about a Samaritan village refusing Jesus hospitality. John's ambitious mother tried to get places of prominence for James and John in Jesus' Kingdom. When the first report of the resurrection reached the disciples, John was first to race to the empty tomb. He was looked up to as one of the leaders among Jesus' followers, and was arrested after healing in Jesus' name and preaching boldly before the authorities. Paul refers to John with respect. John's reverent, eye-witness account of Jesus' life, The Gospel According to John, plus his three Letters and the Revelation make him one of the literary greats of history. There are many traditions outside of the New Testament about John's subsequent career. These indicate that John left Jerusalem and lived at Ephesus until an incredibly old age. Scholars debate the meaning of the references to "John" at Ephesus in fragments of the writings of early Christian leaders. Many authorities link this John at Ephesus with John "the Elder." MATTHEW 4:21; 10:2; 17:1; MARK 1:19; 2:29; 3:17; 5:37; 9:2—38; 10:35—41; 13:3; 14:33; LUKE 5:10; 6:14; 8:51; 9:28—54; 22:8; JOHN, GOSPEL OF; ACTS 1:13; 3:1—11; 4:13—19; 8:14; 12:2; GALATIANS 2:9; I, II, III JOHN; REVELATION

3 Father of Simon Peter, this John was also known as Jona or Jonah. Possibly, like many Jews, he used the Greek form of his Hebrew name as well as the Hebrew, in which case he would have been called Jona-John. Little is known of this John beyond the fact that he was the father of two apostles, Peter and Andrew, was a pious Jew in Galilee, and probably made his living as a fisherman. MATTHEW 16:17; JOHN 1:42—43; 21:15—17

4 A relative of the high priest, Caiaphas, this John was a Jerusalem blueblood who sat on the council of the Sanhedrin. He is mentioned as one of those who gathered hurriedly when the Sanhedrin met in emergency session to decide what action to take against the powerful preaching of the apostles after the resurrection. ACTS 4:6

5 For the nephew of Barnabas known as John who accompanied Paul and Barnabas for a time, see MARK

JOIADA

1 The son of Paseah, this Joiada was one of the intrepid souls who returned to rebuild Jerusalem after the Exile in Babylon. This Joiada repaired the Old Gate. In the King James Version, he is called Jehoiada. NEHEMIAH 3:6

2 The son of Eliashib, this Joiada was a high priest in Nehemiah's time. His son defied the rules against marrying outside the faith, hinting that Joiada himself might not have been

in complete accord with the narrow-minded view then prevailing in Jerusalem after the Exile. NEHEMIAH 12:10, 11, 22; 13:28

JOIAKIM One of the sons of Jeshua, the high priest who returned to Jerusalem with Zerubbabel after the Exile, Joiakim also served as a high priest. NEHEMIAH 12:10, 12, 26

JOIARIB
1 One of the leading men among the exile Jews living in Babylon, this Joiarib was sent by Ezra to the seminary of Iddo to ask for priests to accompany the groups planning to return to rebuild Jerusalem. EZRA 8:16
2 A member of the tribe of Judah, this Joiarib was an ancestor of Maaseiah, one of those who returned to live in Jerusalem after the Exile in Babylon. NEHEMIAH 11:5
3 A priest at the time of the Exile, this third Joiarib was the father of Jedaiah, one of the priests who returned to the devastated Jerusalem with Zerubbabel and agreed to live in the holy city. NEHEMIAH 11:10; 12:6, 19

JOKIM A member of the tribe of Judah, Jokim is the name of a descendant of Judah's son, Shelah, and was a tribal chieftain remembered by the chroniclers of the family tree. I CHRONICLES 4:22

JOKSHAN A son of Abraham and his concubine, Keturah, Jokshan was an ancient desert sheik who was remembered as the father of the tribes of Sheba and Dedan. GENESIS 25:2, 3; I CHRONICLES 1:32

JOKTAN A descendant of Noah through his son, Shem, Joktan was believed to be the progenitor of a number of ancient peoples in the Arabian peninsula. GENESIS 10:25—29; I CHRONICLES 1:19—23

JONADAB See **JEHONADAB**

JONA For the father of Simon Peter, see JOHN 3

JONAH The prophet who went reluctantly to Nineveh to preach repentance, Jonah rebelled at God's commission and tried to escape responsibility by taking a ship to Tarshish. After a storm threatened the safety of the ship, the superstitious crew tossed Jonah overboard. After a terrifying adventure with a monster in the sea, Jonah was cast upon the shore, and grudgingly went ahead with his preaching. Peevish because Nineveh repented, Jonah sulked under a gourd plant. When the gourd, to Jonah's grief, died, God convinced Jonah that He felt the same concern for the Ninevehites. Jonah, the reluctant missionary, was one of the minor prophets in the Old Testament. II KINGS 14:25; THE BOOK OF JONAH; MATTHEW 12:39—41; LUKE 11:29—32

JONATHAN
1 A Levite who was an opportunist, this first Jonathan was a son of Gershom, and lived shortly after the tribes settled in Canaan. Although he was a priest, he hired himself out to Micah, an Ephraimite, as promoter of Micah's Baal cult. Later, when a group of marauding tribesmen from the tribe of

Dan passed by, Jonathan not only stood by while they robbed Micah, but joined the group. This unscrupulous priest was the founder of the Danite priesthood and the founder of the idolatrous cult in Dan. JUDGES 17—18

2 Saul's oldest son and David's closest friend, Jonathan is one of the noblest heroes of the Old Testament. A strapping warrior like his father, Jonathan fought valiantly in the battles against the Philistines, and snatched victory out of defeat at the Pass of Michmash by a bold commando attack. Saul, already showing signs of insanity, ordered that no one was to eat until the following evening. Jonathan, ignorant of the order, grabbed a few handfuls of wild honey while pursuing the enemy, and would have been put to death for disobedience by the unbending Saul had the troops not threatened mutiny. Although heir to Saul's throne, Jonathan was a constant friend of David, even when Saul insisted that David was his arch-rival and tried to hunt David down. Jonathan put David ahead of his own interests and literally saved David's life, yet never was disloyal to his father. His tragic death in Saul's bloody finale at Mount Gilboa led David to compose a moving elegy in Jonathan's memory. I SAMUEL 13, 14, 18—20, 23, 31; II SAMUEL 1:4—26; 4:4; 9:1—7; 21:7—14; I CHRONICLES 8—10

3 The son of Abiathar, one of the high priests during David's reign, this Jonathan was a message carrier for David during the grim days of Absalom's revolt. He also broke the news to Adonijah that Solomon, not Adonijah, had been picked as David's successor on the throne. II SAMUEL 15:27, 36; 17:17, 20; I KINGS 1:42—43

4 David's nephew, this Jonathan was a son of Shimea, David's brother. This Jonathan made a name for himself by killing one of the giants from Gath in man-to-man combat, and served in David's forces. II SAMUEL 21:21; I CHRONICLES 20:7

5 The son of Shagee the Hararite, this Jonathan earned immortality as a fighter by being elected to the exclusive ranks of "The Thirty," David's elite corps. II SAMUEL 23:32; I CHRONICLES 11:34

6 A descendant of Jerahmeel in the tribe of Judah, this Jonathan was the only son of Jada to carry on the family line. He was an ancient chieftain of a clan in the tribe. I CHRONICLES 2:32—33

7 An important official in the treasury department in David's kingdom, this man named Jonathan (known in some translations as Jehonathan) was a son of one Uzziah, and supervised the treasuries in the towns and villages outside of Jerusalem. I CHRONICLES 27:25

8 An uncle of David, this Jonathan was a scholarly man, a scribe, who was noted for his wise counsel and understanding. David appointed him as one of the two tutors for his sons. I CHRONICLES 27:32

9 A scribe who lived in Jerusalem in the days when Judah's time was running out, this Jonathan was the owner of a house which had been converted into a prison. Jeremiah was confined in this place for a time. JEREMIAH 37:15, 20; 38:26

10 In some translations, a man named Jonathan is a leader of one of the small, independent detachments of Judean troops that came to Gedaliah at Mizpah after Jerusalem fell to the Babylonians. This Jonathan, a son of Kareah, was one of the small-bore leaders in the country whom the Babylonians had not bothered to deport. JEREMIAH 40:8

11 Another Jonathan, this man lived during the Exile in Babylon and was the father of Ebed, one of those who returned to Jerusalem with Ezra. EZRA 8:6

12 One of those who returned to Jerusalem after the Exile, this Jonathan, a son of Asahel, bitterly protested Ezra's scheme banning all interfaith marriages and forcing men who had married outside the faith to renounce their non-Jewish wives. EZRA 10:15

13 For the man named in some translations of Nehemiah 12:11 as "Jonathan," see JEHOHANAN 4

14 A son of Malluchi, a priest, this Jonathan, also a priest, was one of those who returned to live in ruined Jerusalem after the Exile in Babylon. NEHEMIAH 12:14

15 Another priest in Jerusalem after the Exile, this Jonathan, a son of Shemaiah, was the father of a man named Zechariah, who played his trumpet at the impressive service when Nehemiah rededicated the walls of Jerusalem. NEHEMIAH 12:35

JORAH A Jew who lived in Babylon during the Exile, Jorah was the father of a family that returned to Jerusalem with Zerubbabel. EZRA 2:18

JORAI An ancient clan chieftain in the tribe of Gad, Jorai is remembered in the family records by the Chronicler. I CHRONICLES 5:13

JORAM

1 Son of Toi, the king of Hamath in Syria, this Joram was sent as an emissary from his father to congratulate David on his victory over Toi's enemy, Hadadezer. II SAMUEL 8:10

2 For the son of King Jehoshaphat whose name is given as "Joram" in some translations, see JEHORAM 2

3 For the son of King Ahab whose name is given as "Joram" in some translations, see JEHORAM 1

4 A son of Elizer, this Joram was a Levite who held a position in the sanctuary treasury office in Jerusalem in David's time. I CHRONICLES 6:25

JORIM This name appears among Jesus' ancestors in Luke's list. LUKE 3:29

JORKEAM A son of Raham, Jorkeam was a member of the tribe of Judah who was descended from Caleb, the spy, and Hezron. He was a clan chieftain remembered in the tribal roll. I CHRONICLES 2:44

JORKOAM   See JORKEAM

JOSAPHAT   See JEHOSHAPHAT

JOSE A distant ancestor of Jesus who was remembered in Luke's genealogy. LUKE 3:29

JOSECH Another name on the list of Jesus' ancestors in Luke's genealogy. LUKE 3:26

JOSEDECH See **JEHOZADAK**

JOSEDEK See **JEHOZADAK**

JOSEPH

1 The next to the youngest son of Jacob, Joseph was his father's favorite. He brashly told his brothers of his dreams in which he was made prominent over them. The brothers jealously planned to murder him, but decided at the last minute to sell him as a slave to a caravan going to Egypt, and reported to Jacob that Joseph had been killed by a marauding animal. In Egypt, Joseph served an army officer named Potiphar. He was industrious and reliable, and soon was promoted to look after all of Potiphar's affairs. Potiphar's wife, meanwhile, began to make advances to Joseph. When Joseph repeatedly refused to betray Potiphar's trust in him and turned down the wife, Potiphar's wife, furious at being scorned, concocted accusations against Joseph. Joseph was fired and jailed. In prison he quickly gained a reputation as an interpreter of dreams. When the Pharaoh was troubled by bad dreams, Joseph was brought to counsel the Pharaoh. Joseph correctly forecast seven fat years of abundant harvests in Egypt, to be followed by seven years of famine. The Pharaoh installed Joseph as prime minister of Egypt. Under Joseph's energetic leadership, ample crop surpluses were raised and stored. When the famine years struck, Egypt sold grain to the hungry. The most touching scenes in Joseph's story occurred when his brothers came to buy food. Although they did not recognize Joseph, he knew them. Joseph forgave them and magnanimously moved his father and brothers to Egypt. Joseph's two sons, Ephraim and Manasseh, were given the same prominence as Joseph's brothers in the affairs of the tribes of Israel. GENESIS 30:24—25; 33:2—7; 35:24; 37—50; EXODUS 1:5—8; 13:9; also references in NUMBERS, DEUTERONOMY, JOSHUA, JUDGES, II SAMUEL, I KINGS, I CHRONICLES, PSALMS, EZEKIEL, AMOS, AND OBADIAH

2 A man in the tribe of Issachar, this Joseph was the father of Igal, one of the spies sent to Canaan by Moses. Joseph advised against trying to invade the land. NUMBERS 13:7

3 One of the sons of the great musician, Asaph, this Joseph, in David's time, played a prominent part in the services, in which he prophesied with lyre, harp, and cymbals. I CHRONICLES 25:2, 9

4 One of the many descendants of Bani who, during the Exile in Babylon, married outside the faith, this Joseph agreed to Ezra's strict rule against interfaith marriages to keep the faith pure. EZRA 10:42

5 One of the family of the priest Shebaniah, this Joseph was also a priest in Jerusalem, and served at the time of the high priest Joiakim, after the return from Exile in Babylon. NEHEMIAH 12:14

6 One of the remote ancestors of Joseph, Jesus' earthly father, this sixth Joseph is listed in Luke's genealogy. LUKE 3:24

7 Another in the genealogy of Jesus, this man is also carried in the roll of ancestors by Luke. LUKE 3:30

8 The kindly carpenter of Nazareth who agreed to go ahead with wedding plans although he knew his betrothed, Mary, was to have a baby, this Joseph was Jesus' earthly father. He was a conscientious Jew who adhered faithfully to the Law, but was considerate enough to plan to spare Mary the indignities required by the Law. When he learned the Divine origin of her unborn Child, he immediately trusted God's promise and married Mary. After the birth of Jesus in Bethlehem and the harrowing flight to Egypt to escape Herod's slaughter of male babies, Joseph resettled his family at Nazareth and lived the quiet life of a village builder-repairman. He was the father of several other children, but apparently died before Jesus began His active ministry. Although the references to Joseph are sparse, he obviously left a deep imprint on Jesus. Not only did Jesus follow Joseph's trade, but He deliberately adopted the name "Father" for God. MATTHEW 1:16—24; LUKE 1:27; 2:4—43; 3:23; 4:22; JOHN 1:45; 6:42

9 One of Jesus' brothers, this man is also known as "Joses." Embarrassed and annoyed by the publicity and controversy Jesus was stirring up, Joseph was probably part of the family delegation which tried to bring Jesus home to Nazareth. Unlike Jesus' other brothers, James and Jude, Joseph never grew to believe in Jesus.

MATTHEW 13:55; 27:56; MARK 6:3; 15:40, 47

10 A well-to-do member of the Jewish council of the Sanhedrin who had deep sympathy for Jesus, this Joseph came from Arimathea. Although he took Jesus seriously, he hesitated to profess his discipleship openly for fear of reprisals. He technically was absolved of any role in the Sanhedrin's part in the crucifixion, but he obviously felt guilty over his timid allegiance to Jesus. The sight of Jesus on the cross stirred Joseph to ask Pilate for Jesus' body and to provide a dignified burial in his own personal tomb. Legends abound about Joseph of Arimathea—the most popular being that he later settled at Glastonbury in Britain. Historians dismiss all of these. MATTHEW 27:57—59; MARK 15:43; LUKE 23:50; JOHN 19:38

11 An early member of the Christian community shortly after the resurrection, this Joseph was known as Joseph Barsabbas, and was nicknamed "Justus." He was one of two men nominated to fill Judas' vacant position in the Twelve but lost to Matthias. We are told that he had been with Jesus during His entire public ministry, and was highly esteemed among the other followers. ACTS 1:23

12 For the companion of Paul who was called "Joseph Barnabas," See BARNABAS.

JOSES See JOSEPH

JOSHAH A chieftain in the tribe of Simeon at the time of King Hezekiah,

Joshah was one of those who drove the Amalekites out of the valley of Gedor and took it over for themselves. I CHRONICLES 4:34

JOSHAPHAT
1 One of David's boldest warriors, this Joshaphat was from the town of Methon, and earned himself a place on the roll of "The Thirty," David's elite corps of guards. I CHRONICLES 11:43
2 A priest at the time of David, this Joshaphat was one of the trumpet players in the ceremonies when David brought the Ark up to Jerusalem after his coronation. I CHRONICLES 15:24

JOSHAVIAH A valiant fighter in David's army, Joshaviah earned himself a place in the annals of heroes in Judah through his exploits, and was elected to the roll of "greats," "The Thirty." I CHRONICLES 11:46

JOSHBEKASHAH One of the sons of the great musician in David's sanctuary, Heman, Joshbekashah chose the lot to head the seventeenth contingent of singers and instrumentalists in the worship services. I CHRONICLES 25:4, 24

JOSHIBIAH A chieftain in the tribe of Simeon at the time of King Hezekiah, this bold leader Joshibiah joined others of his tribe and displaced the Amalekites from the lush vale of Gedor, taking over for himself. I CHRONICLES 4:34

JOSHUA
1 The military genius whose lightning campaigns carved out living space in Canaan for the Israelites, Joshua was the successor to Moses. He was the son of Nun, and was originally known as Osgea, but was renamed Joshua (meaning "God saves") by Moses. As Moses' commander, Joshua brought the Israelites a startling victory over the Amalekites at Sinai, and was invited by Moses to be part of the small party to go up Mount Sinai at the time the Law was given. While Moses ascended to the top, Joshua looked after the Tent of Meeting. When Moses wanted to have spies to reconnoiter the Promised Land, Joshua represented his tribe, Ephraim, and with Caleb, brought in the unpopular minority report that Canaan could be invaded immediately. Dissension followed, but Joshua was finally appointed to succeed the aging Moses and lead the tribes. His strategy and tactics in conquering Canaan are still classics in military science. After distributing the conquered territory, Joshua retired to devote himself to strengthening the worship of the Lord at a time when most Israelites were straying from the faith. His last appearance was at a mammoth mass rally at which he persuaded the people to covenant themselves again to God. EXODUS 17, 24, 32, 33; NUMBERS 11, 13, 14, 26, 27, 32, 34; DEUTERONOMY 1, 3, 31, 34; JOSHUA; JUDGES 1, 2; I KINGS 16:34
2 A man in Bethshemesh at the time of Samuel, this Joshua owned the field in which the Ark was set after it was returned by the frightened Philistines, who believed the Ark had brought a plague into their camp. I SAMUEL 6:14, 18

JOSIAH

3 The governor of Jerusalem in the reign of King Josiah, this Joshua occupied a mansion with gates near the city gates. There had been some shocking idolatrous carryings-on near Joshua's gates which were stopped by Josiah's reform. II KINGS 23:8

4 A high priest at the time Zerubbabel returned with the first contingent of exiles from Babylon to the devastated city of Jerusalem, this fourth Joshua, the son of Jehozadak, helped Zerubbabel rule the people in the early days after the return. HAGGAI 1:1, 12; 2:2, 4; ZECHARIAH 3:1—9; 6:11

JOSIAH

1 The king of Judah whose reform staved off the collapse of the kingdom for a few years, Josiah was the son and successor of the notorious King Amon. He was crowned when he was only eight, after his father's assassination, and began his active rule when he was eighteen. At the suggestion of the high priest, Hilkiah, Josiah ordered the Temple repaired. During the repairs, a lost book of the Law was discovered (what we call Deuteronomy). When this was read to the King, he ordered its requirements observed, and took active steps to clean up the mess in Judah. Josiah effectively closed down the dozens of local shrines (which had degenerated into sites of vice and cults of idols) and centralized all worship in Jerusalem. Had Josiah not died prematurely, he might have brought about more lasting changes in his kingdom. He died as boldly as he lived: when Neco, the Egyptian pharaoh, invaded northern Palestine, Josiah recklessly

jumped into battle and lost his life at Megiddo. I KINGS 13:2; II KINGS 21:24—26; 22:1—3; 23: 16—34; I CHRONICLES 3:14—16; II CHRONICLES 33:25; 34:1, 33; 5:1—26; 36:1; JEREMIAH 1:1—3; 3:6; 22:11, 18; 25:1—3; 26:1; 35:1; 36:1—9; 37:1; 45:1; 46:2; ZEPHANIAH 1:1; MATTHEW 1:10—11

2 A son of Zephaniah, this second Josiah lived at Jerusalem at the time of the prophet Zechariah, in the waning days of the kingdom of Judah. ZECHARIAH 6:10

JOSIBIAH See JOSHIBIAH

JOSIPHIAH
One of those who lived at Babylon during the Exile, Josiphiah was the father of one of Ezra's friends, Shelomith, who accompanied Ezra to Jerusalem. EZRA 8:10

JOTHAM

1 The youngest of Gideon's seventy sons, Jotham was the only one who escaped when Abimelech killed off all his brothers in order to seize power for himself. Jotham boldly appeared at Abimelech's coronation at Shechem, and denounced his usurper brother with the famous parable of the trees having to choose the bramble for their king. Before Jotham made his getaway, he predicted doom for Shechem and its new king. He was forced to live as an exile the rest of his life. JUDGES 9

2 A contemporary of the prophets Hosea, Isaiah, and Micah, this Jotham ruled as *de facto* king during the last years of King Uzziah's life, when Uzziah was ill. After the death of his illustrious father Uzziah, Jotham succeeded to the throne of Judah and proved to be an able administrator. He subdued the Ammonites, built the upper gate of the Temple, and was highly regarded by the Hebrew historians. II KINGS 15; I CHRONICLES 3:12; 5:17; II CHRONICLES 26:21, 23; 27:1—9; ISAIAH 1:1; 7:1; HOSEA 1:1; MICAH 1:1

3 An ancient chieftain in the tribe of Judah, this third Jotham, son of Jahdai, is one of those listed in the tribal genealogy among the descendants of Caleb, Jerahmeel's brother. I CHRONICLES 2:47

JOZABAD

1 A warrior from Gederah, this first Jozabad was one of those from the tribe of Benjamin who grew tired of Saul and signed on with David at Ziglag. Like his cohorts, Jozabad could fight equally well with either hand, and was deadly with both the bow and sling. I CHRONICLES 12:4

2 Another tough soldier, this Jozabad was one of two from the tribe of Manasseh named Jozabad who left Saul and joined David at Ziglag. Jozabad was a leader in his detachment of troops, and was made an officer in David's forces. I CHRONICLES 11:20

3 Another from the tribe of Manasseh who joined David at Ziglag, this Jozabad was also commissioned in David's army. I CHRONICLES 11:20

4 One of six Levites all bearing the name Jozabad, this man lived in King Hezekiah's time and was given a post in the treasurer's office in the Temple. II CHRONICLES 31:13

5 Another Levite named Jozabad, this person lived in King Josiah's time.

He was prominent among the Levites in Jerusalem and had an active part in celebrating the great Passover—the first properly observed for many years—following Josiah's reform. II CHRONICLES 35:9

6 This Levite named Jozabad was a son of Jeshua, and lived in Ezra's time. He helped weigh the sacred utensils returned from Babylon to Jerusalem after the Exile. EZRA 8:35

7 Still another Levite named Jozabad who lived in the time of Ezra after the Exile, this one was remembered because he had married outside the faith and had to give up his non-Jewish wife to keep the faith pure. EZRA 10:23

8 A priest named Jozabad who lived at the same time as **7**, this man also broke the Law by marrying a non-Jew, and decided to heed Ezra's command to leave his wife. EZRA 10:22

9 Another Levite named Jozabad who was associated with Ezra, this was one of the team of instructors in the meaning of the Law. He stood on the platform when Ezra called a mass meeting of all those who had returned from Babylon to Jerusalem after the Exile to hear the Law read. NEHEMIAH 8:7

10 One of the chief Levites in Jerusalem in Nehemiah's time, this last Jozabad was one of the superintendents of outside construction of the Temple at the time the returned exiles were rebuilding Jerusalem. NEHEMIAH 11:16

JOZADAK See JEHOZADAK

JUBAL Lamech's son and Cain's descendant, Jubal was the originator of all musical arts, including instruments and songs. GENESIS 4:21

JUCAL   See JEHUCAL

JUDA   See JUDAH

JUDAH
1 Jacob's fourth son, Judah was the progenitor of the tribe known by his name. He was involved with his brothers in selling Joseph into slavery; in some accounts he is credited with preventing the murder of Joseph by the other brothers. In Egypt, Judah pleaded that Joseph release their youngest brother, Benjamin, even offering to take Benjamin's place, when Joseph pretended to frame his brothers with charges of non-payment for grain. Judah later received the privileges of the oldest son after his older brothers, Reuben, Simeon, and Levi, disgraced themselves. He was married first to a Canaanite woman, Shua, and later to Tamar. His family, known as the tribe of Judah, wandered with Moses in the wilderness and ultimately settled in the hill country of southern Palestine. GENESIS 29, 35, 37, 38, 43, 44, 46, 49; EXODUS 1:2; NUMBERS 26: 19; RUTH 4:12; I CHRONICLES 2, 4, 5, 9; NEHEMIAH 11:24; MATTHEW 1:2 —3; LUKE 3:33
2 A Levite who lived at the close of the Exile in Babylon, this Judah was the father of some of those who served as overseers in the rebuilding of the ruined Temple in Jerusalem after the exiles returned. He was also known as Hodavah or Hodaviah. EZRA 2:40; 3:9; NEHEMIAH 7:43
3 Another Levite named Judah who

lived about the same time as 2, this man was one of those who married foreign women during the Exile and later agreed to annul the marriage to keep the faith pure. EZRA 10:23
4 The son of Senuah, this Judah was one of the tribe of Benjamin who returned to Jerusalem after the Exile in Babylon. He was selected to be second-in-command of the city in Nehemiah's time. NEHEMIAH 11:9
5 Perhaps the same man as 3, this Judah is recorded as being among the group of Levites who were part of the first party to return to Jerusalem after the Exile in Babylon. NEHEMIAH 12:8
6 One of the nobility who returned to Jerusalem after the Exile in Babylon, this Judah helped rebuild the walls and, with the other princes, took a prominent part in Nehemiah's impressive service of rededicating the walls. NEHEMIAH 12:34
7 A priest by the same name who lived in Jerusalem at the same time as 6, this Judah also participated in Nehemiah's service rededicating the rebuilt walls by playing the musical instruments from David's sanctuary. NEHEMIAH 12:36

JUDAS
1 The disciple of Jesus who betrayed Him, this Judas hailed from Kerioth, which made him the only non-Galilean among the apostles. His name is the Greek form of the Hebrew "Judah," an honorable Jewish name for centuries. He had such outstanding promise that Jesus selected him to be one of the Twelve, and his fellow disciples elected him to handle

the funds from the common purse. No one knows for certain what soured Judas. Perhaps he wanted Jesus to conform to the popular idea of the Messiah. His motive for betraying Jesus was certainly more than money, although he sold out to the authorities for thirty pieces of silver. He coolly attended the Last Supper and left only when Jesus identified him as the betrayer. His treachery was compounded when he identified Jesus to the guards by giving Jesus the customary greeting of disciple to teacher, a kiss. Although Jesus knew the depths to which Judas had sunk, He nevertheless greeted him as "friend." Struck by remorse when he realized what he had done, Judas tried to return the silver, and committed suicide. MATTHEW 10:4; 26:14—27; 27:3; MARK 3:19; 14:10, 43: LUKE 6:16; 22:3—48; JOHN 6:71; 12:4; 13:2—29; 18:2—5; ACTS 1:16—25

2 JUDAS BARSABBAS
See BARSABBAS

3 The man who lived in Damascus on the street called Straight, this Judas was the owner of the house to which Paul went after he was blinded while on his way to Damascus to persecute Christians. Ananias, the Christian sent to befriend Paul, was directed to Judas' house. Nothing more is known of him. The identification of the house pointed out to tourists today in Damascus as "Judas' house" is based only on shaky tradition. ACTS 9:11

4 A super-patriot who was fanatically opposed to Roman taxation, this man is known as Judas the Galilean. When the Roman governor, Quirinius, in A.D. 6 or 7 ordered everyone to register in order to prepare a tax roll, Judas and Saddoc, a Pharisee, fanned the resentment in Galilee into a violent insurrection. The revolt was put down cruelly, and Judas the Galilean was killed. The members of the movement, however, turned into an underground group of guerrillas called "The Zealots." ACTS 5:37

5 For the Judas who was Jesus' brother, see JUDE.

6 One of the Twelve, this Judas must not be confused with Judas Iscariot. One of the least known of the apostles, this Judas was also known as Thaddaeus or Lebbaeus. He was also referred to as Judas, the son of James. In the two lists of disciples where his name Judas, is included, this Judas is either last or next to the last, indicating the minor part he played. He emerged only one time from the lists to a place in the Gospel narrative—when he asked the question at the Last Supper on the subject of how Jesus would reveal Himself to them. LUKE 6:16; JOHN 14:22; ACTS 1:13; as LEBBAEUS: MATTHEW 10:3; as THADDAEUS: MATTHEW 10:3; MARK 3:18

JUDE One of Jesus' brothers, Jude was sometimes called Judas. Like his brothers, Jude took a very dim view of his brother Jesus' claims and ministry at first, and did not believe in Jesus until after the resurrection. He then became a staunch member of the small, harassed group of believers, but never gained the prominence that James, his brother, did. In fact, Jude preferred to refer to himself modestly as "James' brother." He wrote the brief letter preserved in the New Testament in which he warned believers against the libertines who had sneaked into the church and were pretending that Christ's grace released them from all authority or restraint. From the letter, it is obvious that Jude was well-versed in Old Testament scriptures and traditions. The historian Eusebius reported that Jude's grandsons were hailed before the emperor Domitian on charges of sedition because they were Christians, but contemptuously dismissed when Domitian saw that they were poorly dressed Syrian peasants. MATTHEW 13:55; MARK 6:3; JUDE

JUDITH One of Esau's wives, Judith was the daughter of Beeri the Hittite. She and Esau's other wife, Basemath, were such nuisances to their in-laws that the author of Genesis was moved to comment, "and they made life bitter for Isaac and Rebekah." GENESIS 26:34—35

JULIA One of the Christians living in Rome to whom the Apostle Paul sent greetings in his letter to the Romans, Julia was probably the wife of Philogogus, mentioned in the same group of names. The name "Julia" was the most common of all names for women in Rome, and appears so frequently among slaves and freedmen in Rome that nothing certain can be added about the identity of this Julia. ROMANS 16:15

JULIUS A Roman soldier, Julius was an officer, a "centurion," of the Au-gustan Cohort, the corps of offic er-couriers. He was in charge of a group of political prisoners which included Paul, who was being brought to Rome. Obviously considerate of Paul, Julius allowed him to go ashore at Sidon to visit friends. Although Julius disregarded the warning of the experienced traveler, Paul, against sailing from Crete during the winter storms, he listened when Paul warned him to cut loose the lifeboat to prevent the sailors from abandoning ship. When the ship foundered, Julius saved Paul's life by forbidding the soldiers to indulge in their usual practice of slaughtering prisoners. Julius was undoubtedly instrumental in securing private quarters and special privileges for Paul in Rome. ACTS 27, 28

JUNIA See JUNIAS

JUNIAS Because the name occurs in the accusative form in the Greek, it is impossible to tell whether Junia or Junias was a woman or a man. Some think that the name refers to a woman because it appears with Andronicus and means a person named Junia, wife of Andronicus. They point out that many women are referred to by name in the Letter from Paul to the Romans. On the other hand, it seems more likely that Junias was a man because of the terms Paul used to describe Andronicus and Junias: "kinsmen and my fellow prisoners . . . of note among the apostles." Junias as Paul's "kinsman" was a fellow-Jew, not necessarily a relative, and was a Christian believer long before Paul. ROMANS 17:6

JUSHABHESED A descendant of David, Jushabhesed was not only a member of the royal family of Judah but the son of Zerubbabel, the leader of the first contingent of exiles from Babylon to Jerusalem. I CHRONICLES 3:20

JUSTUS

1 For the Justus who was also known as Judas Barsabbas, see BARSABBAS.

2 A convert to Judaism in Corinth, this Justus was known as Titius Justus or Titus Justus. He lived next door to the Corinth synagogue. His name implies that he was a Roman citizen or person of Latin background, not a Jew. Paul made his home with Justus for some time in Corinth. Obviously Justus became a Christian believer. ACTS 18:7

3 For the Justus who was called "Jesus," surnamed "Justus," see JESUS 2

Addendum

JEZREEL

1 An early clan chieftain in the tribe of Judah, this Jezreel was listed in the genealogies as one of the sons of Etam. I CHRONICLES 4:3.

2 The prophet Hosea's first child by the faithless Gomer, Jezreel carried a name which meant "God soweth," recalling the terrible slaughter at the town of Jezreel when King Jehu took over the kingdom, and warning of divine vengeance on Jehu's dynasty for the bloodshed at Jezreel. Hosea's son, Jezreel, served as a living reminder of God's retributive justice. HOSEA 1:4.

K

KADMIEL
1 The head of a family that was among the original band returning to devastated Jerusalem with Zerubbabel, Kadmiel was a Levite who probably lived before the Exile. EZRA 2:40; NEHEMIAH 7:43
2 A Levite in Jerusalem after the Exile in Babylon, this Kadmiel was perhaps a descendant of **1** and, with his sons, was an overseer of construction when the Temple was rebuilt. EZRA 3:9
3 Perhaps the same as **2**, this Kadmiel, another Levite, took a prominent part in the impressive worship services when Nehemiah led the people in the Day of Humiliation and sealed the covenant. NEHEMIAH 9:4, 5; 10:9; 12: 8, 24

KALLAI A priest in the time of Nehemiah, Kallai was head of the Sallai family of priests during Jeshua's term

as high priest in Jerusalem after the Exile. NEHEMIAH 12:20

KAREAH One who lived near Jerusalem during the deportations by the Babylonians, Kareah was remembered as the father of Johanan, the Jewish captain of a band of diehard fighters in Jeremiah's time, after the fall of Jerusalem. II KINGS 25:23; JEREMIAH 40:8—16; 41:11—16; 42:1, 8; 43:2 —5

KEDAR One of Abraham's grandsons through his son, Ishmael, Kedar was the ancestor of a tribe which lived in southern Arabia in ancient times. GENESIS 25:13; I CHRONICLES 1:29

KEDEMAH Another grandson of Abraham through his son Ishmael, Kedemah was Ishmael's youngest son and the progenitor of an obscure clan. GENESIS 25:15; I CHRONICLES 1:31

KELAIAH A Levite who married out-

209

side the faith during the Exile, Kelaiah went along with the strict instructions to keep the faith pure, and left his non-Jewish wife. He was also known as Kelita, and is mentioned as one of those who signed the covenant and helped Ezra tutor the people who returned to Jerusalem in the meaning of the Law. EZRA 10:23; NEHEMIAH 8:7; 10:10

KELITA   See KELAIAH

KEMUEL
1 Abraham's nephew, Kemuel was one of Nahor's sons and was listed in the family genealogy. GENESIS 22:21
2 A leader from the tribe of Ephraim, this Kemuel was the one chosen from his tribe when Moses asked for representatives of the twelve tribes to help him divide the Promised Land fairly. NUMBERS 34:24
3 A Levite, this Kemuel was the father of Hashabiah, the head of the Levites in David's time. I CHRONICLES 27:17

KENAN   The name of Enoch's son, "Kenan" is a variation of the name "Cain" and is the same as the "Cainan" in some translations. In the genealogies Kenan is listed as the father of Mahalelel. GENESIS 5:9, 12; I CHRONICLES 1:1, 2

KENAZ
1 One of Esau's grandsons, this Kenaz was Eliphas' fourth son and an early Edomite chieftain. His descendants, the Kenizzites, were a clan living on the borders of Judah. GENESIS 36:11, 15, 42; I CHRONICLES 1:36, 53

2 A member of the tribe of Judah, this Kenaz was remembered because he was related to famous leaders in Israel's history. His brother was Caleb, the great spy, and his son was Othniel, one of the judges. JOSHUA 15: 17; JUDGES 1:12; 3:9, 11; I CHRONICLES 4:13
3 A grandson of Caleb, son of Jephunneh, the famous spy, this Kenaz was listed in Caleb's family tree in the records of the tribe of Judah. I CHRONICLES 4:15

KENEZ   See KENAZ

KEREN-HAPPUCH   Job's youngest daughter, Keren-Happuch was born after Job's affairs took a turn for the better. Her name means literally "horn of antimony," referring to the paint made from antimony that women used to tint their eyelashes, and indicates that she had lovely eyes. JOB 42:14

KEROS   A Temple servant who lived at the time of the Exile in Babylon, Keros was one of the first to return to Jerusalem as a member of the group under Zerubbabel. EZRA 2:44; NEHEMIAH 7:47

KETURAH   Abraham's second wife, Keturah married the great patriarch after Sarah's death. She was the mother of six sons, each of whom became the head of well-known desert tribes. GENESIS 25:1—4; I CHRONICLES 1:32—33

KEZIA   See KEZIAH

KEZIAH   One of Job's daughters, Keziah was born after Job's fortunes were restored and life was looking up again. JOB 42:14

KISH

1 A well-to-do farmer of the tribe of Benjamin, this Kish was best remembered as the father of Saul, the first king of Israel. I SAMUEL 9:1—3; 10:11, 21; 14:51; II SAMUEL 21:14; I CHRONICLES 8:33; 9:39; 12:1; 26:28

2 The uncle of **1**, this Kish was also a Benjaminite. He was the son of Jeiel and the brother of Gibeon. I CHRONICLES 8:30; 9:36

3 A Levite, this Kish was one of Merari's grandsons in the early days of the kingdom. I CHRONICLES 23:21—22; 24:29

4 Another Levite of the Merari side of the tribe, this Kish lived in King Hezekiah's time and helped renovate the Temple during Hezekiah's reform. II CHRONICLES 29:12

5 One of the tribe of Benjamin, this Kish was remembered as an ancestor of Mordecai, Queen Esther's cousin. ESTHER 2:5

KISHI A Levite of the Merari branch of the tribe, Kishi was the father of the great singer and musician, Ethan, David's song leader in worship services. He was also known as Kushaiah. I CHRONICLES 6:44; 15:17

KITTIM One of the sons of Javan, Noah's grandson, Kittim is the legendary name of the founder of the peoples that inhabited the islands of the eastern Mediterranean, especially Cyprus. GENESIS 10:4; I CHRONICLES 1:7

KOHATH Levi's second son, Kohath was one of Moses' forebears and the legendary founder of a great branch of the tribe of Levites, the Kohathites, or "sons of Kohath." In spite of the prominence given to his family in later times, no personal details about Kohath are known. GENESIS 46:11; EXODUS 6:16—18; NUMBERS 3:17, 19; references to Kohath's descendants in NUMBERS, JOSHUA, and I CHRONICLES.

KOLAIAH

1 One of the tribe of Benjamin, Kolaiah was the father of a family that returned and settled in Jerusalem after the Exile in Babylon. NEHEMIAH 11:17

2 A second Kolaiah, this man was remembered as the father of the false prophet, Ahab, the man who glibly predicted deliverance from the Babylonians and was put to death. JEREMIAH 29:21

KORAH

1 The ringleader of a revolt against Moses while the tribes were in the desert, this Korah was the son of Izhar. Korah conspired with Dathan and Abiram to challenge the authority of Moses and Aaron, but died suddenly when an earthquake dramatically swallowed up the disgruntled troublemakers. In spite of his infamous ending, this Korah was the ancestor of a distinguished line of Levites who were respected as Temple doorkeepers and singers. EXODUS 6:21, 24; NUMBERS 16:1—49; 26:9—11; 27:3; I CHRONICLES 6:22; 37; 9:19

2 One of Esau's sons, this Korah was an ancient Edomite clan chieftain. GENESIS 36:5, 14, 18; I CHRONICLES 1:35

3 One of Esau's grandsons, this Korah was a son of Eliphaz and was also an early clan chieftain of the Edomites. I CHRONICLES 36:16

4 A member of the tribe of Judah, this Korah was a son of Hebron and was mentioned in the tribal genealogy by the Chronicler. I CHRONICLES 2:43

KORE

1 A Levite of the Korah branch of the tribe, this Kore was the father of Shallum, a gatekeeper in David's sanctuary in Jerusalem. I CHRONICLES 9: 19; 26:1, 19

2 A son of Imnah, this Kore was also a Levite. He was responsible for counting and distributing the free will offerings in the Temple in the time of King Hezekiah. II CHRONICLES 31:14

KOZ See HAKKOZ

KUSHAIAH See KISHI

L

LAADAH One of Judah's grandsons, Laadah was recorded as the father of Mareshah. I CHRONICLES 4:21

LAADAN See **LADAN**

LABAN Jacob's wily father-in-law, Laban was the father of Rachel and Leah, and the brother of Rebekah, Jacob's mother. His greediness showed first when Abraham's servants appeared with gifts in payment for Laban's sister, Rebekah. Laban, years later, negotiated with Jacob, his nephew, to give Rachel to Jacob as a bride in return for seven years' service. When the seven years were up, Laban tricked Jacob by passing off Leah as the bride, and giving Jacob Rachel as a wife only after Jacob had promised to work another seven years. At the end of this second seven years, Jacob planned to return home. Laban, hoping to hold on to Jacob, asked him to name his terms. Jacob outsmarted his uncle by saying that he would take only the speckled flocks—and departing with most of the sheep and goats, which happened to be speckled. Laban angrily chased Jacob, but was kept from a battle after being warned by God in a dream. The two settled their differences by a covenant in which Jacob promised not to mistreat Rachel or Leah, and in which Laban and Jacob agreed not to transgress on each other's territories. GENESIS 24, 25, 27—32, 46

LADAN
1 An Ephraimite, this Ladan was an ancestor of Joshua in the family genealogy. I CHRONICLES 7:26
2 A descendant of Gershom, Levi's son, this Ladan was the ancestor of a group of Levites who were known as Libnites. This Ladan was also known as Libni. EXODUS 6:17; NUMBERS 3:18;

213

I CHRONICLES 6:17, 20; 23:7—9; 26: 21

LAEL A Levite of the Gershon side of the tribe, Lael was remembered as the father of Eliasaph, the man Moses appointed to be responsible for the tabernacle and the tent covering it. NUMBERS 3:24

LAHAD One of Judah's great-great-grandsons, Lahad was remembered as the head of a clan in the tribe of Judah. I CHRONICLES 4:2

LAHMI A Philistine giant who was one of Goliath's brothers, Lahmi was slain by Elhanan of Bethlehem, one of David's heroes, in the wars with the Philistines. I CHRONICLES 20:5

LAISH A member of the tribe of Benjamin during Saul's reign, Laish was the father of Paltiel, the man who was given David's wife, Michal, by Saul. I SAMUEL 25:44; II SAMUEL 3:15

LAMECH
1 The first to practice polygamy in the Bible, this Lamech was descended from Cain. His wife Adah bore him Jabal and Jubal, and his wife Zillah, Tubalcain. Jubal became the first musician, and Tubalcain the first metal worker and weapon maker, making Lamech the father of two of civilized man's distinctive interests. Lamech's song boasts that his weapons kill his enemies, and that he does not have to rely on God as did Cain. GENESIS 4:18 —24

2 A descendant of Seth and the son of Methuselah, this Lamech was the father of Noah. GENESIS 5:25; 31

LAPIDOTH See **LAPPIDOTH**

LAPPIDOTH The husband of Deborah, the great prophetess, Lappidoth was so completely eclipsed by his wife that we do not even know the name of his tribe. JUDGES 4:4

LAZARUS
1 The brother of Mary and Martha, Lazarus was raised from the dead by Jesus. Undoubtedly the youngest of the family, Lazarus was overshadowed by his older sisters, bustling Martha and contemplative Mary. He knew Jesus well, for Jesus made their house in Bethany, near Jerusalem, His home whenever He visited Jerusalem. Lazarus' sudden tragic death threw his sisters into bitter despair. Jesus Himself was moved to weep for His friend. John's gospel account emphasizes the fact that Lazarus was actually dead by pointing out that his body was in the tomb for four days. Jesus' raising of Lazarus convinced so many Jews of Jesus' unique powers that the authorities decided to take steps, according to John, to silence Jesus for good. Significantly, nothing whatsoever is recorded of Lazarus' reactions, nor are there any sensational details of his resurrection. He sinks back into obscurity in the Gospel record. A tradition is preserved that he and his sisters were deported in a leaky boat which eventually landed at Marseilles, and that Lazarus became a bishop there. JOHN 16:20—25

2 The Lazarus mentioned in Jesus' parable of Lazarus and the rich man was a fictional character, and had no relationship to **1**. LUKE 16:20—25

LEAH Laban's oldest daughter, Leah was passed off to Jacob as a wife by her deceitful father in place of her younger sister, Rachel. She bore Jacob six sons (Reuben, Simeon, Levi, Judah, Issachar, Zebulun) and a daughter (Dinah). She loyally accompanied Jacob when he fled from Laban, and patiently endured being second to her sister in Jacob's affections. GENESIS 29 —31; 33—35; 46; 49; RUTH 4:11

LEBANA A Temple servant, Lebana was the ancestor of one of the families that returned to Jerusalem with Zerubbabel after the Exile in Babylon. EZRA 2:45; NEHEMIAH 7:48

LEBANAH See LEBANA

LEBBAEUS See Judas 6

LEBBEUS See Judas 6

LECAH One of Judah's great-grandsons and one of Er's sons, Lecah was an ancient clan chieftain. Some scholars are inclined to think that Lecah may refer to the place where Er lived. I CHRONICLES 4:21

LEHABIM Mizraim's third son, Lehabim was the reputed ancestor of an ancient tribe related to the Egyptians. Some scholars think that the reference may be to the Libyans. GENESIS 10:13; I CHRONICLES 1:11

LEMUEL The name of the king to whom his mother dedicated the poem in Proverbs 31:2—9, Lemuel is assumed by most scholars to be either the name of a king in "Massa" (or Arabia) or another name for Solomon. PROVERBS 31:1—4

LETUSHIM One of the sons of Dedan, Letushim was an ancient desert tribal chieftain descended from Abraham. GENESIS 25:3

LEUMMIM Another of Dedan's sons, and brother of Letushim, Leummim was also a great-grandson of Abraham (through Abraham's wife, Keturah) and an early clan sheik. GENESIS 25:3

LEVI
1 The third son of Jacob and Leah, Levi was the founder of the family-tribe that served as Temple ministers. Hot-tempered and treacherous, Levi and his brother Simeon fiercely resented Shechem's interest in their sister Dinah and, in spite of Shechem's honorable intentions, slaughtered Shechem and his followers. Levi and his followers were forced to seek refuge among the tribe of Judah to escape the vengeful Canaanites. The descendants of Levi were scattered among the various other tribes for several generations. Because of the importance and prestige of Moses, a Levite, Levi's family became associated with the religious functions of Israel, and by the time of the judges, became the hereditary order of priests. GENESIS 29:34; 34:25—30; 35:23; 46:11; 49:5; EXODUS 1:2; 6:16; NUMBERS 3:17; 16:1; 26:59; I CHRONICLES 2:1; 6:1—47; EZRA 8:18
2 For Levi, son of Alphaeus the Apostle, see MATTHEW
3 Great-grandfather of Joseph, Jesus' earthly father, this Levi is named in Luke's genealogy of Jesus. LUKE 3:24
4 Another obscure ancestor of Jesus,

this Levi is also in Luke's list. LUKE 3:29

LIBNI

1 See LADAN 2

2 A Levite, this second Libni was a grandson of Merari and a member of that branch of priests. I CHRONICLES 6:29

LIKHI A member of the tribe of Manasseh, Likhi was listed in the tribal genealogy as a son of Shemidah and was an early clan chieftain. I CHRONICLES 7:19

LINUS A Christian who lived at Rome at the time of Paul's imprisonment, Linus was one of four who joined Paul in sending greetings to Timothy. The early Christian writer, Irenaeus, states that Linus succeeded Peter as Bishop of Rome. One early tradition tells of his ability to cast out demons; another, that he would not permit women in church without veils; still another, that he was beheaded after serving as bishop for eleven years. II TIMOTHY 4:21

LOAMMI Hosea's second son, Loammi was remembered because his prophet-father named him "not my people," symbolizing Hosea's insistence that Israel could no longer be considered God's people. No personal details about Loammi are known. HOSEA 1:9

LOIS See page 218

LORUHAMAH Daughter of the prophet Hosea, Loruhamah, like her two brothers, Jezreel and Loammi, was given a name to illustrate Hosea's message to Israel. Loruhamah meant "not pitied," indicating that Israel, not pitied any longer by the Lord, would be permitted to fall into the hands of enemies. HOSEA 1:6, 8; 2:23

LOT Abraham's nephew, Lot accompanied Abraham when the patriarch emigrated to Canaan. When their herds grew too large for the land, Abraham generously allowed Lot to choose the portion of Canaan he preferred. Lot grabbed the lushest for himself, the fertile Jordan valley. He was abducted by marauding desert chiefs, but rescued by Abraham and returned to Sodom. Angels warned Lot of the Lord's intention to destroy the wicked city. Lot and his daughters left, but his scoffing sons-in-law and his reluctant-to-leave wife died in the conflagration. After a sojourn at Zoar, Lot and his daughters moved to a cave in the hills where his daughters made him drunk and seduced him. Moab and Ben-ammi were the children born from these incestuous relations. GENESIS 11—14, 19

LOTAN A son of Seir the Horite, Lotan was an ancient clan chieftain in Arabia. GENESIS 36:20; 22, 29; I CHRONICLES 1:38, 39

LUCAS See LUKE

LUCIFER The only reference in the Bible to anyone named Lucifer is in Isaiah 14:12, where the prophet writes of the meteoric fall of "the shining one" ("Lucifer"), the king of Babylon, who conceitedly predicted that he would ascend to heaven and be exalted above the stars of God. Not until the Middle Ages did "Lucifer" come to be associated with the name for Satan. ISAIAH 14:12

LUCIUS
1 A leading Christian at Antioch, this Lucius was a native of Cyrene. He is mentioned third in the list of prophets and teachers in the church at Antioch, and apparently was a key man in the creative mission program of that dynamic congregation. ACTS 13:1
2 Perhaps the same as **1**, this Lucius was one of those living at Rome who joined Paul in sending greetings to Timothy. Paul calls Lucius his kinsman, meaning that he was a fellow-Jew. ROMANS 16:21

LUD One of the four sons of Shem, Lud was the legendary founder of the Lydians in Asia Minor. GENESIS 10:22; I CHRONICLES 1:17

LUKE "The beloved physician," Luke was one of the Apostle Paul's co-workers, and the author of the third Gospel and the Acts of the Apostles. He was an educated non-Jew who was converted to Jesus Christ without first becoming a Jew. Some think he might have come from Philippi, others from Antioch in Syria. Luke joined Paul at Troas on the Apostle's second missionary journey, and went to Philippi with him. Six years later he accompanied Paul on his third missionary journey, which ended at Jerusalem, and faithfully stayed with Paul on the wretched voyage to Rome. Luke's diary of these trips gives a you-are-there realism to much of the Book of Acts. Loyal Luke was the only companion to stay with Paul until the very end of the Apostle's final imprisonment in Rome. There are numerous traditions—all unreliable—about Luke: he was a painter, he was one of the Seventy, he had no wife or children, he lived in Bithynia, he lived in Alexandria and Achaia, he died in Bithynia, he died in Achaia, he died a natural death, he was martyred by Domitian. From the records in the New Testament, we know that he was a cultured, well-educated doctor-scientist with outstanding literary abilities. LUKE; THE ACTS; COLOSSIANS 4:14; II TIMOTHY 4:11; PHILEMON 24

LYDIA A woman from Thyatira, Lydia was one of Paul's converts in Europe. Lydia worked at Philippi, selling the famous purple dye from her native area that was so much in demand in the ancient world, and had prestige and money. She had associated with the local synagogue, and spent the Sabbaths by the riverside on the outskirts of Philippi with other women proselytes, at prayer. Paul encountered her there and won her to Christ. Lydia and her friends were the nucleus of the congregation at Philippi. Paul and his companions made Lydia's house their headquarters before and after their stay in the Philippi jail. We can not be certain of Lydia's subsequent career. Some surmise that because she was not mentioned by name in Paul's letter at Philippi, she might have died or left the city. ACTS 16:14, 40

LYSANIAS The "tetrarch of Abilene"

217

LYSIAS

at the time John the Baptist began his ministry, Lysanias was the Roman-appointed governor of the territory around the city of Abila, located between Damascus and Heliopolis in Syria. This Lysanias was actually Lysanias II, and should not be confused with the son of Ptolemy, called Lysanias I, who was killed by Mark Antony in 36 B.C. LUKE 3:1

LYSIAS The officer in command of the Roman garrison at Jerusalem at the time of Paul's arrest, Lysias permitted Paul to address the crowd, then took him into custody to protect him from the mob, and finally sent him secretly and under heavy guard to Caesarea. Lysias was proud of having secured his Roman citizenship, and was deeply impressed to learn that Paul had been born a Roman citizen. Lysias was known as Claudius Lysias, meaning that he was a freedman who took the name of the emperor—possibly because the emperor conducted a flourishing business in selling citizenship papers. ACTS 23:26; 24:7, 22

Addendum

LOIS Grandmother of Timothy and mother of Eunice, Timothy's mother, Lois was a devout Jewish woman who lived with her daughter in Lystra, in Asia Minor. She helped look after Paul when he and Barnabas were nearly killed by the angry mob, and through Paul became a Christian believer. A woman of "unfeigned faith," she taught her daughter and grandson the Jewish Scriptures. She was held in high esteem by Paul, and was referred to by Paul when he wrote to Timothy to bolster his faith. II TIMOTHY 1:5

M

MAACAH

1 Abraham's nephew, this Maacah was a son of Nahor, Abraham's brother. He was the chieftain and founder of a tribe of Aramaeans known as Maacathites. GENESIS 22:24

2 One of David's wives, this Maacah was the daughter of King Talmai of Geshur. Jewish tradition holds that she was captured in war with the Geshurites. David's marriage to Maacah might have been for diplomatic purposes, to seal a treaty between her father and David. She was the mother of David's rebel son Absalom. II SAMUEL 3:3; I CHRONICLES 3:2

3 The father of Achish, king of Gath, this Maacah lived at the time of David and Solomon. I KINGS 2:39

4 One of the wives of Rehoboam, king of Judah, this Maacah was Rehoboam's favorite. A careful study of her genealogy bears out the ancient historian Josephus' statement that this Maacah was a granddaughter of Absalom, and was, undoubtedly, named after Maacah **2**, Absalom's mother. This Maacah was the mother of Abijah, king of Judah. I KINGS 15:2; II CHRONICLES 11:20—22; II CHRONICLES 13:2, where she is named MICAIAH.

5 Another queen mother of Judah, this Maacah was the mother of King Asa of Judah. The records are confusing, leading some scholars to identify Maacah **4** and **5** as one person. In any case, King Asa was forced to remove Maacah as queen mother because of her involvement with the disgusting cults so rampant at the time. I KINGS 15:10, 13; II CHRONICLES 15:16

6 One of the concubines of Caleb, son of Hezron, this Maacah was the mother of four sons and a daughter listed in the family genealogy. I CHRONICLES 2:48

7 A Benjaminite woman, this Maacah was married to Machir, the son of Manasseh. I CHRONICLES 7:15—16

8 Another woman named Maacah, this one was married to Jeiel and was remembered as the mother of Gibeon. I CHRONICLES 8:29; 9:35

9 Another by the same name, this Maacah was the father of Hanan, one of David's mighty heroes. I CHRONICLES 11:43

10 A member of the tribe of Simeon, this Maacah was remembered as the father of Shephatiah, the head of the Simeonites in David's time. I CHRONICLES 27:16

MAACHAH See MAACAH

MAADAI One of the many sons of Bani who married outside the faith during the Exile in Babylon, Maadai agreed to Ezra's rigid decree and put away his non-Jewish wife to keep the faith pure. EZRA 10:34

MAADIAH A priest who lived at the time of the Exile in Babylon, Maadiah and his family were among the contingent to return to Jerusalem with Zerubbabel. NEHEMIAH 12:5; 12:17, where the name is MOADIAH.

MAAI A Levite musician in Jerusalem after the return from Exile in Babylon, Maai took an active part in the ceremonies in which Nehemiah dedicated the rebuilt wall of the city. NEHEMIAH 12:36

MAASAI A priest at the close of the Exile in Babylon, Maasai was one of those who took his family and returned to davastated Jerusalem to live. I CHRONICLES 9:12

MAASEIAH

1 A Levite in Jerusalem in the early days of David's reign, this Maaseiah was appointed to take part in the festivities when David brought the Ark to Jerusalem. Maaseiah sang and played a harp. I CHRONICLES 15:18—20

2 A bold captain in Judah's army, this Maaseiah joined the high priest Jehoiada in deposing the psychotic Queen Athaliah and crowning the young Joash as king. II CHRONICLES 23:1

3 An outstanding organizer, this Maaseiah was one of King Uzziah's top army men in Judah. He was ranked as a cabinet officer as well as officer, and helped develop Uzziah's force to awesome strength. II CHRONICLES 26:11

4 The son and heir of the infamous King Ahaz of Judah, this Maaseiah was slain as a youth by Zichri of Ephraim when Syria and Israel invaded Judah. II CHRONICLES 28:7

5 The governor of Jerusalem at the time of King Josiah, this Maaseiah was one of the leading citizens sent by Josiah with money to repair the Temple. In the course of the repairs, the document we know as Deuteronomy was discovered, triggering a reform movement in Judah. II CHRONICLES 34:8

6 A priest who married outside the faith at the time of the Exile in Babylon, this Maaseiah agreed to Ezra's strict rules against interfaith marriages and put away his non-Jewish wife. EZRA 10:18

7 Another priest who married a non-Jewish girl during the Exile, this man was from the family of Harim. EZRA 10:21

8 Still another priest who broke the Law by marrying outside the faith, this one was from the family of Pashur. EZRA 10:22

9 Another priest who went through the heartbreak of leaving his non-Jewish wife in order to keep the faith pure, after returning to Jerusalem, this man was from the family of Pahath-moab. EZRA 10:30

10 A man who lived shortly after the close of the Exile, this Maaseiah was remembered as the father of Azariah, one who helped rebuild the wall of Jerusalem in Nehemiah's time. NEHEMIAH 3:23

11 A priest in Jerusalem after the return from the Exile in Babylon, this Maaseiah stood at Ezra's right on the platform and took an active part in the ceremonies when the people heard the Law read at the national assembly. NEHEMIAH 8:4

12 Possibly the same as **11**, this Maaseiah was one of the team of teachers sent out to instruct the people in the meaning of the Law during Ezra's crash program of adult education. NEHEMIAH 8:7

13 A prominent citizen of Jerusalem after the Exile, this man named Maaseiah joined Nehemiah in the impressive national service of signing a covenant promising to observe the Law. NEHEMIAH 10:25

14 The son of Baruch of the tribe of Judah, this Maaseiah was one of the tribal chieftains selected to live in Jerusalem after the return from Exile in Babylon. NEHEMIAH 11:5

15 Another chosen to reside in devastated Jerusalem after the return from Exile in Babylon, this Maaseiah was a leader in the tribe of Benjamin. NEHEMIAH 11:7

16 Possibly the same as **11**, this Maaseiah was a priest who took part in the elaborate services when Nehemiah dedicated the rebuilt wall of Jerusalem after the return from Exile. NEHEMIAH 12:41

17 Another priest in Jerusalem in Nehemiah's time, this man also participated in the service dedicating the rebuilt wall. NEHEMIAH 12:42

18 A priest, this Maaseiah was the father of Zephaniah, whom King Zedekiah sent to ask Jeremiah what was the word from the Lord. JEREMIAH 21:1; 29:25; 37:3

19 Another who lived at the same time as **18**, this Maaseiah was the father of the false prophet, Zedekiah, who was roundly denounced by Jeremiah. JEREMIAH 29:21

20 An important Temple official in Jerusalem in King Jehoiakim's time, this Maaseiah had a room near the chamber in which Jeremiah met with the Rechabite Jaazaniah and his brothers. JEREMIAH 35:4

MAASIAI See MAASAI

MAATH One of Jesus' ancestors on Joseph's side of the family, Maath is mentioned in Luke's genealogy of Jesus. LUKE 3:26

MAAZ An early chieftain of the tribe of Judah, Maaz was Ram's son and Jerahmeel's grandson, according to the Chronicler's family tree of the tribe. I CHRONICLES 2:27

MAAZIAH
1 A priest in Jerusalem, this Maaziah was chosen by lot to head up the twenty-fourth contingent of priests in David's sanctuary. I CHRONICLES 24:18
2 Another priest, this Maaziah signed the covenant with Nehemiah promising to keep the Law after the return from Exile in Babylon. NEHEMIAH 10:8

MACHBANAI See **MACHBANNAI**

MACHBANNAI A fierce mountain fighter from Gad, Machbannai was one of the contingent from his tribe that left Saul to join David, who was at that time an outlaw, at Ziglag. I CHRONICLES 12:13

MACHI A member of the tribe of Gad, Machi was remembered as the father of Geuel, one of those selected by Moses to act as a spy in the Promised Land. NUMBERS 13:15

MACHIR
1 Manasseh's son, Machir was a warrior-chieftain in the tribe of Manasseh who took his clan and settled in Gilead after Moses apportioned the land among the various tribes. His descendants, the Machirites, were well-known in subsequent history of Israel. GENESIS 50:23; NUMBERS 26:29; 27:1; 32:39—40; 36:1; DEUTERONOMY 3:15; JOSHUA 13:31; 17:1, 3; JUDGES 5:14; I CHRONICLES 2:21—23; 7:14—17

2 A well-to-do landowner in Manasseh, this Machir protected Jonathan's lame son, Mephibosheth, from murder at the hands of the vengeful Gibeonites. Later, in the crisis during Absalom's rebellion, Machir came to David's rescue by furnishing his army with badly needed supplies. II SAMUEL 9:4; 17:27

MACHNADEBAI One of those who married a non-Jewish bride during the Exile in Babylon, Machnadebai agreed to keep the faith pure and leave his foreign wife upon returning to Jerusalem in Ezra's time. EZRA 10:40

MADAI Japheth's son and Noah's grandson, Madai was thought by the ancients to be the ancestor of the Medes. This ancient sheik was believed to have wandered to the area south of the Caspian Sea. GENESIS 10:2; I CHRONICLES 1:5

MAGDIEL An ancient Edomite desert chief, Magdiel is listed in the genealogy of the rulers of Edom. GENESIS 36:43; I CHRONICLES 1:54

MAGOG Japheth's second son and one of Noah's grandsons, Magog was thought by the ancients to be the ancestor of the fierce tribesmen of Armenia in eastern Asia Minor who spread havoc from time to time in the ancient world. The name first came to refer to any wild northern tribe about which little was known, then later to any enemy of Israel, and finally to the forces opposing Christ. GENESIS 10:2; I CHRONICLES 1:5; EZEKIEL 38:2; 39:6; REVELATION 20:8

MAHALAH See MAHLAH 2

MAHALALEEL See MAHALALEL

MAHALALEL

1 Seth's great-grandson and Kenan's son, this Mahalalel was an ancient patriarch listed in the early pre-Flood genealogies. GENESIS 5:12—17; I CHRONICLES 1:2

2 A member of the tribe of Judah, this Mahalalel was the ancestor of Athaiah, one of those who returned to Jerusalem after the Exile. NEHEMIAH 11:4

MAHALATH

1 Ishmael's daughter, this Mahalath was one of Esau's wives. In some of the accounts, Esau's wife is called "Basemath," and in Genesis 36:3 is described as the daughter of Ishmael. Scholars are puzzled about the confusion in names of Esau's wife or wives. GENESIS 28:9

2 David's granddaughter, this Mahalath married King Rehoboam of Judah. She was one of several wives of Rehoboam, her cousin. II CHRONICLES 11:18

MAHALI See MAHLI

MAHARAI A fearless soldier, Maharai won a place on the rolls of "The Thirty," David's elite corps of fighters, and a commission in David's army. II SAMUEL 23:28; I CHRONICLES 11:30; 27:13

MAHATH

1 A Levite of the Kohath branch of the family, this Mahath was an ancestor of the great Temple musician, Heman. I CHRONICLES 6:35

2 Another Levite, this Mahath was also a Kohathite. He took an active part in Hezekiah's reform in Judah and held an important position in the Temple treasury office. II CHRONICLES 29:12; 31:13

MAHAZIOTH One of the sons of the great Temple musician, Heman, Mahazioth was put in charge of the twenty-third contingent of singers in David's sanctuary. I CHRONICLES 25:12, 30

MAHER-SHALAL-HASH-BAZ Isaiah's son, Maher-Shalal-Hash-Baz was born at the critical time in Israel's history when the Assyrian King Tiglath-Pileser was poised to crush Damascus and Samaria. Maher-Shalal-Hash-Baz in Hebrew means, "the booty hastens, the spoil speeds," and the name symbolized the doom that the prophet Isaiah expected to fall on the northern kingdom. ISAIAH 8:1, 3

MAHLAH

1 The oldest of the five daughters of the chieftain Zelophehad of the tribe of Manasseh, this Mahlah and her sisters protested the custom in use at that time whereby a man's property was not passed on to his daughters if he should die without male heirs. Mahlah, who had no brothers, carried her claims to Moses. Moses decreed that as long as the sisters married within their tribe, they—and others like them—should receive the family inheritance. NUMBERS 26:33; 27:1; 36:11; JOSHUA 17:3

2 One of Manasseh's great-grandsons, this Mahlah is significant primarily because his lineage to Manasseh was traced through his mother, Hammolecheth, Manasseh's granddaughter. Ordinarily, genealogies were traced through the male line of the family. I CHRONICLES 7:18

MAHLI
1 Levi's grandson, this Mahli was a son of Merari and the founder of one of the branches of the Levites, "the sons of Mahli" or the Mahlites. EXODUS 6:19; NUMBERS 3:20; I CHRONICLES 6:19, 29; 23:21; 24:26, 28; EZRA 8:18
2 Grandson of 1, this Mahli was a son of Mushi. He was another early member of the tribe of Levi of the Merari branch of the house. I CHRONICLES 6:47; 23:23; 24:30

MAHLON Naomi's oldest son, Mahlon was Ruth's husband. See CHILION RUTH 1:2, 5; 4:9, 10

MAHOL An unknown ancient, Mahol was spoken of as the father of the three great sages, Heman, Chalcol, and Darda, to whose wisdom Solomon's was compared. I KINGS 4:31

MAHSEIAH A pious priest in Jerusalem, Mahseiah was remembered as the grandfather of Jeremiah's loyal personal secretary, Baruch. JEREMIAH 32:12; 51:59

MALACHI The name of the author of the last book in the Old Testament, Malachi means in Hebrew "my messenger." Some scholars suggest that this may be a title of a prophet rather than a personal name. Ancient traditions (including the old Jewish Targum of Jonathan ben-Uzziel and the writings of St. Jerome have insisted that Ezra was the actual author. Others state that the "messenger" was Nehemiah or Zerubbabel. Whoever Malachi was, he obviously lived at the same time as Zerubbabel, Ezra, and Nehemiah, when the Jews were starting to return to Jerusalem after the Exile in Babylon. Malachi writes about God's faithfulness and his people's faithlessness, and saves his choicest words to denounce the priests who break the Law and other Jews who have married outside the faith. At the same time, Malachi points to a new beginning. Although it was not the last book to be written in the Old Testament, and although it does not cover the last events in Old Testament history, it was placed at the end of the Old Testament because it does seem to point to a new beginning. MALACHI 1:1

MALCAM One of the sons of Shaharaim who was born in Moab, Malcam was an ancient clan chieftain in the tribe of Benjamin. I CHRONICLES 8:9

MALCHAM See MALCAM

MALCHIAH
1 A Levite of the Gershon side of the tribe, this Malchiah was an ancestor of Asaph, the great musician in David's sanctuary. I CHRONICLES 6:40
2 One descended from Aaron, this Malchiah was a priest whose descendants were among those returning to Jerusalem after the Exile. His son, Pashur, served as King Zedekiah's

messenger to Jeremiah. I CHRONICLES 9:12; NEHEMIAH 11:12; JEREMIAH 21:1; 38:1

3 Perhaps the same as **2**, one named Malchiah was the ancestor of the group that made up the fifth contingent of priests in David's sanctuary. I CHRONICLES 24:9

4 One of the descendants of Parosh who married a non-Jewish bride, this Malchiah agreed to obey Ezra's strict rule against interfaith marriage to keep the faith pure. EZRA 10:25

5 Another named Malchiah who did the same thing as **4**, this man was a relative of **4**. EZRA 10:25

6 Still another who broke the Law by marrying outside the faith, this Malchiah was one of the sons of Harim. EZRA 10:31

7 Perhaps the same as **6**, this Malchiah returned to Jerusalem after the Exile in Babylon and helped Nehemiah rebuild the wrecked walls of the city. NEHEMIAH 3:11

8 Another Malchiah who worked with Nehemiah in rebuilding, this man was a son of Rechab. He was recorded as rebuilding the Dung Gate. NEHEMIAH 3:14

9 A goldsmith, this Malchiah was still another of the same name who helped Nehemiah in devastated Jerusalem after the Exile. NEHEMIAH 3:31

10 A leading citizen, probably a Levite, this man named Malchiah stood at Ezra's left on the platform when the prophet gathered all the people to hear a reading of the Law at a great national assembly after the return from Exile. NEHEMIAH 8:4

11 A priest who lived in Jerusalem after the Exile, this Malchiah had a prominent part in the impressive service when Nehemiah led the people in signing a covenant to keep the Law. NEHEMIAH 10:3

12 Another priest by the same name in Nehemiah's time, this Malchiah participated in the service dedicating the rebuilt wall of the city. NEHEMIAH 12:42

MALCHIJAH See **MALCHIAH**

MALCHIEL Asher's grandson and Beriah's son, Malchiel was an early chieftain in the tribe of Asher and the founder of the clan known as Malchielites. GENESIS 46:17; NUMBERS 25:45; I CHRONICLES 7:31

MALCHIRAM One of the sons of Jeconiah, Malchiram was one of the descendants of David listed in the family tree of the royal family of Judah. I CHRONICLES 3:18

MALCHISHUA See **MELCHISHUA**

MALCHUS The man whose right ear was sliced when Peter struck out with a sword in Gethsemane on the night of Jesus' arrest, Malchus was the servant of the high priest. He was part of the group of Temple police and household staff of the high priest that was armed and sent to seize Jesus. Apparently he was overly aggressive in carrying out his orders and provoked Peter. Peter's blow did not completely sever Malchus' ear. Luke, the physician, gives the clinical detail that Jesus "touched it and healed him." MATTHEW 26:51; MARK 14:47 and LUKE 22:50 record the incident but not Malchus' name; JOHN 18:10

MALELEEL One of Jesus' ancestors, Maleleel is included in Luke's genealogy. LUKE 3:37

MALLOTHI One of the sons of the famous Temple musician Heman, Mallothi was a skilled singer and cymbal, harp, and lyre player. Like others in his family, he had a prominent part in David's worship services. I CHRONICLES 25:4, 26

MALLUCH
1 A Levite of the Merari branch of the tribe, this Malluch was remembered as an ancestor of David's famous song leader, Ethan. I CHRONICLES 6:44
2 One of the many in the family of Bani who married a non-Jewish bride during the Exile in Babylon, this Malluch agreed to Ezra's strict rule to put away "strange" wives in order to keep the faith pure. EZRA 10:29
3 Another who married outside the faith during the Exile, this man named Malluch was of the family of Harim. EZRA 10:32
4 A priest and leading citizen in Jerusalem after the Exile, this Malluch was one of those who signed the covenant with Nehemiah to keep the Law. There is a possibility that there were actually two persons named Malluch who signed the covenant at the service with Nehemiah. NEHEMIAH 10:4, 27; 12:2, 14

MALLUCHI See MALLUCH

MANAEN One of the leaders in the powerful congregation of Christians at Antioch, Manaen was one of the prophets and teachers led by the Holy Spirit to set apart Paul for his first missionary journey. Manaen was raised at the royal court with Herod Antipas, probably because his grandfather or an older relative also named Manaen, a famous Essene, was held in high respect at the court of Herod the Great. Manaen undoubtedly supplied many details about the Herods to Luke. Although we know little about his conversion or his life, we do know that the Antioch church was a dynamic congregation. As one of the leaders, Manaen was aparently a man of unique insights and abilities. ACTS 13:1

MANAHATH The grandson of Seir and the son of Shobal, this Manahath was an ancient ancestor of the chiefs of the Edomites. GENESIS 26:33; I CHRONICLES 1:40

MANASSEH
1 Joseph's oldest son, this Manasseh was the ancestor of one of the twelve tribes. When Joseph brought his two sons, Manasseh and Ephraim, for their grandfather Jacob's blessing, Jacob upset Joseph by giving first place to Ephraim instead of Manasseh. Jacob adopted both of the boys, giving them the same prominence as his own sons. Part of the tribe of Manasseh's descendants insisted on settling in territory east of the Jordan after traveling from Egypt to the Promised Land; the other half of the tribe assisted in invading Canaan. GENESIS 41:51; 48:1—20; 50:23; NUMBERS 26:28, 29; 27:1; 32:39—41; 36:1; DEUTERONOMY 3:14; JOSHUA 13:31; 17:1—3; I KINGS 4:13; I CHRONICLES 7:14—17

2 A member of the tribe of Levi who lived with the tribe of Dan, this Manasseh was the grandfather of Jonathan, the priest who turned his back on the Lord to go along with the wishes of the people of Dan when they voted to erect an idol. JUDGES 18:30

3 The son and successor of King Hezekiah of Judah, this Manasseh became king at the age of twelve, upon his father's death. The anti-reform group used the boy to stop the reforms in worship and morals begun by Hezekiah. For many years, Manasseh outdid himself to accommodate the cults and please their adherents. He even practiced human sacrifice, using his own son. The prophets attributed the fall of Jerusalem to the cruelty and superstition that was allowed to flourish during most of Manasseh's reign. Not even Josiah's reform, according to the prophets, could undo the damage done in Manasseh's long 55-year reign. According to the Chronicler, Manasseh was taken prisoner briefly by the Assyrians in his later years, finally realized his disobedience to God, and was allowed by God to return to Jerusalem, where he mended his ways before he died. II KINGS 20, 21, 23, 24; I CHRONICLES 3:13; II CHRONICLES 32:33; 33:1—23; JEREMIAH 15:4

4 One of the family of Pahath-moab, this man named Manasseh was one of those who married a non-Jewish woman during the Exile in Babylon, and was forced to leave her upon returning to Jerusalem, in order to keep the faith pure. EZRA 10:30

5 Another Manasseh who married outside the faith during the Exile, this man was of the family of Hashum. EZRA 10:33

MANASSES See **MANASSEH**

MANOAH A man who lived at Zorah of the tribe of Dan, Manoah was remembered as the father of the great strongman, Samson. Manoah and his wife had been childless, but were told by an angel that they would have a son who would deliver the tribes from the ravages of the Philistines, and who was to be raised as a Nazirite, that is, who must vow never to shave. After Samson grew up, Manoah allowed Samson to marry a woman of Timnah, (against Manoah's better judgment, according to a legend preserved by the ancient Jewish historian Josephus). JUDGES 13:2—22; 16:31

MAOCH A Philistine, Maoch was the father of Achish, ruler of the city-state of Gath to whom David fled when chased by Saul. See also MAACHAH **3** I SAMUEL 27:2

MARA The name Naomi took for herself after losing her sons, the word means "bitter" in Hebrew, and was in contrast to the word "Naomi," which means "pleasant." RUTH 1:20

MARCUS See **MARK**

MARESHAH

1 The son of Caleb, who was the brother of Jerahmeel, this Mareshah was an ancient chieftain in the tribe of Judah who was remembered as the father of Hebron. I CHRONICLES 2:42

MARK

2 Another member of the tribe of Judah, this Mareshah was listed among the descendants of Caleb, the great spy, and was the son of Laadah. 1 CHRONICLES 4:21

MARK Author of the second Gospel, Mark was a companion of both Paul and Peter. "John" was his Jewish name; "Mark," a Latin or Gentile name. His mother, Mary, was apparently a woman of some means and influence in Jerusalem. Her house was a meeting place for the earliest followers after the resurrection, and Mark was part of the Christian community from the first. After Barnabas, Mark's uncle, and Paul came to Jerusalem with money from the church at Antioch, Mark returned to Antioch with them, and a year later accompanied them on the first missionary journey. Mark, however, decided to return home after the trio had visited Cyprus and had landed in southern Asia Minor preparatory to going inland to the wild interior. Paul was so annoyed at Mark's desertion that he refused to take Mark on the second missionary trip, and parted company with Barnabas. Mark went to Cyprus with his uncle a second time. The next several years of Mark's career are obscure. Ten or twelve years later, Paul, writing to the Colossians, asked them to welcome Mark—indicating that Mark was in Rome, that Mark and Paul were cordial toward one another again, and that Mark was about to leave for a tour of the churches in the East. A couple years after this, we can tell by Paul's second letter to

Timothy, Mark was away from Rome but needed by Paul at Rome. From I Peter it would seem that Mark joined Peter at Rome, possibly before Paul's execution. Both Paul and Peter used affectionate terms for Mark, indicating that he was a close associate of both great apostles. Most scholars think that Mark spent considerable time with Peter, especially during the time after the second trip to Cyprus and the reference in Colossians by Paul. Most of the early historians state that Mark was with Peter at Rome when Peter died. Nearly all scholars agree that Peter's reminiscences of Jesus were gathered by Mark to form the basis of the earliest gospel account. As would be expected, there are traditions galore about Mark's later career: that he was the first bishop of Alexandria, that his body was transported to Venice. All ancient traditions agree that Mark died a martyr. ACTS 12:12, 25; 15:37—39; COLOSSIANS 4:10; II TIMOTHY 4:11; PHILEMON 24

MARSENA One of the seven wise men in the court of Persian King Ahasuerus, Marsena was one of the inner circle of privileged advisors who were permitted to look at the king's face. ESTHER 1:14

MARTHA The sister of Lazarus and Mary at Bethany, Martha was hostess to Jesus whenever He visited Jerusalem during His ministry. She was apparently the oldest of the family and ran the household. On one occasion, she grew irritated that Mary, her sister, was listening to Jesus and not helping with the dinner, and demanded that Jesus chide Mary. Instead, Jesus gently reproved Martha for being too busy with non-essentials. When her brother Lazarus died, Martha turned to Jesus as the only One on whom she and Mary could lean. Martha, practical and down-to-earth, warned Jesus that her brother's body would be badly decomposed after four days. In most of her appearances in the New Testament, Martha is busy in the kitchen, serving. A tradition from the Middle Ages has it that Martha, Mary, and Lazarus were put on board a leaky boat and set adrift on the Mediterranean, and finally landed at Marseilles, where they preached and founded congregations. LUKE 10, JOHN 11, 12

MARY

1 The mother of Jesus, this Mary was a chaste young Jewish girl betrothed to a devout Jewish carpenter, Joseph. The accounts in Matthew and Luke state the familiar facts of the announcement that she would have a child through the intervention of the Holy Spirit. Undoubtedly, Mary suffered embarrassment and loneliness as a result of being the person picked by God to be the mother of God's Chosen One. In spite of his initial intentions to end the betrothal, Joseph married her and took her to Bethlehem for a government census. Mary's first baby, Jesus, was born in a cave for animals near the inn. Apart from the familiar Christmas story, Mary is not a prominent figure in the New Testament. She carried out the Jewish rituals of presenting herself at the Temple at

the proper times, such as after childbirth and for Passover. By the fact that Joseph is not mentioned further, we deduce that, after giving birth to a large family—James, Joses, Judas, Simon, and at least two daughters— Mary was left a widow. Some of the appearances of Mary in the gospel records did not flatter her. At the wedding at Cana, she appeared anxious and bossy. Once, early in Jesus' ministry, she and others from the family tried to talk Jesus into going home with them, thinking that Jesus was "beside Himself." Jesus gently pointed out to the onlookers that whoever does the will of God is His relative. Mary bravely went to Jerusalem, however, and even stood by the cross. Some of Jesus' last words were to her and John, entrusting them to one another's care. The final mention of Mary is in the little community of believers in the risen Christ. Mary was one of this group of apostles and others who continued in prayer after the resurrection before Pentecost. Her portrait in the New Testament is that of a devout woman with very human traits who knew suffering, heartache, and victory. A wealth of apocryphal material quickly grew up about Mary, most of it wildly improbable, reflecting the popular interest and esteem toward the mother of Jesus. Some of these traditions eventually became Roman Catholic dogma, such as her supposed "immaculate conception" by her own parents, her supposed perpetual virginity, her supposed translation bodily to heaven, and her supposed

229

appointment as co-redemptrix with Jesus. Scholars point out that much of the Mariolatry grew out of the devotion to the female cults so extant in the Mediterranean world in the early centuries of Christianity. MATTHEW 1, 2, 13:55; MARK 6:3; LUKE 1, 2; ACTS 1:14

2 A woman from the village of Magdala along the Sea of Galilee, this Mary was popularly known as Mary Magdalene. Jesus healed her of seven demons—which was understood to mean not only physical and emotional problems, but moral ones as well. Many believe that Mary Magdalene was the "sinner" who invaded the banquet at the house of Simon the Pharisee to anoint Jesus. However, there is no certainty of this. Mary Magdalene was one of the group of women who gave money and provisions to Jesus and the disciple band, and accompanied them on some of their preaching and healing tours. She was with the group that went with Jesus from Galilee to Jerusalem on His final trip and witnessed the crucifixion. She went to the tomb expecting to perform some of the funeral arrangements and was amazed to be confronted by the risen Lord. Mary Magdalene was the first to know of the resurrection. As would be expected, a host of legends sprang up about Mary Magdalene, most of them of a sensational nature. It is impossible to find any consistent or historic details about her subsequent life in these legends. MATTHEW 27:56—61; 28:1; MARK 15:40—47; 16:1—9; LUKE 8:2; 24:10; JOHN 19:25; 20:1—18

3 The mother of James and Joses, this Mary was one of the women who joined Jesus' party in His tours of Galilee, and provided Him with food and money. There is confusion about the identity of this Mary. Many think that she was Mary, "wife of Clopas," the person mentioned in the gospel accounts as "the other Mary." It is impossible to determine exactly how many women from Galilee named Mary were present at the crucifixion and resurrection, and scholars from St. Jerome in the third century A.D. until the present have been debating this point. The James referred to would probably have been James "the Less" of the apostle band. If this James was the same as the "son of Alphaeus," the Mary called "the mother of James and Joses" could have been the Mary "the wife of Clopas," since the names "Alphaeus" and "Clopas" in Aramaic are identical. Like the other women who were the first witnesses of the resurrection, this Mary was frightened and surprised by the unexpected news. MATTHEW 27:56, 61; 28:1; MARK 15:40, 47; 16:1; LUKE 24:10

4 Probably the same as **3**, the gospel records mention a woman named Mary, "wife of Clopas." Scholars disagree on who the wife of Clopas is. Some say that this means that she was the wife of "Cleopas." Others say that the words should be translated to mean that Mary was the "daughter" of Clopas. The greater number today, however, are inclined to think that Mary "mother of James and Joses" and "wife of Clopas" are the same Mary.

5 The contemplative sister of Martha

and Lazarus, this Mary lived at Bethany, where Jesus often visited. In one notable passage, Mary was listening to Jesus while Martha was busy preparing the meal. When Martha disgustedly asked Jesus to speak to Mary, Jesus gently told Martha that Mary had chosen the more essential thing to do. Mary and Martha provided Jesus with the nearest thing that He had to a home during His ministry. When Lazarus died, Mary, like Martha, bitterly repoached Jesus for not coming earlier. A few days later, she devotedly anointed Jesus' feet with expensive ointment and wiped them with her hair, to the disgust of Judas. Most scholars do not think that the Mary who anointed Jesus' feet is the same person as Mary Magdalene or as the woman who was a sinner and intruded upon Simon the Pharisee's dinner party to anoint Jesus. Nothing more is known of Mary, Martha, and Lazarus. One tradition says that they were set adrift in a leaky boat which eventually landed them at Marseilles, where they went ashore and preached and later died. LUKE 10:39—42; JOHN 11:1—45; 12:1—8

6 The mother of John Mark, this Mary was a well-to-do woman in Jerusalem who became one of the earliest followers of Jesus. Her house became the unofficial meeting place for the earliest band of believers after the resurrection, and was probably the location of the "Upper Room" in which the Last Supper was located. The disciples congregated there after the crucifixion and resurrection, prayed together at the time of Pentecost, and were worshipping there when James was put to death and Peter imprisoned. Mary was probably a widow because the house was in her name and not her husband's, according to New Testament accounts. As Barnabas' sister, she was related to one of the leaders of the church at Antioch. Tradition claims that Mary's house was not destroyed when Titus took Jerusalem in 70 A.D., but was used as a church in later years. ACTS 12:12

7 The friend of Paul, this Mary is one of the twenty-four people to whom Paul sent special greetings at the close of his letter to the Church at Rome. By the fact that her name appears near the top of the list and that Paul singles her out as one who "has worked hard among you," it is obvious that this Mary in Rome was a beloved and valuable leader in the Roman Christian community. Possibly this Mary was a deaconess. ROMANS 16:6

MASH Noah's great-grandson, Shem's grandson, and Aram's son, Mash was an ancient tribal chief. GENESIS 10:23

MASSA One of the sons of Ishmael, who was the son of Hagar, Massa was an ancient ancestor of the chiefs of the Edomites and the head of an early Ishmaelite clan. GENESIS 25:14; I CHRONICLES 1:30

MATHUSALA See METHUSELAH

MATRED As mother of Mehetabel, Matred was the mother-in-law of Hadar, last of the old kings of Edom. GENESIS 36:39; I CHRONICLES 1:50

MATRI A member of the tribe of Benjamin, Matri was the head of the clan of which Saul, some generations later, was a member. I SAMUEL 10:21

MATTAN

1 One of the priests of the infamous Baal cults imported to Jerusalem by Queen Athaliah, daughter of Jezebel, Mattan was probably a Phoenician. He was butchered at the same time Queen Athaliah was killed, in Jehoiada's coup which crowned young Joash. II KINGS 11:18; II CHRONICLES 23:17

2 A citizen of Jerusalem, this Mattan was the father of Shephatiah, one of those who accused the prophet Jeremiah of subversion and dumped him in a cistern to die. JEREMIAH 38:1

MATTANIAH

1 The original name of Zedekiah, the last king of Judah, Mattaniah was a brother of King Jehoiakim and managed to succeed him as king by edging out Jehoiakim's son, also named Jehoiakim. II KINGS 24 17

2 A descendant of the great Temple singer Asaph, this Mattaniah was a Levite singer whose descendants were among those who returned to Jerusalem after the Exile in Babylon. I CHRONICLES 9:15; II CHRONICLES 20:14; NEHEMIAH 11:17, 22; 12:8, 25, 35

3 A son of the famous musician in David's sanctuary, Heman, this Mattaniah also sang and played the cymbals, harp, and lyre. Because of his father's skill and talents, Mattaniah and his brothers and their families were given positions of prominence leading the music during worship services in Jerusalem. I CHRONICLES 25:4, 16

4 A Levite who was descended from Asaph, this Mattaniah took a prominent role in cleaning up the Temple during King Hezekiah's time. II CHRONICLES 29:13

5 One of the family of Elam who married outside the faith during the Exile at Babylon, this Mattaniah obeyed Ezra's strict rule against interfaith marriages upon returning to Jerusalem, and left his foreign wife. EZRA 10:26

6 Another named Mattaniah who went through the same experience as **5**, this man was a son of Zattu. EZRA 10:27

7 Still a third named Mattaniah who married a non-Jewish bride during the Exile, this man was one of the family of Pahath-moab. EZRA 10:30

8 A fourth who married outside the faith during the Exile, this Mattaniah was one of the sons of Bani. EZRA 10:37

9 A Levite in Jerusalem after the Exile, in Nehemiah's time, this Mattaniah was one of those appointed to supervise the collection and counting of the offerings in the Temple. NEHEMIAH 13:13

MATTATHA

One of Jesus' ancestors, Mattatha is listed in Luke's genealogy. LUKE 3:31

MATTATHAH

One of the family of Hashum, Mattathah was one of the many who married a non-Jewish bride at Babylon during the Exile, and who was made to leave his wife behind upon returning to Jerusalem, by the order of Ezra. EZRA 10:33

MATTATHIAS

1 A "son of Amos," this Mattathias is one of the names listed by Luke in Jesus' family tree. LUKE 3:25

2 Another in Luke's genealogy of Jesus, this Mattathias was the son of Semein. The name was popular at the time of the Maccabean wars, but there is apparently no connection between the famous men named Mattathias at that time and these two ancestors of Joseph, Jesus' earthly father. LUKE 3:26

MATTATTAH See MATTATHAH

MATTENAI

1 One of the many from the family of Hashum who married outside the faith during the Exile at Babylon, this Mattenai agreed to abide by Ezra's rigid rule against interfaith marriages upon returning to Jerusalem. EZRA 10:33

2 Another Mattenai who went through the same experience as 1, this man was one of the family of Bani. EZRA 10:37

3 A priest who lived at Jerusalem after the Exile, in Nehemiah's time, this Mattenai served under the high priest Joiakim and represented the priestly family of Joiarib. NEHEMIAH 12:19

MATTHAN One of Jesus' ancestors, according to Matthew's list, Matthan is listed as Joseph's grandfather. He is undoubtedly the same man as "Matthat," whom Luke names as Joseph's grandfather. MATTHEW 1:15

MATTHAT

1 The grandfather of Joseph, Jesus' earthly father, according to Luke's records, Matthat is the same as "Matthan" in Matthew's list. LUKE 3:24

2 A still more obscure ancestor of Jesus, this Matthat is carried as one of the names in Luke's genealogy. LUKE 3:29

MATTHEW The son of Alphaeus, this man, originally named Levi, was a turncoat tax collector who was called from his tax office at Capernaum to be given a new life and a new name, Matthew. He was chosen by Jesus to be one of the Twelve, to the disgust of the scribes and Pharisees who could not understand how Jesus would associate with an irreligious turncoat. Matthew's name is carried on all the lists of the Twelve, on two of them together with Thomas and on two of them with Bartholomew. If Matthew is accepted as the author of the first Gospel, it is obvious that he had an intimate knowledge of Jewish traditions and had once been a practicing Jew before selling out to the Romans as a tax collector. Trained at careful record-keeping, Matthew preserved many of Jesus' sayings, such as most of the text of the Sermon on the Mount, which is found only in his Gospel account. Although there are many apocryphal stories about Matthew's subsequent career as a Christian, none of these have any historical basis. MATTHEW 9:9; 10:3; MARK 2:14 (where he is called "Levi"); 3:18; LUKE 5:27—29 ("Levi"); 6:15; ACTS 1:13

MATTHIAS One of two men nominated to take Judas' place, Matthias was selected by lot to fill the ranks of the Twelve after the resurrection and before the day of Pentecost. He was one of the group who had been with Jesus during His earthly ministry and was considered competent to witness to the meaning of Jesus as Christ. The appointment of Matthias instead of Barsabbas, the other man nominated to take Judas' place, depended entirely on the choice of lots, the only time this method was used in the early church. After Pentecost, the leaders depended upon the leading of the Holy Spirit. Although Matthias was inducted as an apostle, nothing more is heard from him in the New Testament records. Eusebius, the ancient Christian historian, states that Matthias was one of the Seventy sent out by Jesus and described in Luke 10:1. Various apocryphal writings in the second and third century are listed under Matthias' name, including a "gospel" and Traditions. Matthias had nothing to do with any of these heretical works. ACTS 1:23, 26

MATTITHIAH

1 A Levite of the Kohath branch of the tribe, this Mattithiah returned to Jerusalem after the Exile at Babylon and was in charge of baking the flat cakes used in the Temple. I CHRONICLES 9:31

2 Another Levite, this Mattithiah was a singer and gatekeeper in the sanctuary in Jerusalem in David's time. He took an active part as a musician in the ceremonies when David brought the Ark up to Jerusalem at the start of his reign as king of the united kingdom. I CHRONICLES 15:18, 21; 16:5

3 Still another Levite musician in David's day named Mattithiah, this one was a son of Jeduthun. He prophesied with a lyre and led in the services of praise, and headed the family group that was picked by lot to take the fourteenth turn in leading in worship at David's sanctuary. I CHRONICLES 25:3, 21

4 A descendant of Nebo, this Mattithiah married outside the faith during the Exile at Babylon and later obeyed Ezra's strict injunction by leaving his non-Jewish wife when returning to Jerusalem. EZRA 10:43

5 A leading citizen at Jerusalem shortly after the return from Exile, this Mattithiah stood on the platform at Ezra's right when Ezra called a great national assembly to hear a reading of the Law. NEHEMIAH 8:4

MEBUNNAI A great fighter in David's army, Mebunnai distinguished himself by slaying the Philistine giant, Sippai, in the wars with the Philistines. This valiant man hailed from the family of Hushah in the tribe of Judah. He was also known in the Bible as "Sibbecai" or "Sibbechai." II SAMUEL 21:18 (where he is called "Sibbecai"); 23:27; I CHRONICLES 11:29; 20:4; 27:11 (called "Sibbecai" in all of the Chronicles passages)

MEDAD One of the two who were not called to the tent when Moses called seventy elders during a crisis in the wilderness, Medad and Eldad began to prophesy in the camp. Joshua indignantly wanted to stop them, but Moses said gratefully that he wished that all the camp would be turned into prophets such as Medad. NUMBERS 11:26, 27

MEDAN One of Abraham's sons by his second wife, Keturah, Medan was an obscure desert sheik listed in the ancient genealogies. GENESIS 25:2; I CHRONICLES 1:32

MEHETABEEL See MEHETABEL

MEHETABEL
1 The wife of Hadar, Mehetabel was one of the last of the ancient queens of Edom. GENESIS 36:39; I CHRONICLES 1:50
2 Another by the same name, this Mehetabel was the grandfather of Shemaiah, the man hired by Sanballat and Tobiah to intimidate Nehemiah so he would not rebuild the walls of Jerusalem. NEHEMIAH 6:10

MEHIDA A Temple servant, Mehida was the ancestor of a family that returned with Zerubbabel from Exile in Babylon to Jerusalem. EZRA 2:52; NEHEMIAH 7:54

MEHIR One of Chelub's sons, Mehir was listed in the genealogy of the tribe of Judah among the descendants of Caleb, son of Hur. I CHRONICLES 4:11

MEHUJAEL One of Cain's descendants listed in the records of the earliest tribes, Mehujael was the father of another ancient clan-founder, Methusael. GENESIS 4:18

MEHUMAN One of the seven advisors to Persia King Ahasuerus, Mehuman was one of the privileged few permitted to look his king in the face. ESTHER 1:10

MEHUNIM A Temple servant, Mehunim was remembered as the ancestor of one of the families that returned to devastated Jerusalem with Zerubbabel after the Exile at Babylon. EZRA 2:50; 7:52

MELATIAH A member of the tribe of Gibeon, Melatiah was part of his tribe's contingent that helped Nehemiah repair the ruined walls of Jerusalem after the Exile. NEHEMIAH 3:7

MELCHI
1 One of Jesus' ancestors, this Melchi is listed as Joseph's great-great-grandfather in Luke's genealogy. LUKE 3:24
2 Another of Jesus' ancestors, this one is farther removed than **1.** LUKE 3:28

MELCHISEDEC See MELCHIZEDEK

MELCHISHUA King Saul's third son, Melchishua stayed loyally with his increasingly mad father, and died with him in the bloody battle at Mount Gilboa. I SAMUEL 14:49; 31:2; I CHRONICLES 8:33; 9:39; 10:2

MELCHIZEDEK A combination priest and king, Melchizedek was the ideal ruler of Israel according to later Jewish thought. Mechizedek himself was king of Salem, the early name for Jerusalem, and "priest of the Most High God." After Abraham decisively defeated Chedolaomer and the other kings of the east, Melchizedek gave Abraham bread and wine and his

235

blessing. In turn, Abraham offered Melchizedek a tithe of the loot. The writer of Hebrews picked up the Old Testament idealization of Melchizedek as one who combined the kingly and priestly offices, and spoke of Jesus as a priest on the order of Melchizedek. GENESIS 14:18; PSALM 110:4; HEBREWS 5—7

MELEA Another obscure ancestor of Jesus, Melea is one of the names in Luke's genealogy. LUKE 3:31

MELECH One of Saul's descendants, Melech was Jonathan's grandson and one of Micah's sons, and was carried in the rolls of the clan of Gibeonites. I CHRONICLES 8:35; 9:41

MELICU See MALLUCH 4

MELZAR A member of the Persian court at the time of the Jewish captivity, Melzar was in charge of young men being groomed for service in Nebuchadnezzar's court. Daniel and his three friends were among his proteges. In spite of Melzar's efforts, however, Daniel and his companions would not forsake their Hebrew heritage. DANIEL 1:11, 16

MEMUCAN An important official in the court of King Ahasuerus of Persia, Memucan was one of the seven royal advisors and one of the few permitted to look the king in the face. ESTHER 1:14, 16, 21

MENAHEM Military governor at the city of Tirzah during King Zechariah's brief rule in Israel, Menahem refused to recognize Shallum as king after Shallum murdered Zechariah. Menahem marched against Samaria, conquered Shallum, then cruelly quashed all opposition. To prop up his regime, he turned to Assyria. Assyria's aid cost Israel dearly. In addition to draining the country of money, it put Israel so completely under Assyria's domination that a few years after Menahem's death, Assyria took over completely. II KINGS 15

MENAN See MENNA

MENNA One of Jesus' more obscure ancestors, Menna is a name in Luke's genealogy. LUKE 3:31

MEONOTHAI A member of the tribe of Judah mentioned in the genealogies, Meonothai was an early clan chief who was descended from Caleb, son of Hur. I CHRONICLES 4:14

MEPHIBOSHETH
1 The last surviving member of the house of Saul, Mephibosheth was Jonathan's son. He was only five when his father and grandfather perished at Mount Gilboa; Mephibosheth fell in fleeing with the others and suffered injuries which left him crippled for life. Out of esteem for Jonathan, David not only spared Mephibosheth's life, but restored all of Saul's personal property to the boy, plus the services of Saul's servant, Zibah, and a place of honor at the royal court. During Absalom's revolt, Zibah apparently tried to gain favor with both sides by spreading stories to David of Mephibosheth's disloyalty. After returning to Jerusalem, David heard from Mephibosheth who swore he had never

wavered in his loyalty. II SAMUEL 4:4; 9:6—13; 16:1—4; 19:24—30; 21:7

2 A second Mephibosheth, this was a son of Saul's concubine, Rizpah, whom David permitted the Gibeonites to put to death with the rest of Saul's survivors, except for Jonathan's lame son, Mephibosheth **1**. II SAMUEL 21:8

MERAB Saul's oldest daughter, Merab was promised by her father to the man who killed Goliath. When David stepped up to claim his reward, Saul went back on his promise, and gave her instead to Adriel. Later, in the bloodbath following Saul's defeat and death, Merab's five sons were executed by the Gibeonites with David's knowledge. I SAMUEL 14:49; 18:17—19

MERIAH A priest in Jerusalem after the return from Exile, Meriah served under the high priest Joiakim and represented the family of Seraiah in the Temple services in Nehemiah's time. NEHEMIAH 12:12

MERAIOTH

1 Like the others of the same name, this first Meraioth was a Levite. He was remembered as an early ancestor of the Azariah who was well-known in Solomon's temple. I CHRONICLES 6:6, 7, 52; EZRA 7:3

2 A distant relative of **1** who was also a priest, this Meraioth was listed as a son of Ahitub, a chief priest in the Temple, and was an ancestor of a group of well-known priests that returned to Jerusalem after the Exile. I CHRONICLES 9:11

3 Perhaps another of the same clan of priests as **1** and **2**, this Meraioth was remembered as the forbear of Helkai, a priest in the time of Nehemiah. NEHEMIAH 12:15

MERARI The third and youngest of Levi's sons, Merari was the ancestor-founder of a great branch of the tribe of Levites, the Merarites. Merari accompanied his father and his grandfather, Jacob, to Egypt when the entire clan emigrated there in Joseph's time. Merari's sons, Mahli and Mushi, were born in Egypt and were the heads of families which later joined Moses in the exodus from Egypt to the Promised Land. Merari's descendants, the Merarites, eventually became a clan of priests who held important assignments in the Temple. GENESIS 46:11; EXODUS 6:16—19; NUMBERS 3:17—36; 4:29—45; 7:8; 10:17; 26:57; JOSHUA 21:7—40; I CHRONICLES 6:1—77; 9:14; 15:17; 23:6—21; 24:26—27; 26:10, 19; II CHRONICLES 29:12; 34:12; EZRA 8:19

MERED A member of the tribe of Judah, Mered is listed among the descendants of the great spy Caleb, son of Jephunneh. I CHRONICLES 4:17 —18

MEREMOTH

1 One of the first priests to return to Jerusalem after the Exile in Babylon, Meremoth counted and weighed the gold and precious utensils brought back from Babylon by Ezra's party. This Meremoth was the son of Uriah the priest. EZRA 8:33; NEHEMIAH 3:4, 21

2 Another priest named Meremoth,

this man joined Nehemiah in the impressive service in Jerusalem in which the people covenanted again to keep the Law. NEHEMIAH 10:5; 12:3

3 One of the many members of the family of Bani who married outside the faith during the Exile at Babylon, this Meremoth obeyed Ezra's rule against interfaith marriages in order to keep the faith pure when returning to Jerusalem. EZRA 10:36

MERES One of the seven top advisors to Persian King Ahasuerus, Meres was one of the privileged few permitted to look the king in the face. ESTHER 1:14

MERIBAAL See MERIBOSHETH

MERODACH-BALADAN A Chaldean chieftain in southern Persia, Merodach-Baladan was able to grab control of Babylon twice briefly. The first time, Sargon of Assyria deposed him before aid from King Hezekiah of Judah and others could arrive. After Sargon's death, Merodach-Baladan made a brief comeback, but was pushed out a second time by Sennacherib of Assyria. II KINGS 20:12; ISAIAH 39:1

MESECH See MESHECH

MESHA

1 A king of Moab at the time of Kings Ahab, Ahaziah, and Jehoram of Israel, Mesha was for a time a vassal of Israel and paid heavy tribute in wool. Mesha refused to pay after Ahab's death, and triggered an independence movement against Israel among most of the tribes of Moab.

Jehoram of Israel finally got Jehoshaphat of Judah and the leader of the Edomites to join him in a war against the Moabites. Mesha was left with a completely devastated country and a defeated tribe. II KINGS 3:4

2 An early clan chieftain in the tribe of Judah, this Mesha was the oldest son of Caleb the brother of Jerahmeel, a descendant of Perez. I CHRONICLES 2:42

3 A member of the tribe of Benjamin, this third Mesha was a son of Shaharaim and was born in Moab. I CHRONICLES 8:9

MESHACH Originally named Mishael, Meshach was one of the young Hebrews who, with Daniel, were carried into captivity in Babylon and specially selected for indoctrination to become a Babylonian. Mishael was renamed Meshach by Nebuchadnezzar's staff, trained, and put in charge of the province of Babylon. He never forgot his Hebrew heritage and refused to worship the golden image. Although he and his companions were cast into the fiery furnace, they emerged unscathed. DANIEL 1:7; 2:49; 3:12—30

MESHECH

1 One of Noah's grandsons, this Meshech was a son of Japheth and was regarded by the ancients as the founder of a fierce group of tribes in the area of Armenia that later were troublesome to the Assyrians. GENESIS 10:2; I CHRONICLES 1:5

2 Another grandson of Noah, this Meshech was one of Shem's sons, according to the Chronicler. This name, however, does not appear in the genealogy of Shem in Genesis 10, leading most scholars to assume that Meshech 1 and Meshech 2 were the same man. I CHRONICLES 1:17

MESHELEMIAH A Levite, Meshelemiah was remembered as the father of Zechariah, one of the gatekeepers of the Temple after the Exile. I CHRONICLES 9:21; 26:1, 2, 9

MESHEZABEEL See MESHEZABEL

MESHEZABEL
1 Meshezabel was the grandfather of Meshullam, who was one of those who worked to repair the walls of devastated Jerusalem after the Exile in Babylon. NEHEMIAH 3:4
2 A member of the same family as 1, this Meshezabel signed the covenant with Nehemiah, promising to keep the Law. NEHEMIAH 10:21
3 Perhaps the same as 2 and certainly closely related to him, one named Meshezabel was the father of Pethahiah, one of the advisors to the king in Jerusalem after the return from Exile. NEHEMIAH 11:24

MESHILLEMITH
See MESHILLEMOTH 2

MESHILLEMOTH
1 An Ephraimite, Meshillemoth was the father of the compassionate Berechiah, who refused to go along with his king in selling prisoners from the southern kingdom of Judah into slavery. II CHRONICLES 28:12
2 A priest from the family of Immer, this Meshillemoth was the ancestor of Amashai, one of those who returned

to Jerusalem after the Exile in Babylon. I CHRONICLES 9:12; NEHEMIAH 11:13

MESHOBAB A member of the tribe of Simeon, Meshobab was one of those who pushed out the Amalekites living in the rich vale of Gedor and settled there himself during Hezekiah's time. I CHRONICLES 4:34

MESHULLAM
1 This Meshullam was remembered primarily because he was the grandfather of Shaphan, a secretary and administrative assistant to King Josiah of Judah. II KINGS 22:3
2 One of Zerubbabel's sons, and a descendant of the kings of Judah, this Meshullam came with his father in the first party to return to Jerusalem after the Exile. I CHRONICLES 3:19
3 A member of the tribe of Gad, this Meshullam won mention as a clan chieftain in the tribal genealogy. I CHRONICLES 5:13
4 A member of the tribe of Benjamin, this man was a member of the clan of Elpaal. I CHRONICLES 8:17
5 Another by the same name in the tribe of Benjamin, this Meshullam was the father of Sallu, one of the first to return to Jerusalem after the Exile at Babylon. I CHRONICLES 8:17; NEHEMIAH 11:7
6 A third Benjaminite with the same name, this man was a son of Shephatiah, and one of the first to return to Jerusalem after the Exile at Babylon. I CHRONICLES 9:8
7 A priest with an illustrious ancestry, this Meshullam was the grandfather of a well-known priest named

Azariah who returned to Jerusalem after the Exile. I CHRONICLES 9:11; NEHEMIAH 11:11

8 An ancestor of Adaiah, another priest who moved back to devastated Jerusalem after the Exile, this Meshullam was also a priest. I CHRONICLES 9:12

9 A Levite of the Kohath branch of the tribe, this man was appointed by King Josiah to be a supervisor of the renovation program in the Temple during Josiah's reform in the last days of Judah. II CHRONICLES 34:12

10 One of the leaders of the Hebrew community in exile at Babylon, this Meshullam was one of the party sent by Ezra to the "seminary" operated by Iddo to recruit priests to return to Jerusalem. EZRA 8:16

11 A Levite, this Meshullam opposed Ezra's strict rule against allowing anyone with a non-Jewish wife to return to Jerusalem. EZRA 10:15

12 One of the many members of the family of Bani that married outside the faith during the Exile at Babylon, this man agreed to abide by Ezra's rigid rule against interfaith marriages. EZRA 10:29

13 A son of Berechiah, this Meshullam helped rebuild the ruined walls of Jerusalem after the return from the Exile. His son-in-law, Tobiah, however, was one of those who caused Nehemiah trouble. NEHEMIAH 3:4, 30; 6:18

14 Another who assisted Nehemiah in rebuilding Jerusalem after the Exile, this Meshullam, a son of Besodeiah, was recorded as one of those who repaired the Old Gate. NEHEMIAH 3:6

15 A leading citizen of Jerusalem shortly after the return from Exile, this Meshullam stood on the platform at Ezra's left during the great national assembly when Ezra brought together all the people to hear a reading of the Law. NEHEMIAH 8:4

16 A priest in Jerusalem in Nehemiah's time, this Meshullam participated in the service and joined Nehemiah in signing a solemn covenant promising to keep the Law. NEHEMIAH 10:17

17 Another outstanding man of the Jerusalem community in the period following the Exile, this Meshullam took part in the ceremonies when Nehemiah led the people in signing the covenant. NEHEMIAH 10:20

18 Another Meshullam who lived in Jerusalem after the Exile, this one walked in the procession as one of the priests and leading citizens when Nehemiah led the city in an impressive dedication service. NEHEMIAH 12:33

19 Another priest in Ezra's time in Jerusalem, this Meshullam served under the high priest Joiakim as a representative of the priestly family of Ezra. NEHEMIAH 12:13

20 A priest in the same capacity as **19**, this man represented the priestly family of Ginnethon. NEHEMIAH 12:16

21 A Levite who lived after the return to Jerusalem from Exile in Babylon, this final Meshullam was a gatekeeper in the Temple. NEHEMIAH 12:25

MESHULLEMETH Daughter of Harus of Jotbah, Meshullemeth married King Manasseh of Judah and reigned during one of the low points in the religious and moral life of the nation. Her son, Amon, succeeded Manasseh and perpetuated the idolatry of his father for two years before he was assassinated. II KINGS 21:19

METHUSAEL See **METHUSHAEL** or **METHUSELAH**

METHUSELAH The man reputed to have lived the longest—969 years, according to the Bible—Methuselah was a son of Enoch and the father of Lamech, Noah's father. He is listed in the genealogy of Seth, Adam's son, and is also known by the name "Methushael." The name means "man of the dart" or "man of the javelin," according to some scholars, and "man of Shelah" (the name of a Babylonian goddess), according to other scholars. Methuselah lived at such an ancient time that little can be known about him. GENESIS 4:18 (where the name is Methushael); 5:21—27; I CHRONICLES 1:3

METHUSHAEL The form of the name Methuselah in the genealogy traced back to Cain, Methushael was the same as "Methuselah" (which see).

MEZAHAB An ancient obscure patriarch, Mezahab was recorded as the grandfather of Mehetabel, wife of the Edomite King Hadar. GENESIS 36:39; I CHRONICLES 1:50

MIAMIN See **MIJAMIN**

MIBHAR A mighty fighter in David's army, Mibhar earned himself a place in the ranks of "The Thirty," David's

elite corps of warriors, and a commission in the royal army. I CHRONICLES 11:38

MIBSAM
1 A son of Ishmael, Hagar's son, this Mibsam was an ancient chieftain of an Ishmaelite desert clan, and was remembered because of his relationship to Abraham. GENESIS 25:13; I CHRONICLES 1:29
2 One of Simeon's sons, this Mibsam was listed in the tribal genealogy as an early clan head of the tribe of Simeon. I CHRONICLES 4:25

MIBZAR An obscure ancient clan chief of the Edomites, Mibzar could also have been the name of a tribe or a place. GENESIS 36:42; I CHRONICLES 1:53

MICA, MICAH, MICAIAH, or MICHAIAH The Hebrew name "Micah" was common in the Old Testament, and means literally "who is like Jehovah." The name appears variously as "Mica," "Micah," "Micaiah," or "Michaiah" (which see), and can cause confusion among Bible readers, especially when Old Testament writers refer to the same person using different spellings, or when different translators spell the name in different ways.

MICA
1 A great-grandson of Saul, a grandson of Jonathan, and a son of the crippled sole survivor of Saul's family, Mephibosheth, this man named Mica appears in the genealogy of the tribe of Benjamin in the list of Saul's

MICAH

descendants. The name is frequently spelled "Micah." II SAMUEL 9:12; I CHRONICLES 8:34—35; 9:40—41

2 A Levite singer with an illustrious family background, this Mica was the father of Mattaniah, one of the Levites who returned to Jerusalem after the Exile in Babylon. He was the son of Zichri or Zaccur or Zabdi, depending upon which account is read, and was also known as Micaiah. I CHRONICLES 9:15; NEHEMIAH 11:17, 22; 12:35 (where he is listed as MICAIAH)

3 Another Levite named Mica, this man was a leader in Jerusalem in Nehemiah's day and had an active part in the meaningful service when Nehemiah led the people in signing a covenant to keep the Law. NEHEMIAH 10:11

MICAH

1 The prophet from Moresheth in Judah in the eighth century B.C., Micah is considered one of the "minor prophets." He was a contemporary of Hosea, Amos, and Isaiah, and denounced the kingdoms of both Israel and Judah for the greed and injustice of their leaders. Like the other spokesmen for God, Micah warned that a day of reckoning was soon to come for the nations, and used vivid imagery to illustrate his point. After chastisement, however, Micah announced that the people could look forward to a new age in which the Deliverer would come. Micah's picture of the Deliverer as one from the house of David is familiar to all Christians. Micah's public career spanned the reigns of Jotham, Ahaz, and Hezekiah of Judah. Practically nothing is known of Micah's personal life. JEREMIAH 26:18; MICAH 1:1

2 For the Micah who was the son of Mephibosheth or Merib-baal, see MICA 1

3 A man from the mountains of Ephraim, this Micah robbed his mother of eleven hundred silver shekels, but secretly returned the money when he heard her curse against the thief. She had part of the silver made into an idol and presented it to Micah. Micah then hired a wandering Levite to forsake his faith and be a priest for the silver god. Micah enjoyed the services of his apostate Levite until a group from the tribe of Dan stole Micah's idol and persuaded the Levite to join them. JUDGES 17—18

4 A Levite of the Kohath branch of the tribe, this Micah was selected to represent his family of priests, the descendants of Uzziel, in duties in David's sanctuary in Jerusalem. I CHRONICLES 23:20; 24:24, 25

5 A member of the tribe of Reuben descended from Joel, this Micah was an ancestor of Beerah, chief of the tribe when the Reubenites were carried away as captives by the Assyrian conqueror, Tiglath-Pileser. I CHRONICLES 5:5

6 This Micah was the father of Abdon or Achbor, one of those sent by King Josiah of Judah to Huldah the prophetess to ask God's will after the Book of the Law was found during Temple renovations. II CHRONICLES

34:20; II KINGS 22:12 (where he is called MICAIAH)

MICAIAH

1 For the woman listed in II Chronicles 13:2 as the mother of Abijah, see MAACAH **4**

2 A respected leader in Judah, this Micaiah was one of those selected by King Jehoshaphat to conduct an intensive program of religious indoctrination throughout all the cities of Judah. II CHRONICLES 17:7

3 The blunt, outspoken prophet who was a son of Imlah, this Micaiah made a name for himself in Israel as one who refused to be a yes man to the king or the majority. Although he appears only once in the Bible, he was well-known to his contemporaries. When King Jehoshaphat of Judah was asked by King Ahab of Israel to march with him against the Syrians, Jehoshaphat asked what the word of the Lord was. Ahab brought in his four hundred "prophets," who used the methods and vocabulary of prophets of the Lord and predicted success for the venture. Suspicious of these sycophants, Jehoshaphat pressed for another prophet. Ahab reluctantly brought in Micaiah. At first, Micaiah sarcastically imitated the four hundred false prophets, but finally he boldly denounced the campaign and graphically foretold disaster and doom. The interview was dramatically ended when the leader of the false prophets, Zedekiah, struck and ridiculed Micaiah, and Ahab ordered Micaiah thrown into prison. The heroic dissenter, supported only by the Lord, suffered loneliness and imprisonment. His warnings to Jehoshaphat and Ahab, however, proved to be correct. I KINGS 22; II CHRONICLES 18

4 For the man named Micaiah in Jeremiah 26:18, see MICAH **1**

5 A leading citizen of Jerusalem, this Micaiah, a son of Gemariah, was one of the first to hear Jeremiah's writings read aloud by Baruch, Jeremiah's secretary. Micaiah rushed to the palace to tell King Jehoiakim's staff of advisors about Jeremiah's prophecies, and they in turn summoned Baruch to read the scroll to them, and later to the king. JEREMIAH 36:11, 13

6 For the man known as the father of Achbor in II Kings 22:12, see MICAH **6**

7 For the man known as the son of Zaccur in Nehemiah 12:35, see MICA **2**

8 A priest in Jerusalem after the return from Exile in Babylon, this Micaiah took part in the services when Nehemiah dedicated the rebuilt wall of the city. NEHEMIAH 12:41

MICHA See MICA

MICHAEL

1 An early member of the tribe of Gad, this Michael was the father of Sethur, one of the twelve spies selected by Moses to reconnoiter in Canaan. NUMBERS 13:13

2 Another member of the tribe of Gad, this Michael was the head of a family from the tribe who settled in Bashan when the tribes ended their

MICHAIAH

wandering in the wilderness. I CHRONICLES 5:13

3 An ancient ancestor of **2**, this Michael is recorded in the tribal genealogy of Gad. I CHRONICLES 5:14

4 A Levite of the Gershon branch of the tribe, this Michael was the great-grandfather of Asaph, a noted singer in David's sanctuary. I CHRONICLES 6:40

5 One of the tribe of Benjamin, this man was an early clan chieftain and warrior who was one of Izrahiah's sons. I CHRONICLES 7:3

6 A member of the tribe of Benjamin, this early clan head was a son of Beriah and settled at Jerusalem. I CHRONICLES 8:16

7 A well-known soldier, this Michael was one of the contingent from the tribe of Manasseh that left Saul to join David at Ziglag. This Michael was made an officer in David's army and distinguished himself in battle. I CHRONICLES 12:20

8 A member of the tribe of Issachar, this Michael was the father of Omri, the head of the tribe at the time of David's census in the kingdom. I CHRONICLES 27:18

9 One of King Jehoshaphat's sons, this prince inherited lavish holdings when his father died. His brother, Jehoram, however, got the throne, and promptly slew Michael and his brothers as possible rivals or troublemakers. II CHRONICLES 21:1—4

10 One who lived in Babylon during the Exile, this Michael was the father of Zebediah, a member of the brave band that determined to return to rebuild Jerusalem with Ezra. EZRA 8:8

11 Michael, in late Jewish thought, ranked as greatest of the four great archangels, and was the special protector of Israel. In early Hebrew thinking, angels were simply executors of God's will, and carried out His judgments or delivered his warnings, calls to duty, or interpretation of some circumstance. The emphasis was upon God and His will, not on the messenger. After the Jews had close contact with Babylonian culture during the Exile in Babylon, 586 B.C. to 536 B.C., they picked up Babylonian ideas about angels in their popular thinking. By 200 B.C. Michael and the other six "archangels" were given great emphasis. In the non-Biblical writings of the time, Michael and the other angels were ascribed a role and powers that nearly eclipsed God. Daniel referred to Michael as "Prince," meaning the Prince of Israel or divine guardian, and the one who would intercede to God for Israel in the last days when the end of time drew near. In the New Testament, the writer of Jude quoted from the non-Biblical writing "The Assumption of Moses," in which Michael was described as one of those who took Moses' body when Moses died. Revelation described Michael and his hosts as warring against the Devil, and echoed early Jewish thinking about angels. DANIEL 10:13, 21; 12:1; JUDE 9; REVELATION 12:7

MICHAIAH For those listed in some translations as "Michaiah," see MICA, MICAH and MICHAIAH

MICHAL King Saul's daughter, Michal infuriated her father by falling in love with David. She has the distinction of being the only woman in the Bible to take the initiative in getting her man. David, flattered by her attention, and perhaps anxious to patch things up with Saul, offered twice the dowry required. After their marriage, Michal once saved David's life by helping David escape out a window and rigging a dummy in his bed. By the time David became ruler of the united kingdom, however, his marriage to Michal had turned sour. When David danced with joy as the Ark was brought into his new capital of Jerusalem, Michal publicly mocked him. Undoubtedly, the reason for her bitterness was that she had married Palti, son of Laiah, during David's outlaw days, and was later torn from her second husband by David when he emerged as king, and then made to share David's favors with several other royal wives. She died childless —a great disgrace in Old Testament times. I SAMUEL 14:49; 18:20—28; 19:11—17; 25:44; II SAMUEL 3:13— 14; 6:16—23; 21:8; I CHRONICLES 15:29

MICHRI A man of the tribe of Benjamin, Michri was remembered as the ancestor of Ibneiah, one of the first of his tribe to return to Jerusalem after the Exile in Babylon. I CHRONICLES 9:8

MIDIAN One of Abraham's sons by Keturah, Midian was the ancestor of a powerful tribe of nomads and traders, the Midianites. Midian and his descendants were, of course, related to Abraham's other descendants, the Israelites. Nothing else is known of Midian except that he was listed in the ancient genealogical tables. GENESIS 25:2, 4; I CHRONICLES 1:32, 33

MIJAMIN
1 A well-known priest in Jerusalem in David's time, this Mijamin chose the lot to head the sixth contingent of priests in David's sanctuary. His descendants inherited the office and were named in the lists of those who returned to Jerusalem after the Exile. I CHRONICLES 24:9
2 Perhaps a descendant or a representative of the family of 1, a man named Mijamin was among those who returned with Zerubbabel to Jerusalem in the first group of returned exiles, and who participated in the service with Nehemiah in signing the covenant to keep the Law. NEHEMIAH 10:7; 12:5
3 A member of the family of Parosh who married outside the faith during the Exile in Babylon, this Mijamin agreed to obey Ezra's stringent rules against "foreign" wives upon returning to Jerusalem. EZRA 10:25

MIKLOTH
1 A son of Jeiel of the tribe of Benjamin, this Mikloth was Saul's uncle and was mentioned in the family tree by the Chronicler. I CHRONICLES 8:32; 9:37, 38
2 One of the officers in David's guards, according to some ancient texts, one named Mikloth is named with Dodai the Ahohite as commander

of the group on duty the second month. I CHRONICLES 27:4

MIKNEIAH A Levite musician, Mikneiah was one of those who led the procession playing on lyres on the gala occasion when David brought the Ark to Jerusalem. I CHRONICLES 15:18—21

MILALAI A priest who lived in Jerusalem after the return from Exile, Milalai assisted Nehemiah in the elaborate ceremonies when the rebuilt walls of Jerusalem were dedicated. NEHEMIAH 12:36

MILCAH
1 Abraham's niece, Milcah was the daughter of Haran, Abraham's brother. According to the genealogy, she married her uncle, Nahor. Her granddaughter was Rebekah, Isaac's wife. Some interpreters think that Milcah perhaps represents the name of a tribe. GENESIS 11:29; 22:20, 23; 24:15, 24, 47
2 A daughter of Zelophehad, a man of Manasseh, Milcah and Zelophehad's other "daughters" are generally understood to have been the names of towns in ancient Israel as well as the names of persons. NUMBERS 26:33; 27:1; 36:11; JOSHUA 17:3

MINIAMIN
1 A Levite in King Hezekiah's time, this Miniamin was appointed to the Temple treasury office to assist in record keeping and offering distribution. II CHRONICLES 31:15
2 A priest who returned to Jerusalem after the Exile with Zerubbabel, and worked with Nehemiah in re-building the walls, this Miniamin may be the same as MIJAMIN **2**. NEHEMIAH 12:17, 41

MIRIAM The older sister of Moses and Aaron, Miriam was such an important figure in the Exodus of the tribes from Egypt and the wanderings in the wilderness that her death was mourned as a public calamity. She was probably the sister who kept watch over her infant brother Moses in the bulrushes and brought her mother to act as nurse after the Egyptian princess found the baby. In the Exodus, Miriam was known as "the prophetess." Her paean of praise after the defeat of the Egyptians in the Red Sea is one of the earliest and most famous Hebrew literary pieces. She exceeded her authority, however, when she criticized Moses for his interracial marriage. Her punishment was leprosy. After she begged Moses' forgiveness, she was cured. She was held in such high esteem in Israel's history, that a form of her name, Mary, was given to many Jewish girls, including the mother of Jesus. EXODUS 15:20—21; NUMBERS 12:1—15; 20:1; 26:59; DEUTERONOMY 24:9; I CHRONICLES 6:3; MICAH 6:4
2 A woman of the tribe of Judah, this Miriam was listed as one of Ezra's daughters. I CHRONICLES 4:17

MIRMA See MIRMAH

MIRMAH A member of the tribe of Benjamin, Mirmah was one of Shaharaim's sons, and an ancient clan head in his tribe. I CHRONICLES 8:10

MISHAEL
1 Kohath's grandson and Uzziel's son, this Mishael was an ancient descendant of Levi. Mishael was one of those who removed the corpses of Nadab and Abihu after they were struck dead for their impertinence toward God. EXODUS 6:22; LEVITICUS 10:4
2 A leading citizen in Jerusalem after the return from Exile, this Mishael supported Ezra in his reform efforts and stood on the platform with Ezra at the great national assembly when Ezra read the Law to the people. NEHEMIAH 8:4
3 One of Daniel's companions in Babylon, this man was better known by his Babylonian name, Meshek (which see). DANIEL 1:6—19; 2:17

MISHAM One of Elpaal's sons, Misham was an early clan chieftain in the tribe of Benjamin whose name was recorded in the tribal genealogy. I CHRONICLES 8:12

MISHMA
1 One of the sons of Ishmael, Abraham's son by Hagar, Mishma was an ancient desert sheik related to the Israelites. He was probably the founder of a now-forgotten clan. GENESIS 25:14; I CHRONICLES 1:30
2 An ancient member of the tribe of Simeon, this Mishma was another early obscure head of a family-clan with the tribe. I CHRONICLES 4:25—26

MISHMANNAH An outstanding warrior, Mishmannah was one of the brigade from the tribe of Gad that deserted Saul and enlisted with David at Ziglag. He was given a command in David's army and was remembered as a distinguished leader. I CHRONICLES 12:10

MISPAR One of those who returned in the first contingent with Zerubbabel to Jerusalem after the Exile in Babylon, Mispar was a leader in Jerusalem in the intrepid little community trying to rebuild the ruined city. He was also known as "Mizpar" and "Mispereth." EZRA 2:2

MISPERETH See MISPAR

MITHREDATH
1 The royal treasurer of Persia under Cyrus, Mithredath was ordered by Cyrus to hand over the Jews returning from the Exile the sacred utensils, which had been removed from the Temple at Jerusalem when Nebuchadnezzar sacked the city. EZRA 1:8
2 Another Persian official, this Mithredath was part of Artaxerxes' foreign service in the provinces near Jerusalem. He joined others in writing to Artaxerxes to try to stop the Jews from rebuilding the walls of Jerusalem. EZRA 4:7

MIZPAR See MISPAR

MIZRAIM The second son of Ham, Noah's son, Mizraim was reputed by the ancients to be the ancestor-founder of Egypt. His name in Hebrew is the same as the ancient word for Egypt. His descendants inhabited lower Egypt. GENESIS 10:6, 13; I CHRONICLES 1:8, 11

MIZZAH

MIZZAH One of Esau's grandsons, Mizzah was a son of Reuel and an early chief among the Edomites, the group of clans that descended from Esau. GENESIS 36:13, 17; I CHRONICLES 1:37

MNASON Paul's host on his fateful last visit to Jerusalem, Mnason was one of the earliest members of the Christian community — which may have meant that he was a Christian from the time of Pentecost. He would have then been an elderly man when Paul visited him. He was a native of Cyprus and, because his name was Greek, probably originally a Gentile. Nothing more is known of his life. ACTS 21:16

MOAB The product of Lot's incestuous relationship with his older daughter while drunk, Moab was the reputed ancestor of the people called Moabites who lived in the area east of the Dead Sea. Like the life stories of other men of ancient times, Moab's history, scholars point out, may be the personification of the history of the tribe, rather than the literal biography of a single man. The Moabites were a strong, wealthy, proud people who maintained themselves as a separate nation for over a thousand years. The history of the Moabites was inevitably interwoven with their neighbors and distant kinsmen, the Israelites. GENESIS 19:37, and references to Moab, the tribe, throughout most of the rest of the Old Testament.

MOADIAH See MAADIAH

MOLID An early chieftain in the tribe of Judah, Molid is recorded in the family tree as a grandson of Jerahmeel, the great-grandson of Judah. I CHRONICLES 2:29

MORDECAI
1 One of the tribe of Benjamin whose family had been carried away by Nebuchadnezzar, Mordecai raised his orphaned cousin, Esther, in the Persian capital. Lovely young Esther was taken into the royal harem, but Mordecai was able to keep in contact with her. Through Esther, Mordecai warned the king of a plot on his life. When Haman, the prime minister, decreed that everyone was to bow down before him, Mordecai refused. The irate Haman got a royal order for the mass murder of all Jews and prepared to have Mordecai hanged from a public gallows for his stubborn refusal to bow. When Esther heard of the planned pogrom against the Jews, she risked everything by going to the king and interceding for Mordecai and all the Jews. The king had Haman hanged and the massacre called off. Mordecai was honored and elevated to prime minister. The Jews still observe their deliverance from mass murder by Haman at the feast of Purim. ESTHER
2 A leading citizen of the exile band in Babylon, this Mordecai was one of the leaders who went back to devastated Jerusalem with Zerubbabel in the first contingent to begin to rebuild the nation. EZRA 2:2; NEHEMIAH 7:7

MOSES The great personality who was God's agent in delivering the Hebrews from the slave labor camps of Egypt and molding them into the nation of Israel, Moses was born near the Egyptian capital, Memphis, at the

248

time the oppressive measures against the Hebrews were being intensified. The Pharaoh had decreed that all male Hebrew babies were to be murdered. The infant Moses was saved by a strategem in which he was set in the bulrushes along the Nile where the princess walked, found by the princess, and raised in the Egyptian court. In spite of his status and training as an adopted Egyptian prince, Moses had a sense of justice and an awareness of his Hebrew background. One day, when he saw an Egyptian beating a Hebrew, he impetuously struck the Egyptian and killed him. When he learned that he was known as the murderer, he fled to Midian, married into the family of Jethro, the priest, and settled into the life of a nomad shepherd. There God confronted Moses and commissioned the reluctant, stammering, excuse-making fugitive to go back to Egypt to lead the Hebrews out of captivity. Moses took Aaron, his brother, into his confidence and persuaded Aaron to do the talking. The interviews with the Pharaoh were unsuccessful. In spite of pleas and threats, the Pharaoh refused to give up his slave laborers. Finally, after God sent a series of ten increasingly ghastly plagues, the Pharaoh relented. The rag-tag group of Hebrew fugitives followed Moses eastward toward Suez, but the Pharaoh angrily changed his mind and sent armored columns to herd them back. The mighty act of God's deliverance followed, in which the Hebrews, under Moses' leadership, crossed the waters, and the pursuing Egyptians were drowned. The following forty years were full of crises as Moses molded his motley assembly of complaining, unbelieving, and rebellious tribesmen into a nation. At Sinai, God, through Moses, entered into a solemn covenant with the wanderers. God and Israel pledged to be faithful to one another and rules of conduct were drawn up, describing how Israel should respond to God's goodness. Moses' strength of character in spite of discouragements marks him as an all-time "great" among men. After bringing his people to the edge of the Promised Land, Moses died. He had welded the whining, faithless refugees into a disciplined, dedicated community, however, and had made Israel aware of its destiny as being God's chosen people. There are references to Moses in nearly every book in the Bible.

MOZA
1 One of the sons of the great spy, Caleb, son of Jephunneh, this Moza was listed in the family tree of the great leaders of the tribe of Judah. I CHRONICLES 2:46
2 One of Saul's descendants, this Moza is mentioned among the chieftains of the tribe of Benjamin. I CHRONICLES 8:36—37; 9:42—43

MUPPIM Jacob's grandson, Muppim was one of Benjamin's sons, and an ancient clan chieftain in the tribe. He was born in Canaan, but moved to Egypt with the rest of Jacob's family during the famine when Joseph welcomed his father and brothers to the land of Goshen. GENESIS 46:21

N

NAAM One of the sons of Moses' great spy, Caleb, son of Jephunneh, Naam was an early chieftain in the tribe of Judah. I CHRONICLES 4:15

NAAMAH
1 A daughter of Lamech, one of Cain's descendants, and his wife, Zillah, this Naamah was a sister of Tubalcain, the first metalworker. GENESIS 4:22
2 One of Solomon's wives, this Naamah was an Ammonite princess, a daughter of King Ana or Hanun. Her son, Rehoboam, was the tactless successor to Solomon. I KINGS 15:21—31; II CHRONICLES 12:13

NAAMAN
1 An important Syrian official under King Ben-hadad of Syria, Naaman came down with leprosy. A slave girl in his household told him of Elisha, the prophet of Israel. With Ben-hadad's permission, Naaman came to Israel. At first, he sneered at Elisha's instructions to bathe seven times in the insignificant Jordan, but finally obeyed and was cured of the dread disease. He gratefully professed his faith in the Lord, and even took two mule loads of earth home with him in order to continue his worship on the soil of Israel. Naaman's courtesy in retracing his steps some thirty miles to express his personal thanks was used as an example by Jesus. The ancient historian Josephus quotes the legend that Naaman was the warrior whose arrow fatally wounded King Ahab of Israel at the battle of Ramoth-gilead. II KINGS 5:1—27; LUKE 4:27
2 One of Benjamin's grandsons, this Naaman was a son of Bela who accompanied the family when Jacob's entire clan moved to Egypt during the famine. He was head of a family which became known as the Naamites.

NAARAH

GENESIS 46:21, 26; NUMBERS 26:38—40; I CHRONICLES 8:3, 4
3 Another early member of the tribe of Benjamin, this third Naaman was a son of Ehud, Benjamin's great-grandson. I CHRONICLES 8:7

NAARAH One of the wives of Ashhur, an ancient clan chieftain in the tribe of Judah, Naarah was an ancestor of several early families of the tribe on the side descended from Caleb, son of Hur. I CHRONICLES 4:5, 6

NAARAI Sometimes called Paarai, Naarai was one of David's toughest warriors. His prowess in battle earned him a place in "The Thirty," the roll of David's greatest soldiers. I CHRONICLES 11:37; II SAMUEL 23:35 (where he is called Paarai)

NAASHON See NAHSHON

NAASON See NAHSHON

NAASSON See NAHSHON

NABAL A hard-drinking, wealthy sheepman from Hebron married to the lovely Abigail, the drunken Nabal insultingly refused to contribute to the support of David's outlaw band. When David marched against Nabal, Abigail saved her insolent husband's life by her gifts and personal charm. The next day, sobered-up Nabal heard what had happened, collapsed, and died of shock. Abigail later married David. I SAMUEL 25:3—39; 27:3; 30:5; II SAMUEL 2:2

NABOTH The man who owned a vineyard coveted by King Ahab of Israel, Naboth probably lived near the royal palace at the capital, Jezreel. He turned down Ahab's offer to buy or trade the vineyard because of his strong sense of family ties to the property. When Ahab sulked over not getting the land, his wife, Jezebel, had Naboth executed on framed charges of blasphemy. The prophets and people were incensed at this injustice and use of naked power. Elijah warned the rulers that they would die disgracefully for seizing Naboth's vineyard. I KINGS 21:1—19; II KINGS 9:21—26

NACHON See NACON

NACHOR See NAHOR

NACON A member of the tribe of Benjamin at the time David became king of the united kingdom, Nacon was the owner of the threshing floor where the priest, Uzzah, presumptuously took hold of the Ark during the celebration when David brought it to Jerusalem. II SAMUEL 6:6

NADAB

1 One of Aaron's sons, Nadab was a priest, as were his brothers. He was one of the privileged few permitted with Moses on Mount Sinai. He and his brother Abihu, however, took matters into their own hands by using unauthorized practices in the ceremonies. It was believed that their deaths were punishment for disobedience. EXODUS 6:23; 24:1, 9; 28:1; LEVITICUS 10:1; NUMBERS 3:2, 4; 26:60—61; I CHRONICLES 6:3; 24:1—2

2 One of King Jeroboam's sons, this Nadab was briefly king of Israel.

While attacking the Philistine city of Gibbethon, he was murdered by Baasha. Baasha not only seized the throne, but wiped out every trace of Jeroboam's family. I KINGS 14:20; 15:25—31

3 One of Jerahmeel's great-grandsons, this Nadab was a clan chieftain remembered in the records of the tribe of Judah. I CHRONICLES 2:28, 30

4 A relative of King Saul on the Gibeonite side of the tribe of Benjamin, this Nadab is listed among the other family heads in the tribal genealogy. I CHRONICLES 8:30; 9:36

NAGGAI See NOGAH

NAGGE See NOGAH

NAHAM An obscure but once famous member of the tribe of Judah, Naham was the brother of Hodiah's wife. He was mentioned as an uncle to Hodiah's sons in the complicated genealogical list. I CHRONICLES 4:19

NAHAMANI One of the twelve leaders of the Jewish community in Exile in Babylon, Nahamani returned with Zerubbabel and the first group to devastated Jerusalem. NEHEMIAH 7:7

NAHARAI A man from Beeroth in the area of the tribe of Benjamin, Naharai was Joab's armor-bearer, and became one of the great heroes in David's army. He was elected to the list of "The Thirty," David's elite corps, and commissioned an officer. II SAMUEL 23:37; I CHRONICLES 11:39

NAHARI See NAHARAI

NAHASH

1 King of the Ammonites, the rugged tribes northeast of the Jordan, Nahash beseiged Jabesh-gilead, the Israelite city, and offered to spare it only if he could gouge out the right eye of every inhabitant. This inhuman offer was the crisis that brought Saul into prominence for the first time. Saul rallied the tribes of Israel and sent Nahash running. Later, Nahash assisted David when they were both fighting Saul. In return, David generously overlooked the insult of one of Nahash's sons, Hanun. Another son, Shobi, helped David during Absalom's revolt. I SAMUEL 11:1—3; 12:12; II SAMUEL 10:2; 17:27; I CHRONICLES 19:1, 2

2 A second Nahash, this one was the grandmother of Amasa, the man chosen by Absalom to head his rebel army instead of Joab. She was also Joab's aunt. II SAMUEL 17:25

NAHATH

1 One of Esau's grandsons, this Nahath was a son of Reuel, and an ancient chieftain in the tribe of Edomites. GENESIS 36:13, 17; I CHRONICLES 1:37

2 A Levite of the Kohath branch of the tribe, this Nahath was also known as "Toah" and "Tohu," and was an ancestor of the prophet Samuel. I CHRONICLES 6:26, 34 (where he is called Toah); I SAMUEL 1:1 (where he is called Tohu)

3 Another Levite, this Nahath lived in King Nehemiah's time and was appointed to an important position in the Temple treasury, where he was

one of the supervisors of the offerings.
II CHRONICLES 31:13

NAHBI One of the twelve spies picked to reconnoiter the Promised Land before Moses' death. Nahbi represented the tribe of Naphtali. Nahbi was one of those bringing in the majority report advising against any invasion attempt. NUMBERS 13:14

NAHOR
1 Abraham's grandfather, this Nahor was an ancient chieftain descended from Shem, or perhaps the personification of an early Semite tribe. His name is given in the involved genealogies of the earliest inhabitants of the East, showing the relationship of Israel to nearly all the ancient tribes. GENESIS 11:22—25; I CHRONICLES 1:26
2 The grandson of 1, this Nahor was Abraham's brother. Nahor married his niece Milcah, the daughter of Haran, an ancient chieftain among northern Semitic tribes and an ancestor of many later Aramean tribes. Nahor was the grandfather of Rebekah and Laban. GENESIS 11:26—29; 22:20—23; 24:10—47; 29:5; 31:53; JOSHUA 24:2

NAHSHON Aaron's brother-in-law and a descendant of Judah, Nahshon was a "prince" of Judah who was an ancestor of David and of Jesus. He was also known as "Naashon," "Naasson," and "Naason." EXODUS 6:23; NUMBERS 1:7; 2:3; 7:12, 17; 10:14; RUTH 4:20; I CHRONICLES 2:9—11; MATTHEW 1:4; LUKE 3:32

NAHUM
1 The minor prophet from the now forgotten town of Elkosh, Nahum bitterly denounced the Assyrian capital of Nineveh as the great enemy of God's Chosen People. From the book of Nahum, it is obvious that Nahum came from the southern kingdom of Judah and prophesied sometime after the capture of Thebes by the Assyrians (663 B.C.) and the fall of Nineveh (606 B.C.). His song of hate toward the Assyrians reveals Nahum as a patriot; his detailed catalogue of Assyria's vices and cruelties tells us he was a man with a profound sense of justice and of God's power. No personal details about Nahum are known. Like most prophets, he was anxious simply to be a spokesman for God. NAHUM 1:1
2 An ancestor of Jesus, this Nahum is listed in Luke's genealogy. LUKE 3:25

NAOMI Driven by a famine, Naomi, her husband, Elimelech, and their two sons, Mahlon and Chilion, left Bethlehem and emigrated to Moab. First her husband died; then her two sons. Naomi decided to return to her own people near Bethlehem and urged her daughters-in-law, Ruth and Orpah, to return to their parents and remarry. Orpah listened to the advice, but Ruth, the other daughter-in-law insisted on going with Naomi. When they arrived at Bethlehem, Naomi told the surprised family and neighbors that her name was no longer Naomi (which means "pleasant" in Hebrew) but Mara ("bitter"). After Ruth married Boaz, Naomi's relative, Naomi was the nurse for their child. RUTH 1—4

NAPHISH A son of Ishmael, Abraham's son by Hagar, Naphish was an obscure ancient desert chieftain whose descendants were a tribe known as the Nephusim, Nephisheshim, or Nephushesim. GENESIS 25:15; I CHRONICLES 1:31

NAPHTALI The fifth son of Jacob and his second by Bilhah, Rachel's maid, Naphtali was Dan's full brother. The childless Rachel had been jealous of her sister Leah, who had borne Jacob several sons, and so she considered herself a mother-by-proxy to Dan and Naphtali. Naphtali's name was a gloating exclamation by Rachel: "wrestlings of God have I wrestled." When the family emigrated to Egypt during the famine in Canaan, Naphtali and his four sons went along. Traditions in Jewish writings report that Naphtali was the fleetest of Jacob's sons and the first to report to Jacob that Joseph was alive and a prominent leader in Egypt, and that Naphtali was later presented to the pharaoh by Joseph. He died and was buried in Egypt. His family became known as the Naphtilites, and was one of the twelve tribes of Israel. GENESIS 30:8; 35:25; 46:24; 49:21; EXODUS 1:4; I CHRONICLES 2:2; 7:13

NARCISSUS The name Narcissus was common among slaves and freed slaves in ancient Rome, and the "Narcissus" referred to by Paul in his list of greetings in Romans might have been a believer who was a slave. Most scholars think, however, that Paul was referring to the household or family of the infamous Narcissus who was a crony of the Emperor Claudius, and was executed when Nero became emperor. This Narcissus' staff and property, including slaves, would have been confiscated by Nero and added to his entourage. Some of the household of Narcissus, attached to Nero's place, were probably Christians and were the ones to whom Paul sent greetings. ROMANS 16:11

NATHAN

1 David's fearless and upright adviser, Nathan the prophet was Samuel's successor as public servant and spokesman for God. He had the unenviable responsibility of opposing David on at least two occasions. The first was after David announced his grandiose plans for the Temple—a clever means of consolidating worship and power in the new capital of Jerusalem. Nathan recognized the dangers and convinced David that the time was not ripe for such an ambitious project. The second and most famous interview between Nathan and David occurred after David's affair with Bathsheba and his murder of Bathsheba's husband, Uriah. Nathan, one of the finest examples in history of a man of God carrying out his commission, made David see the heinousness of his sin. At the same time, Nathan was David's loyal supporter. Nathan was the one who warned the royal family of Adonijah's plan to usurp the throne, and suggested that Solomon be crowned before David's death. Nathan's son, Zabud, was later chosen by Solomon as a special royal advisor. II SAMUEL 7:2—17; 12:1—25; I KINGS

255

NATHANAEL

1:8—45; 4:4—5; I CHRONICLES 17: 1—15; 29:29; II CHRONICLES 9:29; 29:25; PSALM 51

2 One of David's sons by Bathsheba, this Nathan was born in Jerusalem and was an older brother of Solomon. Little mention is made of him, apart from a listing in the royal genealogy and a reference by Luke as an ancestor of Jesus. II SAMUEL 5:14: I CHRONICLES 3:5; 14:4; ZECHARIAH 12:12; LUKE 3:31

3 A relative of one of David's fighters, the records state that he was either the father of Igal or the brother of Joel. The texts are confusing, but refer to the same Nathan. II SAMUEL 23:36; I CHRONICLES 11:38

4 Another Nathan, this man was a son of Attai and was listed in the records of the tribe of Judah as a chieftain in the Jerahmeel clan. I CHRONICLES 2:36

5 One of the twelve leading men in the Jewish community in exile in Babylon, this Nathan was sent by Ezra to Iddo's "seminary" to recruit priests to return to Jerusalem and restore worship in the Temple. EZRA 8:16

6 One of the descendants of Banni who married outside the faith during the Exile in Babylon, this Nathan agreed to abide with Ezra's strict dictum against interfaith marriages upon returning to Jerusalem. EZRA 10:39

NATHANAEL One of those called by Jesus as a follower, Nathanael was a native of Cana, a village near Nazareth in Galilee. Like many, he was dubious that any Messiah could ever spring from insignificant Nazareth, but was an earnest seeker and a devout Jew. Jesus described Nathanael as "an Israelite in whom is no guile." Nathanael's encounter with Jesus came about because of the urging and persistence of Philip. Nathanael, the account in John hints, had gone through some sort of spiritual crisis which Philip and Jesus knew. After his introduction to Jesus, Nathanael became a staunch follower, and was one of those in the fishing boat to whom Jesus revealed Himself after the resurrection. Many scholars identify Nathanael with Bartholomew in the list of the Twelve. JOHN 1:45—49; 21:2

NATHAN-MELECH An official in King Josiah's court in Judah, Nathan-Melech lived near the entrance to the Temple. During Josiah's reform, the statues of horses erected by previous kings that stood near Nathan-Melech's quarters were removed. II KINGS 23:11

NAUM See NAHUM 2

NEARIAH

1 One of David's descendants, this Neariah is listed in the family tree of the royal family of Judah as a grandson of Shechaniah. I CHRONICLES 3:22—23

2 A tough leader from the tribe of Simeon, this Neariah and his cohorts headed the force of five hundred Simeonites that routed the last of the Amalekites on Mount Seir and seized the area for their tribe in Hezekiah's time. I CHRONICLES 4:42

NEBAIOTH Ishmael's oldest son,

Nebaioth, like other grandsons of Abraham was the founder of wandering desert tribes in Arabia who were distant relatives of the Jews. GENESIS 25: 13; 28:9; 36:3; I CHRONICLES 1:29

NEBAJOTH See NEBAIOTH

NEBAT Nebat was remembered as the father of Jeroboam, the man who led the secession of the ten northern tribes against Rehoboam and set himself up as king of the northern kingdom of Israel. I KINGS 11:26; 12:2, 15; 15:1; 16:3, 26, 31; 21:22; 22:52; II KINGS 3:3; 9:9; 10:29; 13:2, 11; 14:24; 15:9; 17:21; 23:15; II CHRONICLES 9:29; 10:2, 15; 13:6

NEBUCHADNEZZAR The mighty king of Babylon who overran the Middle East and deported the cream of Judah's population, Nebuchadnezzar was the oldest son of King Nabopolassar, founder of the Chaldean Empire. He beat Necho II of Egypt at Carchemish in 605 B.C. and went on to win a string of victories that made him master of the civilized world. Under Nebuchadnezzar, Babylon became the greatest cultural, commercial, religious, and political center of southwest Asia. The Bible notes that Nebuchadnezzar beseiged and captured Jerusalem, destroyed the Temple, and carried off most of the inhabitants to Babylon after the leaders of Judah foolishly allowed themselves to be involved in intrigues against the Babylonian overlords. The Exile in Nebuchadnezzar's Babylon was one of the greatest catastrophes to befall the Jews. This energetic and powerful monarch ruled from 604 to 561 B.C. II KINGS 24, 25; I CHRONICLES 6:15; II CHRONICLES 36; EZRA 1, 2, 5, 6; NEHEMIAH 7:6; ESTHER 2:6; JEREMIAH 21, 22, 24, 25, 27, 28, 29, 32, 34, 35, 37, 39, 43, 44, 46, 49, 50, 51, 52; EZEKIEL 26, 29, 30; DANIEL 1, 2, 3, 4, 5

**NEBUCHADREZZAR
See NEBUCHADNEZZAR**

**NEBUSHASBAN
See NEBUSHAZBAN**

NEBUSHAZBAN The "rab-saris" or commander of the Babylonian army, Nebushazban supervised the seige, capture, and ravage of Jerusalem in 586 B.C. He made certain his troops thoroughly destroyed the city, and sent columns of captured refugees on the long walk eastward to Babylon. JEREMIAH 39:13

NEBUZARADAN The chief of Nebuchadnezzar's bodyguard and personal staff, Nebuzaradan was assigned to oversee the long lines of captives deported from Jerusalem to Babylon. He was deputized to select captives, and dragged the supporters of Zedekiah to Nebuchadnezzar at Riblah. On Nebuchadnezzar's personal orders, however, Nebuzaradan showed some favors to Jeremiah. Five years after the fall of Jerusalem, he was sent back to Jerusalem when trouble broke out, and carried away another contingent of 745 people. II KINGS 25:8—20; JEREMIAH 39:9—13; 40:1; 41:10; 43:6; 52:12—26

NECHO The Egyptian pharaoh of the 26th Dynasty from 610 B.C. to 594

B.C., Necho ambitiously tried to regain Egyptian prestige in western Asia, and succeeded briefly in a campaign which killed King Josiah of Judah at the battle of Megiddo. Necho advanced as far as the Euphrates River, returned to Egypt, and settled back to carry out his schemes of canal building, with tribute flowing in from his subjugated countries. Judah was among the nations paying heavy tribute to Necho. The Chaldeans Empire suddenly appeared to challenge Necho. Necho was totally defeated at the decisive battle of Carchemish and retired to Egypt to end his days as head of a second-rate Egypt. II CHRONICLES 35

NECO See **NECHO**

NECOH See **NECHO**

NEDABIAH Grandson of Jehoiakim, the last king of Judah, Nebabiah was one of the royal family listed in the genealogy of David's descendants. I CHRONICLES 3:18

NEHEMIAH

1 The son of Hacaliah, this Nehemiah was the great patriot and pious leader who tirelessly pushed the group of dispirited Jews returned from Exile in Babylon to rebuild the walls of devastated Jerusalem. He originally held the high post of cupbearer in the Babylonian court at Susa. When he heard the discouraging reports from his brother, Hanani, and others about the ruined condition of Jerusalem and Ezra's difficulties, Nehemiah got permission to take a leave of absence to work at Jerusalem.

He brought vital material aid and important letters of introduction. Uniting a discouraged and apathetic hodgepodge of returned exiles into an enthusiastic, dedicated population, and overriding jealousy and opposition by Persian officials and disgruntled Jews, Nehemiah rebuilt the walls from the charred rubble. Nehemiah returned to his post at Babylon, but came back to Jerusalem when he heard of the moral decline of the community. He vigorously cleaned up the abuses and supported Ezra in the strict measures set down to preserve the community of Jews. EZRA; NEHEMIAH

2 The son of Azbuk, this Nehemiah was a contemporary of **1** and helped rebuild the walls of Jerusalem. NEHEMIAH 3:16

3 This Nehemiah (or Nehemias) was one of the twelve leaders of the Jewish community in exile in Babylon. He returned to Jerusalem after the Exile with a contingent of Jews. EZRA 2:2; NEHEMIAH 7:7

NEHUSHTA Queen of Judah during its final days, Nehushta was the wife of King Jehoiakim and the mother of Jehoiachin. She was deported to Babylon with her son after the fall of Jerusalem, and spent the rest of her life there. II KINGS 24:8

NEHUM One of the twelve leaders of the Jewish community in exile in Babylon, Nehum was one of those who led a contingent back to resettle in Jerusalem. He worked closely with Ezra, Nehemiah, and Zerubbabel. NEHEMIAH 7:7; EZRA 2:2 (where the name is listed as REHUM)

NEKODA

1 A Temple lackey, Nekoda was the ancestor of a family which returned to Jerusalem with Zerubbabel after the Exile in Babylon. EZRA 2:48; NEHEMIAH 7:50

2 Another forebear of a family returning to Jerusalem, this Nekoda was not fortunate enough to be able to trace his ancestry—a cause for regret among those in the ancient Middle East. EZRA 2:60; NEHEMIAH 7:62

NEMUEL

1 One of the early members of the tribe of Reuben, this Nemuel was a son of Eliab and a brother of Dathan and Abiram, two who conspired against Moses. NUMBERS 26:9

2 One of Simeon's sons, and one of Jacob's grandsons, this Nemuel was the ancestral head of a clan known as Nemuelites. He journeyed with his father and grandfather when the family emigrated from Canaan to Egypt during the famine. NUMBERS 26:12; I CHRONICLES 4:24 See also JEMUEL

NEPHEG

1 Grandson of Kohath and son of Izhar, this first Nepheg was a brother of Korah and Zichri. He was the ancestor of an ancient Levite family in the Kohath branch of the tribe. EXODUS 6:21

2 One of David's sons, this Nepheg was one of the large family of princes born in Jerusalem after David became king of the united kingdom. There is no mention of Nepheg beyond the inclusion of his name in the records of the royal family. II SAMUEL 5:15, I CHRONICLES 3:7, 14:6

NEPHISH See NAPHISH

NER King Saul's grandfather according to the Chronicler, and Saul's uncle according to the writer of I Samuel, Ner's relationship is not clear. The ancient historian Josephus wrote that Ner and Kish, Saul's father, were brothers. Ner's son, Abner, was one of Saul's greatest generals. I SAMUEL 14:50—51; 26:5, 14; II SAMUEL 2:8, 12; 3:23, 25, 28, 37; I KINGS 2:5, 32; I CHRONICLES 8:33; 9:36, 39; 26:28

NEREUS A Christian who lived in Rome, Nereus and his sister were among those greeted by name by Paul at the close of his letter to the Romans. Many scholars think that the clump of names "Philologus and Julia, Nereus and his sister and all the saints that are with them" was probably a family or household of believers. In later times, after the Bible was written, one named Nereus was linked with a believer named Achilleus. "The Acts of Nereus and Achilleus," an apocryphal account of the lives of these two men, describes Nereus as a member of the household staff of the emperor Vespasian's niece. An ancient inscription, however, states that Nereus and Achilleus were soldiers who were converted to Christianity, and executed because of their views. ROMANS 16:15

NERGAL-SHAREZER A powerful Babylonian prince and general, Nergal-Sharezer was one of the leaders of the occupation army in Jerusalem after its fall in 586 B.C. He and other Babylonians rescued the prophet Jeremiah from prison. After the murder of King

Evil-Merodach of Babylon in 559 B.C., Nergal-Sharezer grabbed power and ruled Babylon for four years until his death. He was called Neriglissar by many ancient writers. JEREMIAH 39:3, 13

NERI One of Jesus' ancestors, according to Luke's genealogy, Neri is a variation of the name Neriah. See NERIAH LUKE 3:27

NERIAH A priest in the last days of the kingdom of Judah, Neriah was the father of Jeremiah's loyal secretary, Baruch. JEREMIAH 32:12, 16; 36:4—32; 43:3—6; 45:1; 55:59

NETHANEEL See NETHANEL

NETHANEL

1 The son of Zuar in the tribe of Issachar, Nethanel was the one selected to represent his tribe when Moses sent twelve spies into Canaan to reconnoiter the Promised Land. Nethanel, however, was one of the ten who were cowed by the difficulties in conquering Canaan and brought back the majority report advising against attempting a conquest. NUMBERS 1:8; 2:5; 7:18, 23; 10:15

2 One of David's brothers, this Nethanel was Jesse's fourth son. With David's seven older brothers, Nethanel was passed over by Samuel when Jesse presented his sons to Samuel for anointing. I SAMUEL 16; I CHRONICLES 2:14

3 A priest in David's time, this Nethanel played a trumpet in the festivities when David brought the Ark to his new capital of Jerusalem. I CHRONICLES 15:24

4 A Levite, this Nethanel was the father of Shemaiah, the Levite David selected to keep the records of the service of the Levites in David's sanctuary. I CHRONICLES 24:6

5 One of Obed-Edom's sons, this Nethanel was appointed by David as a doorkeeper in the sanctuary. I CHRONICLES 24:6

6 One of the leading citizens of Jerusalem in Jehoshaphat's time, this Nethanel was related to the royal family and was one of those selected by King Jehoshaphat to instruct the citizens of Judah in the Law. II CHRONICLES 17:7

7 A leader of the Levites in King Josiah's reign, this man by the name of Nethanel took an active part in celebrating the first Passover for many years in Judah after Josiah's reform began. II CHRONICLES 35:9

8 A priest during the Exile in Babylon, this Nethanel married outside the faith, but agreed to leave his non-Jewish wife upon returning to Jerusalem to keep the faith pure. EZRA 10:22

9 A priest who returned to Jerusalem after the Exile in Babylon, this man represented the family of Jedaiah during the tenure of the high priest Joiakim in the rebuilt Temple. NEHEMIAH 12:21

10 A musician in Jerusalem after the Exile in Babylon, this Nethanel was a Levite who participated in the impressive service when Nehemiah dedicated the rebuilt walls of the city. NEHEMIAH 12:36

NETHANIAH

1 One who lived in the stormy days

of the collapse of Judah during the Babylonian invasion, this Nethaniah was the father of the misguided super-patriot. Ishmael, who assassinated Gedaliah, the Babylonian-appointed governor, and unleashed a new wave of reprisals and deportations. II KINGS 25:23, 25; JEREMIAH 40:8—15; 41: 1—18

2 A Levite musician from the Asaph branch of the tribe, this Nethaniah led the fifth group of singers in the choirs in David's sanctuary. I CHRON-ICLES 25:2, 12

3 A well-known Levite in King Je-hoshaphat's day, this Nethaniah was one of the hand-picked group sent by the king to teach the Law to the people of Judah. II CHRONICLES 17:8

4 One who lived in the time of the prophet Jeremiah, this Nethaniah was the father of Jehudi, a member of the court sent to summon Jeremiah's secretary, Baruch, to read Jeremiah's prophecy. JEREMIAH 36:14

NEZIAH A Temple flunkey near the time of the fall of Jerusalem, Neziah was remembered as the ancestor of one of the families that returned to live in devastated Jerusalem with Ze-rubbabel after the Exile in Babylon. EZRA 2:54; NEHEMIAH 7:56

NICANOR A member of the Seven, Nicanor was one of those chosen by the early Christian community in Jerusalem to look after the less for-tunate members of the church after complaints had been raised that some of the Greek-speaking widows were being neglected. Nicanor was thus one of the first "deacons" or ones who served or ministered, as con-trasted to the apostles, who preached. Apart from Stephen and Philip, the seven deacons were not mentioned again. The name Nicanor was a fairly common Greek name. In spite of the rash of legends about Nicanor the Deacon, nothing apart from the ref-erence in Acts is known about him. ACTS 6:5

NICODEMUS The puzzling rabbi who visited Jesus secretly one night, Nicodemus was a nationally-known religious leader. He was not only a Pharisee but a member of the San-hedrin, the council of the seventy most outstanding Jews. From the lav-ish donation of myrrh and aloes he brought at Jesus' burial, it is obvious that Nicodemus was wealthy. Bible students continue to ponder over Nic-odemus' reasons for coming to Jesus at night. Whatever the motive, the in-terview had a profound effect on Nicodemus. Later, when Jesus visited Jerusalem at the Feast of the Taber-nacles, some of the Sanhedrin pro-posed to arrest Jesus. Nicodemus spoke out for just treatment by the court. Bible students still argue whether or not Nicodemus did all he could have done for Jesus on this occasion, or at the time of Jesus' ar-rest and trial a few months later. Some dismiss Nicodemus as a timid, half-hearted man who wanted to play it safe. Others insist that Nicodemus was a convinced but secret disciple of Jesus all along. Nicodemus and Joseph of Arimathea, a fellow member of the Sanhedrin, at least had the courage to ask for Jesus' body after the crucifixion to give it a decent burial. There are many unsubstantiated stories of Nicodemus' subsequent career as a zealous follower of Jesus. JOHN 3:1—9; 7:50; 19:39

NICOLAS A convert from Antioch in Syria in the earliest days of the church, Nicolas was one of the first deacons. He and six others were selected for service after complaints arose in the Christian community that some of the elderly widows were being neglected in the daily distribution of food. Originally, Nicolas had been a pagan who had embraced Judaism at Antioch. Some think that Nicolas reverted to his earlier position and was the promoter of the immoral and heretical sect known as Nicolaitans referred to in Revelation 2:6, 16. Some of the early church fathers state this as fact; others refute it. Apart from the passing reference in Acts, nothing more is mentioned in the Bible about this member of the Seven. ACTS 6:5

NIGER The gentile name of Simeon, the teacher and prophet in the Christian congregation at Antioch, Niger was an early friend and supporter of Paul. He was apparently one of those instrumental in sending the relief fund to fellow Christians at Jerusalem during the famine, and in commissioning Paul and Barnabas to go on their first missionary journey. ACTS 13:1

NIMROD Cush's son, Ham's grandson, and Noah's great-grandson, Nimrod was a powerful ancient ruler in the Tigris-Euphrates area and the legendary first empire builder in history. Although his name has been associated mostly with hunting, Nimrod was also a great conqueror and able king. Many scholars identify Nimrod with the Babylonian herodeity, Merodach or Marduk. GENESIS 10:8—9; I CHRONICLES 1:10

NIMSHI Nimshi was the grandfather of Jehu, the warrior who killed King Joram of Israel and reigned in his place. I KINGS 19:16; II KINGS 9:2, 20; II CHRONICLES 22:7

NOADIAH
1 The son of Binnui, this Noadiah was one of four Levites who were entrusted with the care of the money and sacred Temple utensils which were brought from Babylon to Jerusalem by Ezra after the Exile. EZRA 8:33
2 A woman who vociferously opposed Nehemiah's efforts to rebuild the walls of Jerusalem after the Exile in Babylon, this Noadiah joined with Sanballat and Tobiah to protest to the Persian authorities that Nehemiah's program was a threat to the peace. NEHEMIAH 6:14

NOAH
1 The son of Lamech, Noah was the hero who trusted God enough to make preparations for the disastrous flood that he knew was coming as God's judgment upon disobedient, depraved men. The great catastrophe known as the Flood divided ancient history into two distinct eras. Noah, taking pairs of every living creature into the ark,

was the agent by which God made a new beginning with His world. In spite of the new start that God made possible, the best Noah could do was to get drunk (it is Noah's dubious distinction to have discovered the process of fermentation). His sons, Ham, Shem, and Japheth, were the legendary ancestors of the tribes of the ancient Middle East. GENESIS 5:10; I CHRONICLES 1:4

2 One of the daughters of Zelophehad, this Noah, with her sisters, persuaded Moses to change the old inheritance laws so that when a father died without sons his daughters could inherit the estate for their children. NUMBERS 26:33; 27:1; 36:11; JOSHUA 17:3

NOBAI One who lived in Jerusalem after the return from Exile in Babylon, Nobai joined Nehemiah in signing the covenant, promising to keep the Law in rebuilt Jerusalem. NEHEMIAH 10:19

NOE See NOAH 1

NOGAH One of David's sons, Nogah was born after his father moved the capital to Jerusalem. Nogah was remembered in the lists of members of the royal family of Judah. I CHRONICLES 3:7; 14:6

NOHAH The fourth son of Benjamin, Nohah was the ancestor-founder of the clan and town of Benjaminites bearing his name. I CHRONICLES 8:2

NON See NUN

NUN A man of the tribe of Ephraim, Nun was the father of Joshua, the great leader and military genius who succeeded, after Moses' death, in inspiring the tribes of Israel to invade and settle Canaan. EXODUS 33:11; NUMBERS 11:28; 13:8, 16; 14:6, 30; 26:65; 27:18; 32:12, 28; 34:17; DEUTERONOMY 1:38; 31:23; 32:44; 34:9; JOSHUA 1:1; 2:1, 23; 6:6; 14:1; 17:4; 19:49, 51; 21:1; 24:29; JUDGES 2:8; I KINGS 16:34; NEHEMIAH 8:17

NYMPHAS A woman in the little Christian congregation at Laodicea, Nymphas was remembered by name by Paul in his list of personal greetings at the close of his letter to the Colossians. She was apparently a woman of prominence and means in the community, inasmuch as her house was the meeting place for the church at Laodicea. Possibly Paul mentioned Nymphas by name because he knew that his letter would be read in her house. COLOSSIANS 4:15

O

OBADIAH

1 The God-fearing member of King Ahab's household staff, this Obadiah managed to save the lives of one hundred prophets during one of Queen Jezebel's persecutions by hiding them in a cave and sneaking food to them. While hunting pastures for Ahab's animals during a drought, Obadiah encountered Elijah the prophet, who had a price on his head. Obadiah was reluctant to take Elijah's message to Ahab because he was certain Ahab would kill him for seeing Elijah. I KINGS 18

2 A Levite who was a son of Shemaiah, this Obadiah was one of those who returned to Jerusalem after the Exile in Babylon. I CHRONICLES 9:16

3 An obscure member of the royal family of Judah, this Obadiah was one of David's descendants through Zerubbabel and Hananiah. I CHRONICLES 3:21

4 One of Izrahiah's sons in the tribe of Issachar, this Obadiah was a descendant of Tola, and an early clan chieftain in the tribe. I CHRONICLES 7:3

5 One of Azel's six sons in the family of King Saul, this Obadiah was head of a family in the tribe of Benjamin and, like his relatives, undoubtedly a doughty warrior. I CHRONICLES 8:38; 9:44

6 One of the shaggy-faced, fleet-footed mountain men from Gad who were such formidable fighters in Saul's army, this Obadiah and his cohorts finally grew disgusted with Saul and joined David at Ziglag. I CHRONICLES 12:9

7 A member of the tribe of Zebulun, this Obadiah was the father of Ishmaiah, head of the tribe of Zebulun at the time of David's census. I CHRONICLES 27:19

8 A leading citizen and relative of

the royal family of Judah, this Obadiah was one of those selected by King Jehoshaphat to conduct an intensive program of teaching the people of Judah's villages the Law. I CHRONICLES 17:7

9 A Levite of the Merari branch of the tribe, this person was one of those in charge of the work crews repairing the Temple at Jerusalem during King Josiah's reform in the last days of Judah. II CHRONICLES 34:12

10 One of Jehiel's sons, this Obadiah was in the party of exiled Jews that returned with Ezra from Babylon to Jerusalem. He was respected as one of the leaders of the Jewish community during the Exile. EZRA 8:9

11 Another by the same name who lived at the same time as 10, this man was a prominent citizen of Jerusalem and took part in Nehemiah's impressive service in which the people promised to keep the Law in a covenant-signing. NEHEMIAH 10:5

12 A doorkeeper in the rebuilt Temple in Jerusalem after the return from Exile, this Levite named Obadiah was the head of a family who inherited his title and duties after him. NEHEMIAH 12:25

13 The minor prophet, this Obadiah is the author of the book in the Bible bearing his name. It is obvious that he lived and wrote after the fall of Jerusalem in 586 B.C., but no personal details are given in his book. The entire message of the twenty-one verses in the book is that the nation of Edom has received its long-deserved punishment from God for gloating over Jerusalem's destruction.

The ancient historian Josephus carelessly assumed that this Obadiah was the same as 1, but this would have been impossible because Obadiah 1 lived in Ahab's time (9th century B.C.) and Obadiah 13 lived in Nebuchadnezzar's time (6th century B.C.). Obadiah was one of the few prophets who was never quoted in the New Testament. OBADIAH 1

OBAL See EBAL 1

OBED

1 The grandfather of David, Obed was born to Ruth and Boaz near Bethlehem. Ruth's mother-in-law by her first marriage, Naomi, looked after the young Obed. Obed was fondly remembered as the father of Jesse, David's father, and an ancestor of Jesus. RUTH 4; I CHRONICLES 2:12; MATTHEW 1:5; LUKE 3:32

2 A member of the tribe of Judah, this Obed had a part-Egyptian background because one ancestor, Sheshan, had no sons and was forced to marry his daughter to his Egyptian slave, Jarha. I CHRONICLES 2:37—38

3 One of King David's most valiant soldiers, this hero earned himself a commission in David's army and a place among "The Thirty," David's roll of greatest fighters. I CHRONICLES 11:47

4 A Levite of the Korah branch of the tribe, this Obed, a son of Shemaiah, was appointed as a gatekeeper in the sanctuary at Jerusalem in David's time. He had a distinguished background and, like his brothers, was regarded as a man "of great ability." I CHRONICLES 26:1—7

5 Another Obed, this man was the father of Azariah, the great army leader and patriot who joined the high priest Jehoiada in the conspiracy to depose the wicked Queen Athaliah and crown young Joash as king of Judah. II CHRONICLES 23:1

OBED-EDOM
1 A Philistine originally from the city of Gath, Obed-Edom lived near Jerusalem in David's time. David left the Ark of the Covenant in Obed-Edom's house for three months after Uzzah had died from touching it. After receiving God's blessings for looking after the Ark, Obed-Edom and his sons helped David move it to Jerusalem and took a prominent part in the festivities. Because of Obed-Edom's care of the Ark, he and his sons were given prominent positions in the sanctuary at Jerusalem and were even referred to as "Levites." II SAMUEL 6:10—12; I CHRONICLES 13:13—14; 15:18—20, 22—24; 16: 38; 26:4, 8, 15; II CHRONICLES 25:24
2 Perhaps a second Obed-Edom, this man was the ancestor of a prominent family of Levites that served as musicians in David's sanctuary. I CHRONICLES 15:21; 16:5

OBIL An Ishmaelite, Obil was put in charge of David's camels. I CHRONICLES 27:30

OCHRAN A member of the tribe of Asher, Ochran was the father of Pagiel, the man selected by Moses to help him count the people in the tribes and serve as a representative of his tribe in advising Moses. NUMBERS 1:13; 2:27; 7:72, 77; 10:26

OCRAN See OCHRAN

ODED
1 A man of Judah, this Oded was the father of the prophet Azariah, the man who encouraged King Asa of Judah to mend his ways and conduct a reform. II CHRONICLES 15:1, 8
2 An outspoken prophet from the northern kingdom in Pekah's time, this Oded protested the plan to sell captives from a raid into Judah as slaves. His plea was listened to by several chieftains from Ephraim, and the captives were not only treated kindly but returned to their homes and families. This humane prophet from Samaria deserves notice for his brave stand for justice and compassion. II CHRONICLES 28:9—15

OG A powerful king and physical giant who ruled Bashan, a strong territory with the two well-fortified cities of Edrei and Ashtaroth in the Trans-Jordan, Og suffered an unexpected and complete defeat by Moses and the Israelites. Og's downfall was regarded as one of the great events in the early history of Israel, and was attributed to God's intervention. The area of Og's kingdom was assigned to the tribe of Manasseh. Og's enormous bed (probably a sarcophagus) was a curiosity for many years. NUMBERS 21:33; 32:33; DEUTERONOMY 1:4; 3:1 —13; 4:47; 29:7; 31:4; JOSHUA 2:10; 9:10; 12:4; 13:12, 30, 31; I KINGS 4:19; NEHEMIAH 9:22; PSALMS 135:11; 136:20

OHAD

OHAD Simeon's third son, Ohad emigrated with the family from Canaan to Egypt during the famine. His descendants were a clan within the tribe of Simeon. GENESIS 46:10; EXODUS 6:15

OHEL A member of the royal family of Judah, this descendant of David was also the son of a famous leader, Zerubbabel, who led the first group of exiles home to Jerusalem from Babylon. I CHRONICLES 3:20

OHOLIAB See AHOLIAB

OHOLIBAMAH See AHOLIBAMAH

OLYMPAS A Christian at Rome, Olympas was one of the select few singled out by Paul for special greetings at the close of his letter to the Church at Rome. His name was the shortened form of Olympiodorus. He is another of the faceless names who made up the roll of the saints in the early church. ROMANS 16:15

OMAR Esau's grandson, Omar was Eliphaz's son and an ancient Edomite chieftain. Like other clans of Edom, his family lived as nomads in the desert on the eastern side of the Jordan. GENESIS 36:11, 15; I CHRONICLES 1:36

OMRI
1 An army commander stationed at Gibbethon, Omri rushed to Tirzah, the capital of Israel, when Zimri assassinated King Elah. Omri promptly killed Zimri and took over as king of Israel himself. His dynasty, the house of Omri, was respected for years in the Middle East. He quickly quelled opposition by a disgruntled group under Tibni, and organized Israel into a well-governed, strongly fortified kingdom. Omri moved the capital to Samaria, a central location yet easily defended, and forced the tribes of Moab to pay him tribute money. Even Syria, Omri's powerful neighbor, avoided provoking him. Omri's name was famous enough to be inscribed on the great black obelisk of Shalmaneser II. The Bible states that Omri ruled only twelve years, but some scholars think that the writer of Kings might have been mistaken, judging from the great influence Omri had and from the data of the ancient inscriptions from the period. Omri's son, the notorious Ahab, succeeded him. I KINGS 16:16—30; II KINGS 8:26; II CHRONICLES 22:2; MICAH 6:16

2 One of Benjamin's grandsons, this Omri was a son of Becher and an ancient clan chieftain in the tribe of Benjamin. I CHRONICLES 7:8

3 A member of the tribe of Judah descended from Perez, this man was remembered as the ancestor of a family which returned to Jerusalem after the Exile in Babylon. I CHRONICLES 9:4

4 The son of Michael, this Omri was the head of the tribe of Issachar at the time of David's census of the tribes of his kingdom. I CHRONICLES 27:18

ONAM
1 Shobal's second son, Onam was an ancient Seirite or Edomite clan head in the desert who was remem-

bered mainly because of the tribe's relationship to the Israelites. GENESIS 36:23; I CHRONICLES 1:40

2 A great-great grandson of Judah, this Onam was a son of Jerahmeel and an early leader of a family-clan in the tribe of Judah. I CHRONICLES 2:26, 28

ONAN One of Judah's sons, Onan was responsible for marrying the widow of his deceased older brother, Er. Onan's sin was not so much a sexual aberration, as some have interpreted it, as a breach of contract with the entire community. GENESIS 38:4, 8, 9; 46:12; NUMBERS 26:19; I CHRONICLES 2:3

ONESIMUS The runaway slave belonging to Philemon who became a Christian under Paul, Onesimus was the subject of Paul's short epistle to Philemon. Onesimus had stolen some of his master's money and left. He encountered Paul, probably at Rome, and ministered to Paul as a servant. Although Paul would have liked to have kept Onesimus with him, Onesimus was returned to his owner, Philemon, at Colossae, probably in the company of Tychicus. Onesimus was commended to Philemon and the other Christians as a Christian brother, not as a slave, because of his conversion to Christ under Paul. Onesimus' name means "profitable," and Paul makes a play on words on how unprofitable Onesimus once was, but how, after his conversion, Onesimus truly began to live up to his name. Tradition has it that Onesimus became a trusted and respected leader in the church, al-

though the legends are confusing and could refer to several persons of the same name. COLOSSIANS 4:9; PHILEMON 10

ONESIPHORUS A loyal friend of Paul, Onesiphorus took the risks and effort of hunting up Paul in prison at Rome at a time when others were avoiding Paul or deserting him. Onesiphorus hailed from Ephesus and was an active member of the Christian congregation there. Paul's recollections of Onesiphorus' ministry at Ephesus suggest that Onesiphorus was a deacon in that church. Onesiphorus' kindnesses to Paul in the Roman prison came at a time when Paul was alone and friendless, and were deeply appreciated. The references in II Timothy to the household of Onesiphorus, and not to Onesiphorus himself, suggest that Onesiphorus had died before Paul wrote to Timothy. II TIMOTHY 1:16; 4:19

OPHIR One of Shem's descendants and one of Joktan's thirteen sons, Ophir was an early ancestor of a tribe and area which scholars cannot locate with certainty. GENESIS 10:29; I CHRONICLES 1:23

OPHRAH Meonothai's son, Ophrah was an ancient family head in the tribe of Judah. Perhaps Ophrah or his clan gave their name to one of the villages known as Ophrah or Ephron. I CHRONICLES 4:14

OREB A leader and general in the tribe of Midianites at the time of Gideon's astounding victory, Oreb tried to flee after the defeat of his

OREN

forces, but was intercepted by a fleet detachment of Ephraimites sent by the canny Gideon. Oreb and Zeeb, the other Midianite chief were both trapped and slain by the Jordan. Their deaths ended the bullying by the Midianites of the tribes of Israel. JUDGES 7:24—25; 8:3; PSALM 83:11

OREN A direct descendant of Judah and the third son of Jerahmeel, Oren was the ancient head of a clan within the tribe of Judah. I CHRONICLES 2:25

ORNAN The man whose threshing place became the site of the Jewish Temple, Ornan was leader of the clan of Jebusites which originally inhabited the area in which Jerusalem is located. Ornan agreed to sell the threshing floor to David after David was instructed by the prophet Gad to buy the area for an altar, to make amends for his disobedience in numbering the people. Ornan's name was sometimes known as ARAUNAH (which see). I CHRONICLES 21:15—25; II CHRONICLES 3:1; II SAMUEL 24:16 (where he is called Araunah)

ORPAH A girl from Moab, Orpah married Naomi's son Chilion. After the deaths of Mahlon and his father, Naomi decided to return home to Bethlehem, and urged her two daughters-in-law, Orpah and Ruth, to return to their families in Moab. Orpah remained in Moab, but Ruth went with Naomi. RUTH 1:4, 14

OSNAPPAR See **ASNAPPAR**

OTHNI One of Shemaiah's sons, Othni was a Levite who was appointed a gatekeeper in the sanctuary at Jerusalem in David's time. I CHRONICLES 26:7

OTHNIEL The first of the strongmen who presided as judges over the loose confederation of tribes of Israel after the invasion of Canaan, Othniel succeeded Joshua as the leader of the tribes. He was a nephew of Caleb the spy, and married Caleb's daughter as a reward for killing the Canaanite leader Kiriath-sepher. Part of the dowry included some precious springs of good water which helped establish Othniel as a wealthy man. Othniel was an able general and gave the tribes a much needed breathing-space of peace. His rule lasted forty years. JOSHUA 15:17; JUDGES 1:13; 3:9, 11; I CHRONICLES 4:13; 27:15

OZEM
1 One of David's older brothers, Ozem, with Jesse's other older sons, was passed over when the prophet Samuel came to anoint David. Apart from a record of his name in the family tree, there is no further mention of Ozem in the Bible. I CHRONICLES 2:3; I SAMUEL 16 (describes the anointing of David without referring by name to Ozem)
2 One of Jerahmeel's sons, this Ozem was an early chieftain of a clan in the tribe of Judah. I CHRONICLES 2:25

OZIAS The name used by Matthew for King Uzziah, Ozias is listed as one of Jesus' ancestors in Matthew's genealogical account. MATTHEW 1:8, 9

OZNI One of Jacob's grandsons,

Ozni was a son of Gad. He accompanied the family when it moved during the famine from Canaan to Egypt. His family became known as Oznites, a clan within the tribe of Gad. Ozni was also known as EZBON (which see). NUMBERS 26:16; GENESIS 46:16 (where the name is Ezbon)

P

PAARAI One of David's greatest fighters, Paarai was elected to the roll of "The Thirty," David's top warriors, and commissioned an officer in the royal army. He was also known by the name "Naarai." II SAMUEL 23:35; I CHRONICLES 11:37 (where he is called Naarai)

PADON A Temple lackey, Padon was remembered as the ancestor of a family that returned with the first contingent of exiles from Babylon to Jerusalem under Zerubbabel. EZRA 2: 44; NEHEMIAH 7:47

PAGIEL A son of Ochran, Pagiel was the man chosen by Moses to represent the tribe of Asher in numbering the tribes and advising Moses. NUMBERS 1:13; 2:27; 7:72, 77; 10:26

PAHATH-MOAB An obscure person whose descendants were mentioned frequently at the time of the return

from Exile in Babylon, Pahath-moab himself is not mentioned in the Bible. Scholars are not certain what the word "Pahath" means, and can shed little light on his identity. Over twenty-eight hundred men from his clan, divided into two branches, Jeshua's and Joab's, returned from Babylon to Jerusalem. EZRA 2:6; 8:4; 10:30; NEHEMIAH 3:11; 7:11; 10:14

PALAL A son of Uzai or Uzzai, Palal worked with Nehemiah in rebuilding the walls of devastated Jerusalem after the return from Exile in Babylon. Palal constructed part of the tower on the king's house. NEHEMIAH 3:25

PALLU Reuben's second son, and one of Jacob's grandsons, Pallu went with the family when it emigrated from Canaan to Egypt during the famine. Later, he was the ancestor-founder of the clan in the tribe of

273

PALTI

Reuben known as Palluites. GENESIS 46:9; EXODUS 6:14; NUMBERS 26:5, 8; I CHRONICLES 5:3

PALTI

1 A son of Raphu of the tribe of Benjamin, Palti was chosen to represent his tribe as one of the twelve spies sent by Moses to reconnoiter the Promised Land. Palti, however, like most of the other spies except Caleb and Joshua, was frightened by the difficulties of invading Canaan, and advised strongly against the attempt. NUMBERS 13:9

2 A son of Laish in the tribe of Benjamin, and a distant relative of Saul, this Palti was awarded David's wife Michal after David was forced to flee from Saul's court. Apparently, he was a good husband to Michal. When David became king and forced Michal to leave Palti and join the royal harem, she despised David. I SAMUEL 25:44; II SAMUEL 3:15 (where he was called PALTIEL)

PALTIEL

1 A son of Azzan in the tribe of Issachar, this Paltiel was chosen when Moses asked for representatives from each tribe to advise him on how to divide the Promised Land fairly after the wanderings in the desert. NUMBERS 34:26

2 For the husband of Michal mentioned in II Samuel 3:15, see PALTI 2

PARMASHTA One of Haman's ten sons, Parmashta, together with his father and brothers, conspired to plan a grisly bloodbath against all Jews in Persia during Ahasuerus' reign. The butchery was averted only because Queen Esther intervened. Parmashta and his family were hanged. ESTHER 9:9

PARMENAS Parmenas was one of the seven deacons, or servers, selected by the Jerusalem church in the early days, after there were complaints that some of the Greek-speaking Christians' widows were going hungry. Parmenas was probably a Greek-speaking Jew himself; his name is the shortened form of Parmenides. Parmenas was another respected leader in the early church who was given only a brief reference in the writings. One tradition holds that he later died a martyr at Philippi. ACTS 6:5

PARNACH A man in the tribe of Zebulun, Parnach was remembered as the father of Elizaphan, the representative of the Zebulun selected to help Moses divide the Promised Land among the tribes. NUMBERS 34:25

PAROSH An unknown Hebrew clan head, Parosh was the ancestor of a large group calling itself "children of Parosh" which returned with Zerubbabel in the first contingent of exiles from Babylon to Jerusalem, and of another group which returned with Ezra. Parosh's descendants assisted Nehemiah in rebuilding the walls and joined in signing the covenant to keep the Law. EZRA 2:3; 8:3; 10:25; NEHEMIAH 3:25; 7:8; 10:14

PARSHANDATHA The oldest son of Haman, Parshandatha, together with his father and brothers, planned

274

a brutal reprisal against all the Jews in Persia during Ahasuerus' rule. The massacre was headed off when Mordecai told his cousin, Queen Esther, about it, and she, in turn, interceded for her people to the king. Parshandatha and his family were executed in disgrace. ESTHER 9:7

PARUAH A man from the tribe of Issachar, Paruah was the father of Jehoshaphat, one of Solomon's twelve commissary officers. I KINGS 4:17

PASACH Great - great - grandson of Asher, Pasach was a son of Japhlet, and an early clan chieftain in the tribe of Asher. I CHRONICLES 7:33

PASEAH
1 A clan chieftain in the tribe of Judah, this Paseah traced his ancestry through his father, Eshton, and grandfather, Chelub, to Caleb, son of Hur. I CHRONICLES 4:12
2 A Temple flunkey, this Paseah was the ancestor of a family which returned with Zerubbabel in the first group of exiles to Jerusalem from Babylon. EZRA 2:49; NEHEMIAH 7:51
3 A Jew who lived during the Exile in Babylon, this man was the father of the Jehoiada who helped repair the walls of Jerusalem with Nehemiah. NEHEMIAH 3:6

PASHHUR
1 A close adviser of King Zedekiah during the last days of Judah, Pashhur was one of those sent to ask Jeremiah what the outcome of Nebuchadnezzar's attack on Jerusalem would be. Later, when he heard that Jeremiah was pointing out the futility of fighting the Babylonians, Pashhur urged King Zedekiah to execute Jeremiah as a subversive, but failing to persuade Zedekiah to kill Jeremiah, he joined with others in throwing Jeremiah into a deep cistern. This Pashhur was the son of Malchiah. JEREMIAH 21:1; 38:1—13; I CHRONICLES 9:12; NEHE-MIAH 11:12
2 Another Pashhur who lived at the same time as 1, this man was the son of Immer, the priestly head of the Temple. This Pashhur so resented Jeremiah's prophecy of the downfall of Judah that he had Jeremiah beaten and imprisoned in stocks for a day. Jeremiah, refusing to be intimidated, reiterated his warnings, adding that Pashhur would die in exile in Babylon. This Pashhur, a swaggering Temple bigwig, confidently prophesied that Judah would never be taken by the Babylonians. JEREMIAH 20:1—6
3 The father of Gedaliah, this Pashhur might have been the same as either 1 or 2, or perhaps an entirely different individual. JEREMIAH 38:1
4 This Pashhur was a priest, and the head of a numerous clan which was prominent in the community returning to Jerusalem from Babylon after the Exile. His descendants returned with Ezra and helped Nehemiah repair the walls and sign the covenant. EZRA 2:38; 10:22; NEHEMIAH 7:41; 10:3

PATROBAS A member of the Christian community at Rome, Patrobas was singled out for special greetings by Paul in his letter to the Romans. There was a person by the name of Patrobas who secured his freedom as one of Nero's slaves and was executed by Galba, according to the early historian Tacitus, but whether this Patrobas was the same man that Paul knew is not certain. His name was the abbreviated form of "Patrobius." ROMANS 16:14

PAUL The great apostle to the Gentiles, Paul was born at Tarsus of Cilicia into a proud and strict Pharisee family and given the Jewish name "Saul." He was proud of being born a Roman citizen. A highly educated Jew, Paul studied in Jerusalem under the great Rabbi Gamaliel, and rigorously observed the requirements of the Law. Paul, however, had misgivings about his ability to keep every part of the Law and believed that legalism could not bring about the right relationship with God. Although Paul never met Jesus during His earthly ministry, he encountered the earliest believers in the risen Christ. He immediately recognized the threat that belief in Jesus posed to Judaism. Paul quickly became the most ardent persecutor of the new sect. He was an approving onlooker at Stephen's martyrdom and was carrying lists of suspected Christian believers in Damascus when he experienced a radical change. His conversion on the Damascus road changed the course of the Christian faith—and civilization itself. Temporarily blinded, Saul, the persecutor who had been confronted by the Living Lord was led to Ananias' house, baptized "Paul," then smuggled out of town to escape reprisals. After a brief sojourn in Arabia, Paul visited Jerusalem and stayed briefly with Peter and James, Jesus' brother. After this visit, Paul apparently lived quietly for several years in Cilicia, preaching the gospel and supporting himself by weaving the black goat hair material for tents that was a famous product of the area near Tarsus. He was called by Barnabas, his acquaintance from Jerusalem, to help the dynamic congregation of Antioch carry out its ministry. Paul and Barnabas carried a special famine relief offering to the Jerusalem church, then returned to Antioch. Shortly afterward, the Antioch Christians sent Paul and Barnabas on a preaching mission through Cyprus and Asia Minor. On this and subsequent missionary journeys, Paul stirred up heated opposition by his preaching. His presentation of the gospel was resented in Jewish circles because it usually split local synagogues. On the other hand, his efforts were quickly opposed by members of the Christian community, who insisted that it was necessary to keep the requirements of the Jewish Law before one could be a Christian believer. The infant church was ripped with controversy over Paul's preaching. Paul insisted that man is saved by what God has done through Jesus Christ, not by what man does in keeping the Law. The controversy was partially resolved by a church council in Jerusalem when the leaders agreed that Paul's point was valid, and that he could continue to welcome Gentiles to the faith without compelling them to be circumcised. Paul's subsequent career was packed with high adventure, heavy responsibilities, and deep suffering. As the greatest missionary, he organized and encouraged young congregations throughout Asia Minor, and even crossed over to Europe. Much of the New Testament was written by Paul in the form of letters dashed off to his "problem" churches or to his friends needing advice. Against the advice of his associates, he insisted on going in person to Jerusalem with a special offering collected for the poor. Extremists among the Jewish authorities arranged his arrest and imprisonment. After languishing two years under arrest without a trial, Paul insisted on a hearing before the emperor. He had a harrowing trip to Rome, was apparently acquitted, then re-arrested. All traditions agree that Paul was beheaded after another lengthy imprisonment, probably during Nero's bloody persecution. ACTS 13:38; ROMANS; I AND II CORINTHIANS; GALATIANS, EPHESIANS, PHILIPPIANS, COLOSSIANS, I AND II THESSALONIANS, I AND II TIMOTHY, TITUS, PHILEMON; II PETER 3:15

PEDAHEL A member of the tribe of Naphtali, Pedahel was chosen to represent his tribe when Moses asked for twelve men to assist him in dividing the Promised Land among the twelve tribes. NUMBERS 34:28

PEDAHZUR One of the tribe of Manasseh, Pedahzur was the father of Gamaliel, the man representing his tribe in the group of twelve helping Moses to divide the Promised Land fairly among the tribes. NUMBERS 1:10

PEDAIAH
1 A member of the tribe of Manasseh, Pedaiah was the father of the Joel who was head of the western part of that tribe at the time of David's census of the kingdom. I CHRONICLES 27:20
2 King Josiah's father-in-law, this Pedaiah was the father of Zebidah, one of Josiah's wives, and lived at Rumah. II KINGS 23:36
3 The great-great-grandson of **2**, this man was the son of King Jeconiah, the king of Judah carried away as a captive by the Babylonians. This Pedaiah was born in Babylon after his father's release from prison. He inspired his son, Zerubbabel, to become one of the great leaders among the exiled Jews and to lead the first group back to Jerusalem. I CHRONICLES 3:18—19
4 One of the descendants of Parosh, this Pedaiah helped Nehemiah repair the walls of devastated Jerusalem after the return from Exile in Babylon. NEHEMIAH 3:25
5 Perhaps the same as **4**, this Pedaiah stood on the platform with Ezra as one of the leading citizens of Jerusalem when Ezra convened a great national assembly to hear the Law read and expounded. NEHEMIAH 8:14
6 Possibly identical with **4** and/or **5**, one also named Pedaiah lived at Jerusalem at the same time as **4** and **5** and was a well-known Levite. He was appointed by Nehemiah to a committee of four to take charge of receiving and distributing the offerings. NEHEMIAH 13:13
7 A member of the tribe of Benja-

min, this person was the grandfather of Sallu, a leading man in the community of those who returned to Jerusalem after the Exile. NEHEMIAH 11:7

PEKAH The impatient and ambitious son of Remaliah, Pekah was head of the army in King Pekahiah's Israel. He resented Pekahiah's pro-Assyrian policy and seized the throne in a sudden coup. Pekah immediately lined up allies against Assyria, but could not get Judah to go along. He and Rezin of Damascus angrily invaded and devastated Judah. Judah's King Ahaz, against the advice of Isaiah the prophet, called Assyria in to pull off the invaders. Assyria, happy to oblige, stormed across Pekah's borders, carrying off scores of captives and ruining the country. The northern kingdom had had enough of Pekah's adventures. Hoshea, son of Elah, successfully conspired to slay Pekah and take over as king in his stead. II KINGS 15, 16; II CHRONICLES 28:6; ISAIAH 7:1

PEKAHIAH The son and successor of King Menahem of the northern kingdom of Israel, Pekahiah continued his father's pro-Assyrian policy in national affairs and his tolerance of idolatry in religious affairs. Some of Hosea's poignant words were inspired by Pekahiah's callousness toward injustices and suffering. His undistinguished reign of two years ended abruptly when Pekah, his army commander, stormed in with a hundred and fifty Gileadite troopers, killed Pekah, and seized control of Israel. II KINGS 15:22—26

PELAIAH
1 A descendant of David and a member of the royal family of Judah, this Pelaiah was one of Elioenai's seven sons. I CHRONICLES 3:24
2 A prominent Levite in Jerusalem after the return from Exile in Babylon, this Pelaiah participated in the great national assembly when Ezra called the people together to hear the Law read. Pelaiah helped explain the Law. He also joined Nehemiah in signing the covenant in the impressive ceremony in which the people of Jerusalem promised to keep the law. NEHEMIAH 8:7; 10:10

PELALIAH A priest, Pelaliah was the grandfather of a well-known priest named Adaiah who was a leader among those who returned to Jerusalem after the Exile in Babylon. NEHEMIAH 11:12

PELATIAH
1 The subject of a strange vision by the prophet Ezekiel, this Pelatiah was a well-known leader in Jerusalem. In Ezekiel's vision, twenty-five men, two of whom are mentioned by name (Jaazaniah and Pelatiah), the top national leaders, stand at the gate of the Temple giving evil advice. In the middle of Ezekiel's prophecy, Pelatiah suddenly drops dead for giving wicked counsel. EZEKIEL 11:1—13
2 Another Pelatiah, this man was a descendant of David and a member of the royal family of Judah. His grandfather, Zerubbabel, was a great leader of the Jewish community after the Exile. I CHRONICLES 3:21

3 A warrior and leader of the fighters from the tribe of Simeon, this Pelatiah was one of the clan leaders who led the attack in King Hezekiah's time on the remnant of the Amalekites living near Mount Seir, and grabbed the area for the tribe of Simeon. I CHRONICLES 4:42

4 A leading citizen in Jerusalem after the return from Exile in Babylon, this man joined Nehemiah in the solemn service of signing the covenant promising to keep the Law. NEHEMIAH 10:22

PELEG One of Eber's two sons, and a descendant of Shem, Noah's son, Peleg lived in the era when, the ancients believed, the people of the earth began to separate and disperse to various places in the world and different languages began to appear. GENESIS 10:25; 11:16—19; I CHRONICLES 1:19, 25

PELET

1 An ancient and obscure member of the tribe of Judah, Pelet was a son of Jahdai of the clan of Caleb, son of Hezron, and was included in the tribal lists by the Chronicler. I CHRONICLES 2:47

2 A brave warrior from the tribe of Benjamin, Pelet originally fought for his relative Saul, but, like most others from his tribe, grew disenchanted with Saul and finally joined David at Ziglag. Like others from his tribe, this fighter was a skillful user of the bow and sling, and could fire either weapon with either hand. I CHRONICLES 12:3

PELETH

1 Perhaps the same as Pallu, Reuben's second son, this man named Peleth was listed in some records as a member of Reuben's family. He was best remembered as the father of On one of the ringleaders of the conspiracy against Moses. NUMBERS 16:1

2 A member of the tribe of Judah who could trace his ancestry through such illustrious forbearers as Jerahmeel and Perez, this Peleth was an early clan chieftain of the tribe. I CHRONICLES 2:33

PENIEL   See PENUEL

PENINNAH One of the two wives of Elkanah, father of the prophet Samuel, Peninnah was for many years the only wife fortunate enough to have children. Nonetheless, Elkanah's other wife, Hannah, remained the favorite. Peninnah exacerbated this difficult domestic situation by aiming some bitter comments toward Hannah. I SAMUEL 1:2

PENUEL

1 An ancient chieftain whose name was recorded among the early leaders of the tribe of Judah, this Penuel was the father or clan founder of Gedor. I CHRONICLES 4:4

2 A little-known son of Shashak of the tribe of Benjamin, this Penuel was also a clan chieftain listed in the tribal genealogy. I CHRONICLES 8:25

PERESH A grandson of Manasseh and a son of Machir, Peresh was an early chieftain and clan head in the tribe of Manasseh. I CHRONICLES 7:16

PEREZ

1 Judah's older twin son through his incestuous relations with Tamar, his daughter-in-law, Perez was an ancient clan chieftain in the powerful tribe of Judah. Perez' two sons, Hezron and Hamul, and a host of famous descendants (among them David), gave Perez prominence in the long history of Israel. Nothing of his life, however, is known beyond his parentage. GENESIS 38:29; 46:12; NUMBERS 26:20—21; RUTH 4:12, 18; I CHRONICLES 2:4, 5; 4:1; 9:4; 27:3; NEHEMIAH 11:4, 6; MATTHEW 1:3; LUKE 3:33

PERIDA One of Solomon's staff of servants, Perida was the ancestor of a family that returned in the first contingent of exiles from Babylon to Jerusalem under the leadership of Zerubbabel. EZRA 2:55; NEHEMIAH 7:57

PERSIS A woman who was greatly respected and loved for her tireless ministry, Persis was one of these in the Christian community at Rome to whom Paul sent special greetings at the close of his letter to the Romans. There is a freed slave woman named Persis in an ancient list of Latin inscriptions, but there is no way of identifying this person as the one mentioned by Paul. Although Persis was well-known in the early church, unfortunately she is little more than a name to us today. ROMANS 16:12

PERUDA See **PERIDA**

PETER The Galilee fisherman who with his brother, Andrew, became a member of Jesus' disciple band of twelve, "Peter" was actually a nickname (from the Greek word "petros" for rock) for Simon, son of Jona. He was also known as "Cephas" (from the Aramaic word "kepha" for rock). Both Peter and Andrew were originally from Bethsaida, and were living at Capernaum when summoned by Jesus to be followers. Peter, an enthusiastic, positive man, quickly became one of Jesus' three closest associates, and the names Peter, James, and John, in that order, appear repeatedly in the gospel narratives in such outstanding occasions in Jesus' career as the transfiguration, the raising of Jairus' daughter, and the praying in Gethsemane. Peter impetuously answered Jesus' query, "Who do you say that I am?" with the ringing affirmation at Caesarea-Philippi, "Thou art the Christ, the Son of the Living God." Jesus' comment on Peter's answer was, "Thou art Peter and on this rock I will build my church." The meaning of these words has been hotly debated, the Roman Church insisting that Jesus gave Peter personal primacy above all other leaders in the church; most others saying that it was Peter's *faith*, and not Peter's person, that Jesus was commending. Peter's human qualities are well-known, and endear him to Christians today. He protectively tried to talk Jesus out of going to Jerusalem to die, and received Jesus' curt scolding, "Get thee behind me, Satan." He swaggeringly promised Jesus at the Last Supper that he would never forsake Him, and then promptly fell asleep in the garden when Jesus asked him to sit up with Him in prayer. Peter foolishly swung his sword, wounding a servant, when the arrest party surrounded Jesus. He loudly denied having anything to do with Jesus when accosted by a servant girl in the high priest's courtyard when Jesus was inside being interrogated. Peter, the fickle loudmouth, was, however, transformed by the resurrection. He took charge of the frightened, faltering group of believers and fearlessly preached the news of the resurrection on the streets of Jerusalem. In the early church, Peter emerged as one of the most prominent leaders. With John, Peter suffered imprisonment in Jerusalem. He and John were also sent by the apostle band to visit the new converts in outlying areas of Judea and Samaria. Peter had been born and bred a Jew. At first, he clung to his heritage, insisting with many others, that it was necessary to adhere to the Jewish Law in order to be a Christian. This brought him into conflict with Paul, who was preaching to non-Jews and was not requiring them to be circumcized or observe the dietary laws. Peter, however, was brought closer to Paul's view by a vision at the house of Simon the Tanner and by his mission to Cornelius the Centurion. When Paul visited Peter at Jerusalem, the two were able to reach friendly accord, although many others were angrily denouncing Paul and the inclusion of Gentiles in the church. At the Council of Jerusalem, where the matter of Gentile Inclusion was officially settled, Peter took an active part. From Galatians, however, we learn that

Peter was sharply criticized by Paul for reverting briefly to his old exclusivist position when pressured not to eat with Gentile believers. Peter's later career was a busy one of traveling and preaching. He was married, and took his wife with him. Traditions abound on Peter's work. Some state that he was the first bishop of Antioch, others, of Rome. He had a close connection with the Roman congregation and most certainly lived there for some time in his later years. For a time, Mark was his companion and secretary. Legends persist that he traveled widely from Rome. He was the author of correspondence included in the New Testament. Most scholars accept the tradition of Peter's martyrdom in Rome during Nero's persecution. Recent archaeological work under St. Peter's Church confirms the ancient report that his body was buried at that place. MATTHEW, MARK, LUKE, JOHN, ACTS, GALATIANS, I AND II PETER

PETHAHIAH
1 A priest in David's sanctuary, this Pethahiah was appointed to take charge of the nineteenth contingent of priests. I CHRONICLES 24:16
2 A Levite who married outside the faith during the Exile in Babylon, this man kept Ezra's strict injunction against defiling the faith, and left his "foreign" wife on returning to Jerusalem. EZRA 10:23
3 A third Pethahiah, this man might possibly have been the same as 2. He was a Levite who had a prominent role in Ezra's great national assembly of the returned exiles when the per-

ple heard the Law read and expounded. NEHEMIAH 9:5
4 A son of Meshezabeel and a member of an illustrious family of the tribe of Judah, this Pethahiah was the deputy governor of the area around Jerusalem and advised the king of Persia on matters pertaining to the exiles returning to Jerusalem. NEHEMIAH 11:24

PETHUEL An otherwise unknown man living in the eighth century B.C. in Judah, Pethuel was remembered as the father of the prophet Joel. JOEL 1:1

PEULLETH See PEULTHAI

PEULTHAI A Levite of the Kohath branch of the tribe, Peulthai was a son of Obed-edom and served as a gatekeeper in David's sanctuary at Jerusalem. I CHRONICLES 26:5

PHAATH-MOAB See PAHATH-MOAB

PHALEC See PELEG

PHALLU See PALLU

PHALTI See PALTIEL

PHANUEL A woman of the tribe of Asher, Phanuel was the mother of the prophetess Anna, the elderly widow who gratefully looked at the infant Jesus at the entrance of the Temple. LUKE 2:36

PHARAOH The term is an honorary one, a title for the rulers of Egypt in the times of the Bible, and not a proper name. At least ten pharaohs are referred to in the Bible.
1 The "Pharaoh" in Abraham's time, a king who cannot be identified in Egyptian history, is probably an erroneous title given by a later writer inasmuch as the term was not known until much after Abraham's time, in the Eighteenth Dynasty. This "pharaoh" unwittingly took Abraham's wife into his harem and suffered a series of natural disasters as a result. GENESIS 12:15—20
2 The pharaoh in Joseph's time, probably one of the Hyksos rulers, lived at the site of Heliopolis. It is difficult to identify this pharaoh with a particular ruler in the ancient Egyptian inscriptions. He promoted Joseph, the ex-slave and ex-prisoner, to the post of prime minister, and through Joseph's efforts, saw his kingdom survive seven grim years of famine. GENESIS 37, 39—42, 44—47, 50
3 The pharaoh in Moses' time, undoubtedly Ramses II, held life and death power over every Egyptian for a sixty-seven year rule. This was the great Nineteenth Dynasty, a time of immense building programs and terrible oppression. The Hebrews were forced into slave labor gangs and suffered intolerably. EXODUS 1—2
4 The pharaoh of the Exodus, Merenptah, was Ramses II's successor. Merenptah had a series of dramatic interviews with Moses in which he haughtily refused to accede to Moses' demand to let God's people go. After the last plague swept the kingdom, killing the oldest child in each Egyptian home, Merenptah wavered briefly, then sent out his armored divisions to drive the Hebrews back to the labor camps. The great act of deliverance

by God at the Red Sea wiped out the pursuers, and Moses and the Israelites began their wanderings. Merenptah was the first pharaoh to mention the Hebrews on any inscription found so far by archaeologists. EXODUS 3—15; 18; DEUTERONOMY 6:21, 22; 7:8, 18; 11:3; 29:2; 34:11; I SAMUEL 2:27; 6:6; II KINGS 17:7; NEHEMIAH 9:10; PSALMS 135:9; 136:15; ACTS 7; ROMANS 9:17

5 The pharaoh who became Solomon's father-in-law, this ruler was a Tanite king of the Twenty-first Dynasty. He conquered the city-state of Gezer and presented it to Solomon. His daughter's marriage followed the usual method of sealing an alliance in the international diplomacy of earlier times. I KINGS 2:46; 3:1; 7:8; 9:16, 24; 11:1—13; II CHRONICLES 8:11; Song of Solomon 1:9

6 For Pharaoh Shishak, see SHISHAK.

7 For Pharaoh Necho, see NECHO.

8 Pharaoh Hophra was a contemporary of the Babylonian emperor, Nebuchadnezzar. The prophet Jeremiah correctly predicted Hophra's downfall in the international struggle. Hophra was the fourth king in the Twenty-sixth Dynasty, and had aspirations of recapturing the former glory of his famous kingdom. Nebuchadnezzar, however, cut short Hophra's dreams by subjugating most of the Middle East. Hophra's Egypt was a haven for many refugees from Judah. JEREMIAH 44:30

9 An unnamed pharaoh who gave asylum to Hadad the Edomite, this pharaoh even gave his sister-in-law as a wife to Hadad. Although this pharaoh was a contemporary of David and although his queen's name is given as Tahpenes, scholars cannot identify him clearly with either of the two dynasties which ruled different parts of Egypt simultaneously in the 11th century B.C. I KINGS 11:14—22

10 The pharaoh who was a contemporary of King Hezekiah of Judah, this ruler was the one to whom Hezekiah was strongly tempted to turn for help during the dark days of Sennacherib's seige of Jerusalem. This pharaoh was probably Tirhaka, an Ethiopian who took over Egypt during the late eighth century B.C. II KINGS 18:21; 19:9; ISAIAH 19:11; 30:2, 3, 6

11 The father of Bithiah, the wife of Mered of the tribe of Judah, this pharaoh is another who cannot be identified further. He is mentioned in the genealogy of the tribe of Judah by the Chronicler. I CHRONICLES 4:18

PHARES See PEREZ

PHAREZ See PEREZ

PHAROSH See PAROSH

PHASEAH See PASEAH

PHEBE See PHOEBE

PHICHOL See PHICOL

PHICOL The general of King Abimelech's army, Phicol was present when the Philistine king signed a treaty with Abraham and Isaac after the dispute over rights to use various wells were settled. GENESIS 21:22—32; 26:26

PHILEMON The well-to-do member

of the Christian community at Colossae who owned the runaway slave, Onesimus, Philemon was the recipient of one of Paul's loveliest and most personal letters. The slave, converted to Christianity, was being returned to Philemon. From the letter, it appears that Philemon was a leader of the Colossian church, and had been brought to the faith by Paul himself. Philemon's family or household are named in the letter, implying that Paul knew them well and perhaps had stayed in the home. Tradition insists that Philemon became the bishop of Colossae, and with his wife, son, and faithful slave, Onesimus, was stoned to death during Nero's brutal reign. PHILEMON

PHILETUS An early heretic in the Christian church, Philetus and Hymenaeus were denounced by Paul for distorting the gospel and undermining the belief of others. Specifically Philetus was guilty of the gnostic teachings which tried to "spiritualize" everything, including Jesus' resurrection, death itself, and the life of believers in this world. II TIMOTHY 2:17

PHILIP

1 One of the twelve apostles, this man hailed from Bethsaida of Galilee. He was the fourth to follow Jesus, and undoubtedly had been an earnest listener to John the Baptist's preaching. Immediately after his call to be with Jesus, he communicated the good news of the Messiah to his close friend, Nathanael. He was not discouraged by Nathanael's cool reaction to Jesus, but insisted that Nathanael meet Jesus in person. A practical man, Philip had already figured out the cost of feeding the multitude before Jesus asked about the extent of the disciples' food supply. Apparently he kept his "come and see" viewpoint in regard to Jesus; Philip was the man who introduced Greek-speaking Jews to Jesus when others were hesitant of bringing them to the Master. At the Last Supper, Philip asked to see the Father, indicating either that he was slow to grasp who Jesus was, or that he wanted a private miracle. Philip, after the resurrection, was spoken of as "one of the great lights of Asia," according to Polycrates, the ancient Christian writer. He was frequently confused by early writers with Philip the Evangelist, one of the Seven. Traditions regarding his later career and death are confusing and unreliable. MATTHEW 10:3; MARK 3:18; LUKE 6:14; JOHN 1:43—48; 6:5—7; 12:21—22; 14:8—9; ACTS 1:13

2 One of the Seven, this Philip was frequently confused with 1 because he sprang into prominence as an effective preacher and church organizer at about the same time. He was originally one of the first "deacons," the group of seven set apart to look after the welfare of the elderly and widows following complaints that these were being neglected. Philip and Stephen, however, soon expanded their duties to include evangelistic addresses to the crowds. Philip was one of the first to reach out beyond Jerusalem and to preach to Greek-speaking Jews, especially after Stephen's martyrdom. Philip's work among the Samaritans

brought great numbers into the church and brought about a "bishop's" visit from Peter and John. Always alert for any opportunity to present the claims of Christ, Philip even baptized a high official of the Ethiopian court whom he encountered reading a scroll of Isaiah along the road one day. Philip was instrumental in helping the earliest Christians break out of the cocoon of Judaism, and in insisting that the gospel be proclaimed to non-Jews as well as to Jews. Paul visited Philip and his four daughters at Caesarea before Paul's arrest at Jerusalem, and undoubtedly returned the visit during Paul's two-year imprisonment at Caesarea. Philip and his daughters left Palestine during the Jewish revolt. The most likely of the traditions about his later whereabouts is that he became the beloved bishop of Tralles in Asia Minor. ACTS 6:5; 8:5—40; 21:8

3 Philip the Tetrarch, this Philip was a son of Herod the Great and Cleopatra. In his father's will, he was assigned the territories in southern Syria and given the title of Tetrarch. Philip traveled to Rome to get the Emperor Augustus' approval of the will when old Herod died. Later, he married his niece, Salome, daughter of the much-married Herodias. Unlike his half-brothers, who were ousted from their territories, Philip used his abilities to govern his territory and ruled for almost forty years. Like his father Herod the Great, Philip carried out extensive building programs. MATTHEW 14:3; MARK 6:17; LUKE 3:1, 19

PHILOLOGUS One of the members of the Christian community at Rome, Philologus was singled out by name by Paul for a special greeting at the close of the Letter to the Romans. It is hard to determine who this man was, because the name occurs many times in inscriptions and lists of slaves and freedmen in ancient Rome and was a very common name. Philologus must have been a leader in the early church and a close friend of Paul to have earned the salutation in the Letter. ROMANS 16:15

PHINEHAS
1 Aaron's grandson and Eleazer's son, Phinehas was a decisive leader and high priest during Joshua's time. He recognized the insidious danger of the heathen cults among the Israelites, and took positive steps to prevent Zimri and his zealous pagan wife from bringing her vices into the camp. Phinehas later zealously upheld the cause of the Lord when the Ephraimites began to dally with native rites. He understood more clearly than most the dangers to the community whenever the tribes permitted any vestiges of Canaanite cults to take hold. EXODUS 6:25; NUMBERS 25:7, 11; 31:6; JOSHUA 22:13, 30; 24:33; JUDGES 20:28; I CHRONICLES 6:4, 50; 9:20; EZRA 7:5; 8:2; PSALM 106:30

2 The irresponsible, unscrupulous younger son of the great priest, Eli, this Phinehas, like his brother Hophni, was such a corrupt judge that everyone was relieved when the two brothers were killed in the Philistine wars. The shock of their deaths, however, killed their broken-hearted father. I SAMUEL 1:3; 2:34; 4:4, 17, 19; 14:3

3 A priest who lived during the Exile in Babylon, this Phinehas was the father of Eleazar, one of the priests in Jerusalem after the Exile who received the gifts brought from Babylon by Ezra. EZRA 8:33

PHLEGON A member of the Christian community at Rome, Phlegon was one of the special few singled out by Paul for a personal greeting at the close of his letter to the Church at Rome. Like so many others named by Paul in his list, Phlegon is merely a name. The welter of legends sheds no light on his life. ROMANS 16:14

PHOEBE The deaconess from Cenchrae (the port of Corinth) whom Paul introduced to the Christian community at Rome, Phoebe was undoubtedly the person who carried Paul's Letter to the Romans to Rome. Paul speaks glowingly of her kindnesses to those at Cenchrae, and implies that she was in a financial position to be of great help to the Christian community in her home town. ROMANS 16:1

PHURAH See PURAH

PHUT See PUT

PHUVAH See PUVAH

PHYGELLUS See PHYGELUS

PHYGELUS A one-time enthusiast for the gospel, and one-time supporter of Paul, Phygelus hurt and disappointed Paul by ignoring him during Paul's last imprisonment at Rome. Perhaps it was fear of guilt by asso-ciation, perhaps it was a quarrel over doctrine that led Phygelus and his associate Hermogenes to refuse to help Paul in his hour of need. We unfortunately do not know what Paul had asked Phygelus to do, nor do we know Phygelus' side of the story. II TIMOTHY 1:15

PILATE A hard-boiled army man, Pontius Pilate was the inept fifth Roman procurator of the province of Judea. He was a bad selection for such an explosive area and immediately showed an insensitivity that brought the province to the brink of revolt. Moving his army headquarters to Jerusalem, Pilate offended everyone by needlessly insisting upon bringing the hated and blasphemous Roman eagles and standards into the area overlooking the Temple. A violent five-day demonstration erupted. In the end, Pilate was forced to remove the emblems. Next came the episode of the water mains. Pilate decided to raid the Temple treasury to improve the Jerusalem water system. This time, when the mob gathered in protest, Pilate turned his soldiers loose and massacred many. Third came the episode of the shields, which Pilate had hung in Herod's palace. This time, the emperor himself forced Pilate to back down. His vacillation before the authorities and the crowd during Jesus' trial shows him as an impatient, unsympathetic opportunist. Part of the irony of the crucifixion was the fact that a representative of the best government in the ancient world had such a key role. Pilate was removed from office in 36 A.D. by the Emperor Vitellius after Pilate senselessly wiped out an entire village of Samaritans. His end is the subject of many stories; some say that he was beheaded by Nero, others that he committed suicide, still others that he was banished to Vienna. His body was said to have been dumped in Lake Pilatus in Switzerland. Only the Abyssinian church has made a saint out of Pilate, and this on the flimsy evidence of a tradition that before his death, he prayed to Jesus for forgiveness. MATTHEW 27; MARK 15; LUKE 3:1; 13:1; 23:1—52; JOHN 18—19; ACTS 3:13; 4:27; 13:28; I TIMOTHY 6:13

PILDASH Abraham's nephew, Pildash was one of the six sons of Nahor, Abraham's brother, and the head of an ancient clan in the tribe of Nahor. GENESIS 22:22

PILEHA See PILHA

PILHA One of those brave souls who returned to Jerusalem after the Exile in Babylon, Pilha was a leading citizen and head of a family who joined Nehemiah in the impressive covenant-signing service, promising to keep the Law. NEHEMIAH 10:24

PILIHA See PILHA

PILTAI A priest who returned to Jerusalem after the Exile in Babylon, Piltai was leader of the Moadiah family of priests during the tenure of Joiakim as high priest. NEHEMIAH 12:17

PINON A descendant of Esau, Pinon was an early clan chieftain among the Edomites, the desert nomads distantly related to the Hebrews. GENESIS 36:41; I CHRONICLES 1:52

PIRAM The king of the city-state of Jarmuth in Canaan, Piram allowed himself to be pulled into an alliance with four other kings against the Gibeonites. The Gibeonites had signed a treaty binding Joshua to come to their aid. Piram and the other four kings were defeated and later executed by Joshua at Makkedah. JOSHUA 10:3

PISPAH A member of the tribe of Asher, Pispah is listed in the tribal records as one of Jether's sons. I CHRONICLES 7:38

PITHON One of the few descendants of King Saul, Pithon was the grandson of Jonathan's one surviving son, Mephibosheth, and was listed in the records of the tribe of Benjamin and of the royal family. I CHRONICLES 8:35; 9:41

POCHERETH-HAZZEBAIM A servant of Solomon, Pochereth-Hazzebaim was the ancestor of a group of exiles who returned from Babylon to Jerusalem. EZRA 2:57; NEHEMIAH 9:59

PONTIUS See PILATE

PORATHA The fourth son of the infamous Haman, Poratha, with his father and brothers, conspired to massacre all the Jews in Persia. Fortunately for the Jews, the plot was discovered and reported to King Ahasuerus by Queen Esther. Poratha and his father and brothers were hanged. ESTHER 9:8

PORCIUS FESTUS See FESTUS

POTIPHAR The head of the pharaoh's bodyguard who bought Joseph from the Midianite caravan, Potiphar recognized Joseph's abilities and quickly promoted him to a position of great responsibility in his household. Potiphar's wife, resentful because Joseph had spurned her amorous advances, falsely accused Joseph of improprieties toward her. Potiphar threw Joseph into prison. GENESIS 37:36; 39:1

POTIPHERA Joseph's father-in-law, Potiphera was the father of Joseph's wife, Asenath. Potiphera was the head priest of On and presided at the great Sun Temple. His daughter, Asenath, was presented to Joseph as a token of esteem by the pharaoh. GENESIS 41:45, 50; 46:20

PRISCA The wife of Aquila, Prisca (or Priscilla) was a staunch supporter of Paul and a mature Christian leader in the early church. Prisca and Aquila, as Jews, had been expelled from Rome, and lived at Corinth when Paul met them. They worked together earning their living as tentmakers and getting the small colony of Christians started. They accompanied Paul to Ephesus and stayed there when Paul traveled on to Jerusalem. Prisca showed herself a person of exceptional tact and maturity when she corrected some of the errors in the preaching of the brilliant young Apollos. The church at Ephesus met in their house. After the riots against Christians, they shifted to Rome again, and later back to Ephesus. Prisca apparently was more prominent than her husband (her name precedes her husband's in four out of the six references to them) although both were highly regarded as early missionaries. There are numerous legends about Prisca, none verifiable. ACTS 18:2, 18, 26; ROMANS 16:3; I CORINTHIANS 16:19; II TIMOTHY 4:19

PRISCILLA See PRISCA

PROCHORUS One of the Seven, Prochorus was selected to help the early Jerusalem church administer charity to needy Greek-speaking members of the Christian community. There had been complaints that these were being neglected, and the Seven were appointed to look after the welfare work of the church. Prochorus was himself probably a Greek-speaking Jew, and perhaps originally a convert to Judaism. Tradition claims that he was subsequently the bishop of Nicomedia and a martyr at Antioch. ACTS 6:5

PUA See PUAH

PUAH

1 One of the two Hebrew midwives in Egypt during the oppressive days when Moses was born, Puah and Shiphrah disregarded the pharaoh's order to kill newborn Hebrew male infants. Enraged, the pharaoh ordered all Hebrew boy babies to be thrown into the Nile immediately after birth. EXODUS 1:15

2 A member of the tribe of Issachar,

this Puah was the father of Tola. Tola was one of the judges or strongmen who emerged as a leader of the tribes after the invasion of Canaan. JUDGES 10:1

3 In the genealogical lists of the family of Tola in the tribe of Issachar, there is considerable confusion about the name of Puah. In some lists, Puah appears as the younger brother of Tola the judge, rather than as his father, and as a son of Issachar. Some scholars think that these names may be those of clans, not persons, in the tribe of Issachar. GENESIS 46:13; NUMBERS 26:23; I CHRONICLES 7:1

PUBLIUS The head man on the island of Malta when Paul was shipwrecked enroute to Rome, Publius welcomed Paul to his home. He gave Paul permission to preach after Paul healed Publius' father, who had been seriously ill. Publius, or Polius—the correct form of his name—was said to have been the first bishop of Malta and later bishop of Athens, according to traditions. ACTS 28:7, 8

PUDENS One of the members of the Christian community at Rome who was well-known to most of Paul's circle of friends and co-workers, Pudens asked specifically to be remembered to Timothy when Paul was dictating his second letter to Timothy. "Pudens" was a popular name in Rome, and several distinguished people bore the name, none of whom, however, can be satisfactorily iden-tified with Paul's friend. II TIMOTHY 4:21

PUL See TIGLATH-PILESER

PURAH The personal aide to Gideon, Purah crawled with Gideon to the outskirts of the camp of the Midianites and Amalekites and overheard the frightened conversations of the enemy soldiers. Later that night,

Gideon and Purah organized their three hundred hand-picked commandos to make a surprise raid which routed the Amalekites and Midianites. JUDGES 7:9—10

PUT One of Ham's four sons, this descendant of Noah was believed by the ancients to be the progenitor of one of the peoples of the earth, probably those living along the African coast near the Red Sea. Put's descendants were famous fighters with the bow, and were often hired as mercenaries. GENESIS 10:6; I CHRONICLES 1:8

PUTIEL Father-in-law of Eleazar, Aaron's son, Putiel might have been part Egyptian. EXODUS 6:25

PUVAH See PUAH

PYRRHUS A man of Beroea, Pyrrhus was mentioned as the father of Sopater, one of the party accompanying Paul on his final trip to Rome and bearing the special relief offering for the Christians of Jerusalem. ACTS 20:4

Q

QUARTUS A leader in the church at Corinth, Quartus was one of those who asked to be remembered to the Christian community at Rome in Paul's letter to the Romans. He was another of Paul's associates who is nothing more than a name to us. ROMANS 16:24

QUIRINIUS An able man in the Roman foreign service, Quirinius served many years in the Middle East, first as consul in 12 B.C., then as appointed *legatus Augusti,* or special representative of the emperor, or "governor" of Syria, 6 to 4 B.C., then as proconsul of Asia, 3 to 2 B.C., then a second time as "governor" of Syria, from 6 to 9 A.D. Periodic censuses were undertaken by Roman authorities during Augustus' reign, and Quirinius helped complete an enrollment of his territory about 6 B.C., according to Luke's chronology. Quirinius had some sensitivity about Jewish feelings; he wisely permitted his census to be taken according to Jewish instead of Roman traditions, and took the roll by tribes and households. He died in 21 A.D. LUKE 2:2

R

RAAMA See **RAAMAH**

RAAMAH One of Noah's descendants through Ham, Raamah was Cush's fourth son and an ancient clan head in the Arabian peninsula, probably near the Persian Gulf. Raamah's descendants founded a town which became a well-known business center on the Persian Gulf. GENESIS 10:7; I CHRONICLES 1:9

RAAMIAH One of the twelve leaders of the Jewish community who returned to devastated Jerusalem with Zerubbabel, Raamah lived during the dark days of the Exile in Babylon and courageously agreed to go back to Jerusalem as part of the first group of returnees. NEHEMIAH 7:7

RABMAG One of the titles of Nergal-Sharezer, a leading general in Nebuchadnezzar's army during the capture of Jerusalem, Rabmag means

something like "most wise prince." JEREMIAH 39:3, 13

RABSARIS
1 Like Rabmag, Rabsaris is a title, not a proper name, referring to a top official in the army. The first to carry the honorific title in the Bible narrative was one of Sennacherib's officers in the Assyrian army. This Rabsaris accompanied the Tartan and the Rabshakeh to Jerusalem and tried unsuccessfully to demand the surrender of the city in King Hezekiah's time. II KINGS 18:17
2 This Rabsaris served under Nebuchadnezzar of Babylonia and was also known as Sarsechim. He was present when Jerusalem fell to Nebuchadnezzar's forces. JEREMIAH 39:3
3 Another by the same title, this Rabsaris was also known as Nebushazban, and was a high official in the Babylonian government. As one who

293

was both a military and government leader, he was able to have the prophet Jeremiah released and returned. JEREMIAH 39:13

RABSHAKEH A top man in Sennacherib's Assyrian army, Rabshakeh was the title (meaning "head of the cup-bearers") of the leader of the delegation Sennacherib sent to demand the surrender of Jerusalem at the time the Assyrians were rolling unchecked through Palestine. Rabshakeh was one of the first to use the tricks of psychological warfare, and tried to cow Hezekiah and the leaders of Jerusalem into giving up without a struggle. Part of his cleverness was due to bluster, part was due to his fluency in both Hebrew and Aramaic, as well as his native Assyrian. Hezekiah, however, held firm, and the Rabshakeh's pleas and threats were unsuccessful. II KINGS 18—19; ISAIAH 36—37

RACHEL The beloved wife of Jacob, Rachel was Laban's beautiful younger daughter. Jacob worked seven years for his uncle Laban to win her, then was cheated by the wily Laban on his wedding night when Laban substituted his older daughter, Leah. Jacob, however, was also awarded Rachel after promising an additional seven years' service to Laban. Rachel was childless for many years, and in her disgrace envied her sister for producing a line of offspring for Jacob, their husband. She even allowed Jacob to produce sons-by-proxy for her by giving him her servant-girl, Bilhah, and adopting Bilhah's sons by Jacob

as her own. Finally, she was blessed with a son of her own, Joseph. When Jacob fled from Laban, Rachel cleverly hid some of Laban's household gods, to the anger of Laban. Undoubtedly, Rachel superstitiously hoped these would bring Jacob luck. She died tragically, in childbirth, in Canaan near Bethel. Her second son, Benjamin, was Jacob's youngest. Rachel was later looked upon as the tribal mother of the five northern tribes of Dan, Naphtali, Benjamin, and (Joseph's two sons) Ephraim and Manasseh. After these were carried away captive by the Assyrians, Rachel, was said to weep for her children. GENESIS 29—31, 33, 35, 46, 48:7; RUTH 4:11; I SAMUEL 10:2; JEREMIAH 31:15; MATTHEW 2:18

RADDAI One of David's big brothers, Raddai was Jesse's fifth son. He was passed over by the prophet Samuel when Jesse hopefully paraded all of his stalwart sons except little David for anointment by Samuel. I CHRONICLES 2:14; I SAMUEL 16:6 (not mentioned by name)

RAGAU See REU

RAGUEL Another name for Jethro or Reuel, Raguel was Moses' father-in-law. See JETHRO or REUEL.

RAHAB
1 The harlot of Jericho, who saved the lives of two of Joshua's spies by hiding them under stalks of flax and helping them to escape, Rahab was remembered as one of the great heroines of ancient Israel. Joshua and his men were grateful both for her

military information and her protection of the two spies, and carefully spared the lives of all of Rahab's family when Jericho fell. JOSHUA 2:1, 3; 6:17, 23, 25; HEBREWS 11:31; JAMES 2:25

2 The name of Rahab appears in the genealogy of Jesus in Matthew's account as the wife of Salmon, and the mother of Boaz, Ruth's husband. Rahab would have been an ancestor of David and Jesus. Although scholars are not certain, most lean toward identifying this Rahab with **1**. MATTHEW 1:5

RAHAM A member of the tribe of Judah who traced his family tree through Hebron to Caleb, Perez, and Judah, Raham was a son of Shema and an ancient chieftain of a clan in the Jerahmeel branch of the tribe. I CHRONICLES 2:44

RAKEM One of Manasseh's great-grandsons, Rakem was a son of Sheresh and an early clan head in the tribe of Manasseh. I CHRONICLES 7:16

RAM
1 An early member of the tribe of Judah who was descended through Perez and Hezron, this Ram was the father of Aminadab and either the brother or the son of Jerahmeel (the genealogies differ). He is mainly remembered because he was an ancestor of both David and Jesus. RUTH 4:19; I CHRONICLES 2:9, 10, 25, 27

2 An ancestor of the Elihu who debated theology with the questioning Job, this Ram was said to have been related to Buz. Many scholars are in-

clined to think that this Ram was actually Aram, the nephew of Buz. JOB 32:2

RAMIAH One of the many members of the family of Parosh who married outside the faith during the Exile in Babylon, Ramiah agreed to Ezra's strict rules and left his non-Jewish wife upon returning to Jerusalem. EZRA 10:25

RAMOTH One of the numerous descendants of Bani who married a non-Jewish bride while an exile in Babylon, Ramoth heeded Ezra and kept the faith pure by leaving her. EZRA 10:29

RAPHA Benjamin's fifth son, Rapha was an ancient clan chieftain in the tribe of Benjamin whose name was included by the Chronicler in the family records. I CHRONICLES 8:2

RAPHAH One of Saul's descendants, Raphah was mentioned in the roll of leaders in the tribe of Benjamin. I CHRONICLES 8:37; 9:43 (where he is called REPHAIAH)

RAPHU A member of the tribe of Benjamin, Raphu was the father of Palti, one of the spies sent by Moses to reconnoiter the Promised Land of Canaan. NUMBERS 13:9

REAIA See REAIAH

REAIAH
1 One of Judah's grandsons, this first Reaiah was a son of Shobal and an ancient clan head in the tribe of Judah. I CHRONICLES 4:2
2 An ancient chieftain of a clan of

Reuben, Reaiah was remembered as the grandfather of Beerah, one of the heads of the northern tribes carried away captive by the Assyrians. I CHRONICLES 5:5

3 A lackey who served in the Temple, this Reaiah was the ancestor of a family that returned to Jerusalem in the first party of exiles with Zerubbabel after the Exile in Babylon. EZRA 2:47; NEHEMIAH 7:50

REBA One of the leaders of the horde of Midianites that opposed Moses and the Israelites, Reba was one of the five chieftains who died in the crushing defeat of the Midianites on the plain of Moab by Moses and the Israelites. NUMBERS 31:8; JOSHUA 13:21

REBECCA See REBEKAH

REBEKAH The wife of Isaac, Rebekah was Abraham's great-niece. Abraham, anxious to have his son and heir Isaac marry a girl from Abraham's home instead of from Canaan, sent a trusted servant who picked Rebekah to be Isaac's wife. Rebekah was childless for some years, but finally gave birth to twin sons, Esau and Jacob. She favored Jacob, and connived with him to deceive Isaac into giving Jacob, rather than Esau, his final blessing. When Esau angrily threatened to kill Jacob, Rebekah masterminded Jacob's escape and his trip to her brother, Laban. Her death was not mentioned in the Bible, but she was reported to have been buried in the family cave at Machpelah. GENESIS 22:23; 24—29; 35:8; 49:31

RECHAB
1 A son of a Benjaminite named Rimmon, this Rechab as well as his brother Baanah, led a band of raiders serving under Ishbosheth, King Saul's son. Disillusioned with Saul's suicide on Mount Gilboa and Ishbosheth's timidity, Rechab and Baanah treacherously slew Ishbosheth while he was sleeping, and deserted to David. David, disgusted with them, immediately executed both Rechab and Baanah. II SAMUEL 4

2 A total abstainer who descended from Hammath of the desert tribe to Kenites, Rechab was the father of stalwart, strong-minded Jehonadab, who helped Jehu in the attack on Ahab and the Baal cult in Israel. Rechab's descendants were admired for being faithful to the vow of total abstinence, and survived for many years as a sect which protested the city-type living of later Israelites. II KINGS 10:15, 23; I CHRONICLES 2:55; NEHEMIAH 3:14; JEREMIAH 35

REELAIAH See RAAMIAH

REGEM A member of the tribe of Judah, Regem was a son of Jahdai, a descendant of the great spy Caleb, and was an early clan chieftain in the tribe. I CHRONICLES 2:47

REGEM-MELECH One of those in King Darius' time who was a leading citizen, Regem-melech was delegated by the people to go to the priests of the Temple to ask whether the custom of mourning in the fifth month as a memorial of the destruction of the

Temple should be continued. ZECHA-
RIAH 7:2

REHABIAH Moses' grandson, Rehabiah was one of Eliezer's sons and an
ancestor of several families of Levites.
I CHRONICLES 23:17; 24:21; 26:25

REHOB
1 A contemporary of David, Rehob
was the father of Hadadezer, ruler of
the city-state of Zobah, who was defeated and killed by David. II SAMUEL
8:3, 12
2 A Levite who was a leader in the
community of returned exiles at Jerusalem, this Rehob joined Nehemiah in
the impressive service of covenanting
to keep the Law. NEHEMIAH 10:11

REHOBOAM The stubborn, arrogant
son of Solomon, Rehoboam succeeded
Solomon as king of the nation in 937
B.C. The country was restive after
Solomon's excessive taxes, which supported his ambitious building programs and luxurious tastes. Instead of
reducing some of the more oppressive
burdens, Rehoboam insisted on con-
tinuing Solomon's policies. The northern tribes, never welded to the united
kingdom, promptly seceded. Rehoboam, forced to retire in humiliation
to Jerusalem, wanted to march against
the ten rebellious tribes, but was prevented by the prophet Shemaiah's
warnings and by Shishak of Egypt's
invasion. Rehoboam was further disgraced by having to empty the Temple treasury to buy off Shishak. I KINGS
11—12; 14—15; I CHRONICLES 3:10;
II CHRONICLES 9:31; 10—13; MAT-
THEW 1:7

REHUM
1 One of the twelve leaders of the
community of Jews in Babylon, Rehum
returned with Zerubbabel in the first
contingent to repopulate Jerusalem
after the Exile. EZRA 2:2; NEHEMIAH
12:3
2 A high official in the Persian government, this Rehum was stationed at
Samaria at the time the first Jews were
returning to Jerusalem after the Exile
in Babylon. He joined with other
prominent officials in writing King
Artaxerxes, falsely accusing the group
in Jerusalem with rebellion. This letter
temporarily stopped the program of rebuilding the walls. EZRA 4
3 A well-known Levite in Jerusalem
after the Exile, this Rehum, a son of
Bani, helped Nehemiah rebuild the
walls of the ruined city. NEHEMIAH
3:17
4 The head of a family in Jerusalem
after the Exile in Babylon, this Rehum
joined with Nehemiah in the moving
service of signing the covenant to keep
the Law. NEHEMIAH 10:25

REI A longtime loyal friend of David,
Rei was an officer in David's palace
guards. During David's long, final illness, Adonijah carried on an intrigue
to take over the throne. Rei backed
Solomon, and helped avert Adonijah's
coup by giving Solomon the support of
his troops. I KINGS 1:8

REKEM
1 A chief of the Midianite hordes
that tried to block Moses and the
Israelites, Rekem and four other Midianite leaders were defeated and slain
on the plains of Moab by the children

of Israel. NUMBERS 31:8; JOSHUA 13:21

2 An ancient chieftain of a clan in the tribe of Judah, this Rekem was one of Hebron's sons, and a descendant of Caleb, brother of Jerahmeel. I CHRONICLES 2:43

3 For the man called "Rekem" in some translations of I CHRONICLES 7:16, see RAKEM

REMALIAH A humble man of the northern kingdom, Remaliah was the father of Pekah, the army commander who killed Pekahiah and made himself king of Israel. II KINGS 15; 16; II CHRONICLES 28:6; ISAIAH 7; 8:6

REPHAEL A Levite gatekeeper, the head of a family who held that position in the Temple, Rephael was the son of Shemaiah, the son of Obed-Edom. I CHRONICLES 26:7

REPHAH One of Ephraim's grandsons, Rephah was an early clan chieftain in the tribe. I CHRONICLES 7:25

REPHAIAH

1 One of David's descendants, this Rephaiah was included in the genealogy of the royal family in the records of the tribe of Judah. I CHRONICLES 3:21

2 A chieftain of the tribe of Simeon, this Rephaiah was a leader of the five hundred men from that tribe when they wiped out a remnant of the Amalekites near Mount Seir in Hezekiah's time. I CHRONICLES 4:42

3 A grandson of Issachar and a son of Tola, this third Rephaiah was an early family head in the tribe of Issachar. I CHRONICLES 7:2

4 For the person called "Rephaiah" in I CHRONICLES 9:43, see RAPHAH

5 A member of the Jerusalem community after the Exile in Babylon, this Rephaiah helped Nehemiah repair the walls of the devastated city. NEHEMIAH 3:9

RESHEPH Great-grandson of Ephraim, Resheph was a son of Rephah, and an early clan head in the tribal chronology of Ephraim. I CHRONICLES 7:25

REU A descendant of Shem, Noah's son, Reu was an obscure son of Peleg, and the reputed ancestor of a now-forgotten people in the Arabian peninsula. GENESIS 11:18—21; I CHRONICLES 1:25

REUBEN The oldest son of Jacob and Leah, Reuben forfeited his birthright as the first-born by his incestuous affair with Bilhah, his father's concubine. However, he showed compassion by trying to talk his brothers out of selling their younger brother, Joseph, as a slave, and by being willing to put up his own sons to ransom his youngest brother, Benjamin, from Egypt. His family moved to Egypt with the rest of Jacob's clan during the famine in Canaan, and, years later, went out from Egypt to the wilderness with Moses. The Reubenites were a large, powerful tribe, and took an active part in the subsequent history of the nation. GENESIS 29:32; 30:14; 35:22, 23; 37:21, 22, 29; 42:22, 37; 46:8, 9; 48:5; 49:3; EXODUS 1:2; 6:14; NUMBERS 1:20; 16:1; 26:5; DEUTERONOMY 11:6; JOSHUA 15:6; 18:17; I CHRONICLES 2:1; 5:1, 3, and additional references to Reuben's descendants throughout the Bible.

REUEL

1 One of Esau's sons by Basemath, Ishmael's daughter, this Reuel was an ancient chieftain of the Edomites, the desert-roaming descendants of Esau. GENESIS 36; I CHRONICLES 1:35—37

2 For the father-in-law of Moses, called Reuel in EXODUS 2:18 and NUMBERS 10:29, see JETHRO

3 A leader in the tribe of Gad, this Reuel was the father of Eliasaph, head of the tribe when Moses and Aaron numbered them. This Reuel was also known (NUMBERS 1:14) as "Deuel." NUMBERS 2:14

4 A member of the tribe of Benjamin, this obscure Reuel was remembered as the remote ancestor of Sallu, one of the exiles who returned to Jerusalem. I CHRONICLES 9:8

REUMAH A concubine belonging to Nahor, Abraham's brother, Reumah was mother of four of Nahor's sons. GENESIS 22:24

REZIA   See RIZIA

REZIN

1 The king of the city-state of Damascus, Rezin and King Pekah of Israel teamed up in a revolt against the paying of tribute to Assyria, and tried to force Ahaz of Judah into joining them. When Ahaz refused, Rezin and Pekah angrily swarmed into Judah in retaliation. King Ahaz of Judah called to Assyria for help. Tiglath-Pileser III of Assyria swiftly moved into Syria, crushing Damascus and killing Rezin. II KINGS 15:37; 16:5, 6, 9; ISAIAH 7:1, 4, 8; 8:6; 9:11

2 A Temple lackey, this Rezin was remembered because he was the an-cestor of a family of Temple servants that came with Zerubbabel in the first party of exiles returning from Babylon to Jerusalem. EZRA 2:48; NEHEMIAH 7:50

REZON Eliada's son, Rezon was general of the forces of Hadadezer, ruler of the city-state of Zobah. After David captured Zobah, Rezon was willing to sell his services to David for a time, but he eventually grew restless and headed up a band of outlaw raiders. Eventually, Rezon captured Damascus and founded a dynasty of rulers which held that city and surrounding territory for two centuries. Rezon's raids were a constant nuisance to Solomon. I KINGS 11:23

RHESA One of the royal family of Judah, Rhesa was a descendant of David, a son of Zerubbabel, and an ancestor of Jesus, and was mentioned in Luke's genealogical record of Jesus' family. LUKE 3:27

RHODA A girl at the house of Mary, mother of Mark, at Jerusalem, Rhoda was the person who answered the door when Peter came to the house following his miraculous escape from prison. Rhoda was so surprised that she kept Peter waiting outside while she ran to tell the news to the rest of the gathering. Whether she was a slave, a daughter, a servant, a relative, or one of the assembled Christian community, is not known. "Rhoda" was a common slave name in the Roman world. ACTS 12:13

RIBAI A man of the tribe of Benjamin, Ribai was the father of the stalwart Ittai, one of "The Thirty," David's crew of mightiest warriors. II SAMUEL 23:29; I CHRONICLES 11:31

RIMMON A Benjaminite from Beeroth, Rimmon was remembered as the father of two raiders, Baanah and Rechab, who treacherously killed Saul's son, Ishbosheth. II SAMUEL 4

RINNAH One of the sons of Shimon of the tribe of Judah, and a descendant of the great spy Caleb, Rinnah was an early clan chieftain in the tribe. I CHRONICLES 4:20

RIPHATH A grandson of Japheth, Noah's son, and a son of Gomer, Riphath was the reputed ancestor of the tribes peopling the area of the Riphaean mountains and Carpathian Europe. Some try to trace the Celtic tribes from this group. GENESIS 10:3; I CHRONICLES 1:6

RIZIA A son of Ulla in the tribe of Asher, Rizia was a mighty warrior and clan leader in his tribe. I CHRONICLES 7:39

RIZPAH Saul's concubine and the mother of two of Saul's sons, Rizpah was taken by Abner, Saul's general, after Saul's death. Later, when a famine seared the land, many believed it was a sign of God's disfavor over the unpunished massacre of the Gibeonites by Saul. David finally agreed to hand over seven of Saul's relatives, Rizpah's two sons among them, to be executed by the Gibeonites. Rizpah's devotion to her sons' bodies so touched David that he gave them burial in Kish's tomb. II SAMUEL 3:7; 21:8, 10—11

ROBOAM See REHOBOAM

ROHGAH One of Asher's great-great-grandsons, Rohgah was a son of Shemer and an ancient clan chieftain in the tribe of Asher remembered in the tribal genealogy. I CHRONICLES 7:34

ROMAMTI-EZER One of the sons of the great musician, Heman, Romamti-Ezer was also skillful with the harp, lyre, and cymbals. He was selected by lot to head the twenty-fourth contingent of musicians in David's sanctuary services. I CHRONICLES 25:4, 31

ROSH One of Benjamin's sons, Rosh's name was included in some of the ancient tribal genealogies (but omitted in Numbers 26:38). He was another obscure ancient clan chieftain in the tribe of Benjamin. GENESIS 46:21

RUFUS
1 The son of Simon the Cyrene who carried Jesus' cross, Rufus, as well as his brother, Alexander, was obviously a well-known believer at the time Mark's Gospel was written. It is tantalizing to wonder what Rufus had heard from his father about Simon's conversation with Jesus. Traditions are strong that Rufus and Alexander accompanied Peter and Andrew on some of their missionary trips. MARK 15:21
2 Perhaps the same as 1, Rufus is one of those sent special personal greetings by Paul. The name Rufus was one of the commonest slave names, and means "red." If Mark's Gospel was written in Rome, there is a possibility that Rufus 1 and 2 may

have been the same man. Paul speaks of Rufus as "chosen in the Lord," hinting that he was a leader in the Christian community. Apparently also, judging from Paul's reference to Rufus' mother, Paul held the family in unusual affection because of past kindnesses shown to Paul. There is a profusion of legends about Rufus in which he is represented variously as bishop of Avignon, of Thebes, and of Capua, and a tireless traveler into such areas as Spain and the Alps. ROMANS 16:13

RUTH The girl from Moab who married Naomi's son, Mahlon, Ruth was the faithful daughter-in-law who insisted on staying with Naomi after they were both widowed. Ruth and her sister Orpah had married Naomi's sons, but after a severe famine swept the Bethlehem area, the entire household moved to Moab. Death suddenly carried away all the men of the family. Naomi urged her daughters-in-law to return to their own people, but Ruth insisted on accompanying Naomi back to Bethlehem. There, Ruth attracted the attention of Boaz, a wealthy cousin of Naomi's late husband. When Ruth's next of kin declined to claim her and buy her deceased husband's property rights, as was the custom, Boaz graciously accepted Ruth as his wife. David and Jesus were descended from the son of Ruth and Boaz, Obed. RUTH; MATTHEW 1:5

S

SABTA See **SABTAH**

SABTAH The third son of Cush, Noah's grandson, Sabtah was the founder of an ancient race of desert dwellers in the Arabian peninsula. GENESIS 10:7; I CHRONICLES 1:9

SABTECA The fifth son of Cush, Noah's grandson, Sabteca was also an ancient progenitor of one of the earliest tribes. Scholars are not certain what or where Sabteca's descendants were. GENESIS 10:7; I CHRONICLES 1:9

SABTECHA See **SABTECA**

SACAR
1 A Hararite, this Sacar was remembered as the father of Ahaim, one of David's great fighters. Sacar was also known by the name "Sharar." I CHRONICLES 11:35; II SAMUEL 23:33
2 A Levite of the Korah branch of the family, this Sacar was one of Obed-edom's sons, and, like his father, a gatekeeper in the sanctuary in David's time. His descendants inherited his office and served for years. I CHRONICLES 26:4

SACHIA A Benjaminite, Sachia was a son of Shaharaim, and an early clan chief in the tribe. I CHRONICLES 8:10

SADOC A son of Azor and the father of Achim, Sadoc was a descendant of Zerubbabel, and one of the royal family of Judah. Matthew counts him as an ancestor of Jesus. MATTHEW 1:14

SALA See **SHELAH**

SALAH See **SHELAH**

SALTHIEL See **SHEALTIEL**

SALLAI
1 A well-known member of the tribe of Benjamin, Sallai was one of those

303

who volunteered to move to Jerusalem to help rebuild the ruined city after the Exile at Babylon. NEHEMIAH 11:8

2 A priest, this Sallai was one who returned to Jerusalem with his family in the first party of exiles under Zerubbabel. He was sometimes known as "Sallu" NEHEMIAH 12:20; NEHEMIAH 12:7

SALLU

1 For the priest mentioned in NEHEMIAH 12:20, see SALLAI **2**

2 A son of Meshullam of the tribe of Benjamin, this Sallu was a distinguished member of the tribe who offered to settle in Jerusalem after the Exile in Babylon. I CHRONICLES 9:7; NEHEMIAH 11:7

SALMA   See SALMON

SALMAI A servant in the Temple, Salmai was the ancestor of a family that returned to Jerusalem after the Exile in Babylon. His name is variously given also as "Shamlai" and "Shalmai." EZRA 2:46; NEHEMIAH 7:48

SALMON A descendant of Caleb, the son of Hur, this Salmon was a member of the tribe of Judah and the reputed founder of the town of Bethlehem. Although there seems to be some confusion in the accounts between Salmon and Salma, careful study seems to indicate that they were the same person: the husband of Rahab, the father of Boaz who later married Ruth, and the ancestor of both David and Jesus. RUTH 4:20, 21; I CHRONICLES 2:11, 51, 54; MATTHEW 1:4, 5; LUKE 3:32

SALOME

1 The daughter of Herodias by her first marriage to Philip, Herod Antipas' brother, Salome was both niece and stepdaughter to Herod Antipas. Salome's dance before the drunken Herod Antipas prompted him to promise her anything. On her mother's advice, Salome demanded John the Baptist's head. She later married her kinsman, Herod Philip, tetrarch of Trachonitis, and then another relative, Aristobulus. MATTHEW 14:3—6; MARK 6:17—22

2 A member of the group of women who followed Jesus, this Salome was from Galilee, and was the wife of Zebedee and the mother of James and John, two of the Twelve. As the mother of James and John, she asked for seats of honor for her sons in Jesus' Kingdom, showing her misunderstanding of Jesus' mission at that time. Later, she witnessed the crucifixion and visited the empty tomb. Some shaky traditions identify Salome as a sister of Mary, mother of Jesus. MATTHEW 20:20—23; 27:56; MARK 15:40, 41; 16:1

SALU A member of the tribe of Simeon at the time of the wanderings of Israel in the wilderness, Salu was the father of Zimri, the man killed by Phinehas for brazenly bringing his Midianite lover into the camp. NUMBERS 25:14

SAMGAR-NEBO One of King Nebuchadnezzar's top officers in the Babylonian army, Samgar-Nebo was present when Jerusalem fell, and was one of the Babylonian leaders who sat in the victors' box in the middle gate of the city. JEREMIAH 39:3

SAMLAH Fifth of the ancient kings of Edom, Samlah was an obscure ruler who reigned in the now-unknown city called Masrekah. GENESIS 36:36, 37; I CHRONICLES 1:47, 48

SAMSON The famous strongman from the tribe of Dan, Samson's heroic feats included killing a lion bare-handed, slaughtering thirty Philistines at one time, smashing the strongest bonds, carrying off the huge gates to Gaza, and crushing a thousand people to their deaths. He was dedicated as a Nazirite by his long-childless parents, which meant that he was pledged never to shave or drink intoxicants. His marriage—against his parents' wishes—to a Philistine girl brought him into close contact with the Philistines, and caused him many misfortunes. A harlot, Delilah, finally wheedled from him the secret of his strength: his vow never to shave. She clipped his hair while asleep and turned him over to her Philistine friends, who gouged out his eyes and made him a public exhibit. He ended his life and the lives of one thousand captors by dramatically pushing down the columns of the great temple of Dagon at Gaza. JUDGES 13—16; HEBREWS 11:32

SAMUEL The last of the judges and the first of the prophets, Samuel ruled Israel immediately before the beginning of the kingdom. He was dedicated to God's service at his birth by his grateful mother, Hannah, and raised in the Shiloh sanctuary by Eli the priest. He zealously reformed Israel's idolatrous worship, then rallied the tribes to throw off the Philistines. An energetic saint and seer, Samuel was the acknowledged head of the loose confederation of tribes for years. In his old age, he tried to appoint his worthless sons as judges, but the people demanded to have a king. Samuel reluctantly crowned young Saul, then regretted it when Saul failed to give God absolute obedience. Samuel angrily denounced Saul and secretly anointed David as king. Samuel, the great patriot of Israel and spokesman for God, was the man who made possible the emergence of Israel as a nation. I SAMUEL 1—4, 7—13, 15—16, 19, 25, 28; I CHRONICLES 6:28; 9:22; 11:3; 26:28; 29:29; II CHRONICLES 35:18; PSALM 99:6; JEREMIAH 15:1; ACTS 3:24; 13:20; HEBREWS 11:32

SANBALLAT A man from Beth-horon in Samaria at the time the exiles were returning to Jerusalem from Babylon, Sanballat vindictively tried to defeat Nehemiah's plans to rebuild Jerusalem. He held some office under Artaxerxes Longimanus, the Persian ruler, and had influential relatives at Jerusalem. When his false reports to Persia and his threats failed to stop Nehemiah, he even tried to entice Nehemiah into a murder trap. Apocryphal stories in Jewish lore tie in Sanballat with the beginnings of Samaritan worship on Mount Gerizim. NEHEMIAH 2:10, 19; 4:1, 7; 6:1—14; 13:28

SAPH One of the descendants of

Rapha, the Philistine giant who fathered a clan of huge warriors, including Goliath, Saph was one of four Philistine champions who boastfully challenged David's forces to man-to-man combat, and who were in turn slain by David's heroes. He was also known as "Sippai." II SAMUEL 21:18; I CHRONICLES 20:4

SAPPHIRA Wife of the liar, Ananias, Sapphira was a member of the early Christian community at Jerusalem. She and her husband tried to deceive other church members about their gifts to the church, and collapsed and died within a short time of each other after their falsehood was revealed. ACTS 5:1

SARAH

1 Abraham's half-sister who became his wife, Sarah loyally went with Abraham from the culture and civilization of Ur to a land strange to her, Canaan, and later to Egypt. When the Egyptian pharaoh coveted Sarah, Abraham, fearful of angering him, said that Sarah was his sister and allowed her to be taken into the pharaoh's harem. Fortunately, the pharaoh learned that Sarah was Abraham's wife and, after criticizing Abraham for lying, ordered Sarah and Abraham to leave Egypt. For many years Sarah endured the disgrace of being childless. She even gave her servant-girl, Hagar, to her husband to bear him a son. The union did produce a son, Ishmael, but created as well much jealousy and hard feeling. Sarah's criticism drove Hagar to run away to the wilderness with her infant. To the

amazement of both Sarah and Abraham, God's promise that they would have a son was fulfilled in their old age, when Sarah gave birth to Isaac. Abraham buried Sarah in the cave at Machpelah after her death. GENESIS 11, 12, 16—18, 20, 21, 23—25, 49:31; ISAIAH 51:2; ROMANS 4:19; 9:9; HEBREWS 11:11; PETER 3:6

2 For the person listed in some translations of Numbers 26:46 as "Sarah" see SERAH

SARAI See SARAH

SARAPH A descendant of Judah's son Shelah, Saraph was an ancient clan chief of the tribe of Judah who held sway over some of the desert tribes in the area of Moab, according to some obscure early records referred to by the Chronicler. I CHRONICLES 4:22

SARGON An Assyrian general who seized the throne during the turbulence after Shalmaneser IV's death, Sargon founded the last great Assyrian dynasty, ruling from 722 to 705 B.C. Samaria, capital of the northern kingdom, Israel, was captured by Sargon's forces shortly after his accession. He began the grim policy of deporting entire populations to help quell his restive territories, and uprooted most of the ten northern tribes (known as the "lost tribes" from then on). In turn, he imported colonists from Hamath to the cities of Samaria. Sargon was a ruthless soldier and able organizer. He smashed revolts in Palestine, exacted tribute from Egypt, drove out Merodach-baladan of Babylon and made himself king of Babylon. He barely completed his showplace palace at Khorsabad before he was assassinated by one of his soldiers. ISAIAH 20:1

SARSECHIM One of the top leaders in the Babylonian forces when Nebuchadnezzar captured Jerusalem, Sarsechim was one of the princes with an exalted title who sat at the gates of Jerusalem in a council of victory. JEREMIAH 39:3

SAUL
1 The moody Benjaminite who was the first king of Israel, Saul was summoned to leadership against the Philistines by the prophet Samuel. Saul was an energetic and courageous fighter of striking physical size, and quickly roused the tribes to push out the Philistines from the hill country of central Israel. After his initial successes, however, unpleasant traits began to appear in him—jealousy, rashness, depression. A young musician named David soothed Saul's nerves, but when the musician David became the popular hero David, Saul was moved to outbursts of insanity. The new nation deteriorated with Saul, and the Philistines pounced on Saul's army at Mount Gilboa. Saul, seeing the battle turning against him, committed suicide. In spite of his emotional problems, Saul was deeply beloved, especially by David who refused on several occasions to kill Saul and who lamented Saul's death. I SAMUEL 9—11; 13—29; 31; II SAMUEL 1—7; 9; 12; 16; 19; 21; 22; I CHRONICLES 5:10; 8:33; 9:39; 10—13; 15:29; 26:28; ISAIAH 10:29; ACTS 13:21

2 For the account of Saul of Tarsus, see PAUL

3 The sixth in the list of ancient kings of Edom, this Saul, or Shaul, was supposed to have come from Rehoboth on the Euphrates River. GENESIS 36:37, 38; I CHRONICLES 1:48, 49

SCEVA A Jewish priest at Ephesus, Sceva was the father of seven sons who were impressed with Paul's ability to heal, and tried to use Jesus' name as a magic formula. Their mumbo-jumbo with Jesus' name backfired; the evil spirits they were trying to drive out of a sick man stirred the sick man into such a frenzied mania that Sceva's sons were disgracefully forced to flee. ACTS 19:14

SEBA One of Noah's great-grandsons descended from Ham, Seba was Cush's oldest son. He was the reputed ancestor of one of the races of peoples of the earth. Scholars are puzzled over who Seba's descendants were and where they dwelt, but believe they might have been the inhabitants of the area of Africa south of Ethiopia. GENESIS 10:7; I CHRONICLES 1:9

SECUNDUS A leader in the Christian community at Thessalonica, Secundus was one of the party that accompanied Paul on his final trip to Jerusalem. He had probably been instrumental in collecting the special relief offering that was Paul's pet project at the time, and was commissioned by the congregation at Thessalonica to represent them in presenting the gift to the leaders of the Jerusalem church. There is a Secundus listed among the politarchs or civic leaders of Thessalonica in an inscription from the city, but we cannot be certain it was the same as Paul's companion. ACTS 20:4

SEGUB

1 One of the sons of Hiel of Bethel, Segub died, as did his brother, just as his father finished rebuilding the city of Jericho and was setting up the gates. Whether Segub and his brother died accidentally or were sacrificed in some ceremony is not clear. Everyone at the time, however, understood that their deaths were a fulfillment of Joshua's curse against anyone rebuilding Jericho. I KINGS 16:34

2 A member of the tribe of Judah, this Segub was a clan chieftain in the tribe who was remembered as the son of Hezron, Judah's grandson, and the father of Jair. I CHRONICLES 2:21, 22

SEIR The reputed ancestor of the ancient tribesmen called Horites which lived in the mountainous desert of Arabia, Seir was an obscure chief, or perhaps the personification of the earliest Horites. Seir's name was subsequently associated with the area which eventually was taken over by Esau's descendants and was known as Edom. GENESIS 36:20; 21; I CHRONICLES 1:38

SELED A member of the tribe of Judah, Seled was remembered in the tribal records as a chieftain who was descended from Jerahmeel and Perez. I CHRONICLES 2:30

SEMACHIAH A Levite of the Korah branch of the tribe, Semachiah was a

grandson of Obed-edom and a son of Shemaiah, and, like them, a gatekeeper in the sanctuary in David's time. His descendants inherited the office because of Obed-edom's prominence. I CHRONICLES 26:7

SEMEI See SHIMEI 16

SEMEIN One of Jesus' ancestors, according to Luke's records, this Semein was the father of Mattathias. LUKE 3:26

SEMEIS See SHIMEI 16

SEMIS See SHIMEI 16

SENNACHERIB The brutal son and successor of Sargon, Sennacherib inherited the usual flurry of revolts that followed the death of an Assyrian ruler, especially by assassination. Sennacherib first subdued Merodachbaladan (the persistently rebellious king whom Sargon finally quelled), then marched west. His campaign ravished the cities of Palestine with characteristic Assyrian cruelty. During the siege of Lachish, King Hezekiah of Judah thought he had bought protection for Jerusalem by sending three hundred talents of silver, thirty talents of gold, and lavish gifts. Sennacherib grabbed the presents and insolently sent Rabshakeh or chief emissary to demand the surrender of Jerusalem. The tense days of the siege of Jerusalem and the miraculous withdrawal of Sennacherib's disease-decimated armies are described in the Old Testament. Sennacherib's subsequent career was a constant series of battles against rebellious provinces. Before the end of his bloody reign, he looted and destroyed Babylon, and built a pretentious palace at Nineveh. He was murdered by two of his sons in 681 B.C. II KINGS 18:13; 19:16, 20, 36; II CHRONICLES 32; ISAIAH 36—37

SENUAH A member of the tribe of Benjamin, Senuah was the father of Judah, the second-in-command at Jerusalem in Nehemiah's time. NEHEMIAH 11:9

SEORIM A priest in David's time, Seorim chose the lot to head the fourth contingent of priests serving in the sanctuary. I CHRONICLES 24:8

SERAH A daughter of Asher, Serah and her brothers and parents accompanied Jacob and the clan when everyone left Canaan for Egypt during the famine. GENESIS 46:17; NUMBERS 26:46; I CHRONICLES 7:30

SERAIAH
1 David's scribe or secretary, Seraiah was also known as "Sheva," "Shavsha," and "Shisha." His two sons, Elihoreph and Ahiah, were secretaries to King Solomon. II SAMUEL 8:17; 20:25; I KINGS 4:3; I CHRONICLES 18:16
2 Descended from a long line of distinguished priests, this Seraiah was a son of Azariah and was the high priest in King Zedekiah's reign when Nebuchadnezzar captured Jerusalem. He was executed with a party of notables from Jerusalem at Riblah on Nebuchadnezzar's personal orders. II KINGS 25:18; I CHRONICLES 6:14; EZRA 7:1; JEREMIAH 52:24
3 A son of Tanhumeth the Netopha-

thite, this Seraiah was a leader of a clandestine band of holdouts that had escaped capture when Jerusalem fell to Nebuchadnezzar. He approached Gedaliah, the Babylonian-appointed governor, at Mizpeh, but was advised to turn himself in. II KINGS 25:23; JEREMIAH 40:8
4 Kenaz's second son, this Seraiah was a brother of Othniel and the father of Joab, the head of a famous family of craftsmen. I CHRONICLES 4:13, 14
5 A son of Asiel in the tribe of Simeon, this man was a prince in the tribe, and the grandfather of Jehu. He was one of the party which drove out the inhabitants of the lush vale of Gedor in the days of King Hezekiah and seized it for themselves. I CHRONICLES 4:35
6 A priest who was one of the twelve leaders of the Jewish community in exile in Babylon, this Seraiah returned to Jerusalem with Zerubbabel in the first party. EZRA 2:2; NEHEMIAH 7:7 (where he was called Azariah)
7 Undoubtedly related to **2**, this Seraiah was a priest whose family was the first in the order of those who served in the Temple in the times of Zerubbabel, Joiakim, and Nehemiah. NEHEMIAH 10:2; 12:2, 12
8 The son of Hilkiah, this Seraiah was also a priest who served in Jerusalem in Nehemiah's time after the return from Exile. He was part of the family of **6**. NEHEMIAH 11:11
9 A son of Azriel, this person was a prominent official in the court of King Jehoiakim of Judah who was sent by the king to arrest Jeremiah and his secretary Baruch after reading and burn-

ing the scroll of Jeremiah's stern prophecies. JEREMIAH 36:26

10 Neriah's son and Baruch's brother, this Seraiah held a high office in the court of King Zedekiah. He went with Zedekiah to Babylon in the fourth year of his reign to promise subjection to Babylon. A loyal friend of Jeremiah, Seraiah carried Jeremiah's prophecies to Babylon, read them aloud, then threw the scroll into the river, announcing that Babylon would sink forever just as the scroll would sink. JEREMIAH 50—51

SERED Zebulun's oldest son, Sered accompanied his father and grandfather, Jacob, when the entire clan left Canaan to settle in Egypt. Later, Sered was known as the head of a clan within the tribe of Zebulun. GENESIS 46:14; NUMBERS 26:26

SERGIUS See PAULUS

SERUG An obscure ancestor of Abraham, Serug was Nahor's father. His name is the same as a district north of Haran in Assyrian records. GENESIS 11:20—23; I CHRONICLES 1:26

SETH The third son of Adam and Eve, Seth was born after Abel's death. Seth, the father of Enosh, lived 912 years, according to the ancients. GENESIS 4:25, 26; 5:3—8; I CHRONICLES 1:1; LUKE 3:38

SETHUR One of the spies sent by Moses into the Promised Land, Sethur represented his tribe, Asher. Except for Caleb and Joshua, however, the spies were frightened by the size of the Canaanites and advised against

trying to invade the Promised Land. NUMBERS 13:13

SHAAPH

1 A member of the tribe of Judah, Shaaph was a descendant of Caleb, the brother of Jerahmeel, and a son of Jahdai. I CHRONICLES 2:47

2 Another in the same branch of the tribe, this Shaaph was a son of Caleb, son of Hezron, by Caleb's concubine, Maacah. I CHRONICLES 2:49

SHAASHGAZ The overseer of the royal harem of Persian King Ahasuerus, Shaashgaz had custody over Esther when she was taken into the palace. ESTHER 2:14

SHABBETHAI A prominent Levite in the community of returned exiles at Jerusalem, Shabbethai at first opposed Ezra's strict rule against interfaith marriages. He was also active in the education program to teach the people the Law, and in the worship activities in the Temple. EZRA 10:15; NEHEMIAH 8:7; 11:16

SHACHIA See SACHIA

SHAHARAIM A member of the tribe of Benjamin, Shaharaim had children by his two Hebrew wives, Hushim and Baara, then sent them away and raised families of mixed ancestry by his liaisons with Moabite women. I CHRONICLES 8:8

SHALLUM

1 A king of Israel for one month, this Shallum plotted and murdered Zechariah, Jehu's descendant, to seize the throne, only to be cut down by another conspirator, Menahem. This

Shallum was the son of Jabesh. II KINGS 15:10—15

2 The fourth son of King Josiah of Judah, this Shallum was also known as Jehoahaz. Jeremiah predicted that he would be carried away from his homeland in the coming time of reckoning. I CHRONICLES 3:15; JEREMIAH 22:11

3 The husband of Huldah, the great prophetess, this Shallum was the son of Tikvah. He gracefully lived in the shadow of a wife who was both his intellectual superior and a respected national figure. II KINGS 22:14; II CHRONICLES 34:22

4 A descendant of Perez and Jerahmeel in the tribe of Judah, this Shallum was listed in the tribal genealogy as a son of Sismai. I CHRONICLES 2:40, 41

5 One of Simeon's grandsons, this Shallum was an early clan chieftain in the tribe. I CHRONICLES 4:25

6 A high priest from a distinguished family, this Shallum was a son of Zadok and the father of Hilkiah, the high priest in King Josiah's time who found the lost book of the Law during repairs to the Temple. I CHRONICLES 6:12, 13; EZRA 7:2

7 Naphtali's fourth son, the second by Bilhah, Rachel's maid, this Shallum was also known by the name "Shillem." His descendants were a clan known as Shillemites. Shallum or Shillem was part of the group of Jacob's family that emigrated from Canaan to Egypt during the famine. GENESIS 46:24; NUMBERS 26:49; I CHRONICLES 7:13

8 A Levite of the Korah branch of the tribe, this Shallum served as a gatekeeper in David's sanctuary. His descendants were a well-known family of gatekeepers in the Temple at Jerusalem after the Exile in Babylon. I CHRONICLES 9:17, 19, 31; 26:1, 2, 9, 14 (where he was called Meshelemiah or Shelemiah); EZRA 2:42; NEHEMIAH 7:45

9 A man of the northern kingdom of Israel, this Shallum was the father of the humane Jehizkiah, one of those who refused to sell captives from the southern tribes as slaves. II CHRONICLES 28:12

10 A member of a family of gatekeepers in the Temple, this man was one of the many who married outside the faith during the Exile, but who agreed to leave his wife to keep the faith pure on returning to Jerusalem. EZRA 10:24

11 One of Bani's descendants who also married a non-Jewish bride during the Exile, this Shallum obeyed Ezra's strict rule against bringing non-Jewish dependents back to Jerusalem. EZRA 10:42

12 The son of Hallohesh, ruler of half of the district of Jerusalem, this Shallum, together with his daughters, worked hard with Nehemiah and others to rebuild the wrecked walls of Jerusalem after the return from the Exile in Babylon. NEHEMIAH 3:12

13 A son of Colhozeh, the man in charge of the district of Mizpeh, this Shallum rebuilt the entire Fountain Gate and the wall of the Pool of Shelah after the return of the exiles from Babylon to devastated Jerusalem in Nehemiah's time. NEHEMIAH 3:15

14 Jeremiah's uncle, this Shallum was the father of Jeremiah's cousin, Hanamel, from whom Jeremiah bought the field at Anathoth during the national crisis. JEREMIAH 32:7

15 Probably a Temple servant, this Shallum is mentioned as the father of Maaseiah, one who had a room in the Temple above the one where Jeremiah brought the Rechabites to test their faithfulness. JEREMIAH 35:4

SHALLUN See **SHALLUM 13**

SHALMAI See **SALMAI**

SHALMAN An invader who wrecked the town of Beth-Arbel, according to the prophet Hosea, Shalman could either have been one of the Assyrian rulers named Shalmaneser or a Moabite chief named Salamanu. Scholars are frankly puzzled about Shalman's identity. HOSEA 10:14

SHALMANESER Although there were several Shalmanesers in history, the only one mentioned in the Bible is Shalmaneser IV, the Assyrian king who beseiged Samaria, capital of Israel, in 722 B.C. Shalmaneser originally was a general named Ulula who seized power after Tiglath-Pileser III's death. He allowed King Hoshea of Israel to be his vassal until he caught Hoshea in a plot against Assyria. Shalmaneser swiftly deported Hoshea and began carrying off the northern tribes (known from then on as the "ten lost tribes"). He reigned only five years, dying during the seige of Samaria in 722 B.C. II KINGS 17:3; 18:9

SHAMA A son of Hotham the Aroerite, Shama and his brother, Jeiel, were two of David's great heroes and members of that exclusive band of worthies, "The Thirty." I CHRONICLES 11:44

SHAMARIAH See **SHEMARIAH**

SHAMED See **SHEMED**

SHAMER See **SHEMER**

SHAMGAR A son of Anath, Shamgar was the third judge of Israel after Joshua, and the first of six minor judges, or deliverers, of Israel. He rallied the tribes to drive away the Philistines and once slaughtered six hundred Philistines with an ox-goad. JUDGES 3:31; 5:6

SHAMHUTH An officer in David's forces, Shamhuth was an Izrahite who headed the contingent of troops serving in the fifth month. He was also known as "Shammoth" and "Shammah." I CHRONICLES 27:8; 11:27 (called Shammoth); II SAMUEL 23:25 (called Shammah)

SHAMIR A Levite of the Kohath branch of the tribe, Shamir was a son of Micah and served in David's sanctuary. I CHRONICLES 24:24

SHAMLAI See **SALMAI**

SHAMMA A member of the tribe of Asher, Shamma was a son of Zopha and a respected warrior-chief of a clan in the tribe. I CHRONICLES 7:37

SHAMMAH

1 One of Esau's grandsons, this Shammah was a son of Reuel, and an ancient chief of a clan of Edomites in the Arabian desert. GENESIS 36:13, 17; I CHRONICLES 1:37

2 One of David's older brothers, this Shammah was Jesse's third stalwart son. He fought in Saul's army against the Philistines and was one of those who sneered when young David proposed to take on the giant Goliath. Shammah was passed over by the aged prophet Samuel when Samuel came to select one of Jesse's sons as ruler in Saul's place. I SAMUEL 16:9; 17:13; II SAMUEL 13:3, 32; 21:21; I CHRONICLES 2:13; 20:7

3 Agee the Aharite's valiant son, this Shammah was the second of David's three greatest heroes. He earned immortality by refusing to retreat during a fierce hand-to-hand battle in a lentil patch against the Philistines after the rest of his comrades had fallen or run away. His stand rallied David's faltering forces and swept them to victory. His son, Jonathan, carried on the family's martial tradition and won a place in "The Thirty." II SAMUEL 23:11, 32 (where the words " son of Shammah" are inadvertently omitted); I CHRONICLES 11:34

4 For the Shammah in II Samuel 23:25, see SHAMHUTH

SHAMMAI

1 A member of the tribe of Judah descended from Jerahmeel, this Shammai was a son of Onan, and an early clan chieftain in the tribe. I CHRONICLES 2:28, 32

2 Another in the tribe of Judah, this man traced his ancestry through Caleb, son of Hezron, and was a son of Rekem. I CHRONICLES 2:44, 45

3 Still another Shammai listed in the tribal records of Judah, this one was a descendant of Moses' great spy, Caleb, and was also an ancient clan head in the tribe. I CHRONICLES 4:17

SHAMMOTH See SHAMHUTH

SHAMMUA

1 The son of Zaccur of the tribe of Reuben, Shammua was one of the twelve spies picked out by Moses to reconnoiter the Promised Land. Shammua, however, like everyone in the group of spies except Joshua and Caleb, was so frightened by the size of the Canaanites that he opposed any attempt to invade Canaan. NUMBERS 13:4

2 One of David's sons, Shammua was born in Jerusalem after David was crowned king of the united kingdom. He was listed in the records of the royal family of Judah. II SAMUEL 5:14; I CHRONICLES 3:5 (where he was called Shimea); 14:4

3 A Levite of the family of Jeduthun, this Shammua was the father of Abda, one who led the worship in the Temple in Nehemiah's time. I CHRONICLES 9:16 (where he is called Shemaiah); NEHEMIAH 11:17

4 A priest representing the family of Bilgah, this Shammua headed a contingent of priests in the worship in the Temple in Nehemiah's time. NEHEMIAH 12:18

SHAMMUAH See SHAMMUA

SHAMSHERAI One of the tribe of Benjamin, Shamsherai was another obscure clan chieftain whose name was remembered in the tribal records. He was the son of Jeroham. I CHRONICLES 8:26

SHAPHAM A leader in the tribe of Gad in his day, Shapham was number two man in the tribe when it began to settle in the area of Bashan. I CHRONICLES 5:12

SHAPHAN

1 A scribe who was a highly-placed official in Jerusalem in King Josiah's time, this Shaphan, a son of Azaliah, was the man who took the newly-discovered book of the Law from the high priest Hilkiah to King Josiah. Josiah, deeply stirred by the book, sent Shaphan to consult with Huldah the prophetess about the contents of the book. Shaphan was sympathetic to the reform movement, and was trusted by both the Temple and the palace. His sons, Ahikam, Elasah, and Gemariah, were distinguished patriots and loyal friends to Jeremiah, and his grandson, Gedaliah, took Jeremiah into his home after Jerusalem fell. II KINGS 22; II CHRONICLES 34; JEREMIAH 26:24; 29:3; 36:10—12; 39:14; 40:5; 41:2; 43:6; EZEKIEL 8:11

2 This second Shaphan was the father of Jaazaniah, one of the seventy elders seen by Ezekiel in his vision who offered incense to idols. EZEKIEL 8:11

SHAPHAT

1 A son of Hori of the tribe of Simeon, this Shaphat was one of the twelve spies sent by Moses into Canaan. Shaphat and the other spies,

except for Caleb and Joshua, were frightened by the size of the Canaanites and came back telling Moses and the tribes that it was hopeless to try to invade the Promised Land. NUMBERS 13:5

2 A man of Abel-meholah, this Shaphat was the father of the great ninth century prophet of Israel, Elisha. I KINGS 19:16, 19; II KINGS 3:11; 6:31

3 One of David's descendants, this Shaphat was listed in the royal family of Judah as a grandson of Shechaniah, and lived in the fifth century B.C. I CHRONICLES 3:22

4 A member of the tribe of Gad, this Shaphat was a clan chief who settled in the area of Bashan. I CHRONICLES 5:12

5 A son of Adlai, this Shaphat was superintendent of David's extensive herds in the area of Sharon. I CHRONICLES 27:29

SHARAI One of the descendants of Bani who married outside the faith during the Exile in Babylon, Sharai agreed to abide by Ezra's strict precept against bringing non-Jewish members of families to Jerusalem. EZRA 10:40

SHARAR See SACAR

SHAREZER

1 An Assyrian prince, Sharezer and his brother murdered their father, King Sennacherib, while he was worshipping. Sharezer, however, was not able to grab the throne. A third brother, Esarhaddon, managed to beat out other contenders. Sharezer was

forced to flee to Armenia. II KINGS 19:37; ISAIAH 37:38

2 A contemporary of the prophet Zechariah, this Sharezer was one of the delegation sent from Bethel to ask the priests at Jerusalem whether or not the people should continue to observe the anniversary of the fall of Jerusalem each year. ZECHARIAH 7:2

SHASHAI Another of Bani's many descendants who took a non-Jewish bride during the Exile, Shashai left her when he returned to Jerusalem in order to keep the faith pure. EZRA 10:40

SHASHAK A member of the tribe of Benjamin, Shashak was a son of Elpael and the chief man in the tribe in its early days. His descendants were remembered as leaders who lived in Jerusalem. I CHRONICLES 8:14, 25

SHAUL
1 For the person listed as "Shaul" in I Chronicles 1:48—49, see SAUL **3**
2 One of the sons of Simeon by his Canaanite wife, this Saul emigrated, with all of his grandfather Jacob's clan, to Egypt when famine struck Canaan. His descendants were a clan of mixed ancestry listed with the tribe of Simeon. GENESIS 46:10; EXODUS 6:15; NUMBERS 26:13; I CHRONICLES 4:24
3 An ancient Levite, this Shaul was one of Kohath's descendants. He was remembered primarily because he was an ancestor of the great prophet Samuel. His name was also listed as "Joel." I CHRONICLES 6:24, 29, 36

SHAVSHA See SERIAH

SHEAL One of the numerous members of the family of Bani who married a non-Jewish bride during the Exile at Babylon, Sheal forsook her to keep the faith pure in Jerusalem. EZRA 10:29

SHEALTIEL A descendant of David and a son of King Jeconiah, Shealtiel was best remembered as the father of Zerubbabel, the great leader who led the first contingent of Jews from Babylon to Jerusalem. EZRA 3:2, 8; 5:2; NEHEMIAH 12:1; HAGGAI 1:1, 12, 14; 2:2

SHEARIAH One of Saul's descendants, Sheariah was a son of Azel and member of the tribe of Benjamin. I CHRONICLES 8:38; 9:44

SHEAR-JASHUB One of the sons of the prophet Isaiah, Shear-Jashub's name literally means "a remnant shall return," signifying that Isaiah believed than an invasion would come to carry off the people of Judah, but that God eventually would restore the nation. ISAIAH 7:3

SHEBA
1 A son of Bichri and a member of the tribe of Benjamin who stirred up the resentment of his tribe against David after the collapse of Absalom's revolt, Sheba headed a brief rebellion which was quickly quelled by David's ruthless general, Joab. When Sheba tried to hold out in the town of Abel-beth-maacah, Joab sent the ultimatum to the town's leaders: Sheba's head, or death to the entire town. The townsmen quickly threw down Sheba's

head. II SAMUEL 20

2 A leader in the tribe of Gad, this Sheba was one of the clan leaders who settled in the land of Bashan. I CHRONICLES 5:13

3 A son of Joktan in the family of Noah's son Shem, this Sheba was the reputed ancestor of the Sabaeans, according to one version. The Sabaeans lived in southern Arabia and were known as wealthy traders in later times. GENESIS 10:28; I CHRONICLES 1:22

4 One of Abraham's grandsons through his marriage to Keturah, this Sheba was a son of Jokshan. As in the case of **3**, Sheba was supposed to have been the founder of the Sabaeans. Many scholars question whether either **3** or **4** were actual historic persons, suggesting that these accounts might have been early attempts to explain the spread of the races of mankind. GENESIS 25:3; I CHRONICLES 1:32

SHEBANIAH

1 A priest in David's time, Shebaniah was one of the musicians who took part in the festivities when David brought the Ark from Obed-edom's house to Jerusalem. I CHRONICLES 15:24

2 A Levite who lived in Nehemiah's time, this Shebaniah helped teach the people the meaning of the Law after Ezra read the Law before a great national assembly. This Shebaniah also joined Nehemiah in sealing the covenant. NEHEMIAH 9:4, 5; 10:10

3 Another priest in Nehemiah's day, this man also joined in signing the covenant promising to keep the Law. NEHEMIAH 10:4; 12:14

4 A contemporary of **2** and **3**, this Shebaniah was also a Levite who signed the covenant with Nehemiah. NEHEMIAH 10:12

SHEBER A son of the great spy, Caleb, son of Jephunneh, by his concubine Maacah, Sheber is remembered in the tribal records of Judah as a clan head. I CHRONICLES 2:48

SHEBNA A wealthy and powerful official in King Hezekiah's government, Shebna was a foreigner who adopted Judah as his home. He administered both Hezekiah's household and many of the government departments, and was once one of three top officials chosen to represent Hezekiah in negotiations with Assyria. He was proudly constructing an ostentatious tomb for his eventual burial when Isaiah shattered his hopes and pride by telling him that he would be buried far from Judah. Eventually Eliakim was appointed to Shebna's position. II KINGS 18:18, 26, 37; 19:2; ISAIAH 22:15; 36:3—22; 37:2

SHEBUEL

1 The grandson of Moses and the son of Gershom, this Shebuel was head of his branch of the tribe and administrator of the treasury funds. I CHRONICLES 23:16; 24:20; 26:24

2 One of the sons of the great singer, Heman, this Shebuel was also a musician of note in David's sanctuary. His family were part of the Temple choirs for many generations. I CHRONICLES 25:4, 20

SHECANIAH

1 A member of the royal family of Judah, this Shecaniah was descended from David and Zerubbabel, and was head of a family which later returned to Jerusalem after the Exile. I CHRONICLES 3:21, 22; EZRA 8:3

2 A son of Jahaziel, this Shecaniah was descended from Zattu, and was one of those who returned to Jerusalem with Ezra after the Exile in Babylon. EZRA 8:5

3 A priest serving in the sanctuary in David's time, this Shecaniah was chosen by lot to head the tenth contingent of priests. I CHRONICLES 24:11

4 A well-known priest during King Hezekiah's reign in Jerusalem, this man was responsible for distributing the free-will offerings among his fellow priests. II CHRONICLES 31:15

5 One of Jehiel's sons, this Shecaniah was the first to admit to Ezra that he had broken trust with God by marrying outside the faith during the Exile in Babylon. At Shecaniah's suggestion, Ezra made the leading priests and Levites and other notables sign an oath promising to put away non-Jewish mates before returning to Jerusalem, in order to keep the faith pure. EZRA 10:2—5

6 This Shecaniah was the father of Shemaiah, one of those who helped Nehemiah rebuild the walls of Jerusalem after the Exile. NEHEMIAH 3:29

7 Tobiah's father-in-law, this Shecaniah had the misfortune to find his daughter married to one of Nehemiah's most implacable opponents. NEHEMIAH 6:18

8 For the Shecaniah in Nehemiah 10:4 and 12:3, 14, see SHEBANIAH 3

SHECHANIAH   See SHECANIAH

SHECHEM

1 The son of Hamor, the head man of the Hivites in Canaan, Shechem tried to handle things in an honorable way after getting Dinah, Jacob's daughter, pregnant. Shechem and his followers wanted to marry into Jacob's clan and even consented to have themselves circumcised as a condition of marriage. While recuperating, Shechem and his men were treacherously massacred by Dinah's full brothers, Simeon and Levi. GENESIS 33:18—34:26; JOSHUA 24:32; JUDGES 9:28

2 One of Manasseh's grandsons, this Shechem was a son of Gilead and an early clan chieftain in the tribe. NUMBERS 26:31; JOSHUA 17:2

3 Another obscure early member of the tribe of Manasseh, this Shechem was a son of Shemidah. I CHRONICLES 7:19

SHEDEUR A member of the tribe of Reuben, Shedeur was the father of Elizur, the representative of Reuben selected to help Moses count the tribes. NUMBERS 1:5; 2:10; 7:30, 35; 10:18

SHEERAH The daughter of Ephraim, Sheerah was the reputed builder of the towns of Lower and Upper Beth-horon and a now-unknown place called Uzzen-sheerah. I CHRONICLES 7:24

SHEHARIAH A little-known early member of the tribe of Benjamin,

317

SHELAH

Shehariah is carried in the rolls as one of the six sons of Jeroham, an ancient chieftain. I CHRONICLES 8:26

SHELAH

1 Judah's youngest son by the Canaanite girl, Shua, Shelah's father had promised him in marriage to Tamar, widow of both of Shelah's deceased older brothers. Judah, however, forgot his promise to Tamar. Shelah married another and founded the clan known as Shelanites. GENESIS 38; 46: 12; NUMBERS 26:20; I CHRONICLES 2:3; 4:21

2 The son of Arpachshad, one of Shem's sons, this Shelah's name was one of those in the earliest genealogies of the earth's inhabitants which probably was symbolic of a nation or a people. I CHRONICLES 1:18, 24

SHELEMIAH

1 One of the family of Bani who married outside the faith during the Exile in Babylon, this Shelemiah agreed to observe Ezra's stringent rule against interfaith marriages in Jerusalem. EZRA 10:39

2 Another of the same family, this man had the same experience as 1, EZRA 10:41

3 This Shelemiah was remembered primarily as the father of Hananiah, the perfume-maker, who helped Nehemiah rebuild the wrecked walls of Jerusalem after the Exile. NEHEMIAH 3:30

4 A priest in Jerusalem after the Exile, this man was appointed by Nehemiah to supervise the distribution of the tithes from the Temple treasury. NEHEMIAH 13:13

5 Cushi's son, this Shelemiah was the grandfather of Jehudi, the man sent by the authorities to bring Jeremiah's secretary Baruch to a hearing. JEREMIAH 36:14

6 A son of Abdeel, this man was one of those sent by the angry King Jehoiakim to seize Jeremiah and Baruch after hearing Jeremiah's prophecy. Shelemiah and his party, however, were unable to find the prophet. JEREMIAH 36:26

7 Another Shelemiah who lived through the crises during which Jeremiah wrote and spoke, this man was the father of Jehucal, the messenger sent by King Zedekiah to beg the prayers of Jeremiah. JEREMIAH 37:3; 38:1

8 Still another Shelemiah, this man was the father of Irijah, the captain of the guard at the gate of Jerusalem who arrested Jeremiah on false charges of deserting to the Babylonian enemy. JEREMIAH 37:13

9 For the Shelemiah in I Chronicles 26:14, see SHALLUM 8

SHELEPH
One of Joktan's sons, Sheleph was a descendant of Shem. He was another of those shadowy persons in the ancient genealogies who was believed to have been the ancestor of one of the earth's peoples. GENESIS 10:26; I CHRONICLES 1:20

SHELESH
A member of the tribe of Asher in its early days, Shelesh was a clan leader who was a son of Helem. I CHRONICLES 7:35

SHELOMI
A member of the tribe of Asher, Shelomi was remembered as

318

the father of the tribe chief, Ahihud, who was selected to help Moses divide the Promised Land among the tribes. NUMBERS 34:27

SHELOMITH
1 A daughter of Dibni of the tribe of Dan, this woman married an Egyptian and was the mother of the man who was stoned to death in the wilderness for blasphemy in Moses' time. LEVITICUS 24:11
2 A woman in the royal family of Judah, this Shelomith was a daughter of Zerubbabel and a descendant of David. She accompanied her family to Jerusalem after the Exile. I CHRONICLES 3:19
3 For the Shelomith in I Chronicles 23:18, see SHELOMOTH 1
4 One of King Rehoboam's children by his favorite wife, Maacah, this Shelomith is not even identified as either a man or a woman. II CHRONICLES 11:20
5 The son of Josiphiah, this Shelomith was one of the clan of Bani who was a leader in the exiled community of Jews. Many of his family returned with Ezra to Jerusalem. EZRA 8:10

SHELOMOTH
1 A Levite of the Gershom side of the tribe, this Shelomoth was a son of Shimei, and served in the sanctuary in David's time. I CHRONICLES 23:9
2 Another Levite by the same name, this man was of the Kohath branch of the tribe, and was the number-one representative of his family, the family of Izhar, in the sanctuary services. I CHRONICLES 23:18; 24:22
3 A direct descendant of Moses

through Eliezer, Moses' son, this Shelomoth was another prominent Levite of the same name in David's day. He was appointed a supervisor of the treasury in the House of the Lord. I CHRONICLES 26:25, 26, 28

SHELUMIEL A son of Zurishaddai, Shelumiel was the head of the tribe of Simeon, and helped Moses in his census of the tribes. NUMBERS 1:6; 2:12; 7:36, 41; 10:19

SHEM Noah's oldest son, Shem was the reputed ancestor of all Semitic peoples, including the Hebrews, through his five sons. Shem accompanied Noah on the voyage in the ark and tactfully tried to cover his disheveled father after Noah got drunk. Shem and his brothers, Ham and Japheth, were believed by the ancient historians to be the founders of all of the races and peoples on the earth. GENESIS 5:32; 6:10; 7:13; 9:18—27; 10:1—31; 11:10—11; I CHRONICLES 1:4, 17, 24

SHEMA
1 An early member of the tribe of Judah, Shema was listed as a descendant of Caleb, son of Hezron, and as a son of Hebron. He was one of those early clan chieftains recorded carefully in the Chronicler's genealogies of the tribes. I CHRONICLES 2:43, 44
2 One of the chief men in the tribe of Reuben, this Shema was the grandfather of Bela, a well-known head of a powerful clan of the tribe. I CHRONICLES 5:4, 8
3 One of the fierce sons of Elpaal in the tribe of Benjamin, this Shema and

SHEMAAH

his brothers were warrior chiefs of clans living at Aijalon at the time of the conquest of Canaan. Shema and others of his tribe once won a skirmish in which they drove all the Philistines out of Gath. I CHRONICLES 8:13, 21

4 A distinguished citizen at Jerusalem after the Exile, this man was given a place of honor beside Ezra when Ezra brought all the people together in a great national assembly to hear the Law read. NEHEMIAH 8:4

SHEMAAH A tough Benjaminite, Shemaah was the father of two of David's most famous fighters, Ahiezer and Joash. I CHRONICLES 12:3

SHEMAIAH

1 The prophet of the Lord in the tense days following Solomon's death, Shemaiah talked haughty, hot-tempered King Rehoboam out of war with the ten rebellious northern tribes. Later, he counseled Rehoboam to repent for ignoring God when Shishak of Egypt attacked Judah. The Chronicler mentions that Shemaiah's records, or diary, helped in writing about Rehoboam's reign. I KINGS 12:22; II CHRONICLES 11:2; 12:5, 7, 15

2 A member of the royal family of Judah, this Shemaiah was a son of Shecaniah and the father of Hattush. He was remembered primarily because he was descended from David. I CHRONICLES 3:22

3 A clan chieftain in the tribe of Simeon, this Shemaiah was the head of a clan whose descendants were among those who pushed out the Canaanite inhabitants of the lush val-

ley of Gedor in King Hezekiah's time. I CHRONICLES 4:37

4 For the Shemaiah in I Chronicles 5:4, see SHEMA **2**

5 A Levite of the Merari side of the tribe, this Shemaiah was the son of Hasshub and was one of the first to return to Jerusalem after the Exile in Babylon. I CHRONICLES 9:14; NEHEMIAH 11:15

6 For the Shemaiah in I Chronicles 9:16, see SHAMMUA **3**

7 A Levite musician in David's time, this man participated in the gala festivities when David brought the Ark up to Jerusalem from Obed-edom's house. I CHRONICLES 15:8, 11

8 A scribe who was a son of Nethanel, this Shemaiah kept the records of the assignments of the various priests in David's time in Jerusalem. I CHRONICLES 24:6

9 One of the sons of Obed-edom, the man who kept the Ark before David brought it to Jerusalem, this Shemaiah was appointed a gatekeeper in David's tabernacle and was enrolled as a Levite. I CHRONICLES 26:4, 6, 7

10 A Levite, this man was one of the leaders appointed by King Jehoshaphat to carry out his intensive education program in the cities of Judah on the meaning of the Law. II CHRONICLES 17:8

11 Another Levite by the same name, this person was a son of Jeduthun who took an active part in Hezekiah's reform in which the Temple was renovated. II CHRONICLES 29:14

12 Perhaps the same as **11**, this Levite named Shemaiah served in the

Temple in King Hezekiah's time. He was appointed to supervise the distribution of the offerings to the Levites in the various towns of Judah. II CHRONICLES 31:15

13 A chief Levite in King Josiah's time, this man gave lavish presents to help the priests celebrate the first proper Passover observance in Judah in years. II CHRONICLES 35:9

14 A leader in the Jewish community in exile in Babylon, Shemaiah was one of those sent by Ezra to Iddo's "seminary" to ask for Levites and Temple servants to return with him to Jerusalem. EZRA 8:16

15 Probably the same as **14**, a man named Shemaiah is mentioned as one of the sons of Adonikam who returned with Ezra to Jerusalem after the Exile. EZRA 8:13

16 A priest who was a son of Harim the priest, this person married outside the faith during the sojourn in Babylon, but agreed to leave behind his "foreign" wife upon returning to Jerusalem, in order to keep the faith pure. EZRA 10:21

17 Another who had also married a non-Jewish woman during the Exile, this man was a layman and a member of another family named Harim. EZRA 10:31

18 The son of Shecaniah the keeper of East Gate in Jerusalem, this Shemaiah worked hard with Nehemiah to rebuild the ruined walls of Jerusalem after returning from Babylon. NEHEMIAH 3:29

19 Son of Delaiah, this Shemaiah was hired by Nehemiah's enemies,

Tobiah and Sanballat, to make Nehemiah look like a coward and blasphemer. Shemaiah, probably a priest's son, posed as Nehemiah's friend and protector, but Nehemiah was not taken in by his phony prophecies. NEHEMIAH 6:10—14

20 A priest who was well-known in Jerusalem after the Exile, this man headed a contingent of priests in Zerubbabel's, Joiakim's, and Nehemiah's time, and took an active part in the services when Nehemiah dedicated the rebuilt walls of the city. NEHEMIAH 10:8; 12:6, 18, 34

21 A contemporary of **20**, this Shemaiah was a priest of Asaph's branch of the tribe and a son of Mattaniah. His grandson Zechariah played a trumpet in the elaborate service when Nehemiah dedicated the rebuilt walls of Jerusalem. NEHEMIAH 12:35

22 A musician at the same service mentioned in **20** and **21**, this Shemaiah was a Levite who marched in the procession through the city, playing on the instruments carefully preserved from David's time. NEHEMIAH 12:36, 42

23 A man from the village of Kirjath-jearim near Jerusalem, this man is remembered as the father of the martyred prophet Uriah, who was killed by King Jehoiakim for his outspoken sermons against Jerusalem. JEREMIAH 26:20

24 One of the false prophets who accused Jeremiah of being a false prophet, this Shemaiah had taken the Exile from Jerusalem lightly and predicted a quick return. When Jeremiah wrote the captives warning them of a long sojourn in Babylon, Shemaiah wrote to Zephaniah, the priest in charge of disciplining other priests, demanding suitable punishment for Jeremiah. Jeremiah coolly foretold Shemaiah's lonely death in Babylon. JEREMIAH 29:24—32

25 This Shemaiah was the father of Delaiah, one of the advisors to King Jehoiakim during Jeremiah's ministry. JEREMIAH 36:12

SHEMARIAH

1 One of the bold Benjaminite warriors who deserted Saul and joined David at Ziglag, this Shemariah could fight skillfully with either hand with both the deadly sling and bow. I CHRONICLES 12:5

2 One of King Rehoboam's sons by his wife Abihail, this man was probably one of those appointed by Rehoboam to a responsible position in a fortified city of Judah. II CHRONICLES 11:19

3 A member of Harim's family who married outside the faith during the Exile in Babylon, this man agreed to abide by Ezra's strict rule against interfaith marriages upon returning to Jerusalem. EZRA 10:32

4 Another who broke the Law by marrying a non-Jewish woman in Babylon, this man by the same name was a member of the family of Bani. EZRA 10:41

SHEMEBER An ancient king of the city-state of Zeboim, Shemeber and the kings of Sodom, Gomorrah, Adma, and Bela were attacked by five other kings, led by Chedorlaomer, king of Elam, and defeated in a battle near the Dead Sea. The victors carried away Abraham's nephew, Lot. GENESIS 14:2

SHEMED See **SHEMER 4**

SHEMER

1 The first Shemer was the owner of the hill which was sold to Omri and became the site of the city of Samaria. I KINGS 16:24

2 A Levite of the Merari side of the tribe, this Shemer was remembered primarily because he was an ancestor of Ethan, one of the great singers in David's sanctuary. I CHRONICLES 6:46

3 A member of the tribe of Asher, this man's name was recorded in the tribal annals as an early chieftain of a clan and a mighty warrior. I CHRONICLES 7:32, 34

4 One of the tribe of Benjamin, this Shemer, a son of Elpaal, settled in Canaan after Joshua's conquest and was the founder-builder of the towns of Lod and Ono. I CHRONICLES 8:12

SHEMIDA One of Manasseh's grandsons and Gilead's sons, Shemida was another early clan chieftain listed in the ancient genealogies. His descendants were known as Shemidaites. NUMBERS 36:22; JOSHUA 17:2; I CHRONICLES 7:19

SHEMIDAH See **SHEMIDA**

SHEMIRAMOTH

1 A famous Levite musician in David's time, this Shemiramoth sang in one of the choirs and played the harp in David's sanctuary. I CHRONICLES 15:18, 20; 16:5

2 Another Levite, this man lived in King Jehoshaphat's day. He was sent to teach the people in the towns of Judah the meaning of the Law when Jehoshaphat sent teams of instructors out during a brief flurry of reform. II CHRONICLES 17:8

SHEMUEL

1 A chief of the tribe of Simeon in Moses' time, this Shemuel was selected to represent his tribe as one of Moses' twelve advisors in dividing the Promised Land west of the Jordan fairly among the various clans of the twelve tribes. NUMBERS 34:20

2 For the name given as Shemuel in some translations of I Chronicles 6:33, see SAMUEL.

3 One of Issachar's grandsons, this Shemuel was the ancestor of a clan in the tribe and a mighty warrior in his time. I CHRONICLES 7:2

SHENAZAR See SHENAZZAR

SHENAZZAR One of Jeconiah's sons, Shenazzar was a member of the royal family of Judah descended from David. His father was carried away as a captive to Babylon by Nebuchadnezzar at the age of eighteen, and Shenazzar spent most of his life in Babylon. I CHRONICLES 3:18

SHEPHATIAH

1 David's fifth son, this Shephatiah was obviously overshadowed by his rebellious older brothers, Absalom and Adonijah. He was born in Hebron during David's outlaw days. His mother was Abital. II SAMUEL 3:4; I CHRONICLES 3:3

2 A member of the tribe of Benjamin, this man was remembered primarily as the father of Meshullam, one of the chief men of the tribe who returned to live in Jerusalem after the Exile. I CHRONICLES 9:8

3 One of the fierce detachment of Benjaminites that grew disgusted with Saul and joined David at Ziglag, this Shephatiah, like his buddies, could expertly handle the deadly sling and bow equally well with either hand. I CHRONICLES 12:5

4 The son of Maacah in the tribe of Simeon in David's time, this Shephatiah was head of the tribe when David took his census. I CHRONICLES 27:16

5 One of Jehoshaphat's sons, this Shephatiah was left both power and possessions when his father died. His brother, Jehoram, however, was left the throne. Shephatiah and his other brothers were immediately slaughtered by the mistrustful Jehoram. II CHRONICLES 21:2

6 This Shephatiah was the ancestor of a family, 372 of whom returned to Jerusalem after the Exile with Zerubbabel. EZRA 2:4; NEHEMIAH 7:9

7 One of Solomon's servants, this man was also the ancestor of a large group which decided to return to Jerusalem after the Exile. EZRA 2:37; NEHEMIAH 7:59

8 Perhaps the same as **6**, one named Shephatiah had a number of descendants in the party that came back to Jerusalem after the Exile with Ezra. EZRA 8:8

9 A member of the tribe of Judah descended from Perez, this man was a distant ancestor of Athaiah, one of the

head men in the government in Judah in Nehemiah's time. NEHEMIAH 11:4
10 A nobleman in Jerusalem in Jeremiah's time, this person, a son of Mattan, was one of the civic leaders who determined to silence Jeremiah for good by dropping him down into a cistern. JEREMIAH 38:1

SHEPHI See SHEPHO

SHEPHO Grandson of Seir and Horite and son of Shobal, Shepho was one of the little-known ancient desert chieftains of the Horites, the tribe occupying Arabia before the Edomites ruled it. GENESIS 36:23; I CHRONICLES 1:40

SHEPHUPHAM Benjamin's grandson and Bela's son, Shephupham was sometimes known as "Shuppim" and "Shupham." He was the ancestral head of a clan known as Shuphamites. NUMBERS 26:39; I CHRONICLES 7:12, 15; 8:5

SHEPHUPHAN See SHEPHUPHAM

SHERAH See SHEERAH

SHEREBIAH A Levite who was prominent in the community of Exiles in Babylon, Sherebiah and his family were closely associated with Ezra. Sherebiah was one of the twelve leaders entrusted with the silver, gold, and precious utensils for the Temple in Jerusalem. In Jerusalem, Sherebiah was one of those who stood on the platform with Ezra at the great national assembly, and was a signer of the covenant drawn up in Nehemiah's time. EZRA 8:18, 24; NEHEMIAH 8:7; 9:4, 5; 10:12; 12:8, 24

SHERESH Manasseh's grandson and Machir's son, Sheresh is another who is simply a name in the long tribal lists of ancient clan leaders. I CHRONICLES 7:16

SHEREZER See SHAREZER

SHESHAI One of the descendants of Anak, the giant, Sheshai and his family-clan lived in the area of Hebron at the time of the conquest of Canaan by the tribes of Israel. He was killed by troops from the tribe of Judah under Caleb, and his lands taken over by the Calebites. NUMBERS 13:22; JOSHUA 15:14; JUDGES 1:10

SHESHAN A member of the tribe of Judah descended from Jerahmeel, Sheshan had the misfortune of having no sons to carry on his line. He tried to solve this by marrying his daughter to an Egyptian slave, Jarha, and adopting his grandchildren as members of his own clan. I CHRONICLES 2:31, 34, 35

SHESHBAZZAR A distinguished leader in Jerusalem when the first group of Jews was authorized by Cyprus the Persian to return, Sheshbazzar in certain accounts was reported to have been the man who carried the sacred Temple vessels to Jerusalem and who laid the foundation for the new Temple. Some scholars think that "Sheshbazzar" might have been a Babylonian name for Zerubbabel, the man who, in certain accounts, was responsible for laying the foundations for the new Temple. Still other scholars have conjectured that Sheshbazzar might have been Shenazzar, the son of King Jeconiah, king of Judah carried away by Nebuchadnezzar to Babylon. Shenazzar was an uncle of Zerubbabel, and could have passed on the responsibilities to his nephew. Sheshbazzar, whoever he was, served briefly as governor before Zerubbabel. EZRA 1:8, 11; 5:14, 16

SHETHAR One of the top advisors to King Ahasuerus of Persia, Shethar was one of seven subjects who were allowed to look the king in the face. ESTHER 1:14

SHETHAR-BOZENAI One of those who officiously tried to prevent the Temple from being rebuilt after the Jews returned from exile in Babylon, Shethar-Bozenai was a Persian government official in a district adjoining Judah. A letter from King Darius of Persia forced Shethar-Bozenai to let the people of Jerusalem alone. EZRA 5:3, 6; 6:6, 13

SHEVA
1 For the Sheva mentioned in II Samuel 20:25, see SERAIAH 1
2 A son of the great spy, Caleb, son of Jephunneh, by his concubine, Maacah, Sheva was the head of a clan which settled in Machbena and Gibea after the conquest of the Promised Land. I CHRONICLES 2:49

SHILHI King Asa's father-in-law, Shilhi was remembered as Queen Azubah's father, and the maternal grandfather of King Jehoshaphat. I KINGS 22:42; II CHRONICLES 20:31

SHILLEM See SHALLUM 7

SHILONI In some older translations of Nehemiah 11:5, Shiloni appears as a person's name. Actually, it refers to "the Shilonite," a member of Shelah's family in the tribe of Judah. NEHEMIAH 11:5

SHILSHAH One of the tribe of Asher, Shilshah was an early chief who was ninth of Zophah's sons and a noted warrior. I CHRONICLES 7:37

SHIMEA
1 For David's son, called Shimea in some translations, see SHAMMUA 2
2 A Levite of the Merari branch of the tribe, this Shimea was a son of Uzzah, according to the Chronicler's roll of the tribe. I CHRONICLES 6:30
3 Another Levite, this man was a son of Michael of the Gershom side of the tribe. He was the ancestor of Asaph, David's famous song leader in the sanctuary. I CHRONICLES 6:39
4 For David's older brother, sometimes known as Shimea, see SHAMMAH 2

SHIMEAH
1 A Benjaminite clan chief who was descended from Jehiel and Gibeon, Shimeah was a son of Mikloth and a close relative of Saul. I CHRONICLES 8:32; 9:38
2 In many translations, persons by the name of Shimeah are also known by the name SHIMEA (which see).

SHIMEAM See SHIMEAH 1

SHIMEATH An Ammonite woman, Shimeath was the mother of Jozacar or Zabad, one of those who conspired to kill King Joash of Judah and seize his throne. II KINGS 12:21; II CHRON-ICLES 24:26

SHIMEI

1 Moses' grandson and Gershon's second son, this Shimei was the first of many carrying the name. Shimei was with the tribes during the wanderings in the wilderness. He had four sons who became ancestral heads of ancient houses in the tribe. Their descendants, proud to claim Shimei as their ancestor, were families of prominent Levite musicians in David's time. EXODUS 6:17; NUMBERS 3:18; I CHRONICLES 6:17, 42; 23:7, 10

2 A member of the tribe of Benjamin descended from Gera, this Shimei was a close relative and ardent supporter of Saul who was deeply suspicious of David after Saul's death. During Absalom's rebellion, Shimei publicly insulted David and stirred up trouble against David. After David's victory, Shimei cunningly affected profound regret and was forgiven. David, however, on his deathbed, warned Solomon to watch Shimei. Shimei broke his parole and was executed by Solomon. II SAMUEL 16; 19; I KINGS 2

3 For the Shimei mentioned in II Samuel 21:21, see SHAMMAH **2**

4 Another Shimei who lived during David's reign, this man was one of David's mighty men, one who remained loyal to David even during David's long final illness when Adonijah tried to make himself king. I KINGS 1:8

5 A son of Ela, this Shimei was one of Solomon's twelve commissary officers. Shimei was assigned the territory of the tribe of Benjamin and was responsible for procuring supplies to maintain Solomon's enormous staff for one month each year. I KINGS 4:18

6 A member of the royal family of Judah descended from David, this Shimei was a brother of Zerubbabel, the great colonizer of Jerusalem after the Exile. Shimei probably also returned to Jerusalem. I CHRONICLES 3:19

7 A son of Zaccur of the tribe of Simeon, this Shimei's chief claim to fame was fathering sixteen sons and six daughters, the largest family in his tribe. He was a grandson of Simeon. I CHRONICLES 4:26, 27

8 For the man named Shimei in I Chronicles 5:4, see SHEMA **4**

9 An early member of the Merari family of Levites, this man was a grandson of Merari himself, and was remembered as a clan head in the tribal records. I CHRONICLES 6:29

10 Another Levite by the same name, this one was part of the Gershon side of the tribe and was principally remembered because he was a remote ancestor of David's renowned musician, Asaph. I CHRONICLES 6:42

11 For the man named Shimei named in I Chronicles 8:21, see SHEMA **3**

12 A son of Jeduthun, this was still another Levite Shimei. He chose the lot to head the tenth contingent of singers in David's sanctuary. I CHRONICLES 25:17

13 A Ramathite, this person was supervisor of all of David's vineyards. I CHRONICLES 27:27

14 A descendant of David's outstanding musician, Heman, this Levite served in the Temple in the time of King Hezekiah. He was active in the Temple renovation program during Hezekiah's reform. II CHRONICLES 29:14

15 Possibly the same as 14, one named Shimei was also a Levite in Hezekiah's days. He held a responsible position in the Temple treasury office. II CHRONICLES 31:12, 13

16 Another of the many Shimeris who was a Levite, this man married outside the faith during the Exile, but abided by Ezra's rule against "foreign" wives when the exiles returned to Jerusalem. EZRA 10:23

17 A layman who did the same thing as 16, this man was a member of the family Hashum. EZRA 10:33

18 Still another layman who married a non-Jewish woman, the same as 16 and 17, this Shimei was one of the many descendants of Bani. EZRA 10:38

19 A member of the tribe of Benjamin, this was the grandfather of Mordecai, the man who raised young Esther. ESTHER 2:5

SHIMEON A member of the family of Harim who wed a Babylonian woman during the Exile, Shimeon was one of the many who had to leave his wife behind when returning to Jerusalem. EZRA 10:31

SHIMMA See SHAMMAH 2

SHIMON A descendant of Moses' great spy Caleb, Shimon was one of the many listed in the roll of the tribe of Judah who were prominent heads of houses in their day, but are mere names to us. I CHRONICLES 4:20

SHIMRATH A son of Shema 3 or Shimei 11, Shimrath was another Benjaminite chieftain remembered in the tribal genealogy by the Chronicler. I CHRONICLES 8:21

SHIMRI

1 One of the tribe of Simeon, this Shimri was an ancestor of Ziza, one of the tribal leaders who led an expedition to seize the valley of Gedor during King Hezekiah's reign. I CHRONICLES 4:37

2 This second man by the name was remembered as the father of Jediael, one of David's leading warriors. I CHRONICLES 11:45

3 A Levite of the Merari side of the tribe, this Shimri, a son of Hosah, headed his family's contingent of gatekeepers in David's sanctuary. I CHRONICLES 26:10

4 Another Levite of the same name, this man was a son of Elizaphan and took an active part in King Hezekiah's program of renovating the rundown Temple. II CHRONICLES 29:13

SHIMRITH See SHIMEATH

SHIMRON Issachar's fourth son, Shimron accompanied the family on its move from Canaan to Egypt to escape the famine. Later, Shimron was the ancestral head of a clan, within the tribe of Simeon, the Shimronites, which went out from Egypt to the wilderness with Moses. GENESIS 46:13; NUMBERS 26:24; I CHRONICLES 7:1

SHIMSHAI A Persian official who served under Rehum as secretary, Shimshai wrote to King Artaxerxes I of Persia protesting Nehemiah's rebuilding of the walls of Jerusalem and wrongly accusing Nehemiah and the Jews of treachery. EZRA 4

SHINAB The king of Admah, a city-state in the area of the Dead Sea, Shinab and four other local rulers were attacked and defeated by a coalition of four other kings, led by Chedorlaomer. Chedorlaomer pillaged Admah and kidnapped Lot, Abraham's nephew, after Shinab's death. GENESIS 14:2

SHIPHI A Simeonite clan leader, Shiphi was the father of Ziza, one of the heads of the armed shepherd clans that seized the valley of Gedor for themselves during King Hezekiah's time. I CHRONICLES 4:37

SHIPHRAH One of the two Hebrew midwives at the time of Moses' birth, Shiphrah refused to obey the pharaoh's cruel order to arrange the deaths of Hebrew male babies. She protected her charges by telling the pharaoh that Hebrew women delivered their children before she could get to them. EXODUS 1:15

SHIPHTAN One of the tribe of Ephraim, Shiphtan was the father of the head man of the tribe, Kemuel, who was selected to advise Moses when the land west of the Jordan was divided among some of the tribes. NUMBERS 34:24

SHISHA See SERIAH

SHISHAK King of Egypt who founded the twenty-second Dynasty, Shishak (or Sheshonk I, as the Egyptians called him) swept across Palestine after Solomon's death and forced both Rehoboam of Judah and Jeroboam of Israel to pay heavy tribute. During this expedition, he sacked Jerusalem and plundered the Temple. As a builder, he added spectacular additions to the great temple of Karnak. I KINGS 11:40; 14:25; II CHRONICLES 12:2—9

SHITRAI A herdsman who lived in the lovely valley of Sharon, Shitrai was hired by David to oversee the royal flocks pastured in the vicinity. I CHRONICLES 27:29

SHIZA A tribesman of Reuben, Shiza was listed as the father of Adina, one of David's toughest warriors. I CHRONICLES 11:42

SHOBAB
1 One of the nine sons born to David after he moved to Jerusalem as king of the united kingdom, Shobab never distinguished himself in any way or earned himself any mention in the Bible beyond inclusion in the roll of the royal family. II SAMUEL 5:14; I CHRONICLES 3:5; 14:4
2 One of the early and obscure clan chieftains listed in the records of the tribe of Judah, this Shobab was a son of Caleb, Hezron's son. I CHRONICLES 2:18

SHOBACH When King Hadadezer of city-state of Zobah in Syria recklessly organized an attack against David shortly after David became king, Shobach was appointed general of the entire invading force. David personally led his troops, routed the Shobach army and slew Shobach. II SAMUEL 10:16—18; I CHRONICLES 19: 16, 18

SHOBAI A gatekeeper in the Temple, this Levite was the ancestor of one of the families that returned to devastated Jerusalem with Zerubbabel after the Exile. EZRA 2:42; NEHEMIAH 7:45

SHOBAL
1 One of the little-known chieftains of the Horites, that group that inhabited the Arabian desert before the Edomites, Shobal was a descendant of Seir. GENESIS 36:20, 23, 29; I CHRONICLES 1:38, 40
2 An obscure clan head in the tribe of Judah probably some time in the fifteenth century B.C., this Shobal was a son of Caleb, son of Hur. I CHRONICLES 2:50, 52
3 One of Judah's sons, this shadowy figure is nothing more than a name in the family genealogy. He was the chief of one of the families within the tribe. I CHRONICLES 4:1, 2

SHOBEK A leader in Jerusalem after the Exile, Shobek was one of the prominent men and heads of families that joined Nehemiah in signing the covenant to keep the Law. NEHEMIAH 10:24

SHOBI A son of Nahash, the Ammonite king of the city-state of Rabbah, Shobi had probably been put in charge of the city as David's vassal after David had subdued it. When David was escaping from Absalom, Shobi brought provisions to David's men. II SAMUEL 17:27

SHOHAM An early Levite, Shoham was one of Merari's five sons and the ancestral head of a family of Merari Levites who served through the years in the sanctuary and temples. I CHRONICLES 24:27

SHOMER
1 For the Shomer mentioned in II Kings 12:21, see SHIMEATH

2 for the Shomer mentioned in I Chronicles 7:32, see SHEMER **3**

SHOPHACH See SHOBACH

SHUA
1 Judah's Canaanite father-in-law, Shua lived at Adullam. GENESIS 38:2, 12; I CHRONICLES 2:3
2 One of Abraham's sons by his wife Keturah, this Shua was the founder of a desert people west of the Euphrates GENESIS 25:2; I CHRONICLES 1:32
3 A daughter of Heber, a grandson of Asher, this woman gave her name to a clan in the tribe of Asher. I CHRONICLES 7:36

SHUAH See SHUA

SHUAL Zophah's third son, Shual was recorded in the long list of clan chieftains and warrior-leaders of the tribe of Asher. I CHRONICLES 7:36

SHUBAEL See SHEBUEL

SHUHAM See HUSHIM 1

SHUNI Gad's third son, Shuni emigrated with his father and grandfather, Jacob, when the entire clan went to Egypt to escape the famine in Canaan. Shuni's family, the Shunites, went out with Moses to the wilderness as one of the clans in the tribe of Gad. GENESIS 46:16; NUMBERS 26:15

SHUPHAM See SHEPHUPHAM

SHUPPIM

1 For the Shuppim mentioned in I Chronicles 7:12, 15, see SHEPHUPHAM

2 A gatekeeper in the tabernacle in David's time, this Shuppim was a Levite who was selected by lot to be posted on the west side by the Gate of Shallecheth. I CHRONICLES 26:16

SHUTHELAH

1 The ancestor of the Ephraimite clan known as the Shuthelaites, Shuthelah was a little known ancient clan chieftain who was one of Ephraim's sons. NUMBERS 26:35, 36; I CHRONICLES 7:20

2 A descendant of **1** this Ephraimite was listed as a son of Zabad in the tribal genealogy. I CHRONICLES 7:21

SIA A Temple servant, Sia was the ancestor of a family who returned with Zerubbabel from Babylon to Jerusalem after the Exile. EZRA 2:44

SIAHA See SIA

SIBBECAI See MEBUNNAI

SIBBECHAI See MEBUNNAI

SIDON One of Noah's descendants through Ham, Sidon was Canaan's oldest son. He was the reputed founder of the city of Sidon, the great Phoenician port, and the ancestor of the energetic people of the area. GENESIS 10:15

SIHON Ruler of the surly people at Heshbon near the Arnon River at the time the tribes were preparing to move into the Jordan Valley from the wilderness, Sihon was an Amorite king who had wrested his territory from the Moabites. He turned down the Israelite request to pass through his territory, and attacked the tribes at Jahaz. His defeat was the beginning of the struggle by the tribes to hack out a homeland in Palestine. NUMBERS 21:21—34; 32:33; DEUTERONOMY 1:4; 2:24—32; 3:2, 6; 4:46; 29:7; 31:4; JOSHUA 2:10; 9:10; 12:2, 5; 13:10—27; JUDGES 11; I KINGS 4:19; NEHEMIAH 9:22; PSALM 135:11; 136:19; JEREMIAH 48:45

SILAS Paul's companion on the second missionary journey, Silas was originally part of the early congregation at Jerusalem. He was one of the party bringing greetings and the decision of the Jerusalem council to the Christians at Antioch. He returned to Jerusalem, then came back to Antioch in time to join Paul on the second journey. Like Paul, he was a Roman citizen which, undoubtedly, saved his life during some of the troubles in the towns in Asia Minor and Macedonia. Silas stayed in Beroea for a time, preaching, before joining Paul again at Corinth. Silas was with Paul when the letters were written from Corinth to Thessalonica. It seems, however, that Silas did not stay in Corinth during the year and a half that Paul lived there. The next mention in the New Testament of Silas is in I Peter, where he is identified as the man carrying Peter's letter from Rome to the churches in Asia Minor. Silas was probably associated with Peter after leaving Paul at Corinth. There was no hint of animosity, however, between Silas and Paul. ACTS 15—18; II CORINTHIANS 1:19; I THESSALONIANS 1:1; II THESSALONIANS 1:1; I PETER 5:12

SILVANUS   See SILAS

SIMEON

1 One of Jacob's sons, his second by Leah, Simeon was an ancient tribal chief in Jacob's clan of sons. He and his brother treacherously murdered Shechem and his followers even though Shechem had generously offered to be circumcised and to marry Dinah, Simeon's sister, whom Shechem had violated. Later, during the famine, Simeon was sent by Jacob to buy grain in Egypt. When Joseph (the brother sold as a slave who rose to prime minister of Egypt) insisted on meeting Benjamin, Jacob's youngest son and favorite, Simeon was selected as a hostage to make certain the others would return with Benjamin. His tribe, the Simeonites, was one of the twelve tribes of Israel. GENESIS 29:33; 34:25, 30; 35:23; 42:24, 36; 43:23; 46:10; 48:5; 49:5; EXODUS 1:2; 6:15; NUMBERS, DEUTERONOMY, JOSHUA, JUDGES, I, and II CHRONICLES, etc.
2 Another Simeon, this was a man alleged to be an ancestor of Jesus. LUKE 3:30

3 An aged Jew who devoutly had waited a lifetime in the Temple precincts to catch a glimpse of God's Chosen One, this Simeon recognized the infant Jesus as the One for whom he had been waiting. Simeon was one of "the pious," a pious minority who refused violence but waited humbly for God's deliverance from the oppressive Romans and the clique of high priests and aristocrats. LUKE 2:25—34
4 A well-known leader in the Christian community at Antioch, this Simeon was also known as "Niger." He was a prophet and/or teacher, and was one of those who were led by the Spirit to commission Paul and Barnabas for their evangelistic tour, the first missionary journey. ACTS 15:1
5 For the reference to the Simeon in Acts 15:14, see PETER

SIMON

1 For the disciple of Jesus also known as Peter, see PETER
2 Another of Jesus' twelve disciples, this Simon was "the Canaanite" or "Cananean" or "the Zealot," which meant that he was once a member of the fanatic sect of Jewish nationalists founded by Judas of Gamala. This group terrified the countryside and fanned the resentments against all Romans into frequent bloody outbreaks. Simon deserted these revolutionaries for One who was far more revolutionary. MATTHEW 10:4; MARK 3:18; LUKE 6:15; ACTS 1:13
3 One of Jesus' brothers, this Simon was a stay-at-home member of the

family who apparently never believed in Jesus. Simon was undoubtedly embarrassed by Jesus and, if he was not with other members of Jesus' family when they tried to persuade Him to come home, was probably sympathetic to them. MATTHEW 13:55; MARK 6:3

4 A Simon known as "the Leper," this man lived at Bethany. While Simon was entertaining Jesus, a woman burst in and anointed Jesus' head with an alabaster jar of ointment, to the indignation of the disciples and other guests. MATTHEW 26:6; MARK 14:3

5 A Pharisee, this Simon also entertained Jesus at a dinner party which was interrupted by a notorious local woman weeping uncontrollably and anointing Jesus' feet with ointment. Simon, indignant at the intrusion, was given a lesson both in manners and in the meaning of forgiveness by Jesus. Some Bible scholars identify Simon **5** with **4**. Others, pointing out the differences, maintain they were two separate persons. LUKE 7:36—50

6 The father of Judas Iscariot, Jesus' betrayer. JOHN 6:71; 12:4; 13:2, 26

7 The man whose holiday in Jerusalem was ruined when the Roman guards forced him to carry Jesus' cross, this Simon was apparently so affected by Jesus that he became a believer. His two sons, Alexander and Rufus, were later well-known members of the Christian community. This Simon came from Cyrene, in North Africa. Probably he was a Jewish pilgrim fulfilling a lifetime dream of attending Passover in Jerusalem. MATTHEW 27:32; MARK 15:21; LUKE 23:26

8 A magician at Samaria who enjoyed great prestige, Simon was impressed when Philip evangelized and healed at Samaria. Simon even insisted on being baptized. The gospel, however, was simply a new brand of magic for Simon. He tried to buy the power of the Holy Spirit from Peter and was ringingly denounced. The early Christian fathers devote much space to Simon the Magician. Justin Martyr reports that Simon's miracle-working created such a stir in Rome that he was honored with a statue, and that he was founder of all subsequent Christian heresies. ACTS 8:9—24

9 A tanner who lived at the port of Joppa, this Simon was an early believer who entertained Peter. While Peter was making his headquarters at Simon's house by the sea, he healed Tabitha, had his vision, and received the message from Cornelius. ACTS 9:43; 10:6, 17, 32

SIMRI See SHIMRI

SIPPAI See SAPH

SISAMAI An obscure early clan chief in the tribe of Judah, Sisamai traced his family lineage through Eleasah (his father), Jerahmeel, and Perez. I CHRONICLES 2:40

SISERA

1 A Canaanite warrior, Sisera commanded the armies of Jabin and other Canaanite kings which held the Israelites under their iron heel for twenty years. The prophetess Deborah finally stirred Barak to raise troops for a revolt. Sisera's forces were completely routed. After hiding as a fugitive for a time, Sisera met a disgraceful death when a plucky Israelite woman, Jael, crushed his skull with a hammer blow. JUDGES 4, 5; I SAMUEL 12:9; PSALM 83:9

2 One of the Temple servants known as Nethinim, this man was an ancestor of a family that returned with Zerubbabel from Exile in Babylon to Jerusalem. EZRA 2:53; NEHEMIAH 7:55

SISMAI See SISAMAI

SITHRI An early Levite who headed a family in the Kohath side of the tribe, Sithri was Kohath's grandson and Uzziel's son. EXODUS 6:22

SO The king of Egypt during the final days of Israel, King So was approached by King Hoshea of Israel regarding a possible alliance against the Assyrians. Assyria got wind of the proposal and invaded Palestine, snuffing out the nation of Israel. King So was perhaps one of the Twenty-fifth Dynasty, and might also have been known as King Shabaka or King Shabataka. Egyptian experts today, however, point out that Egyptian records do not agree, but that a general in northern Arabia, Sib'a of Pir'u, was probably the strongman to whom Hoshea turned. II KINGS 17:4

SOCHO See SOCO

SOCO One of Mered's grandsons by his Jewish wife, Soco was a son of Heber. Heber is another man in the tribal roll of Judah who is now simply a name in the lists. I CHRONICLES 4:18

SOCOH See SOCO

SODI An early member of the tribe of Zebulun, Sodi was the father of Gaddiel, one of the twelve spies sent by Moses into the land of Canaan. NUMBERS 13:10

SOLOMON David's tenth son and his successor to the throne, Solomon came to power principally because of the intrigues of his mother, Bathsheba, during David's senility. Immediately after he was anointed by Nathan the prophet, Solomon moved against his rebellious brother Adonijah, then settled some old scores of his father against Joab and Shimei. Solomon relished the luxurious trappings of power that fell to Oriental despots. He introduced the system of forced labor gangs to furnish manpower for his ambitious building programs, and broke down the old system of tribal rule with his well organized administrative districts. He maintained an immense standing army, suppressed all revolts ruthlessly, and made his kingdom respected as a world power during his reign. The great Temple was but one of his ambitious building projects. To finance all this opulence, Solomon taxed his subjects so oppressively that the nation simmered with revolt during his last days. Although his wisdom and piety were extolled by some Biblical writers, Solomon was a shrewd, overbearing, worldly, comfort-loving dictator. II SAMUEL 5:14; 12:24; I KINGS 1—14; II KINGS 21:7; 23:13; 24:13; 25:16; I CHRONICLES 3:5, 10; 6:10, 32; 14:4; 18:8; 22:5—17; 23:1; 28; 29; II CHRONICLES 1—13; 30:26;

33:7; 35:3, 4; NEHEMIAH 12:45; 13:
26; PROVERBS; SONG OF SOLOMON;
JEREMIAH 52:20, and others

SOPATER One of those who accompanied Paul on his last trip to Jerusalem, Sopater was a Christian from the town of Beroea in northern Greece and was the son of Pyrrhus. Sopater and the other members of Paul's party were representatives of congregations which had contributed to the special offering that Paul had collected for the Jerusalem Christians. They sailed from Philippi to Caesarea and were with Paul at the time of his arrest. Many scholars think that Sopater is the same as "Sosipater," who is one of those who joined Paul in sending greetings at the close of Paul's letter to the church at Rome. Sosipater was called a kinsman of Paul, meaning that he, too, was born a Jew. The name of a Sosipater appears in the list of politarchs in an inscription in the city of Thessalonica, not far from Beroea, but there is no way of ascertaining whether or not this was Paul's friend. ACTS 20:4; ROMANS 16:21

SOPHERETH A servant in Solomon's Temple, Sophereth was the ancestor of a family that returned to Jerusalem with Zerubbabel after the Exile. NEHEMIAH 7:57; EZRA 2:55 (where he is called HASSOPHERETH)

SOSIPATER See **SOPATER**

SOSTHENES
1 A leading Jew in Corinth, Sosthenes apparently succeeded Crispus as head man in the local synagogue after Crispus became a Christian. When Paul's opponents tried to bring charges against Paul but had their case thrown out of court, the crowd beat up Sosthenes—either because he had not presented the case against Paul forcefully enough, or because he seemed to be sympathetic to Christianity. ACTS 18:17

2 Perhaps the same as **1**, especially since he was obviously well-known at Corinth, this Sosthenes was a Christian who joined Paul in writing to the Corinthian congregation. Paul affectionately identifies him as "the brother." Sosthenes was living at Ephesus and perhaps served as Paul's secretary when Paul wrote the Corinthian letter. Legends say that he was one of the Seventy, and later Bishop of Colophon. I CORINTHIANS 1:1

SOTAI A servant of Solomon, Sotai was the ancestral head of one of the families that returned with Zerubbabel to Jerusalem after the Exile. NEHEMIAH 7:57

STACHYS One of Paul's closest friends, Stachys is one of those singled out by name for special greetings at the conclusion of Paul's letter to the Romans. Although Stachys was then living in Rome, apparently he had previously been so closely associated with Paul as to earn the term, "my beloved." The name was not common in the Roman world. The Stachys listed among the emperor's household might have been the man mentioned in Romans. The usual unreliable legends surrounding every New Testament figure also were written in later years about Stachys. ROMANS 16:9

STEPHANAS One of the few who had the distinction of being personally baptized by Paul, Stephanas was one of the first believers in Corinth. He quickly rose to be a leader in the young Corinthian congregation. When the troubles among the new converts in Corinth threatened to ruin the church in that area, Stephanas was one of those who journeyed to Ephesus to consult Paul and carried back Paul's messages to the Corinthian church. Paul speaks well of Stephanas in this letter and urges the Corinthian believers to be obedient to Stephanas. I CORINTHIANS 1:16; 16:15, 17

STEPHEN The first Christian to die for his belief, Stephen was one of the Greek-speaking Jews ("Hellenists") who were part of the earliest Christian group in Jerusalem. When there was murmuring that some of the widows and needy were being neglected, Stephen was one of "the Seven," men appointed to administer the social service program of the Jerusalem church. Stephen's talents quickly showed him to be a persuasive public speaker and a powerful miracle worker. He quickly ran afoul of the Jewish authorities in Jerusalem. In spite of a masterful presentation of his faith, Stephen was interrupted by a furious mob, charged with blasphemy, and stoned to death.

One of the approving bystanders was Saul of Tarsus. Stephen was the first to understand the implications of the gospel which were later developed by Paul, the Apostle. ACTS 6:5—7:59; 8:2; 11:19; 22:20

SUAH An ancient and obscure man in the tribe of Asher, Suah was a son of Zophah, and one of the clan chieftains listed by the Chronicler. I CHRONICLES 7:36

SUSANNA One of the group of women who provided for Jesus and His disciples, Susanna was apparently a woman of some means, perhaps a widow. There are unfortunately no records of how she met Jesus, who she was, or what she did. LUKE 8:3

SUSI A member of the tribe of Manasseh, Susi was remembered as the father of Gaddi, the spy representing Manasseh who was one of the twelve spies in the reconnaissance patrol sent into Canaan by Moses. NUMBERS 13:11

SYMEON See SIMEON

SYNTYCHE A woman who was prominent in the Christian congregation at Philippi, Syntyche was urged by Paul to settle her feud with Euodia, also in the Philippian church. Syntyche was probably a well-to-do deaconess. Her disagreement with Euodia had grown to the point where it threatened to split the Philippian church. PHILIPPIANS 4:2

T

TABBAOTH A Temple servant, Tabbaoth was the ancestral head of a family that returned with Zerubbabel to Jerusalem after the Exile. EZRA 2:43; NEHEMIAH 7:46

TABEAL See TABEEL 1

TABEEL
1 The father of an unnamed man whom the rulers of Syria and Ephraim wanted to make king of Judah instead of Ahaz, this Tabeel is a puzzle to scholars. Some think that the "son of Tabeel" might have been Rezin, king of Damascus. Others, pointing out that the Hebrew text was set so that the name was pronounced "Tabeal" or "good for nothing," think that Isaiah may have been punning. ISAIAH 7:6
2 A Persian official stationed at Samaria at the time the Jews were returning to Jerusalem after the Exile, this Tabeel was one of those who wrote King Artaxerxes of Persia a letter with the false accusation that the Jews' rebuilding of Jerusalem's walls was a sign of rebelliousness. EZRA 4:7

TABITHA See DORCAS

TABRIMMON A ruler of the city-state of Damascus, Tabrimmon is best remembered as the father of King Ben Hadad, contemporary to King Asa of Judah. I KINGS 15:18

TAHAN
1 A son of Ephraim, Tahan was the ancestral head of a family-clan in that tribe known as Tahanites. NUMBERS 26:35
2 A descendant of 1 four generations later, this Tahan was another little-known chief in the tribe of Ephraim. He was one of Joshua's ancestors. I CHRONICLES 7:25

TAHASH One of Nahor's sons, Tahash was Abraham's nephew and the reputed founder of an Aramean clan. GENESIS 22:34

TAHATH

1 A Levite of the Kohath side of the tribe, this Tahath was the ancestor of such notables as Samuel, the prophet, and Heman, the singer. I CHRONICLES 6:24, 37

2 A great-grandson of Ephraim, this Tahath is one of the clan chieftains listed in the tribal genealogy by the Chronicler. I CHRONICLES 7:20

3 A grandson of **2**, this man is another person who is simply a name on a list to us. He is carried on the tribal records as a leader of Ephraim. I CHRONICLES 7:20

TAMAH See TEMAH

TAHPENES Wife of an unnamed pharaoh of Egypt at the time of Solomon, Tahpenes and her immediate family were pawns in the international chess game. Tahpenes' sister was married off by the pharaoh to Solomon's enemy, Hadad the Edomite. I KINGS 11:19, 20

TAHREA A descendant of Saul through Jonathan's one surviving son, Mephibosheth, Tahrea is listed in the genealogy of the house of Saul. I CHRONICLES 8:35; 9:41

TALMAI

1 One of the huge sons of the giant Anak, Talmai and his brothers lived in the area of Hebron. When Moses' spies saw Talmai and his family, they were so frightened that all except Caleb and Joshua advised against trying to invade Canaan. In the invasion, however, Talmai was driven out of Hebron by Caleb's clan from Judah. NUMBERS 13:22; JOSHUA 15:14; JUDGES 1:10

2 David's father-in-law, this Talmai was the king of Geshur and father of Maacah. David's marriage to Maacah was most likely engineered to cement cordial relations between Talmai and David. Talmai offered his grandson Absalom refuge after Amnon's murder. II SAMUEL 3:3; 13:37; I CHRONICLES 3:2

TALMON A Levite, Talmon was the head of a family of gatekeepers at the Temple in Jerusalem in Ezra's time. I CHRONICLES 9:17; EZRA 2:42; NEHEMIAH 7:45; 11:19; 12:25

TAMAR

1 Judah's daughter-in-law, Tamar was a Canaanite woman originally married to Judah's son, Er. After Er's death, Tamar was married to Onan until he, too, died. By law and custom, Tamar should have been given to Judah's next surviving son, Shelah. When Judah reneged on his obligation to Tamar, she disguised herself as a harlot to secure her rights, and became the mother of Judah's twin sons, Perez and Zerah. GENESIS 38; RUTH 4:12; I CHRONICLES 2:4

2 The beautiful daughter of David, this Tamar was raped by her half-brother Amnon. Her brother Absalom vowed revenge, and killed Amnon, triggering a chain reaction of domestic problems in David's household which culminated in Absalom's revolt. II SAMUEL 13; I CHRONICLES 3:9

3 A daughter of Absalom, this third Tamar married King Rehoboam, Solomon's son and successor. Some scholars identify this woman with Rehoboam's wife Maacah. II SAMUEL 14:27

TANHUMETH One who lived during the collapse of Judah after the Babylonian invasion, Tanhumeth was the father of Seraiah, one of the leaders of small Israelite detachments which eluded capture by the Babylonians and escaped to Gedaliah at Mizpeh. II KINGS 25:23; JEREMIAH 40:8

TAPHATH One of Solomon's daughters, Taphath married Benabinadab, a top civil servant in Solomon's ranks who had charge of one of Solomon's twelve administrative districts. I KINGS 4:11

TAPPUA See TAPPUAH

TAPPUAH An early leader in the Jerahmeel branch of the tribe of Judah, Tappuah was mentioned in the family tree as a son of Hebron. I CHRONICLES 2:43

TAREA See TAHREA

TARSHISH
1 One of Noah's great-grandsons, this Tarshish was a son of Javan and the alleged ancestor of the peoples who wandered to the then-remote areas of the western Mediterranean. GENESIS 10:4; I CHRONICLES 1:7
2 One of Benjamin's great grandsons, this Tarshish was a son of Bilhan and was a warrior and family-head in the earliest days of the tribe of Benjamin. I CHRONICLES 7:10

3 This Tarshish was one of the seven advisors to King Ahasuerus of Persia, and one of the few privileged to be in the king's presence. ESTHER 1:14

TARTAN The title, not the proper name, of the commander of the Assyrian forces, the Tartan had charge of Sargon's campaign in Palestine and later was one of the trio of arrogant officials who demanded that King Hezekiah surrender Jerusalem to the Assyrian King Sennacherib. The tartans, in Assyrian inscriptions, stood next to the kings themselves. I KINGS 18:17; ISAIAH 20:1

TATNAI See TATTENAI

TATTENAI A Persian governor, Tattenai ruled the area of northern Palestine at the time the Jews were beginning to rebuild Jerusalem after the Exile. Tattenai was uneasy about the designs of the Jews and wrote to Darius asking that he search the records to find out whether or not Cyrus had given permission to rebuild Jerusalem. EZRA 3:5; 6; 6:6, 13

TEBAH One of Abraham's nephews, Tebah was a son of Nahor and was the ancestor-founder of an ancient Aramean clan and town carrying his name. GENESIS 22:24

TEBALIAH A Levite of the Merari side of the tribe, Tebaliah, a son of Hosah, served as a gatekeeper in the Jerusalem sanctuary in David's day. I CHRONICLES 26:11

TEHINNAH An ancient clan head in the tribe of Judah, Tehinnah is listed as the father of Irnahash, and a resident of the village of Recah. I CHRONICLES 4:12

TELAH The father of Tahan 2 Telah was an obscure family chief in the tribe of Ephraim. I CHRONICLES 7:25

TELEM A Levite gatekeeper who married outside the faith during the Exile, Telem agreed to observe Ezra's strict rule against inter-faith marriages when returning to Jerusalem. EZRA 10:24

TEMA One of Ishmael's twelve sons, Tema was the alleged ancestor of the Arabian tribe of traders and founder of the famous oasis-town on the ancient caravan route which carried his name. GENESIS 25:15; I CHRONICLES 1:30

TEMAH A Temple servant, Temah was the ancestral head of a family which returned to Jerusalem after the Exile. EZRA 2:53; NEHEMIAH 7:55

TEMAN A son of Eliphaz, Esau's son, Teman was an ancient chieftain among the Edomites. His family, the Temanites, were a group renowned for their wisdom who lived in the Arabian peninsula. GENESIS 36; I CHRONICLES 1:36, 53

TERAH Abraham's father, Terah left Ur, the cultured and civilized Chaldean capital, after his son Haran's death, with Abraham, Sarah, and Lot. He originally planned to go to Canaan, but settled instead in Haran, where he died at the age of 205. Like everyone else at the time, he "served other gods." GENESIS 11; JOSHUA 24:2, I CHRONICLES 1:26

TERESH One of Persian King Ahasuerus' palace staff, Teresh plotted with Bigthan to kill Ahasuerus. Esther's cousin, Mordecai, discovered the plot and reported it. Teresh was hanged. ESTHER 2:21; 6:2

TERTIUS The man to whom Paul dictated the Epistle to the Romans, Tertius was a companion and secretary of Paul at Corinth. He added his own personal postscript to Paul's letter to send a greeting to the Christians at Rome. ROMANS 16:22

TERTELLUS An attorney well-versed in Roman law, Tertellus was hired by the Sanhedrin at Jerusalem to present charges against Paul before the Roman governor, Felix, at Caesarea. Tertellus was typical of the Italian lawyers who lived in the provinces at the time, selling their services to local people unused to Roman courts. His presentation to Felix was a masterpiece of flattery toward Felix and full of allegations that Paul disturbed the peace and profaned the Temple. ACTS 24:1, 2

THADDAEUS See JUDAS 6

THAHASH See TAHASH

THAMAH See TEMAH

THAMAR See TAMAR

THARA See TERAH

THEOPHILUS The man for whom Luke wrote his gospel account and the Acts of the Apostles, Theophilus was an educated Gentile who was either a serious inquirer or recent convert to Christianity. Luke addresses him respectfully with the words "most excellent," implying that Theophilus was an important Roman official or a member of the equestrian order. LUKE 1:3; ACTS 1:1

THEUDAS A fiery, well-known Jewish nationalist, Theudas whipped a group of fanatics into attempting to revolt against Rome in the early part of the first century A.D. Theudas and four hundred followers were ruthlessly cut down by the troops of the Roman procurator, Fadus. Theudas was mentioned by Gamaliel in a speech before the Sanhedrin when the Sanhedrin was considering reprisals against the earliest Christians. ACTS 5:34—36

THOMAS Jesus' disciple who was known as "the twin," Thomas was more than a sullen skeptic or "doubter." When Jesus announced at Bethany His plans to continue to Jerusalem, Peter fussily protested, but Thomas bravely said, "Let us also go that we may die with Him." At the Last Supper, Thomas, wanting to stay with Jesus, asked how they could know the way. The crucifixion, however, demolished his faith. Thomas was absent when the risen Jesus first appeared to the disciples, and unable to believe their reports. When he was confronted by the living Lord and commanded to touch the wound-prints, Thomas was convinced. An apocryphal book, "The Acts of Thomas," dating from the

second century, tells how Thomas was sent to India as the slave of an Indian merchant, and founded the Christian community there. The Mar Thoma Church in India today maintains that it has descended from this group evangelized by Thomas. MATTHEW 10:3; MARK 3:18; LUKE 6:15; JOHN 11:16; 14:5; 20:24—29; 21:2; ACTS 1:13

TIBERIUS A stepson of the emperor Augustus, Tiberius was the "Caesar" referred to by Jesus. Tiberius, from 12 A.D. to 14 A.D. was military governor of the provinces. Upon Augustus' death in 14 A.D., Tiberius stepped in as successor and, like Augustus, took the title "emperor." He was a gifted administrator and ruled reasonably well during his twenty-three year reign. During his last ten years, however, he lived mostly as a spoiled and sensuous playboy on the Isle of Capri. LUKE 3:1

TIBNI Omri's rival for the throne after Zimbri's seven-day reign, Tibni fought and schemed for four years to grab the throne of Israel. He attracted a large following and kept the country in the turmoil of a civil war until Omri's forces won out and Tibni died. I KINGS 16:21, 22

TIDAL One of the "four kings" who attacked five heads of ancient city-states in the Dead Sea area, Tidal fought under Chedorlaomer and defeated the five opponents. Tidal, the king of Goiim, and his allies were carrying away the loot and prisoners, including Lot, when pursued by Abraham's forces coming to free Lot. GENESIS 14:1—9

TIGLATH-PILESER The name of several Assyrian kings, the ruler in the Bible was Tiglath-Pileser III. He was actually named Pulu or Pul, and assumed the name of the 12th century B.C. king, Tiglath-Pileser, after usurping the throne in 745 B.C. An excellent organizer, he developed the most awesome war machine of the time and established a well-planned and well-administered empire. His campaigns were models of efficiency and ruthlessness. Tiglath-Pileser exacted tribute from every ruler from Babylon to the Mediterranean. When Pekah of Israel and Rezin of Damascus attacked Ahaz of Judah because Ahaz would not join in a revolt against Assyria, Tiglath-Pileser rushed to Ahaz's defense and pulverized Palestine. The large scale deportations of tribes was first used during Tiglath-Pileser's reign. He died in 727 B.C. II KINGS 15:19, 29; 16:7, 10; I CHRONICLES 5:6, 26; II CHRONICLES 28:20

TIKVAH
1 The father-in-law of Huldah the prophetess, this Tikvah was Sallum's father. II KINGS 22:14; II CHRONICLES 34:22
2 This second Tikvah was the father of Jahzeiah, Ezra's associate, who kept the record of those who had married outside the faith during the Exile. EZRA 10:15

TILON A descendant of Caleb, Moses' spy, Tilon was a son of Shimon and was a family head in the tribe of Judah. I CHRONICLES 4:20

TIMAEUS Probably a native of Jericho, Timaeus was the father of a well-known blind beggar who sat by the roadside until healed by Jesus. MARK 10:46

TIMEUS See TIMAEUS

TIMNA
1 The concubine of Esau's son, Eliphaz, Timnah was the mother of Amalek, the ancestral head of the Amalekites. GENESIS 36:12
2 A relative of 1, or perhaps the same as 1, this Timna was the daughter of Seir and a sister of Lotan, ancient tribal chieftains in the area of Arabia later taken over by Esau's descendants, the Edomites. GENESIS 36:22; I CHRONICLES 1:39
3 A chief of the tribes of Edom, this Timna also was one of the shadowy figures in the earliest days of the Biblical narrative who was descended from Esau. GENESIS 36:40; I CHRONICLES 1:51
4 An obscure ancient Edomite clan head, probably the same as 3, this man was a grandson of Esau and a son of Eliphaz. I CHRONICLES 1:36

TIMNAH See TIMNA

TIMON An early member of the Jerusalem church, Timon was probably originally a Greek-speaking Jew, or Hellenist. When there were complaints that some of the needy were being neglected in the Christian community, Timon was one of the seven men set apart as "deacons" to serve the needs of the poor and widowed and handle the arrangements at the common meals. He was one of those quiet Christians who carried out his responsibilities without fanfare, and was not mentioned again in the New Testament. ACTS 6:5

TIMOTHEUS See TIMOTHY

TIMOTHY Son of the devout Jewish woman, Eunice, and a Greek father, Timothy was won to Jesus Christ when Paul preached in Lystra, Timothy's home town. Paul invited the young convert to accompany him on his second missionary journey, but had him circumcised to avoid undue criticism by sensitive Jews. Although young and timid, Timothy stayed behind at Beroea with Silas while Paul moved on to Athens and Corinth. He rejoined Paul, then was sent back to Thessalonica to strengthen the congregation there. After another sojourn with Paul, Timothy was sent to Corinth to straighten out some of the many problems distressing the young congregation there. Timothy later looked after Paul during Paul's imprisonment. Timothy subsequently was asked to go to Ephesus to represent Paul, and received the two letters from Paul that bear Timothy's name. Timothy, these letters reveal, was like a son to Paul. The last word in the New Testament about this sensitive, sickly, but faithful young helper was that he was imprisoned but finally released. ACTS 16:1; 17:14, 15; 18:5; 19:22; 20:4; ROMANS 16:21; I CORINTHIANS 4:17; 16:10; II CORINTHIANS 1:1, 19; COLOSSIANS 1:1; I THESSALONIANS 1:1; 3:2, 6; II THESSALONIANS 1:1; I and II TIMOTHY; PHILEMON 1; HEBREWS 13:23

TIRAS One of Noah's grandsons and one of Japheth's sons, Tiras was probably the alleged ancestor of an ancient maritime people, the "Tursenoi," or perhaps was the founder of Tarsus, Paul's native city. GENESIS 10:2; I CHRONICLES 1:5

TIRHAKAH A resourceful Ethiopian prince who perennially challenged Assyria's claims, Tirhakah governed for Ethiopian Kings Shabaka and Shabataka in the Nile delta. During this assignment, Tirhakah faced three Assyrian armies—first, Sennacherib's, second and third, Esarhaddon's—and was finally defeated. In spite of his defeat, Tirhakah plotted with the delta strongmen to try again to throw out the Assyrians. He died in 663 B.C. without regaining power. II KINGS 19:9; ISAIAH 37:9

TIRHANAH A son of Caleb, son of Hezron, by his concubine, Maacah, Tirhanah was one of the early members of the tribe of Judah who were clan chiefs. I CHRONICLES 2:48

TIRIA A descendant of Moses' great spy, Caleb, Tiria was a member of the tribe of Judah, and was a son of Jehallelel. I CHRONICLES 4:16

TIRZAH Zelophehad's youngest daughter, Tirzah and her sister successfully protested the inequities of the rules then in use regarding distribution of the property of a man who died without sons. Tirzah and her four sisters persuaded Moses to change the custom so that the daughters could receive a man's estate when he died without male issue.

TITUS

TITUS A Greek who was converted to Christianity by Paul, Titus became one of Paul's most trusted and able assistants. Although Paul earlier had insisted that Timothy be circumcised, he refused to allow Titus to be circumcised in order to demonstrate once and for all to the Judaistic party (then undermining Paul's work) that it is faith in Christ that saves. Paul presented Titus as living proof of this doctrine at the Jerusalem council. Titus continued to serve as Paul's preaching companion and trouble-shooter. He was particularly useful in straightening out problems in the churches at Corinth after Timothy had failed, at Ephesus, and later at Crete. The last mention of him in the New Testament, II Timothy 4:10, states that Paul planned to send Titus to Dalmatia. The early fathers and others link Titus closely to Crete, where he was supposed to have served as bishop and died. II CORINTHIANS 2:13; 7:6, 13, 14; 8:6, 16, 23; 12:18; GALATIANS 2:1, 3; II TIMOTHY 4:10; TITUS 1:4

TITIUS JUSTUS See JUSTUS 2

TITUS JUSTUS See JUSTUS 2

TOAH See NAHATH 2

TOB-ADONIJAH A prominent Levite in King Jehoshaphat's time, Tob-Adonijah was one of the party sent to the cities of Judah to give a cram-course in the meaning of the Law during Jehoshaphat's brief reform. II CHRONICLES 17:8

TOBIAH

1 One whose descendants returned to Jerusalem after the Exile, Tobiah and his family had the misfortune and stigma of not being able to trace their ancestry and thus establish their relationship to one of the tribes. EZRA 2:60; NEHEMIAH 7:62

2 A half-Jewish Ammonite who tried to thwart Nehemiah's plans to rebuild Jerusalem after the Exile, this Tobiah had important family connections in Jerusalem and stirred up opposition against Nehemiah. He was thrown out of his quarters in the Temple by Nehemiah, and joined Sanballat, the Persian governor, in protests to the Persian king that Nehemiah was plotting revolt. NEHEMIAH 2:10, 19; 4:3, 7; 6:1—19; 13:4—8

TOBIJAH

1 A well-known Levite in King Jehoshaphat's day, this Tobijah was one of those sent to the villages of Judah to instruct the people on the meaning of the Law when Jehoshaphat belatedly discovered how slack the moral fiber of the nation had become. II CHRONICLES 17:8

2 A member of the party from Babylon which returned to Jerusalem with gifts of silver and gold from the exiled Jews, this man and the others presented their treasures to Zerubbabel, who had an expensive crown fashioned out of them. ZECHARIAH 6:10, 14

TOGARMAH Noah's great-grandson,

Togarmah was descended through Japheth and Gomer and was the alleged ancestor of the people in the area of western Armenia. GENESIS 10:3 I CHRONICLES ˎ1:6; EZEKIEL 27:14; 38:6

TOHU See NAHATH 2

TOI See TOU

TOKHATH See TIKVAH

TOLA
1 One of Issachar's sons, Tola emigrated from Canaan when Jacob's clan went to Egypt because of famine. His family, the Tolaites, were part of the group that went out to the wilderness with Moses. GENESIS 46:13; NUMBERS 26:23; I CHRONICLES 7:1, 2
2 A minor judge of Israel, this Tola was one of the series of tribal strongmen who rallied the loose confederation of tribes from time to time in the period after the conquest of Canaan until the establishment of the monarchy. He was a descendant of **1** in the tribe of Issachar, and spent most of his life in the tribal lands of Ephraim. JUDGES 10:1

TOU A king of the city-state of Hamath in Syria, Tou sent gifts and congratulations to David after David defeated Hadadezer, Tou's longtime enemy. Tou placed himself under David as a vassal-king. II SAMUEL 8:9; I CHRONICLES 18:9, 10

TROPHIMUS One of the two-man delegation from the church at Ephesus chosen to represent that congregation and carry its offerings to Jerusalem, Trophimus and Tychicus joined Paul's party at Macedonia. In Jerusalem, Trophimus was indirectly the cause of Paul's arrest (the mob wrongly assumed that Paul had taken Gentile Trophimus into the Temple). On the voyage to Rome, Trophimus took ill and had to be left at Miletus. Early non-Biblical records state that Trophimus was martyred at Rome during Nero's persecution. ACTS 20:4; 21:9; II TIMOTHY 4:20

TRYPHAENA A woman member of the Christian community at Rome who was respected for her tireless labors for the Lord, Tryphaena was one of those mentioned by name to whom Paul wished special greetings to be given when he wrote to Rome. The name Tryphaena occurs in an inscription of the imperial household in Rome. A wealthy woman of a leading family of rulers in Pontus who was related to the emperor's family was known as "the queen Tryphaena," and received prominent mention in the apocryphal book, "Acts of Paul and Thecla." It is possible that the Tryphaena listed by Paul might have been identical to one or both of these Tryphaenas. ROMANS 16:12

TRYPHOSA Like Tryphaena, Tryphosa was one of the women in the Roman church singled out by name for a personal greeting by Paul at the close of his letter to the Romans, Tryphosa is mentioned in the same Latin inscriptions with Tryphaena as names of members of the imperial household, hinting that she, too, was a believer with high family connections and money who was highly esteemed in the Roman church for her help. ROMANS 16:12

TUBAL Noah's grandson and Japheth's son, Tubal was the reputed ancestor of the race that settled in the mountains southeast of the Black Sea. GENESIS 10:2; I CHRONICLES 1:5

TUBAL-CAIN The first metalworker, according to the ancients, Tubal-Cain was Lamech's son and was skilled at the art of forging copper and iron weapons and tools. GENESIS 4:22

TYCHICUS A Gentile convert from Ephesus, Tychicus was selected with Trophimus to take the offerings from the Ephesian congregation and join Paul's party journeying to Jerusalem. After Paul's arrest, imprisonment, and trip to Rome, Tychicus was a useful messenger and representative for Paul to various churches. He carried Paul's letters to the Ephesians and the Colossians, and possibly the second letter to the Corinthians. Whether Tychicus got to Crete, as Paul hoped, we do not know. Legend has it that Tychicus became bishop of Chalcedon in Asia Minor, and died a martyr. ACTS 20:4; EPHESIANS 6:21; COLOSSIANS 4:7; II TIMOTHY 4:12; TITUS 3:12

TYRANNUS An influential philosopher-teacher in Ephesus who operated a well-known academy, Tyrannus welcomed Paul and allowed him to teach daily after Paul was forbidden to speak in the local synagogue. Tyrannus had some tie with the synagogue and had been impressed with Paul's message. Paul was permitted to use the school during the afternoon hours when the premises would ordinarily be vacant, since classes were usually held during the cooler morning hours. ACTS 19:9

U

UEL One of the family of Bani, Uel married outside the faith during the Exile in Babylon, but consented to put away his wife to keep the faith pure when returning to Jerusalem. EZRA 10:34

ULAM
1 One of Manasseh's great-grandsons, this Ulam, a son of Sheresh, was another early clan head in the tribe. I CHRONICLES 7:16
2 A relative of Saul, this Ulam was the head of a large and fierce family of fighters in the tribe of Benjamin who were noted for their prowess as archers. I CHRONICLES 8:39, 40

ULLA A clan head in the tribe of Asher in the early days, Ulla was a warrior-chief remembered in the tribal genealogy. I CHRONICLES 7:39

UNNI
1 A Levite in David's time, Unni was a well-known musician and gatekeeper who was appointed to a prominent position in the worship services in the Tabernacle. I CHRONICLES 15:18, 20
2 For the Unni mentioned in some translations of Nehemiah 12:9, see UNNO

UNNO A Levite, Unno and his family were members of the first party to return to Jerusalem after the Exile and accompanied Zerubbabel. NEHEMIAH 12:9

URBANE See URBANUS

URBANUS One whom Paul referred to as "our fellow worker," Urbanus was singled out for special personal greeting at the close of Paul's Roman letter. Little is known about him except that he was an active Christian at Rome. Because the name turns up in Roman inscriptions of lists of the emperor's slaves, some have suggested that Urbanus might have been one of the imperial household. Legend has embroidered the brief mention of his name in Romans with improbable exploits. ROMANS 16:9

URI

1 An ancient member of the tribe of Judah, Uri, son of Hur, was the father of Bezalel, the skilled artisan-designer commissioned by Moses to help fashion the tabernacle. EXODUS 31:2; 35:30; 38:22; I CHRONICLES 2:20; II CHRONICLES 1:5

2 This second Uri was remembered as the father of Geber, one of Solomon's twelve commissary officers. I KINGS 4:19

3 A porter from the Temple, Uri was one of the many who married a non-Jew during the Exile in Babylon. He abided by Ezra's strict orders against taking such spouses back to Jerusalem. EZRA 10:24

URIAH

1 An upright, loyal soldier in David's army, Uriah was treacherously allowed to be killed on David's orders so that David could possess Uriah's attractive wife, Bathsheba. He was such an outstanding warrior that he was named to "The Thirty," David's elite troop. When David granted Uriah special leave in a cheap attempt to make Uriah, not David, appear to be the father of Bathsheba's unborn child, Uriah insisted on maintaining his military discipline and thus upset David's tawdry plans. He was a Hittite, a descendant of the earliest inhabitants of Palestine, but loyal to both David's government and David's God. II SAMUEL 11:12; I KINGS 15:5; I CHRONICLES 11:41

2 A high priest in Jerusalem in Ahaz's time, this Uriah willingly went along with King Ahaz' proposal to build an altar in Jerusalem patterned after the pagan altar that had struck Ahaz' fancy during a visit to Damascus. Although he seems to have been Ahaz's yes-man, Isaiah called on Uriah to witness to the fact that Isaiah had written the words "The spoil speeds, the prey hastes" before Isaiah's child was conceived. II KINGS 16; ISAIAH 8:2

3 A son of Shemaiah of Kiriath-jearim, this Uriah was a friend and disciple of Jeremiah. His prophecies against Judah's policies were so critical that he was forced to flee to Egypt during King Jehoiakim's reign. Jehoiakim arranged to have Uriah extradited to Jerusalem, executed, and insulted by burial in the common pit reserved for outcasts. JEREMIAH 26: 20—23

4 A priest, this Uriah was the father of Meremoth, a prominent priest during the Exile who brought the sacred vessels back to Jerusalem and helped rebuild two sections of the wall. EZRA 8:33; NEHEMIAH 3:4

5 Another Uriah in Jerusalem shortly after the return from Babylon, this man was a prominent Levite who was given a place of honor on the platform when Ezra called the great national assembly to read the Law to all the people. NEHEMIAH 8:4

URIJAH See URIAH

URIAS See URIAH

URIEL
1 A Levite who was descended from Kohath, this Uriel, a son of Tahath, took a prominent part in the festivities when David brought the Ark to Jerusalem from Obed-edom's house. I CHRONICLES 6:24; 15:5, 11
2 A man from Gibeah, this Uriel was father of Maacah **3**, and King Rehoboam's father-in-law. II CHRONICLES 13:2

UTHAI
1 A son of Ammihud of the tribe of Judah, this Uthai was the head of a family that was one of the first to return to devastated Jerusalem to rebuild the city and live there. I CHRONICLES 9:4
2 One of the members of the party returning to live in Jerusalem with Ezra after the Exile in Babylon, this Uthai was identified as one of Bigvai's sons. EZRA 8:14

UZAI This man was remembered as the father of Palal, one of those who worked with Nehemiah to rebuild the walls of Jerusalem. NEHEMIAH 3:25

UZAL A descendant of Shem. Noah's son, Uzal was the sixth of Joktan's thirteen sons, and the reputed founder-ancestor of the people who wandered south on the Arabian peninsula and settled near Yemen. GENESIS 10:27; I CHRONICLES 1:21

UZZA See also UZZAH
1 An obscure member of the tribe of Benjamin, this Uzza is listed in the tribal records as a son of Heglam and the head of a family. I CHRONICLES 8:7
2 A Temple servant, this Uzza was the ancestral head of a family which returned after the Exile to Jerusalem with Zerubbabel. EZRA 2:49; NEHEMIAH 7:51
3 An unknown Uzza, this man had a garden which was the burial place for two of Judah's worst kings, Manasseh and Amon. II KINGS 21:18, 26

UZZAH See also UZZA
1 The son of Abinadab who irreverently grabbed the Ark to steady it during the trip from Kiriath-jearim to Jerusalem, Uzzah suddenly collapsed and died. Uzzah's death was popularly believed to be divine punishment for handling the sacred Ark so sacrilegiously, and put a stop for a time to David's plans to bring the Ark to Jerusalem. II SAMUEL 6:3—8; I CHRONICLES 13:7—11
2 A Levite of the Merari branch of the tribe, this Uzzah, a son of Shimei, was an ancient family head in the tribe. I CHRONICLES 6:29

UZZI
1 One of Aaron's descendants through Phinehas, this Uzzi was a priest with an outstanding pedigree who was listed among the roll of notables in the tribe of Levi. I CHRONICLES 6:5, 6, 51; EZRA 7:4
2 One of Issachar's grandsons, Uzzi was one of the earliest clan chiefs recorded in the tribal records. I CHRONICLES 7:2, 3
3 Another early clan chieftain, this man was one of Benjamin's grandsons

and one of Bela's sons. I CHRONICLES 7:7; 9:8

4 A Levite who was part of Bani's family, this Uzzi was placed in charge of all the Levites in Jerusalem after the return from Exile in Babylon in Nehemiah's day. NEHEMIAH 11:22

5 A priest in Jerusalem after the Exile at the time Joiakim was high priest, this Uzzi served in the Temple as a representative of the house of Jedaiah, an illustrious family of priests, and took a leading part in the impressive service when Nehemiah dedicated the rebuilt walls of the city. NEHEMIAH 12:19, 42

UZZIA An Ashterathite, Uzzia was one of David's most valiant fighting men, and was listed in the roll of most outstanding army heroes. I CHRONICLES 11:44

UZZIAH

1 Amaziah's son and successor as king of Judah, Uzziah became king at the age of sixteen and ruled fifty-two years. During his long reign, he successfully defended Judah against the belligerent Ammonites, Philistines, and Arabians, developed a strong standing army, and rebuilt the nation's fortifications. Uzziah even reopened the Red Sea port of Elath for his nation, and promoted commerce. In spite of the continuation of the cults, contemporary historians gave Uzziah high marks for his religious devotion. He was so crippled with leprosy toward the end of his reign that he was forced to turn over the government to his son, Jotham. II KINGS 15; II CHRONICLES 26; 27:2; ISAIAH 1:1; 6:1; 7:1; HOSEA 1:1; AMOS 1:1; ZECHARIAH 14:5

2 A son of Uriel **1**, this Uzziah was also a Levite of the Kohath branch of the tribe, and head of a prominent family in the tribe. I CHRONICLES 6:24

3 This third man was the father of the Jonathan who was overseer of David's warehouses. I CHRONICLES 27:25

4 A priest at the time of the Exile in Babylon, this person made the mistake of marrying outside the faith, but obeyed Ezra in order to keep the faith pure by returning to Jerusalem without his Babylonian wife. EZRA 10:21

5 A member of the tribe of Judah, this Uzziah was remembered as the father of Athaiah, a chief of the province who offered to live in Jerusalem when the exiles returned to Palestine after the sojourn in Babylon. NEHEMIAH 11:4

UZZIEL

1 One of Levi's grandsons, Uzziel was a son of Kohath and the head of one of the oldest and most respected Levite families. His clan, the Uzzielites, were a prominent group within the Kohath Levites. EXODUS 6:18, 22; LEVITICUS 10:4; NUMBERS 3:19, 30; I CHRONICLES 6:2; 15:10; 23:12, 20; 24:24

2 A Simeonite chieftain, this Uzziel was one of the leaders of the armed horde from that tribe which threw the native Amalekites out of the pasturelands near Mount Seir and took the lands over for themselves during

King Hezekiah's reign. I CHRONICLES 4:42

3 One of Benjamin's grandsons, this Uzziel was a son of Bela. In spite of his distinguished ancestry, we know nothing about him except the names of his forbears and descendants, and that he was a clan head. I CHRONICLES 7:7

4 One of the sons of the great musician Heman, this man inherited his father's talents and was assigned a prominent role in David's sanctuary choir program. I CHRONICLES 25:4

5 A Levite who was a son of Jeduthun, this responsible leader helped repair the Temple and carry out a national reform during King Hezekiah's reign. II CHRONICLES 29:14

6 A son of Harhaiah, this man, like his father, was an artisan-craftman, or goldsmith, who pitched in with Nehemiah to rebuild the walls of Jerusalem after the Exile. NEHEMIAH 3:8

V

VAIZATHA One of the ten sons of Haman, the Persian prime minister who plotted a mass extermination of all the Jews in the country, Vaizatha was hung with the rest of his family when the plot was reported to King Ahasuerus by Queen Esther. ESTHER 9:9

VAJEZATHA See **VAIZATHA**

VANIAH A descendant of Bani, Vaniah was one of many in his family who decided to obey Ezra's rigid rule against interfaith marriages in Jerusalem after the Exile. EZRA 10:36

VASHNI The oldest son of the prophet Samuel, Vashni was a Levite of the Kohath branch of the tribe and father of the famous musician, Heman.

(In some translations he is called "Joel.") I CHRONICLES 6:28, 33

VASHTI King Ahasuerus' first queen, Vashti grew disgusted with her husband's boorish behavior and one night, when the king summoned her to display her beauty to his drunken guests at a banquet, refused to come. Enraged, Ahasuerus repudiated her as queen, and ordered his courtiers to find him another. Vashti was replaced by young Esther. ESTHER 1, 2

VOPHSI A man in the tribe of Naphtali, Vophsi was the father of Nahbi, the spy representing Naphtali sent to explore the Promised Land for Moses before leaving the wilderness. NUMBERS 13:14

Z

ZAAVAN A grandson of Seir, the Horite, Zaavan was an early leader of the Horites, the people inhabiting the portion of Trans-Jordan later occupied by Esau and his descendants, the Edomites. GENESIS 36:21; I CHRONICLES 1:42

ZABAD
1 A member of the tribe of Judah who could trace his lineage back through Jerahmeel and Perez, this Zabad had a half-Egyptian grandfather. I CHRONICLES 2:36, 37
2 A man named Zabad, a son of Ahlai, was listed among David's most valiant heroes. Because there is an Ahlai mentioned in the background of Zabad **1**, some have surmised that Zabad **1** and **2** were actually the same man. I CHRONICLES 11:41
3 A son of Tahath, this man was an early chieftain in the tribe of Ephraim who lived at the time of the invasion of Canaan by Joshua. Two of his kinsmen, Ezer and Elead, were killed while stealing cattle from Gath. I CHRONICLES 7:21
4 The son of an Ammonite woman and a Jewish father, this Zabad avenged the death of Jehoiada the priest's son, Zechariah, by helping to murder King Joash. He was a member of the household staff of Joash. II CHRONICLES 24:26
5 A member of Zattu's family who married outside the faith during the sojourn in Babylon, this person decided to abide by Ezra's strict rule against interfaith marriages when returning to Jerusalem, in order to keep the faith pure. EZRA 10:27
6 Another who did the same thing as **5**, this Zabad was a descendant of Hashum. EZRA 10:33
7 One of Nebo's family, this Zabad went through the same experiences as **5** and **6**. EZRA 10:43

ZABBAI

1 A member of Bebai's family who married a non-Jewish wife during the Exile, this Zabbai kept Ezra's regulation and left her behind when returning to Jerusalem. EZRA 10:28

2 Another who lived during the Exile, this Zabbai was the father of Baruch, one of those who helped Nehemiah rebuild the walls of Jerusalem. EZRA 2:9 (where he is called Zaccai); NEHEMIAH 3:20; 7:14 (called Zaccai)

ZABBUD A member of Bigvai's family, a prominent leader in the Jewish community in exile in Babylon, Zabbud was in the party that returned with Ezra to Jerusalem. EZRA 8:14

ZABDI

1 An early member of the tribe of Judah, this Zabdi was remembered primarily as the grandfather of Achan, the man who violated Joshua's strict rule against keeping loot. JOSHUA 1:7, 17, 18; I CHRONICLES 2:6 (where he was called Zimri)

2 One of the nine sons of Shimei, the Benjaminite chief, this Zabdi was a clan head who lived sometime around the time of the conquest of Canaan. I CHRONICLES 8:19

3 A Shiphmite, this Zabdi had charge of the grape production for David's wine cellars. I CHRONICLES 27:27

4 A Levite who was a son of Asaph, David's great musician, this Zabdi was recorded as the grandfather of Mattaniah, the Levite who led the prayers of thanksgiving in the Temple

after the Exile during Nehemiah's time. NEHEMIAH 11:17

ZABDIEL

1 A descendant of Perez in the tribe of Judah, this Zabdiel was proud to be the father of Jashobeam, the man who served as commander-in-chief of David's army division the first month of each year. I CHRONICLES 27:2

2 A son of Haggedolim, this Zabdiel was a priest in Jerusalem after the Exile in Nehemiah's time. He headed a group of one hundred twenty-eight priests who were respected as "mighty men of valor." NEHEMIAH 11:14

ZABUD The son of a priest named Nathan, Zabud was special assistant and confidential advisor to King Solomon. He was a man with tremendous influence in Jerusalem although he had little in the way of titles or power. I KINGS 4:5

ZACCAI   See ZABBAI 2

ZACCHAEUS The head of the well-paying tax office at Jericho, Zacchaeus was a loathed outcast in his home town because he had sold out to the hated Romans and become a tax collector. When Jesus came through Jericho, Zacchaeus was forced to climb a tree to get a glimpse of Him. Jesus shocked everyone by inviting Himself to eat at Zacchaeus' house. Zacchaeus responded later by offering four times as much as he had collected to those whom he had defrauded. As usual, there are a host of unreliable traditions about Zacchaeus' later career, such as that he travelled with Peter and served as bishop of Caesarea. LUKE 19

ZACCHUR See ZACCUR

ZACCUR

1 A member of the tribe of Reuben, this Zaccur was the father of Shammua, one of the twelve spies sent by Moses into the Promised Land. NUMBERS 13:4

2 A son of Hamuel in the tribe of Simeon, this man was the father of the prolific Shimei, the man with sixteen sons and six daughters. I CHRONICLES 4:26

3 A Levite of the Merari side of the tribe, this person headed a family of Levites which served in David's sanctuary. I CHRONICLES 24:27

4 Another Levite, this Zaccur was the son of the distinguished Asaph, David's great musician, and inherited his father's talent and station as head of a family of singers in the Temple. Zaccur was chosen by lot to head the third contingent of musicians who played and prophesied in the worship services. I CHRONICLES 25:2, 10; NEHEMIAH 12:35

5 A son of Imri, this man worked on the walls of Jerusalem near those who were rebuilding some of the gates under Nehemiah's leadership. NEHEMIAH 3:2

6 Another by the same name who lived at the same time as **5,** this Zaccur was a Levite and one who joined Nehemiah in signing the solemn covenant promising to keep the Law. NEHEMIAH 10:12

7 For the Zaccur mentioned in some translations of Ezra 8:14, see ZABBUD

8 Probably the same as **6,** one named Zaccur was the father of Hanan, an assistant treasurer of the Temple storehouses in Nehemiah's time. NEHEMIAH 13:13

ZACHARIAH See ZECHARIAH

ZACHARIAS

1 The father of John the Baptist, Zacharias was a priest belonging to the order or family of Abijah, one of the twenty-four contingents of priests. He served at the Temple in Jerusalem twice a year, for about a week each time. While on duty, he had a vision that he would finally be blessed with a son. The experience left him without speech until after the birth of John the Baptist. Zacharias was unsympathetic to the comfortable, power-loving Sadducee party of priests in Jerusalem. LUKE 1; 3:2

2 For others named Zacharias, see ZECHARIAH

ZACHER See ZECHARIAH 1

ZADOK

1 One of the two head priests who jointly presided in David's sanctuary in Jerusalem, Zadok, like his colleague Abiathar, was a loyal servant of David. Zadok and Abiathar wanted to stay with David when David was forced to flee from his capital during Absalom's revolt, but were sent back to be David's informants. In David's last days, Zadok backed Solomon, while Abiathar backed Solomon's rival, Adonijah. When Solomon became king, Abiathar was retired in disgrace, and Zadok was promoted to a position of great prominence as head of the Jerusalem priesthood. II SAMUEL 8:17;

357

15:24—36; 17:15; 18:19, 27; 19:11; 20:25; I KINGS 1; 2:35; 4:2, 4; I CHRONICLES 6:8, 53; 15:11; 16:39; 18:16; 24:3, 6, 31; 27:17; 29:22; II CHRONICLES 31:10; EZRA 7:2; EZEKIEL 40:46; 43:19; 44:15; 48:11

2 King Uzziah's father-in-law and King Jotham's maternal grandfather, this Zadok was father of Uzziah's wife, Jerusha. He must have been a person of prominence in Jerusalem, since such names were not usually given on the mother's side of the family. II KINGS 15:33; II CHRONICLES 27:1

3 A son of Baana, one of the first to settle in Jerusalem after the Exile, this Zadok helped Nehemiah rebuild the ruined walls of Jerusalem. NEHEMIAH 3:4

4 A son of Immer, this Zadok was a priest and scribe in Jerusalem during Nehemiah's time. He, too, helped repair the devastated city, and was later appointed as a member of the staff of the Temple treasury and storehouses. NEHEMIAH 3:29; 13:13

5 Neither a priest nor a Levite, but an important "chief of the people" after the Exile, this Zadok was one of the leaders in Jerusalem who joined Nehemiah in signing the covenant promising to keep the Law. NEHEMIAH 10:21

6 The name of a priest named Zadok appears in the Chronicler's list of top priests in I Chronicles 6:12, yet does not appear in Ezra's or Nehemiah's lists. This Zadok was probably a descendant of **1.** I CHRONICLES 6:12

7 Probably the same as **6,** a priest by the same name was listed as an ancestor of Azariah, one of the leading priests who returned to Jerusalem after the Exile, and a descendant of **1.** I CHRONICLES 9:11

8 A young warrior named Zadok headed a contingent of twenty-two fighters from his father's clan that joined David, then at Hebron struggling against Saul. The person referred to might have been a Levite, and possibly was Zadok **1.** I CHRONICLES 12:28

ZAHAM One of King Rehoboam's sons, Zaham was given passing mention in the list of Rehoboam's offspring. II CHRONICLES 11:19

ZALAPH One who lived during the Babylonian Exile, Zalaph was the father of Hanun, who helped Nehemiah rebuild Jerusalem. NEHEMIAH 3:30

ZALMON See ILAI

ZALMUNNA One of the chiefs of the Midianite hordes that oppressed Israel until Gideon's hand-picked three hundred drove them away, Zalmunna, with Zebah, another chief, complacently thought he had gotten away safely and congratulated himself on holding on to his loot. However, Zalmunna and Zebah were surprised by Gideon at Karkor, captured, returned to Gideon's home, and personally executed by Gideon in retaliation for the murder of his brothers. JUDGES 8; PSALM 83:11

ZANOAH An early descendant of Moses' spy Caleb, Zanoah, the son of Jekuthiel, was the alleged founder of the town in Judah by the same name. I CHRONICLES 4:18

ZARA See **ZERAH**

ZARAH See **ZERAH**

ZATTHU See **ZATTU**

ZATTU The ancestral head of a prominent family in Jerusalem after the Exile. Zattu's descendants were in the first party to return to Jerusalem and later joined with Nehemiah in sealing the covenant promising to keep the Law. EZRA 2:8; 10:27; NEHEMIAH 7:13; 10:14

ZAVAN See **ZAAVAN**

ZAZA A member of the tribe of Judah, Zaza is one of the names in the tedious genealogies of the tribe. He was a descendant of Jerahmeel. I CHRONICLES 2:33

ZEBADIAH
1 A chief of a family-clan in the tribe of Benjamin, this Zebadiah was a son of Beriah. I CHRONICLES 8:15
2 Another Benjaminite chief, this Zebadiah was a son of Elpaal. I CHRONICLES 8:17
3 One of the two sons of Jeroham of Gedor who joined David at Ziglag during David's struggle against Saul, this Zebadiah was one of a detachment of fierce Benjaminites, all of whom could fight expertly with either hand as archers and slingmen. I CHRONICLES 12:7
4 A Levite gatekeeper in David's sanctuary in Jerusalem, this Zebadiah was the third son of Meshelemiah and was a member of the Korah branch of his tribe. I CHRONICLES 26:2
5 A nephew of Joab, David's general, and a son of Asahel, this Zeba-diah was appointed a commander in David's standing army and put in charge of the fourth contingent on active duty. I CHRONICLES 27:7
6 A Levite, this man was one of those leading men of Judah appointed to conduct an intensive training program in the towns of Judah to instruct the people in the Law during Jehoshaphat's reform. II CHRONICLES 17:8
7 The son of Ishmael, a prominent official in Judah, this Zebadiah was head of the court to which all appeals dealing with non-religious matters were directed in King Hezekiah's time. II CHRONICLES 19:11
8 This man by the same name was a member of the second party of exiles to return to Jerusalem with Ezra. EZRA 8:8
9 One of the family of Immer who married a non-Jewish wife in Babylon, this Zebadiah obeyed Ezra and left her behind when returning to Jerusalem after the Exile. EZRA 10:20

ZEBAH A Midianite chief, Zebah, like Zalmunna, thought he had escaped with his life, and his loot, after Gideon routed the Midianite hosts. Zebah and Zalmunna, however, were surprised by another commando attack by Gideon, captured, returned to Gideon's home, and personally slain by Gideon in reprisal for their murder of Gideon's brothers. JUDGES 8; PSALM 83:11

ZEBEDEE The father of James and John, two of Jesus' closest associates in the disciple band, Zebedee was a fisherman on the Sea of Galilee. He apparently was a mildly successful businessman, and had hired servants and provided his wife, Salome, with money to help care for the needs of Jesus and His followers. He must have had dealings in Jerusalem, because John, his son, was known in the high priest's house. Some think that Zebedee died shortly after his sons became followers of Jesus. Some also think that like his sons, Zebedee might have been a disciple of John the Baptist. MATTHEW 4:21; 10:2; 20:20; 26:37; 27:56; MARK 1:19; 20; 3:17; 10:35; LUKE 5:10; JOHN 21:2

ZEBINA One of Nebo's family who married outside the faith during the Exile, Zebina returned to Jerusalem without his wife to keep the faith pure. EZRA 10:43

ZEBIDAH The wife of King Josiah of Judah, Zebidah was the mother of King Jehoiakim. II KINGS 23:36

ZEBUDAH See ZEBIDAH

ZEBUL The head of the occupation government placed by Abimelech in the city of Shechem, Zebul dealt with Gaal and a group of insurrectionists at Shechem by devising a clever ambush which ended the threat to Abimelech's power. JUDGES 9

ZEBULUN Jacob's tenth son, his sixth by Leah, Zebulun together with his three sons, emigrated with the rest of Jacob's clan to Egypt during the famine in Canaan. Jewish lore states that Zebulun was the first to be presented to the pharaoh by Joseph. His family, the Zebulunites, became known as one of the ten tribes, and

went out with Moses to the wilderness thus playing a role in the subsequent history of Israel. GENESIS 30:20; 35: 23; 46:14; 49:13; EXODUS 1:3; I CHRONICLES 2:1; numerous references to his tribe

ZECHARIAH
1 The eleventh of the twelve "minor prophets," Zechariah was the son of Berechiah and the grandson of Iddo, and lived and wrote in the days of Darius the Persian, when the exiled Jews were beginning to return to Jerusalem. His writings in the first eight chapters of Zechariah call on the returning Jews to be loyal to the Lord, reminding them of the judgment visited on their fathers. In eight visions, rich with symbolism, Zechariah prophesies that Israel's hopes of an age of the Messiah will come to pass, in spite of the discouraging setbacks. Zechariah helped inspire the forlorn band of returned exiles to rebuild Jerusalem and recreate a nation. Later writers, especially the author of Revelation, used Zechariah's apocalyptic material. ZECHARIAH 1:8; NEHEMIAH 12:16
2 Saul's uncle, this Zechariah was one of Jehiel's ten sons and a Benjaminite chief living at Gibeon. I CHRONICLES 8:31 (where he was called Zecher); 9:37
3 Meshelemiah's oldest son, this Zechariah was a Levite who served as a gatekeeper in David's sanctuary. I CHRONICLES 9:21; 26:2, 14
4 Another Levite by the same name, this man was a harp-player who served in the second order of musicians in

David's sanctuary. I CHRONICLES 15:18, 20; 16:5

5 A prominent priest in David's sanctuary, this Zechariah was one of seven who were permitted to blow the trumpet before the Ark of the Lord. I CHRONICLES 15:24

6 Another Levite in David's service, this person represented the family of Isshiah of the Kohath clan of Levites in the rotating roster of duty in the sanctuary. I CHRONICLES 24:25

7 A son of Hosah, this man was one of the Merarite Levites who chose the fourth turn of serving in the sanctuary. His shift was assigned a position at the west gate. I CHRONICLES 26:11

8 A member of the half tribe of Manasseh living east of the Jordan, this Zechariah was the father of Iddo, chief of the tribe when David conducted his census of the tribes. I CHRONICLES 27:21

9 One of the leaders of Judah, this prince by the same name was sent by King Jehoshaphat to conduct classes for adults in the towns of Judah. He taught the meaning of the Law during Jehoshaphat's reform. II CHRONICLES 17:7

10 A Levite, this Zechariah was the father of Jahaziel, the brave prophet who rallied King Jehoshaphat and the people of Judah during a national assembly called because of the threat of invasion by the desert tribes. II CHRONICLES 20:14

11 One of Jehoshaphat's sons who received a rich inheritance when his father died, this unfortunate prince was killed by his uneasy brother, Jehoram, who felt that any living brother might threaten to depose him as king and successor to Jehoshaphat. II CHRONICLES 21:2

12 The fearless son of the priest, Jehoiada, this Zechariah became a martyr and a deeply respected hero in Judah for his blunt words of warning to the nation. King Joash and other leaders engineered Zechariah's death by stoning in the Temple courtyard. II CHRONICLES 24:20; MATTHEW 23:35; LUKE 11:51

13 An advisor to King Uzziah in the first part of his long reign, this Zechariah was a prophet who tutored young Uzziah and influenced him to respect the Lord. II CHRONICLES 26:5

14 A son of King Jeroboam II of Israel, this Zechariah after ten years finally won the struggle for the throne of Israel. He scored low on morals and justice, however, and died as a result of Shallum's coup against him after ruling only six months. II KINGS 14:29; 15:8, 11

15 A contemporary of Isaiah, this Zechariah, a son of Jeberechiah, attested that Isaiah had indeed given his child the name "the spoil speeds, the prey hastes" even before the child was conceived as a dramatic way of warning the nation. Some scholars think this man may be the same as either **13, 16,** or **17.** ISAIAH 8:2

16 King Hezekiah's maternal grandfather, this man's daughter, Abi, married King Ahaz of Judah. II KINGS 18:2; II CHRONICLES 29:1

17 A Levite who was a descendant of Asaph, the great Temple musician in David's time, this Zechariah helped promote King Hezekiah's reform and assisted in repairing the Temple. II CHRONICLES 29:13

18 One of those who was carried off by the Assyrians in the mass deportations after the fall of Samaria and the collapse of the northern nation of Israel, this Zechariah was a relative of Beerah and a clan chief of the tribe of Reuben. I CHRONICLES 5:7

19 Another of the many Levites named Zechariah, this man was of the Kohath family in the tribe. He was appointed a supervisor of Temple renovations when King Josiah launched his intensive reform movement. II CHRONICLES 34:12

20 A contemporary of **19**, this Zechariah was a priest and a leading citizen in Judah. He was undoubtedly second-in-command (after Hilkiah, the chief priest) at the Temple in Josiah's time. II CHRONICLES 35:8

21 A friend of Ezra who joined Ezra's first party of exiles to return from Babylon to Jerusalem, this man was a descendant of Parosh and the head of a family of well-known Jews. EZRA 8:3

22 Another by the same name who lived at the same time as **21** and also accompanied Ezra back to Jerusalem, this Zechariah was one of the family of Bebai. EZRA 8:11

23 A distinguished leader of the Jewish community in exile at Babylon, this man was one of the group which Ezra sent to Iddo's "seminary" to request Levites to return to Jerusalem so that worship in the Temple could be resumed. EZRA 8:16

24 A member of the family of Elam, this individual was one of the many who married outside the faith during the Exile, but who obeyed Ezra's strict rule against interfaith marriage upon returning to Jerusalem. EZRA 10:26

25 A notable in Jerusalem after the Exile, this distinguished citizen was given a place of honor on the platform at Ezra's left when the great national assembly was held to hear Ezra read the Law. NEHEMIAH 8:4

26 The son of Amariah, scion of a distinguished family in the tribe of Judah, this Zechariah was the ancestor of Athaiah, one of those who returned to Jerusalem after the Exile. NEHEMIAH 11:4

27 Another blueblood in the tribe of Judah named Zechariah, this man was descended from Shelah, and was a forebear of Maaseiah, a clan head who brought his family back to Jerusalem after the Exile. NEHEMIAH 11:5

28 A priest who was a son of Pashur, a well-known priest when Zedekiah was king in Judah, this Zechariah was the ancestor of Adaiah, a priest in Nehemiah's time in Jerusalem. NEHEMIAH 11:12

29 Still another of the many Levites bearing the name, this one, a descendant of the musician Asaph, took a leading part in the impressive services when Nehemiah dedicated the rebuilt walls of Jerusalem. This Zechariah played one of the instruments carefully preserved from David's time. NEHEMIAH 12:35

30 One of the seven priests who were appointed to play trumpets at the rededication of the walls after the return from Babylon, this man might have been the same as **29.** NEHEMIAH 12:41

ZECHER See ZECHARIAH 2

ZEDEKIAH

1 One of King Ahab's four hundred paid yes-men "prophets," this Zedekiah willingly blessed Ahab's and Jehoshaphat's proposed invasion of Ramoth-gilead, using the usual prophets' religious jargon and props. When King Jehoshaphat insisted on hearing the report of any other prophets, Micaiah was brought in. Zedekiah mocked Micaiah and convinced the kings that Micaiah was the false prophet. As it turned out, Micaiah's dour predictions came true, and Zedekiah was revealed as the false prophet. I KINGS 22:11—24; II CHRONICLES 18:10—23

2 Another false prophet, this man, a son of Maaseiah, aroused Jeremiah's ire for his loose living and his glib prediction of a speedy return of the captive Jews to Jerusalem from Babylon. Nebuchadnezzar finally burnt this Zedekiah alive, probably for subversive activities in Babylon as a captive, just as Jeremiah had warned. JEREMIAH 29:21—23

3 One of the noblemen in King Jehoiakim's Jerusalem, this Zedekiah was a son of Hananiah. He was one of the audience that first heard Jeremiah's prophecy read, and urged that it be passed on to the king. JEREMIAH 36:12

4 The timid, inexperienced youngest son of Josiah who was put on the throne of Judah by the Babylonian conqueror, Nebuchadnezzar, this Zedekiah was the final king of Judah. He could not decide at first whether to listen to the anti-Babylon party of nobles who wanted to plot with others, or to Jeremiah and the prophets, cooler heads who advocated patience. He finally went along with the plans for a revolt. Nebuchadnezzar returned, smashed the rebellion, slew Zedekiah's family before his eyes, then blinded Zedekiah and kept him a prisoner in Babylon the rest of his life. II KINGS 24, 25; I CHRONICLES 3:15; II CHRONICLES 36:10—11; JEREMIAH 1:3; 21:1—7; 24:8; 27:3, 12; 28:1; 29:3; 32; 34; 37—39; 44:30; 49:34; 51:59; 52

5 A leader in Jerusalem after the Exile, this man joined Nehemiah in signing the covenant. NEHEMIAH 10:1

ZEEB See OREB

ZELEK An Ammonite, Zelek was one of David's greatest fighters. His prowess won him a place in "The Thirty," David's finest warriors, and a commission in the royal army. II SAMUEL 23:37; I CHRONICLES 11:39

ZELOPHEHAD A member of the tribe of Manasseh who had five daughters but no sons, Zelophehad died during the stay in the wilderness. His daughters persuaded Moses to change the old rules whereby daughters were denied the father's property when he died without sons. NUMBERS 26:33; 27:1, 7; 36:2—11; JOSHUA 17:3; I CHRONICLES 7:15

ZEMIRA One of Benjamin's grandsons, Zemira was a son of Becher and one of the many little-known ancient chieftains whose names appear in the tribal genealogies. I CHRONICLES 7:8

ZEMIRAH See **ZEMIRO**

ZENAS A Christian believer staying in Crete, Zenas was a lawyer, an expert in either Roman or Jewish law (we cannot be sure which), whose services were needed by Paul. Paul wrote to Titus asking that Zenas and Apollos be sent to him at Nicopolis, where Paul planned to spend the winter. TITUS 3:13

ZEPHANIAH
1 The ninth of the twelve minor prophets, Zephaniah was a son of Cushi and a descendant of King Hezekiah. He wrote during King Josiah's reign. His book is an awesome announcement of the day of the Lord which was fast approaching, and a call to repentance. In spite of Josiah's reform, Zephaniah and every other perceptive person knew that a time of reckoning was inevitable as a result of Judah's idolatry and moral deterioration. ZEPHANIAH 1:1
2 A son of Tahath, a Levite in the Kohath branch of the tribe, this Zephaniah was an ancestor of the prophet Samuel and of David's great musician, Heman. I CHRONICLES 6:36
3 One of King Zedekiah's advisers and messengers in the troublesome last days of Judah, this Zephaniah was a son of a well-known priest, Maaseiah. Zephaniah was a member of the party opposing Jeremiah's policies and urging a revolt against Babylon, and

served as King Zedekiah's emissary to Jeremiah. After the revolt fizzled, Zephaniah and the other plotters were taken to Riblah and executed. II KINGS 25:18; JEREMIAH 21:1; 29:25, 29; 37:3; 52:24
4 One who lived during the Exile, this Zephaniah was the father of Josiah, the priest living in Jerusalem who received the representatives from the Jewish community taken to Babylon. ZECHARIAH 6:10, 14

ZEPHI A son of Eliphaz, Zephi was an ancient chieftain of a tribe of Edomites, the desert-dwelling descendants of Esau distantly related to the Jews. GENESIS 36:11, 15; II CHRONICLES 1:36

ZELPHO See **ZEPHI**

ZEPHON Gad's oldest son, Zephon gathered his family and emigrated to Egypt with Jacob's clan. His family, the Zephonites, were part of the tribe of Gad that went out to the wilderness with Moses. NUMBERS 26:15; GENESIS 46:16 (where he was called ZIPHION)

ZERAH
1 A grandson of Esau and a son of Reuel, this Zerah was an early Edomite chief. GENESIS 36:13, 17; I CHRONICLES 1:17
2 Perhaps the same as 1, one named Zerah was the father of Jobab, an ancient king of the Edomites, (the desert tribe descended from Esau which was distantly related to the Hebrews). GENESIS 36:33; I CHRONICLES 1:44
3 Tamar's youngest twin son by her father-in-law, Judah, this Zerah was

Perez's brother. His descendants were the Zerahites. GENESIS 38:30; NUMBERS 26:20; JOSHUA 7:1, 24; 22:20; I CHRONICLES 2:4, 6; 9:6; N᷿ ᷿EMIAH 11:24

4 One of Simeon's sons, this Zerah was head of a clan, also called Zerahites, in the tribe of Simeon. He emigrated to Egypt during the famine when all of Jacob's sons and their families left Canaan. NUMBERS 26:13; I CHRONICLES 4:24

5 One of the Levites named Zerah in the Bible, this first man belonged to the Gershon branch of the tribe, according to the Chronicler's genealogy. I CHRONICLES 6:21

6 Another Levite, this Zerah was recorded as part of the Kohath side of the tribe. I CHRONICLES 6:41

7 An Ethiopian king, this Zerah headed a large army that invaded Judah in King Asa's time, but was repelled with horrendous losses at Mareshah. Egyptian scholars suggest that Zerah might have been either Osorkon I or II of the Twenty-second Dynasty. II CHRONICLES 14:9

ZERAHIAH

1 A priest with an impeccable family history stretching back to Aaron, this Zerahiah was one of Ezra's ancestors. I CHRONICLES 6:6, 51; EZRA 7:4

2 A descendant of Pahath-moab, this Zerah was the father of Eliehoenai, one of the party that returned to Jerusalem with Ezra after the Exile. EZRA 8:4

ZERESH The wife of Haman, the Persian prime minister who plotted to exterminate the Jews, and the mother of Haman's ten sons who were accomplices in the nefarious scheme, Zeresh saw her husband and sons hanged after the plot was uncovered. ESTHER 5:10, 14; 6:13

ZERETH A son of Helah and a descendant of Caleb, son of Hur, Zereth was one of the names of family chieftains carried in the rolls of the tribe of Judah. I CHRONICLES 4:7

ZERI See IZRI

ZEROR Saul's great-grandfather, Zeror was a Benjaminite family head. I SAMUEL 9:1

ZERUAH The mother of King Jeroboam, first king of the northern ten tribes when the kingdom split. Zeruah was the widow of Nebat and lived in the hill country of Ephraim. I KINGS 11:26

ZERUBBABEL The man who led the first group of dispirited exiles back to Jerusalem from Babylon, Zerubbabel was the governor of Jerusalem in the dismal days at the close of the Exile. Zerubbabel directed the resumption of the worship, the rebuilding of the altar, and the foundation construction for the new Temple. A descendant of David, he was a member of the royal family, and was thought by many to be the Messiah of Davidic origin. Scholars are puzzled as to why Zerubbabel later seemed to fade in importance in the Biblical records. One Jewish tradition has it that he went back to Babylon and died. Some students theorize that Zerubbabel, as a royal prince, might have been regarded as a threat by the Persian rulers, and removed from Jerusalem for political reasons. He was not present at the dedication of the rebuilt Temple. I CHRONICLES 3:19; EZRA 2:2; 3:2, 8; 4:2, 3; 5:2; NEHEMIAH 7:7; 12:1, 47; HAGGAI 1:1, 12, 14; 2:2, 4, 21, 23; ZECHARIAH 4

ZERUIAH David's sister, Zeruiah was the mother of three sons who were placed in important positions in David's forces—Joab, Asahel, and Abishai. Strangely, Zeruiah's husband's name is not given, suggesting perhaps that Zeruiah was widowed, or that she, as David's sister, was more prominent than her spouse. I SAMUEL 26:6; II SAMUEL 2:13, 18; 3:39; 8:16; 14:1; 16:9, 10; 17:25; II SAMUEL 18:2; 19:21, 22; 21:17; 23:18, 37; I KINGS 1:7; 2:5, 22; I CHRONICLES 2:16; 11:6, 39; 18:12, 15; 26:28; 27:24

ZETHAM A Levite of the Gershon branch of the tribe, Zetham, a son of Jehieli, was placed in the office of the treasury in David's sanctuary in Jerusalem. I CHRONICLES 23:8; 26:22

ZETHAN One of Benjamin's great-grandsons, Zethan was an ancient and obscure warrior-chieftain named in the annals of the tribe by the Chronicler. I CHRONICLES 7:10

ZETHAR One of the seven top advisors to Ahasuerus, King of Persia, Zethar was one of the few privileged to speak face-to-face with the king. ESTHER 1:10

ZIA A little-known member of Gad, Zia is included in the tribal genealogy among those who headed families. I CHRONICLES 5:13

ZIBA Originally one of Saul's servants, Ziba presented himself to David after Saul's death. David, wanting to express his personal appreciation for Jonathan, gave Saul's estate to Jonathan's only surviving heir, the young, lame Mephibosheth. Ziba was made supervisor of the estate. During Absalom's rebellion, Ziba cleverly managed to protect his own interests, and accused Mephibosheth of treachery against David. In spite of Mephibosheth's denials, David divided Saul's estate and gave half to Ziba. II CHRONICLES 9; 16; 19

ZIBEON A chieftain of the Horites, the ancient people superseded by Esau's descendants in the desert, this Zibeon was a son of Seir the Horite. He is listed as an ancestor of Adah, one of Esau's wives. GENESIS 36; I CHRONICLES 1:38, 40

ZIBIA One of Shaharaim's sons by Hodesh, Zibia was an early minor chieftain in the tribe of Benjamin. I CHRONICLES 8:9

ZIBIAH The mother of King Joash of Judah, Zibiah had the heavy responsibility of raising her young son after her husband, Ahaziah, was assassinated and during the queen mother Athaliah's bloody reign. Joash was crowned when he was a boy of seven, and Zibiah must have had considerable influence in Judah for a time. II KINGS 12:1; II CHRONICLES 24:1

ZICHRI

1 A son of Izhar and a grandson of

Kohath, Zichri was an ancient clan ancestor in the tribe of Levi. EXODUS 6:21

2 One of four obscure chiefs in the tribe of Benjamin named Zichri, this man was a son of Shimei. I CHRONICLES 8:19

3 Another Benjaminite, this man was a son of Shishak. I CHRONICLES 8:23

4 Still another from the same tribe, this Zichri was a son of Jeroham. I CHRONICLES 8:27

5 A fourth Benjaminite Zichri, this man was the father of Joel, the head of the tribe in Jerusalem after the Exile. NEHEMIAH 11:9

6 A Levite, this Zichri was a son of the well-known musician in David's sanctuary, Asaph, and the ancestor of the distinguished Shemaiah, a leader in the post-Exile community in Jerusalem. He was probably the same as ZADDI 4. I CHRONICLES 9:15

7 A Levite descended from Moses' son Eliezer, this man served in the treasury office of David's sanctuary in Jerusalem. I CHRONICLES 26:25

8 A member of the tribe of Reuben, this Zichri was father of Eliezer, the head of the Reubenites when David took his census of the tribes. I CHRONICLES 27:16

9 A member of the tribe of Judah, this man was the father of Amasiah, a commander of a large fighting force in King Jehoshaphat's army. II CHRONICLES 17:16

10 This Zichri was remembered as the father of Elishaphat, one of those who conspired to depose the infamous Queen Athaliah and crown young Joash. II CHRONICLES 23:1

11 A powerful warrior from Ephraim, this Zichri fought in the Israelite-Syrian army that wiped out the forces of King Ahaz of Judah. Zichri personally slew the king's son and two top officials of Judah. II CHRONICLES 28:7

12 A priest of Abijah's family, this Zichri served under chief priest Joiakim in the community of returned exiles in Jerusalem. NEHEMIAH 12:17

ZIDKIJAH See ZEDEKIAH 5

ZIDON Canaan's oldest son and Ham's grandson, this man was the reputed founder-ancestor of the people living along the Phoenician coast, and the alleged founder of the oldest city of the area, Sidon. GENESIS 10:15; I CHRONICLES 1:13

ZIHA

1 A obscure Temple servant, Ziha was the ancestor of a family which was recorded among those that returned from Babylon to Jerusalem after the Exile. EZRA 2:43; NEHEMIAH 7:46

2 Probably a descendant of 1, this Ziha was appointed to head a contingent of Temple servants from his family-clan. NEHEMIAH 11:21

ZILLAH Methuselah's daughter-in-law, Zillah was one of Lamech's wives and the mother of history's first metalworker, Tubal-cain. GENESIS 4:19—23

ZILPAH A slave girl belonging to Leah, one of Jacob's wives, Zilpah had been presented to Leah by her father, Laban. Later, Leah passed on Zilpah to Jacob for use as a concubine. She was the mother of two of Jacob's sons, Gad and Asher. GENESIS 29:24; 30:9—12; 35:26; 37:2; 46:18

ZIPHION See **ZEPHON**

ZILLETHAI

1 One of Shimei's sons in the tribe of Benjamin, this Zillethai was one of those clan chiefs who are only names in the tribe's genealogy. I CHRONICLES 8:20

2 Head of a detachment of fighters from the tribe of Manasseh, this Zillethai and his cohorts grew disenchanted with Saul and deserted to join David's outlaw band at Ziglag. I CHRONICLES 12:20

ZILTHAI See **ZILLETHAI**

ZIMMAH A great-grandson of Gershom, Levi's son, Zimmah was head and ancestor of a distinguished family in the Gershonite branch of the Levites. Later members of the family referred to themselves as "sons" of Zimmah. I CHRONICLES 6:20, 42; II CHRONICLES 29:12

ZIMRAN One of Abraham's sons by Keturah, Zimran was the head of a now-forgotten tribe in the Arabian peninsula. GENESIS 25:2; I CHRONICLES 1:32

ZIMRI

1 The brazenly disobedient son of a Simeonite chief during the wanderings in the wilderness, Zimri brought his pagan girl friend into camp to live with him. The priest Phinehas was so incensed that he killed both Zimri and the woman. NUMBERS 25:14

2 For the man called Zimri in some translations of I Chronicles 2:6, see ZABDI 1

3 One of Saul's descendants, this Zimri was a Benjaminite family head remembered chiefly because of his relationship to Saul. I CHRONICLES 8:36; 9:42

4 King of Israel for seven days, this Zimri was a brutal opportunist who killed King Elah when the latter was in a drunken stupor. Previously Zimri had been commander of half of Elah's chariot forces. His deed, however, was not favorably received, and he died in the flames of the palace when Omri marched against him a week later. I KINGS 16

ZINA See **ZIZA**

ZIPH

1 An early member of the tribe of Judah, this Ziph was one of Jehallelel's sons, and a relative of Moses' great spy, Caleb. I CHRONICLES 4:16

2 A son of Maresha, in the Jerahmeel branch of the tribe of Judah, this Ziph was reputed founder of the town bearing his name southeast of Hebron. I CHRONICLES 2:42

ZIPHAH One of Jehallelel's sons, Ziphah was another of the tribe of Judah who was proud to be related to Moses' great spy, Caleb, and was a family head. I CHRONICLES 4:16

ZIPPOR An early Moabite, Zippor was the father of King Balak, the adversary of the Israelites who hired the prophet Baalam to curse the tribes of Israel. NUMBERS 22:2—16; 23:18; JOSHUA 24:9; JUDGES 11:25

ZIPPORAH The daughter of a priest of Midian, Zipporah was Moses' wife. Zipporah was the person who introduced her tribal practice of circumcision to the Hebrews when she insisted upon circumcising her son Gershom. She stayed with her father while Moses was contending with the Pharaoh in Egypt and leading the tribes out of the slave labor camps, but brought her two sons and joined Moses in the wilderness. EXODUS 2:21; 4:25; 18:2

ZITHRI See SITHRI

ZIZA
1 One of the leaders from the clan of Simeon who led a land-grab raid into the lush vale of Gedor during King Hezekiah's time, Ziza and his family settled in Gedor after dispossessing the Amalekites living there. I CHRONICLES 4:37
2 One of King Rehoboam's sons by his favorite wife, Maacah, Ziza was not mentioned except in the brief family tree of Rehoboam. II CHRONICLES 11:20

ZIZAH A Levite who was one of the Gershom side of the tribe, Zizah, a son of Shimei, headed a family of Levites serving in David's sanctuary. I CHRONICLES 23:11

ZOBEBAH A son of Koz, an early clan chieftain related to Hur, Zobebah was a name in the annals of the tribe of Judah. I CHRONICLES 4:8

ZOHAR
1 An ancient Hittite living in Canaan, Zohar was the father of Ephron, the man from whom Abraham bought the cave of Machpelah for use as a family tomb. GENESIS 23:8; 25:9
2 For the Zohar who was Simeon's son, see ZERAH **4**

ZOHETH A descendant of the famous spy, Caleb, son of Jephunneh, Zoheth was another obscure family head who was remembered in the records of the tribe of Judah. I CHRONICLES 4:20

ZOPHAH One of Asher's great-great-grandsons, Zophah was a family head in the tribe of Asher remembered in the tribal genealogy. I CHRONICLES 7:35—36

ZOPHAI A Levite belonging to the Kohath branch of the tribe, Zophai, also known as Zuph, was remembered principally as an ancestor of the great prophet Samuel. I SAMUEL 1:1; I CHRONICLES 6:26, 35

ZOPHAR One of Job's three moralistic friends who philosophized and "explained" Job's woes to him, Zophar was from Naamah, a locality somewhere east of the Jordan, perhaps in Arabia. Like Bildad and Elihu, the others of the trio of visitors, Zophar interpreted Job's misfortunes as a sign of God's disfavor because of Job's

, and urged Job to confess it. JOB 2:11; 11:1ff; 20:1ff; 42:9

ZOROBABEL See ZERUBBABEL

ZUAR A member of the tribe of Issachar, Zuar was the father of Nethanel, the man selected as Issachar's representative when Moses asked for a delegate from each tribe to help count and govern the people in the wilderness. NUMBERS 1:8; 2:5; 7:18, 23; 10:15

ZUPH See ZOPHAI

ZUR

1 The father of Cozbi, the Midianite woman whom Zimri brazenly brought into the camp in open violation of rules, Zur was an ancient chief of the Midianites in Moses' time. He, his daughter, and Zimri were all put to death by the priest Phinehas. NUMBERS 25:15; 31:8; JOSHUA 13:21

2 Saul's great-uncle, this Zur was one of the family of Benjaminites who lived at Gibeon. I CHRONICLES 8:30; 9:36

ZURIEL An early Levite of the Merari side of the tribe, Zuriel headed a family whose duty it was to camp on the north side of the tabernacle during the days when the tribes wandered in the wilderness. NUMBERS 3:35

ZURISHADDAI An ancient member of the tribe of Simeon, Zurishaddai was noted as the father of Shelumiel, head of the Simeonites in Moses' time and the man chosen to assist Moses in numbering the people in the tribes. NUMBERS 1:6; 2:12; 7:36, 41; 10:19